Understanding Nancy, Understanding Modernism

Understanding Philosophy, Understanding Modernism

The aim of each volume in **Understanding Philosophy, Understanding Modernism** is to understand a philosophical thinker more fully through literary and cultural modernism and consequently to understand literary modernism better through a key philosophical figure. In this way, the series also rethinks the limits of modernism, calling attention to lacunae in modernist studies and sometimes in the philosophical work under examination.

Series Editors:
Paul Ardoin, S. E. Gontarski, and Laci Mattison

Volumes in the Series:
Understanding Bergson, Understanding Modernism
Edited by Paul Ardoin, S. E. Gontarski, and Laci Mattison
Understanding Deleuze, Understanding Modernism
Edited by S. E. Gontarski, Paul Ardoin, and Laci Mattison
Understanding Wittgenstein, Understanding Modernism
Edited by Anat Matar
Understanding Foucault, Understanding Modernism
Edited by David Scott
Understanding James, Understanding Modernism
Edited by David H. Evans
Understanding Rancière, Understanding Modernism
Edited by Patrick M. Bray
Understanding Blanchot, Understanding Modernism
Edited by Christopher Langlois
Understanding Merleau-Ponty, Understanding Modernism
Edited by Ariane Mildenberg
Understanding Nietzsche, Understanding Modernism
Edited by Douglas Burnham and Brian Pines
Understanding Derrida, Understanding Modernism
Edited by Jean-Michel Rabaté

Understanding Adorno, Understanding Modernism
Edited by Robin Truth Goodman
Understanding Flusser, Understanding Modernism
Edited by Aaron Jaffe, Rodrigo Martini, and Michael F. Miller
Understanding Marx, Understanding Modernism
Edited by Mark Steven
Understanding Barthes, Understanding Modernism
Edited by Jeffrey R. Di Leo and Zahi Zalloua
Understanding Kristeva, Understanding Modernism
Edited by Maria Margaroni
Understanding Žižek, Understanding Modernism
Edited by Jeffrey R. Di Leo and Zahi Zalloua
Understanding Nancy, Understanding Modernism
Edited by Cosmin Toma
Understanding Cavell, Understanding Modernism (forthcoming)
Edited by Paola Marrati
Understanding Bakhtin, Understanding Modernism (forthcoming)
Edited by Philippe Birgy
Understanding Badiou, Understanding Modernism (forthcoming)
Edited by Arka Chattopadhyay and Arthur Rose

Understanding Nancy, Understanding Modernism

Edited by
Cosmin Toma

BLOOMSBURY ACADEMIC
NEW YORK • LONDON • OXFORD • NEW DELHI • SYDNEY

BLOOMSBURY ACADEMIC
Bloomsbury Publishing Inc
1385 Broadway, New York, NY 10018, USA
50 Bedford Square, London, WC1B 3DP, UK
29 Earlsfort Terrace, Dublin 2, Ireland

BLOOMSBURY, BLOOMSBURY ACADEMIC and the Diana logo are
trademarks of Bloomsbury Publishing Plc

First published in the United States of America 2023
Paperback edition published 2024

Copyright © Cosmin Toma, 2023

Each chapter copyright © by the contributor, 2023

Cover design: Eleanor Rose
Cover image © Getty Images

All rights reserved. No part of this publication may be reproduced or
transmitted in any form or by any means, electronic or mechanical, including
photocopying, recording, or any information storage or retrieval system,
without prior permission in writing from the publishers.

Bloomsbury Publishing Inc does not have any control over, or responsibility for,
any third-party websites referred to or in this book. All internet addresses given in
this book were correct at the time of going to press. The author and publisher
regret any inconvenience caused if addresses have changed or sites have
ceased to exist, but can accept no responsibility for any such changes.

A catalogue record for this book is available from the British Library.

A catalog record for this book is available from the Library of Congress.

ISBN: HB: 978-1-5013-7012-0
       PB: 978-1-5013-7016-8
       ePDF: 978-1-5013-7014-4
       eBook: 978-1-5013-7013-7

Series: Understanding Philosophy, Understanding Modernism

Typeset by Integra Software Services Pvt. Ltd.

To find out more about our authors and books visit www.bloomsbury.com
and sign up for our newsletters.

Contents

Notes on Contributors   ix
List of Abbreviations   xiv
Series Preface   xvi

Introduction   *Cosmin Toma*   1

Part 1   Conceptualizing Nancy

1   Jean-Luc Nancy's *Expectation*: Rephrasing "Philoliterature"
    Ginette Michaud   17

2   *Fort-Pflanzung*: The Literary Absolute's Botanic Afterlife   *Stefanie Heine*   39

3   Back to *The Muses*: A Di-versation on the World(s) and the Plurality of Arts   *Nicholas Cotton*   57

4   After *Listening*: Music, Musicians, and Modernity   *Sarah Hickmott*   73

5   *Fabula, Bucca, Humanitas*: On *Ego Sum*   *Andrea Gyenge*   88

6   From *Dis-Enclosure* to *Adoration*: Literature and the Deconstruction of Christianity   *Schalk Gerber*   109

Part 2   Nancy and Modernity

7   Before the Abyss   *Jean-Luc Nancy*   127

8   *Noli me operare*: Reading Nancy (Re-)Reading Blanchot   *Aukje van Rooden and Andreas Noyer*   131

9   "Close Relations": Nancy and the Question of Psychoanalysis   *Jean-Michel Rabaté*   147

10a   Streams of Consciousness: River Poetry from Heidegger to Nancy and Lacoue-Labarthe   *John McKeane*   162

10b   Altus   *Philippe Lacoue-Labarthe*   176

11	The Regime of Technique: Nancy, Science, and Modernism *Ian James*	178
12	*Le fond du film*: Worlds, Images, and the Machining of Grounds (or: Blanchot Not/Beyond Nancy) *Jeff Fort*	197
13	Nancy('s) Surfaces *James Martell*	220
14	The Poetics and Politics of Disenclosure: Nancy, Mbembe *Michael Krimper*	237
15	Between Modernism and *Modernité*: An Interrupted Dialogue with Jean-Luc Nancy *Jean-Luc Nancy and Cosmin Toma*	252

Part 3 Glossary

16	Art (and Its Deliverance) *John McKeane*	265
17	Body *Juan Manuel Garrido*	268
18	Exscription *John Paul Ricco*	271
19	Globalization/*Mondialisation* *Barnaby Norman*	274
20	Sense *Isabelle Perreault*	278
21	With *Jérôme Lèbre*	282

Index   286

Contributors

Nicholas Cotton teaches French literature at the Collège Édouard-Montpetit (Longueuil, Quebec). He was Visiting Postdoctoral Fellow (Fonds de recherche du Québec – Société et culture) at Princeton University from 2020 to 2021. His doctoral thesis, which he defended at the Université de Montréal in 2020, analyzes the concept of "perversion" in the work of Jacques Derrida, and will be published under the title *Penser la « pervertibilité » – Avec Jacques Derrida*. He is also the co-editor, with Ginette Michaud, of Derrida's seminar *Le parjure et le pardon* (Galilée, 2019–20), as well as the author of several pieces on the poetry of Charles Baudelaire.

Jeff Fort is Associate Professor of French at the University of California, Davis. His research explores the relation between fiction and autobiography, critical theory, aesthetics, French film, and translation. He is the author of *The Imperative to Write: Destitutions of the Sublime in Kafka, Blanchot, and Beckett* (Fordham UP, 2014) and the working title of his current research project is *Effacements: Blanchot, the Deathly Image, and the Cinema of Disfiguration*. He has also translated a number of literary and philosophical works into English, including Jean-Luc Nancy's *The Ground of the Image* (Fordham UP, 2005).

Juan Manuel Garrido is Professor of Philosophy at Alberto Hurtado University (Chile). His research interests include the philosophical concept of life as well as the philosophy of knowledge production and scientific practice. He is the author of *Producción de conocimiento* (Metales Pesados, 2018), *On Time, Being and Hunger: Challenging the Traditional Way of Thinking Life* (Fordham UP, 2012), *Chances de la pensée. À partir de Jean-Luc Nancy* (Galilée, 2011), and *La Formation des formes* (Galilée, 2008).

Schalk Gerber is currently completing a PhD in philosophy at Stellenbosch University (South Africa) and the Vrije Universiteit Amsterdam (The Netherlands). His doctoral thesis is a sustained inquiry into the problem of ontological reparation, in dialogue with Jean-Luc Nancy and Achille Mbembe. He has published articles on Nancy, Mbembe, and Richard Kearney.

Andrea Gyenge is Postdoctoral Fellow in Visual Studies at the University of Toronto. Her main research project, *Swallow: The Mouth in Cinema*, an extension of her doctoral thesis at the University of Minnesota, is a sustained exploration of the motif of the mouth in philosophy, art, and technology. She is also working on a study of film and video media during the HIV/AIDS crisis in the early 1990s provisionally entitled *The Life-Image: An Essay in Biopolitical Resistance*. Gyenge's writings have been published in *Angelaki* and *Cultural Critique*, among other journals.

Stefanie Heine is Assistant Professor of Comparative Literature at the University of Copenhagen. Her research focuses on modernist literature, intermediality, and psychoanalysis. She is the author of *Poetics of Breathing: Modern Literature's Syncope* (SUNY Press, 2021) and *Visible Words and Chromatic Pulse: Virginia Woolf's Writing, Impressionist Painting, Maurice Blanchot's Image* (Turia + Kant, 2014). She has also co-edited several volumes, including *Reading Breath in Literature* (Palgrave, 2018), *Transaktualität. Ästhetische Dauerhaftigen und Flüchtigkeit* (Wilhelm Fink, 2017), and *Die Kunst der Rezeption* (Aisthesis, 2014).

Sarah Hickmott is Assistant Professor in the School of Modern Languages and Cultures at Durham University. Her research focuses on the relationship between contemporary French thought and ecological, social, cultural, and political concerns. Her first book is entitled *Music, Philosophy and Gender in Contemporary French Thought: Nancy, Lacoue-Labarthe, Badiou* (Edinburgh UP, 2020) and it explores the way music has been used, understood, or characterized in recent French thought.

Ian James is Professor of Modern French Literature and Thought at the University of Cambridge. His research focuses on twentieth-century and contemporary French literature and philosophy. He is the author of *The Technique of Thought: Nancy, Laruelle, Stiegler and Malabou after Naturalism* (Minnesota UP, 2019), *The New French Philosophy* (Polity, 2012), *Paul Virilio* (Routledge, 2007), *The Fragmentary Demand: An Introduction to the Philosophy of Jean-Luc Nancy* (Stanford UP, 2006), and *Pierre Klossowski: The Persistence of a Name* (Oxford Legenda, 2000). He is also co-editor of *Exposures: Critical Essays on Jean-Luc Nancy* (*Oxford Literary Review*, vol. 27, 2005).

Michael Krimper teaches comparative literature at New York University. He specializes in twentieth- and twenty-first-century and Francophone Anglophone literature, with a particular emphasis on the intersection of aesthetics and politics in transatlantic modernisms. His articles, reviews, and translations have been published in *New Literary History*, *SubStance*, *The Los Angeles Review of Books*, and the *Journal of Italian Philosophy*, among other venues. He is also the editor of the April 2022 issue of the *Journal of Beckett Studies*, on Beckett and Sade.

Philippe Lacoue-Labarthe was Professor of Philosophy at the Université de Strasbourg. A close friend and colleague of Jean-Luc Nancy, they wrote several books together, including *The Title of the Letter: A Reading of Lacan* (1973) and *The Literary Absolute: The Theory of Literature in German Romanticism* (1978). He is also the author of *The Subject of Philosophy* (1979), *Poetry as Experience* (1986), and *Musica Ficta: Figures of Wagner* (1991), among other important volumes.

Jérôme Lèbre teaches philosophy at the Lycée Hélène Boucher (Paris). His research focuses on German idealism and contemporary French philosophy, as well as on the quest for stability in the twenty-first century. He is the author of several books, including *Scandales et démocratie* (Desclée de Brouwer, 2019), *Une pensée voisine. Lectures françaises de la philosophie allemande* (Hermann, 2018), *Éloge de l'immobilité* (Desclée de Brouwer, 2018), *Les Caractères impossibles* (Bayard, 2014), *Derrida – la justice sans condition* (Michalon, 2013), *Vitesses* (Hermann, 2011) and, with Jean-Luc Nancy, of *Signaux sensibles* (Bayard, 2017).

James Martell is Assistant Professor of Romance languages at Lyon College. He is the author of *Modernism, Self-Creation, and the Maternal: The Mother's Son* (Routledge, 2019) and co-editor of *Tattooed Bodies: Theorizing Body Inscription across Disciplines and Cultures* (Palgrave Macmillan, 2022) and *Samuel Beckett and the Encounter of Philosophy and Literature* (Roman Books, 2013). His writing has also appeared in *Samuel Beckett Today/Aujourd'hui*, *Mosaic* and *Oxford Literary Review*.

John McKeane is Lecturer in Modern French Literature at the University of Reading. His research looks at literary and philosophical thought in French and comparative contexts. He is the author of *Philippe Lacoue-Labarthe: (Un)timely Meditations* (Oxford Legenda, 2014), and the co-editor of *Sarah Kofman and the Relief of Philosophy* (*Paragraph* 44, 2021) and *Blanchot romantique* (Peter Lang, Oxford, 2010). He has also translated Jean-Luc Nancy's *Adoration: The Deconstruction of Christianity II* (Fordham UP, 2013) and Christophe Bident's *Maurice Blanchot: A Critical Biography* (Fordham UP, 2018).

Ginette Michaud is Professor Emerita of French Literature at the Université de Montréal. Her research focuses on twentieth-century French literature and critical theory, particularly the work of Jacques Derrida, whose writings she has extensively commented and edited. More recently, she is the co-author, with Isabelle Ullern, of *Sarah Kofman et Jacques Derrida. Croisements, écarts, differences* (Hermann, 2018) and the author of several monographies, including *Ekphraser. Nouvelles poétiques de l'ekphrasis en déconstruction* (Les Presses de l'UdeM, 2022), *Lire dans la nuit et autres essais. Pour Jacques Derrida* (Les Presses de l'UdeM, 2020), *Derrida, Celan. Juste le poème, peut-être* (Hermann, 2017), *Cosa volante. Le désir des arts dans la pensée de Jean-Luc Nancy* (Hermann, 2013), *Battements du secret littéraire. Lire Jacques derrida et Hélène Cixous, Volume 1* and *« Comme en rêve... » Lire Jacques Derrida et Hélène Cixous, Volume 2* (Hermann, 2010). She is also the co-editor of Jean-Luc Nancy's *Expectation: Philosophy, Literature* (Fordham UP, 2017), among other volumes.

Jean-Luc Nancy was Professor of Philosophy at the Université de Strasbourg. His research, which has elicited in-depth commentaries from scholars and writers across multiple disciplines, focuses on deconstruction, aesthetics, ontology, politics, and theology. He is the author or co-author of numerous books, such as *The Literary Absolute: The Theory of Literature in German Romanticism* (SUNY Press, 1988; with Philippe Lacoue-Labarthe), *The Inoperative Community* (Minnesota UP, 1991), *The Muses* (Stanford UP, 1996), *Being Singular Plural* (Stanford UP, 2000), *Listening*

(Fordham UP, 2007), *Dis-Enclosure: The Deconstruction of Christianity* (Fordham UP, 2008), and *Expectation* (Fordham UP, 2017).

Barnaby Norman is a translator and independent scholar. He is the author of *Mallarmé's Sunset: Poetry at the End of Time* (Routledge, 2014) and has translated works by Bernard Stiegler, Laurent de Sutter, and Jean-Hugues Barthélémy.

Andreas Noyer holds a master's degree in philosophy from the University of Amsterdam. His research interests include Georges Bataille, Maurice Blanchot, and Pierre Klossowski, as well as the concept of work throughout the history of philosophy.

Isabelle Perreault is Postdoctoral Fellow at the Université du Québec à Rimouski. Her doctoral thesis, on the relationship between musical imagination and the novel in twentieth-century France, is currently being prepared for publication with Vrin. Her postdoctoral research is primarily concerned with "memories of modernity" as they manifest themselves through musical references in the work of contemporary French novelists. Her writing has appeared in *Études littéraires*, *Musicorum*, and *Acta Fabula*, among others.

Jean-Michel Rabaté is Professor of English and Comparative Literature at the University of Pennsylvania. His research is primarily concerned with modernism, psychoanalysis, contemporary art, philosophy, and literature. Recent monographs include *Beckett and Sade* (Cambridge UP, 2020), *Rust* (Bloomsbury, 2018), *Think, Pig!: Beckett at the Limit of the Human* (Fordham UP, 2016), *The Pathos of Distance: Affects of the Moderns* (Bloomsbury, 2016), and *The Cambridge Introduction to Literature and Psychoanalysis* (Cambridge UP, 2014). He has also edited *Knots: Post-Lacanian Psychoanalysis, Literature and Film* (Routledge, 2021), *The New Samuel Beckett Studies* (Cambridge UP, 2019), *Understanding Derrida, Understanding Modernism* (Bloomsbury, 2019), *After Derrida: Literature, Theory and Criticism in the 21st Century* (Cambridge UP, 2018), and *1922: Literature, Culture, Politics* (Cambridge UP, 2018), among many other volumes.

John Paul Ricco is Professor of Contemporary Art, Queer Theory, Aesthetics and Ethics at the University of Toronto. His research draws connections between late twentieth century and contemporary art, architecture, continental philosophy, and issues of gender and sexuality, bodies and pleasures, pornography and eroticism. He is the author of *The Decision Between Us: Art and Ethics in the Time of Scenes* (U of Chicago Press, 2014) and *The Logic of the Lure* (U of Chicago Press, 2003) and has published several articles and book chapters on Jean-Luc Nancy. He is currently working on two separate projects: *The Outside Not Beyond: Pornographic Faith and the Economy of the Eve* and *The Collective Afterlife of Things*.

Cosmin Toma is British Academy Postdoctoral Fellow at the University of Oxford's Faculty of Medieval and Modern Languages/St Hugh's College. He has primarily published on modern and contemporary French literature, critical theory, music, and aesthetics. His first book, *Neutraliser l'absolu. Blanchot, Beckett et la chose littéraire* (Hermann, 2019), is an inquiry into what remains of the literary absolute when it is neutralized by modernity. A second monograph in progress, provisionally entitled *Maurice Blanchot au siècle de sa mort. Des espaces numériques et littéraires*, reckons with Blanchot's twenty-first-century legacy.

Aukje van Rooden is Assistant Professor in Philosophy of Art and Culture at the Philosophy Department of the University of Amsterdam. Her work is concerned with contemporary continental philosophy, comparative literature, and literary and cultural theory. She is the author of *L'Intrigue dénouée. Mythe, littérature et communauté dans la pensée de Jean-Luc Nancy* (Brill, 2022) and *Literature, Autonomy and Commitment* (Bloomsbury, 2019). She co-edited *Re-treating Religion: Deconstructing Christianity with Jean-Luc Nancy* (Fordham UP, 2012), as well as *De nieuwe Franse filosofie: Denkers en thema's voor de 21e eeuw* (Boom, 2011).

Abbreviations

Selected Works of Jean-Luc Nancy Translated into English

A   *Adoration (The Deconstruction of Christianity II)*, trans. John McKeane (New York: Fordham University Press, 2013).

C II   *Corpus II – Writings on Sexuality*, trans. Anne O'Byrne (New York: Fordham University Press, 2013).

CW   *The Creation of the World or Globalization*, trans. David Pettigrew and François Raffoul (Albany: SUNY Press, 2007).

DC   *The Disavowed Community*, trans. Philip Armstrong (New York: Fordham University Press, 2016).

DE   *Dis-Enclosure (The Deconstruction of Christianity)*, trans. Bettina Bergo, Gabriel Malenfant, and Michael B. Smith (New York: Fordham University Press, 2007).

E   *Expectation: Philosophy, Literature*, ed. with the assistance of Ginette Michaud, trans. Robert Bononno (New York: Fordham University Press, 2018).

ES   *Ego Sum: Corpus, Anima, Fabula*, trans. Marie-Ève Morin (New York: Fordham University Press, 2016).

GI   *The Ground of the Image* (New York: Fordham University Press, 2005).

IC   *The Inoperative Community*, ed. Peter Connor, trans. P. Connor, Lisa Garbus, Michael Holland, and Simona Sawhney (Minneapolis and Oxford: University of Minnesota Press, 1991).

L   *Listening*, trans. Charlotte Mandell (New York: Fordham University Press, 2007).

LA   Philippe Lacoue-Labarthe and Jean-Luc Nancy, *The Literary Absolute: The Theory of Literature in German Romanticism*, trans. Philip Barnard and Cheryl Lester (Albany: State University of New York Press, 1988).

M   *The Muses*, trans. Peggy Kamuf (Stanford: Stanford University Press, 1996).

SW   *The Sense of the World*, trans. Jeffrey S. Librett (Minneapolis and London: University of Minnesota Press, 1997).

TL   Philippe Lacoue-Labarthe and Jean-Luc Nancy, *The Title of the Letter: A*

Reading of Lacan, trans. François Raffoul and David Pettigrew (Albany: State University of New York Press, 1992).

UC   *The Unavowable Community,* trans. Pierre Joris (Barrytown, NY: Station Hill Press, 1988).

Selected Works of Jean-Luc Nancy in French

FI   *Au fond des images* (Paris: Galilée, 2003).

LM   *Les Muses* (Paris: Galilée, 2001).

Series Preface

Sometime in the late twentieth century, modernism, like philosophy itself, underwent something of an unmooring from (at least) linear literary history in favor of the multi-perspectival history implicit in "new historicism" or, say, varieties of "presentism." Amid current reassessments of modernism and modernity, critics have posited various "new" or alternative modernisms—postcolonial, cosmopolitan, transatlantic, transnational, geomodernism, or even "bad" modernisms. In doing so, they have not only reassessed modernism as a category, but also, more broadly, rethought epistemology and ontology, aesthetics, metaphysics, materialism, history, and being itself, opening possibilities of rethinking not only which texts we read as modernist, but also how we read those texts. Much of this new conversation constitutes something of a critique of the periodization of modernism or modernist studies in favor of modernism as mode (or mode of production) or concept. Understanding Philosophy, Understanding Modernism situates itself amid the plurality of discourses, offering collections focused on key philosophical thinkers influential both to the moment of modernism and to our current understanding of that moment's genealogy, archaeology, and becomings. Such critiques of modernism(s) and modernity afford opportunities to rethink and reassess the overlaps, folds, interrelationships, interleavings, or cross-pollinations of modernism and philosophy. Our goal in each volume of the series is to understand literary modernism better through philosophy as we also better understand a philosopher through literary modernism. The first two volumes of the series, those on Henri Bergson and Gilles Deleuze, have established a tripartite structure that serves to offer both accessibility to the philosopher's principle texts and to current new research. Each volume opens with a section focused on "conceptualizing" the philosopher through close readings of seminal texts in the thinker's oeuvre. A second section, on aesthetics, maps connections between modernist works and the philosophical figure, often surveying key modernist trends and shedding new light on authors and texts. The final section of each volume serves as an extended glossary of principal terms in the philosopher's work, each treated at length, allowing a fuller engagement with and examination of the many, sometimes contradictory ways terms are deployed. The series is thus designed both to introduce philosophers and to rethink their relationship to modernist studies, revising our understandings of both modernism and philosophy, and offering resources that will be of use across disciplines, from philosophy, theory, and literature, to religion, the visual and performing arts, and often to the sciences as well.

Introduction

Cosmin Toma

It is all but impossible to introduce the present volume without marking the passage of time. When I first approached Jean-Luc Nancy about this then-nascent *ouvrage collectif*—a set expression that is bound to have sounded odd to his ears due to what it insinuates about work and community—he replied that he was somewhat taken aback by my invitation because the entirety of his *travail* (he would never speak of his *œuvre*) is immersed in modernity and concerned with it. Modernity for him was a given— *our* given—at the furthest possible remove from a polemical claim such as *We Have Never Been Modern*, to quote a well-known title of Bruno Latour. There is thus a sense in which modernity is for us—after Nancy, and with him—that which goes without saying, *pace* Latour or the protracted debates that once pitted modernism against postmodernism, especially in the English-speaking world. For insofar as it harks back to the Latin adverb *modo*—"just now"—modernity is *merely* (to cite another one of its etymon's meanings) an acknowledgment that, in passing, time marks an irrevocable contrast between the then and the now, a seemingly obvious distinction that we are tasked with remarking and reflecting upon.

Modernity is thus a matter of now and then, so to speak, yet this also means that it is a matter of occasion and intermittence. On the one hand, it all too bluntly differentiates between an elapsed span of time and what comes after, thereby entrenching a linear, at times even a teleological view of history. On the other hand, this ostensibly hard border between the then and the now entails the return and foreshadowing of wholly other timelines, every now and then, as if modernity, despite its apparent self-evidence, could not quite shake off the unfinished specters that haunt it, including those that intimate its imminent end. And so to be "immersed" in its element, as Nancy would have it, is to be attentive to these disruptions, which gesture towards something completely different—a deep-seated "disquiet" (*inquiétude*), as he puts it, but also a kind of *ek-stasis*, one that quickens all the senses and, indeed, *sense* (or rather: *le sens*) as such.

***

Even though it is tempting to view them as modern classics, Nancy's writings do not, even now that the passage of time has taken its toll, form a corpus, at least not in the usual sense ascribed to this word. Nancy's "body of work" is a misnomer unless we understand it on his own terms, which may be said to consider the body in its sheer nakedness and therefore in its exposure, *partes extra partes*, to cite one of his favorite Latin leitmotifs. And this emphasis on the prefix *ex-*, which recalls Bataille's excess above all, forms the very heart of *exscription*, a Nancean neologism whose import cannot be understated, as a recent issue of *Parallax* devoted to its figurations rightly reminds us.[1] Indeed, it is exscription that best accounts for the sprawl of Nancy's corpus of writings, because it names a textual body that is written ever out(wards), "its being placed *outside the text* as the most *proper* movement of its text; the text *itself* being abandoned, left at its limit."[2] If there is a "body of work" here, it is given over to abandon and abandonment; it does not seek to embody anything like an authoritative canon that would gather itself into a corpus, clearly distinguishing an inside from an outside, a self from an other. Much like Psyche, which is "extended" yet "knows nothing about it,"[3] to invoke an insight of Freud that Nancy was fond of quoting, the body *is* space, and thus spaces itself (out), as do the countless notes, chapters, books, scribbles, fragments, lectures, poems, letters, emails, etc., that make up the non-totality of Nancy's writings—published no less than unpublished—with this difference that they *know* themselves to be extended.

This is where the second term of the equation comes in: "work" or, better yet, *l'œuvre*. What one might call the boundless "extension" of Nancy's body of work was a knowing decision on his part—a thought-out poetics. After all, the volume that first afforded him a broader readership, *The Inoperative Community* (*La Communauté désœuvrée*, 1986)—featuring a revised version of the title essay, initially published in 1983 in the journal *Aléa*, which would kick off a decades-long and partly posthumous dialogue with Maurice Blanchot, who famously penned *The Unavowable Community* (*La Communauté inavouable*, 1983) in response to Nancy—primarily revolves around the twin notions of work (*œuvre*) and inoperancy/idleness/worklessness (*désœuvrement*), whose political implications Nancy was particularly keen to scrutinize. Without delving into the specifics of this dialogue, which was also a complex quarrel or *différend*, suffice it to say that, for Blanchot, worklessness is something that occurs through the work and by it, according to a logic which posits each term (*œuvre* and *désœuvrement*, respectively) in order to better neutralize them (neither *œuvre* nor *désœuvrement*), thus ensuring that both subsist as shadowy versions of each other, perpetually adumbrating their differences. For Nancy, however, worklessness overwhelms the work, to such an extent that their relationship is one of excess exscribed. Hence the work is written out (of itself), ever touching (on) the edges of other works, which are themselves exscribing and exscribed. There is thus a sense in which Nancy radicalizes Blanchot's own insights (including on the "Outside"), impelling them forward into a space of ever greater movement, a melee or *methexis* of bodies that is inseparable from

---

[1] "Jean-Luc Nancy: Poetics, Politics & Erotics of Exscription," ed. John Paul Ricco, Stefanie Heine, and Philippe P. Haensler, *Parallax* 24, no. 4 (2020).

[2] Jean-Luc Nancy, *Corpus*, trans. Richard A. Rand (New York: Fordham University Press, 2008), 11.

[3] Sigmund Freud, *Schriften aus dem Nachlass* (*Gesammelte Werke*, Band 17) (London: Imago, 1946), 152.

his interpretation of community. Indeed, he parses *désœuvrement* as a precursor to what he would later call, in a context where Blanchot also plays a significant role, *dis-enclosure* (*la déclosion*), emphasizing the extent to which unworking (*désœuvrer*) the work means stressing its opening (*l'ouverture de l'œuvre*), in line, once again, with the preformative *ex-*, which propels his writing outwards. What we are dealing with here, then, is a kind of embodied worklessness, a body whose "work" is exscribed and hence abandoned from the very outset.

It would be remiss of me not to stress the extent to which such a conception of philosophy—and art (writ large) and writing in general, to say nothing of politics and the rest—resists, be it only in part, the work that is ostensibly being done here, via this very volume. First of all, because it is difficult, even in retrospect, to single out those books of his that are the most important or significant to his "oeuvre." We have already begun to see why: perhaps even more so than for other thinkers affiliated with deconstruction, there can be no simple canonical shortlist of essential works by Nancy, veritable *summae* that would be more deserving of attention than other, "lesser" writings. To that we must add a certain degree of defiance towards the book form itself, one that echoes his exacerbation of *désœuvrement* in that it takes Blanchot's "absence of the book" beyond the biblical and Mallarméan fascination with a Book to Come. In this—somewhat unexpectedly, perhaps—Nancy seems even more comfortable with the fragmentation that writing, understood as exscription, necessarily entails, problematizing it less insistently than Blanchot, as though he ultimately viewed it as a given, much like modernity itself, with the proviso that what appears to be given also yields the most crucial questions.

Nancy's lengthy introduction to *The Literary Absolute*, co-authored with his close friend and colleague Philippe Lacoue-Labarthe, betokens a different fragmentary lineage as well, away from the more solitary, Nietzschean frame of reference that was dearer to Blanchot.[4] Here, it is the early German Romantics, whose writings are compiled alongside Nancy and Lacoue-Labarthe's essay, in a French translation by Anne-Marie Lang for the 1978 edition, who occupy the place of honor. Put differently, *The Literary Absolute* is to be understood as a collaborative endeavor, all the more so when one considers that several of the *Frühromantik* texts contained therein are themselves the work of more than one author, thus touching on the relationship between literature and community five years ahead of "The Unavowable Community." This, too, has a bearing on Nancy's "body of work": not only is the commingling of writerly bodies, *partes extra partes*, made obvious by the involvement of various authors (and a translator), both living and dead, the "work" as such is hard to pinpoint here. While it is customary to treat *The Literary Absolute* as a volume by Nancy and Lacoue-Labarthe above all, the Romantic fragments that follow their essay are no less essential to the whole (provided we may confidently speak of such here).

---

4 That being said, Blanchot's 1964 piece on the *Athenaeum*, collected in *The Infinite Conversation*, provided part of the impetus for *The Literary Absolute*.

Other examples of Nancy's collaborative willingness abound across the decades: aside from Lacoue-Labarthe, one may also cite Jean-Christophe Bailly, Aurélien Barrau, Mathilde Monnier, Danielle Cohen-Levinas, and Simon Hantaï, among others. As we can see, he did not limit himself to collaborations with other philosophers: his omnivorous appetite for the arts—the Muses, as he would often call them—makes this plain. While the history of philosophy is rife with thinkers who take a panoptic view of aesthetics, essentially applying a preset interpretive framework to matters of music, painting, film, architecture, dance or, indeed, literature, Nancy always sought to decenter his own philosophical authority, thus emphasizing the extent to which the encounter with art—and with other artists—is an exemplary instance of the *with*, a preposition of which he made much in the course of his career due to what it tells us about being and existence—to speak in Heideggerian terms—beyond *Dasein* construed as a mere singularity. Drawing upon the *Mitsein*, Nancy instead sidestepped the dialectical pull of plurality by thinking the two alongside each other—*with* each other, as the hyphenated, singular-plural coming and going of existence. His body of work is thus singular-plural as well, and to speak of Nancy is also, by metonymy, to invoke a multitude of other names, along *with* that of Nancy.

***

A further difficulty arises on the threshold of this edited volume: that of "modernism" itself. What exactly does this word denote in the context of a collection of essays revolving around a French philosopher whose second language was German? The challenge of thinking modernism relative to philosophy and its notorious tendency to overinterpret or appropriate art (in the broadest sense of the term, which includes literature) is understood from the get-go, and the ensuing dialogue cannot but be fraught to some degree. Yet the incursion into a different linguistic sphere has the effect of complicating matters further, forcing us to reckon with the fact that "modernism" conveys a specifically Anglophone set of assumptions. First of all, as regards the timeline, since we tend to conceive of modernist art as having begun around the end of the nineteenth century at the earliest or, strictly speaking, in the wake of the First World War, which is when the names we most readily associate with the movement— James Joyce, Virginia Woolf, Ezra Pound, T. S. Eliot, Gertrude Stein, William Faulkner for literature, Arnold Schoenberg, Alban Berg, Anton Webern, Igor Stravinsky for music, and a flurry of *-isms* for the visual arts, to say nothing of dance, sculpture, architecture, and more recent artforms like film and photography—became recognized as the standard-bearers of a broader cultural push, one often (and somewhat wrongly) defined as striving to overcome the residual Romanticism of their *fin-de-siècle* forebears. Second, as this deliberately reductive, eminently debatable enumeration suggests, modernism's key figures tend to be drawn from a limited pool of nationalities, betraying an idiosyncratic relationship with French culture in particular.

Beyond the timeworn cliché of the Anglophone expat to Paris elevating their artistry to new heights during the *entre-deux-guerres* while simultaneously indulging in a "Bohemian" lifestyle, French art was often assumed to be ahead of the curve, more modern than modernism itself, as the wholesale import of *avant-garde* into the English language makes clear. The absence of explicitly French names within the litany of writers above is thus not a conspicuous lack so much as it denotes a conscious riposte to already established modern *-isms*, such as Symbolism, or contemporaneous, competing ones, such as Surrealism. A certain degree of taxonomic ambiguity manifests itself here as well: while Marcel Proust and Paul Valéry emerged from the same Symbolist scene before developing a style of their own, the former is likelier to be dubbed "modernist" in English, perhaps because he is better known abroad. More importantly, however, what is at stake here between the Anglosphere and the Francosphere—*mutatis mutandis*—is their divergent apprehensions of the relationship between modernism and modernity or, better yet, between modernism and *modernité*.

Modernisme is not unheard of in French by any means, but its semantic currency is nowhere near as high as that of its English counterpart. Whereas *modernism* conveys the existence of a kind of doctrine of modernity, one that actively furthers the cause of all things modern, the far more common (and commonplace) *modernité* belies a vaster state of affairs, like the English *modernity*, yet with an eye resolutely turned toward art and aesthetics. This is a consequence of Baudelaire's wide-reaching influence, since his 1864 essay "The Painter of Modern Life" explicitly interleaves art and the modern condition, as though to be *moderne* could not but be construed through the lens of aesthetics. Against the backdrop of this alternative timeline, Arthur Rimbaud, Paul Verlaine, and Stéphane Mallarmé are no less "modernist" than Édouard Manet, who tends to be typically applied this descriptor in the English-speaking world, with no need for a hesitant qualifier such as "early." In French, however, such inconsistencies are less likely to occur due to the inherently capacious, even voracious nature of *modernité*.

Jean-Luc Nancy's sense of "immersion" in the modern is thus to be understood more broadly than the title of this volume might indicate. This is not to say that one ought to outright rephrase it as *Understanding Nancy, Understanding* Modernité, since Nancy did also engage with writers and artists canonically deemed "modernist" in English, but that his starting assumptions differed from those of scholars trained in the Anglophone tradition is obvious and should be kept in mind as we read the essays that follow.

***

Before properly introducing the chapters that make up the present volume, I would like to highlight what strikes me as one of the most "modern" traits of Nancy's writings: their embrace of the *trop*—the "too (much)"—per the stark title of a 2006 exhibition[5] devoted to his work (along with those of the visual artist François Martin and the musician Rodolphe Burger) at the Galerie de l'UQÀM, in Montreal; an adverb also foregrounded by one of his final publications, *Un trop humain virus* (*An All Too*

---

[5] Jean-Luc Nancy, Rodolphe Burger, Louise Déry, Isabelle Décarie, Georges Leroux, and Ginette Michaud, *TROP. Jean-Luc Nancy*, ed. L. Déry and G. Michaud (Montreal: Galerie de l'UQÀM, 2006).

Human Virus), on the Covid-19 pandemic. From an etymological standpoint, *trop* is remarkable insofar as it is cognate with the Old English *þorp* and the German *Dorf*, "village." In Frankish, it also doubles as "agglomeration," indicating a large number of dwellings, hence its posterity in modern French. Somewhat counterintuitively, perhaps, its Proto-Indo-European root, **treb-*, may have additionally meant "room," complicating the relationship between the inside and the outside, as well as between the singular and the plural. Be that as it may, *trop* is first and foremost a question of *space*, of bodies clustering together and forming a community. And while it indicates excess in a pejorative sense, as when something (or someone) is said to be *de trop*, it can also be used to reinforce praise (e.g., "il est trop fort") in colloquial French. Indeed, *trop* always implies a critical judgment of sorts.

More specifically, Nancy parses the "too (much)" as that which has the potential to eclipse the general equivalency of commerce, which undergirds the globalized triumph of late capitalism. A 1995 essay on "Human Excess" ("Démesure humaine"), which was appended to the 2013 edition of *Être singulier pluriel*, as well as to its 2000 English translation, *Being Singular Plural*, marks an opportunity for Nancy to lay out a certain theory of the *trop*. What gets rendered as "excess" here in English—*démesure*—may be broken down, quite literally, as "dis-measure," and hence as that which disrupts measure, or even which is disruptive through measure itself. If Protagoras's notorious contention that "man is the measure of all things" can be said to foreshadow a key tenet of early modernity—understood here as "humanism"—ours, Nancy argues, is an age of *démesure* in that we measurelessly measure measurelessness with an unprecedented degree of microscopic accuracy—so much so that the work of measure itself becomes excessive.

Arguing that something has the potential to escape the state of general equivalency in which we find ourselves enmeshed is not tantamount to re-positing the existence of an infinite being such as God, of course. Nancy's two-volume *Deconstruction of Christianity* (*Dis-Enclosure* and *Adoration*) is devoted to disabusing us of precisely that notion, against any and all attempts at reverting the so-called Western world to the religious superstructures of yore. On the contrary, he liked to remind us that we have thus far failed to think "the *humanitas* of man high enough,"[6] per a Heideggerian quip that recurs across his writings. Here too, the call is toward that which exceeds the common measure of being, which also implies reckoning with nothing less than a constitutive lack, particularly that of Oneness or totality—a lack out of which the countless fragments that make up existence continuously emerge. And this outstanding dearth, conventionally presumed to be inseparable from the experience of modernity, is precisely what *trop* seeks to circumscribe.

That said, there is a somewhat paradoxical sense in which techno-capitalism—more or less synonymous with our late modern paradigm—is in fact *incapable* of excess, even as it is routinely condemned for being a system that runs on sheer surplus and

---

[6] Martin Heidegger, "Letter on Humanism," trans. Frank A. Capuzzi and J. Glenn Gray, in *Basic Writings*, ed. David Farrell Krell (New York: HarperCollins, 1977), 210.

utter waste, especially now that its environmental consequences have become plain for all the world to see. Indeed, Nancy contends that within its "order of truth, excess is impossible," for late capitalism "is the perfect domain of large numbers, shifts in scale, incommensurables, all the surpluses with regard to averages, and so forth."[7] This version of modernity only knows measure, even though it is overwhelmed by its very own *démesure*, in keeping with Heidegger's conception of it as *das Riesenhafte* (the gigantic). Nor is it limited to contemporary neoliberalism, since it also lies behind the twentieth century's genocidal legacy: the number 6 million is "indissociable from the Shoah," as Nancy contends; indeed, it is nothing less than one of the key "*semantemes* of modernity."[8]

But it is how we respond to these figures (in every sense of the word), how they beckon us toward *responsibility* that most interests Nancy, for whom the problem of excess as *démesure* is ultimately an ethical one:

> The question is not how many people the Earth or the universe can support, but rather which people it can support, which existences. Number, here, immediately converts its magnitude into moral magnitude: the size of humanity becomes indissociable from its dignity.
>
> But this dignity, this *humanitas*, is not itself given as a measure (to believe that it is constitutes the notorious weakness of all discourses of "measured" and measuring humanism). In a certain way, all calls to "measure" are in vain, since there is no excess that can be determined with relation to a given measure, norm, scale, or mean. Thus, the use and/or rule that gives the measure must itself be invented.[9]

Contra Protagoras, who laid the groundwork for a measure-oriented conception of humanity that was subsequently championed as a model for the West—whether real or fantasized—and who, in some sense, is the precursor of Malthusianism, utilitarianism, as well as of the exterminatory ideologies that are inseparable from the modern age, Nancy argues that "we have set up this model" only for it to get "exhausted ... because it does not take into account ... that the measure of the modern world is itself the 'excessive' mode of infinity."[10] We are thus presented with *two* accounts of modernity here, competing takes that can be construed as flowing from the same chiasmic source, mirroring the finite/infinite split: measureless measure and measured measurelessness. Moreover, we cannot resolve their tension without potentially re-enshrining, on the one hand, a punctilious calculation that is complicit in modern mass murder, or, on the other hand, a pre-mathematical incalculable beyond-measure that ultimately gestures

---

[7] Nancy, *Being Singular Plural*, trans. Robert D. Richardson and Anne E. O'Byrne (Stanford: Stanford University Press, 2000), 177.
[8] Ibid., 178.
[9] Ibid., 180.
[10] Ibid., 181.

back to the divine and hence to another kind of "absolute measure, as an absolutely finished or accomplished infinity,"[11] which Nancy identifies with Hegel.

Now that we are wading ever deeper into the digital age, which cannot but strengthen, be it only microscopically and out of sight, the sway of numbers—and it is worth recalling here that the French word for "digital" is *numérique*—Nancy's description of the *démesure* of modernity and the predicament into which it plunges us is timelier than ever:

> The epoch that appears to us as the epoch of very large numbers, the one we can describe as that of "exponential Being," is in fact the epoch of Being which is exposed to and as its own immensity in the strictest sense: nothing measures it, and it is precisely that which measures the existence which engages it, and which it engages in the mode of a responsibility that is itself immense. "Humanity" and "globalness" ["mondialité"] now mean this engagement without measure [or this measureless engagement].
>
> Either the time to come will know to take the measure [of things], or there will be the loss of all measure, and existence along with it. In both a disturbing and exhilarating way, this is what is immensely grand in what is happening to us today, to the extent [*à mesure*] that we are exposed to it.[12]

Modern exponentiality, which resembles Hegel's "bad" infinity in its endless computation, thus goes so far as to inadvertently promise a potential turn into the "good" infinity. The *too much* becomes so calculably incalculable as to augur something completely, overwhelmingly different, which is "disturbing and exhilarating"[13] in equal measure, and which is the future—*l'avenir*: what is to come—as such.

In a more recent volume, *Dans quels mondes vivons-nous?*, cowritten with the astrophysicist Aurélien Barrau and translated into English as *What's These Worlds Coming To?*, Nancy returns to the matter of (mathematical) excess via "More Than One," an essay that tellingly begins with an epigraph borrowed from Derrida's *Writing and Difference*, which provides what one might call a "neutral" definition of the infinite, described as "neither one, nor empty, nor innumerable. It is of a ternary essence,"[14] for there is always an additional number, a +1 to be reckoned with, which lies in excess, over and above what precedes it, *ad infinitum*. Indeed, "[t]he two divides the one and supplants and supplements it: the one has not taken place; it has only taken place by redoubling and repeating itself."[15] Abstract though it may appear, this equation is for Nancy the very calculus that may help us

---

[11] Ibid., 182.
[12] Ibid., 183.
[13] Ibid.
[14] Jacques Derrida, *Writing and Difference*, trans. Alan Bass (Chicago: University of Chicago Press, 1978), 299.
[15] Jean-Luc Nancy and Aurélien Barrau, *What's These Worlds Coming To?*, trans. Travis Holloway and Flor Méchain (New York: Fordham University Press, 2015), 8.

"[e]xit nihilism"¹⁶ at long last. It is a calculation that perpetually escapes or evades calculation, again and again, and so on, recalling Samuel Beckett's rhythmic recourse to an ever-paradoxical, eminently musical movement of permutation. And it is the very excess that allows us to continue, to go on, since "[e]xcess is given within the nature of the 'one'" much as "'More than one' is multitude—less as proliferation than as efflorescence, overabundance, and finally as excess of sense."¹⁷ In other words, *one* is always *more than one*; *one* is *too* much and *too* little; it blossoms in every direction—or rather: in every sense—like a living, breathing, touching organism: it is the very "dis-measure" of being, its self-subverting mathematics.

This "efflorescence" is precisely what makes Nancy so unique among his contemporaries. His writing can indeed be said to be an art of the +1, an addition that is always too much relative to the One or Oneness that oversaw the work of sense and/or meaning (*le sens*) in premodern times. It is perhaps his most fully modern quality, recalling a certain French poet who famously argued that writing happens "literally, and in every sense."¹⁸ For it is also as a poet that Nancy approached the excess of sense, displaying a catholic reach by writing sympathetic essays on most of the arts—literature, painting, music, film, sculpture, dance, etc.—while simultaneously paying attention to the poetic excess of Art as such, which *The Muses* defines as a distinctly *modern* construct. Indeed, his fundamental belief that "the arts come about against each other"¹⁹ is paradigmatically modern in its emphasis on tension and the impossibility of reconciliation (there is always more than one art), even as it stresses the necessary coexistence of these singular-plural entities, which are *too much* relative to one another. And it is through a process of exscription, which is an art of its own—an art and a writing of excess—that he wrote his way through the measureless, sense-engendering absence of ground of modernity.

***

As we can see, then, to attend to Nancy's complex relationship with modernity and modernism is to be exposed to a profusion of figures, brimming with potential for a thinking that is still to come. In this sense, and despite the caveats I pointed out, the excess that is proper to any edited volume—by dint of the exscriptions it brings together within a single, insuperably differential *with*, at times in translation—remains a meaningful point of entry into Nancy's own proliferating "body of work."

As befits the series' mandate, the opening section is devoted to close readings of key volumes by Nancy, with the proviso, once again, that others could have been selected in their stead, in line with the decentralized movement of his writing. The second section further opens up the volume's stated *topos* via essays that discuss Nancy's connection

---

[16] Ibid., 9.
[17] Ibid., 12.
[18] Attributed to Arthur Rimbaud by his sister, Isabelle Rimbaud, in *Reliques* (Paris: Mercure de France, 1921), 143. My translation.
[19] Nancy, "Les arts se font les uns contre les autres," in *Les Muses* (Paris: Galilée, 1994), 161–74.

to modernism and modernity from a wide range of angles. The third and final section traces the import of specific "keywords" across Nancy's writings.

We begin with what is neither quite the beginning nor quite the end: *Demande* (*Expectation*), a 2015 volume comprising writings on literature penned over a period of nearly forty years. Ginette Michaud, who compiled and co-edited these scattered texts, offers an in-depth reading of Nancy's longstanding practice of "philoliterature," which brings out the rivalry no less than the friendship that binds these two ostensibly separate domains in a single portmanteau. Even as she emphasizes the extent to which Nancy's thinking of literature owes many of its core concerns to early German Romanticism, Michaud is attentive to the sprawl of his engagement, which covers a remarkably broad range of writers deemed "literary," be it Blanchot, Joyce, Celan, Hölderlin, or Valéry, to cite but a few. She singles out three recurring motifs in Nancy's writings on literature: the notion of a radical yet repeating beginning, the theme of orality, and the interaction between sense and the body. In closing, she evokes Nancy's interest in contemporary poetry, which may well be the unacknowledged locus toward which his "philoliterature" ceaselessly gravitates.

The chapter that follows is specifically intent on discussing Nancy's enormous debt to early German Romanticism via a (re)reading of *The Literary Absolute*, co-written with Philippe Lacoue-Labarthe. While it is customary to conceive of modernism as having defined itself in opposition to Romanticism, Stefanie Heine undoes this received narrative by sketching out an unsuspected aspect of the continuity that binds the two, namely their privileged relationship with the lexicon of *engendering*, understood here in primarily botanic terms, thus subverting the distinction between the human and the non-human. Heine makes this connection explicit by analyzing what she calls the "afterlife" of the German notion of *Fort-Pflanzung*—first, in *The Literary Absolute*, where it is tied to the twin problems of genre and becoming; second, in Virginia Woolf's writings, which afford us a glimpse into their explicitly modernist posterity.

Insofar as, for Nancy, "the arts come about against each other," it is impossible to speak of modernism without tackling the problem of art's multiplicity. In his piece, Nicholas Cotton stresses the tension that is proper to the "singular plural" and the extent to which it underpins Nancy's *The Muses*, perhaps his most sustained inquiry into aesthetics. This tension also mirrors that between sense and the senses—without ever being thoroughly reducible to it—and is likewise intertwined with another, no less significant issue, namely that of *la technique*, which denotes both technics and technique, echoing the originary duality of the Ancient Greek *tékhnē*. Furthermore, Cotton is also attentive to the relationship between *la technique* and the process of world-making that is so essential to Nancy's philosophy, beyond aesthetics narrowly understood as *l'art pour l'art*.

Delving into the Muse *par excellence*, music, Sarah Hickmott's chapter begins by attending to Nancy's most well-known work on the art of sounds, *Listening*, which offers a critical analysis of philosophy's difficult—and often ocularcentric—relationship with the ear(s) in general. Having summarized the key points of contention raised by this decisive volume, Hickmott goes on to place them within the broader context of Nancy's subsequent writings on music, with a special emphasis on the political implications of his proposed distinction between *écouter* and *entendre*. She also takes up the question of music's own musicality and/or "musicianliness," as well as that of the role of the amateur in the experience of listening as such, which has much to teach us about what Nancy calls "sense" and its resonance, thus straddling the line between meaning and the sensible.

Through a close reading of *Ego Sum*, Andrea Gyenge's "*Fabula, Bucca, Humanitas*" delves into Nancy's understanding of modernity through the specifically epistemological problem of the mouth, which provides an opportunity to reckon with René Descartes's pioneering conception of the subject, understood here as one of the pillars of a properly modern philosophy. Gyenge thus makes plain the extent to which Nancy's own body of thought is not just a thought of the body but also, more specifically and always more than metonymically, a (non-)thought of the mouth beyond mere speech and so of the mouth as sense, one that finds echoes in a poem by Paul Valéry, evoked by Nancy along the way and taken up by Gyenge, who is attentive to the aesthetic figures that arise when the mouth becomes a pressing motif for modern literature and philosophy.

The first section closes with an essay by Schalk Gerber on the two-volume *Deconstruction of Christianity*, which is one of Nancy's most significant inquiries into modernity, approached here from the perspective of the fraught relationship between Christian theology and literature. First, Gerber retraces how Christianity is itself engaged in a process of self-deconstruction for Nancy, emptying itself out of its own religiousness through a protracted movement that is co-extensive with the work of globalization. Gerber then turns to Nancy's uses of Blanchot across *Dis-Enclosure* and *Adoration* so as to show how the "absenting of God" manifests itself via literature in particular due to its privileged connection with the act of naming, on the one hand, and because literary writing cannot but imitate—even as it openly parodies it—the movement of resurrection, as Nancy argues in his reading of *Thomas the Obscure*. Lastly, Gerber sketches out the import of adoration as a means of overcoming modern nihilism.

A short piece by Jean-Luc Nancy, "Before the Abyss," opens the second section. Written in German and translated into English by Michael Holland, it reflects on the eminently modern figure of the abyss, and the fascination that it continues to elicit to this day.

Aukje van Rooden and Andreas Noyer's chapter tackles one of the most controversial facets of Nancy's work: his decades-long, even partly posthumous, dialogue with Blanchot regarding the question of community. Noyer and van Rooden revisit the various monographs and articles Nancy has written around this thematic over the years in order to better elucidate the broader context for his engagement. They then proceed to show how the ambiguities of Nancy's response to Blanchot have progressively been lifted, leading up to an increasingly more critical, even combative, stance toward the end of his life. More importantly still, van Rooden and Noyer identify the core of the quarrel under discussion, beyond community and *désœuvrement*. Indeed, their argument is that the question of the neutral (*le neutre*) is what lies at the heart of Nancy and Blanchot's disagreement, particularly as regards its political repercussions.

The next chapter, by Jean-Michel Rabaté, retraces Nancy's engagement with psychoanalysis from his earliest writings on the subject, co-authored with Philippe Lacoue-Labarthe, to his more recent titles, which come to grips with the legacy of Jacques Lacan more specifically. First, Rabaté returns to *The Title of the Letter*, a work from the 1970s that drew Lacan's begrudging respect no less than his sarcastic ire. Spurred on by the question of the unconscious, a sidestep is then taken toward the influence of the Jena Romantics on Freud, thus reminding us that the latter's proverbial modernity is also a kind of belated Romanticism, once again complicating the usual chronological narrative. Finally, Rabaté returns to Lacan anew by showing us how the latter may still be fruitfully leveraged today, despite Nancy's erstwhile reservations, to meditate on *jouissance* beyond Freud. A complete overview of psychoanalysis's long-lasting influence on Nancy is thus provided.

The following chapter, by John McKeane, explores the presence of rivers not just in Nancy's work but also in those of a broader constellation of poets and thinkers, from Friedrich Hölderlin to Philippe Lacoue-Labarthe, through Martin Heidegger's own notorious (mis)readings of Hölderlin. Questions pertaining to eco-poetics and eco-technics are taken up along the way, deepening our modernist yet residually Romantic understanding of the fluvial trope in literature and philosophy. Special attention is also afforded to *The Ister*, a 2004 documentary film on the Danube, featuring Nancy and Lacoue-Labarthe, as well as their contemporary Bernard Stiegler, and the German film director Hans-Jürgen Syberberg. Lastly, as a companion piece, McKeane's English translation of Lacoue-Labarthe's "Altus" was appended here to emphasize the indelible influence Nancy's close friend and colleague had on his own thinking of nature, literature, Romanticism, and modernity.

Ian James's contribution takes up the still underacknowledged thread of Nancy's philosophy of technics and science in general, following it back through the seminal oeuvres of Henri Poincaré and Gaston Bachelard in order to help us gain a better understanding of Nancy's characteristically modernist conception of *tékhnē*. Indeed, a wider fresco of modernist (mainly French) philosophy of science is painted here, one that emphasizes the absence of ground, the fragmentation and the singular multiplicity to which Nancy's own epistemological postulates are responding. The final section dwells on what the French philosopher calls "struction," which simultaneously subverts construction, destruction, and deconstruction in order to better account for the regime of technique into which we are embedded in the late modern era, somewhere between cosmological order and its perpetual ruin—and beyond.

Moving back to more explicitly aesthetic considerations, Jeff Fort's chapter attends to that most quintessentially modern(ist) of arts: film. More specifically, Fort revisits Nancy's interest in the cinema through Abbas Kiarostami's *Taste of Cherry*. Yet this also provides an opportunity for a broader meditation on Nancy's approach to the image, undertaken here through the lens of the classic figure/ground distinction, whose Nancean deconstruction is exacerbated and prolonged by Fort's attentiveness to Blanchot's subterranean influence, so to speak. Indeed, the groundlessness that is so characteristic of modernism in general, including for Nancy, is reaffirmed here through its literalization in image form, and by way of the figure of the grave, which is of prime importance to Blanchot, Nancy, and Kiarostami, but also to Heidegger, whose own understanding of the ground (*Grund*) of the image is analyzed along the way.

We then linger within the realm of what Derrida called "the spatial arts" with James Martell's contribution, which further delves into Nancy's approach to the conventional opposition between surface and depth. More specifically, Martell demonstrates the ways in which Nancy deliberately exacerbates the surface, turning it into something like a quasi absolute in order to set up a modernist cosmology of touch and touching, one where all beings and things are contiguous, *with* each other no less than against each other, in a state of general "prepositionality" that also echoes the Platonic *khōra* and its reassessment under a Derridean guise. Indeed, Martell shows us that this motif also appears in Nancy's work, where it fulfills a pointedly aesthetic role, as though art could grant us a privileged access to the problem of space.

Michael Krimper's chapter focuses on another essential facet of Nancy's writings, namely the poetico-political nexus that underlies so much of his thinking. Although the key notion of "dis-enclosure" was leveraged by Nancy to rethink Christian theology in particular, Krimper reminds us that its scope also encompasses politics, especially via the burning question of globalization. This is made abundantly clear by the work of Achille Mbembe, who recasts *déclosion* as a process of *décolonisation*, thus demonstrating the potential of Nancy's body of thought when it is expanded beyond the confines of the "West," providing new opportunities to make sense of the ethical call for justice that gains a newfound resonance as the world more fully becomes world. In closing, Krimper insists on the role modern African music plays in Mbembe's philosophy, as well as what it owes to Nancy's own meditations in *Listening*.

The second section ends on a sadly unfinished interview I conducted with Jean-Luc Nancy over email. It is an attempt to come to grips with the volume's theoretical underpinnings, namely the question of modernism, and its relationship with the French *modernité*.

Lastly, the third and final section is devoted to short essays on a series of characteristically Nancean terms: "Art" (John McKeane), "Body" (Juan Manuel Garrido), "Exscription" (John Paul Ricco), "Globalization/*Mondialisation*" (Barnaby Norman), "Sense" (Isabelle Perrault), and "With" (Jérôme Lèbre). The last word is thus (coincidentally) left to the preposition around which the entirety of this edited volume forms a fragmented community, *in memoriam* Jean-Luc Nancy.

Part One

Conceptualizing Nancy

1

Jean-Luc Nancy's *Expectation*: Rephrasing "Philoliterature"

Ginette Michaud

> *Between literature and philosophy this intertwining is lacking, this embrace... Their distinction is exactly the de-intertwining, the de-embracing. The tangle thus untangled is separated by the sharpest of blades, but the cut itself forever bears the marks of that entanglement. Between them is that which cannot be disentangled.*
> — Jean-Luc Nancy, "'One day the gods withdraw...'"[1]

I

Although literature has never been Jean-Luc Nancy's chief concern, he has often pondered literary matters; indeed, literature acts as a kind of basso continuo in his thinking. In his "Introduction" to the English translation of *Demande, Expectation*, which he unhesitatingly calls a *"summa poetica,"* Jean-Michel Rabaté points out that "[f]or the first time ... Nancy takes his stand both as a philosopher and as a poet facing ... the loaded, enigmatic, and tantalizing interactions between poetic form and abstract thought."[2] He also notes that "[i]n the French tradition, only Paul Valéry comes to mind" (*E*, x) as having tackled literature in both its concrete and theoretical guises. Isabelle Alfandary likewise writes that *"Expectation* is manifestly concerned with the letter and the act that is proper to it, with its *poiéin*. It is concerned with language, with its *tékhnē*, with its singular operation. It is uncommon to encounter such a concern in philosophical discourse, coming from a philosopher."[3] Thus, we can only agree with Rabaté when he asserts that "[i]t is now time to recognize that the

---

[1] Jean-Luc Nancy, "'One day the gods withdraw...,'" in *Expectation: Philosophy, Literature*, ed. with the assistance of Ginette Michaud, trans. Robert Bononno (New York: Fordham University Press, 2018), 26. Hereafter *E*.
[2] Jean-Michel Rabaté, "'Wet the Ropes!': Poetics of Sense, from Paul Valéry to Jean-Luc Nancy," in *Expectation*, ix. All *E* quotations followed by Roman numerals ix–xx are by Rabaté.
[3] Isabelle Alfandary, "'[L]'*ars poetica* en tant que tel': de quelques enjeux philosophiques de la poésie pour elle-même," *Les Cahiers philosophiques de Strasbourg*, no. 42, "Jean-Luc Nancy: penser la mutation" (2017): 205. [Translator's note: my translation throughout unless otherwise noted.]

work of Jean-Luc Nancy ... cannot be reduced to an offshoot, albeit a highly creative one, of deconstruction, even if we know the complicity that links him with Derrida" (*E*, xx). Nancy shares Derrida's point of view regarding writing's repression at the hands of philosophical discourse—a critique which Rabaté summarizes as follows: "first, philosophy breaks with the illusion of transparency condensed in the wish to hear oneself speak; then philosophy has to reckon with form, which should lead to a study of the formal practices and programs offered to philosophers; finally, philosophy can never be fully regulated by the law of pure thinking" (*E*, xvii)—yet writing and philosophical discourse nonetheless differ in their approach to these matters. Nancy insists more than Derrida on the technical or formal dimension of the literary craft, whether it be in his own "exercises as a close reader" (*E*, xix) (of Hölderlin's poetry, for instance) or in his exploration of literary genres, occasionally undertaken in jest (indeed, Nancy often assumes a seriously parodic tone).

Taking up the ancient dialogue between philosophy and literature, wherein "the two domains ... act as sparring partners, each attempting to stare the other down," Nancy shifts this longstanding confrontation toward a different ground, one where poetry and thought "appear less as enemies than rival neighbors" (*E*, x) and "are discussed, following the Schlegelian tradition, with regard to their elective affinities."[4] *The Literary Absolute* obviously comes to mind here, a volume on the Early German Romantics' theory of literature that has become a milestone since its publication in 1978, as well as *The Title of the Letter*, also co-written with Philippe Lacoue-Labarthe and published five years later, already bespeaking their mutual interest in "philoliterature,"[5] a "relationship ... which is intimate, complex, conflictual, seductive, and manipulative all at the same time,"[6] ever exposed to "a sharing that is extremely complex and always in transformation,"[7] as Nancy notes in *Adoration*. In a piece entitled "Pensée psalmodiée" ("Thought Intoned"), which was published in May 2018, Nancy also writes of this sharing or partition between philosophy and literature. He argues that poetry is "a continuous thought, the obstinate reprise of a single thought without any monotony, for it is certain of nothing and forms no concepts. It does not form any because it busies itself with its own uncertain insistence. That is, perhaps, one of the possible definitions of poetry (philosophy would then be the insistence of a certainty)."[8] Although this question stood at the core of the projects jointly undertaken with Lacoue-Labarthe, the two philosopher friends' paths diverged after *The Literary Absolute*, with Lacoue-Labarthe taking up the daunting question of *mimesis* (modernism's imitation without

---

[4] Ibid., 210.
[5] Nancy, "'D'une '*mimesis* sans modèle'. Entretien avec Philippe Choulet au sujet de Philippe Lacoue-Labarthe," *L'Animal*, nos. 19–20, "Cahier 'Philippe Lacoue-Labarthe'" (Winter 2008): 109.
[6] Nancy, "Taking Account of Poetry," trans. Leslie Hill, in *Multiple Arts: The Muses II*, ed. Simon Sparks (Stanford: Stanford University Press, 2006), 12–13.
[7] Nancy, *Adoration (The Deconstruction of Christianity II)*, trans. John McKeane (New York: Fordham University Press, 2013), 110.
[8] Nancy, "Pensée psalmodiée," *Lettres françaises* (supplement to *L'Humanité*), no. 160 (May 17, 2018): VII; online, accessed November 24, 2021: https://www.humanite.fr/sites/default/files/les-lettres-francaises-17-mai-2018.pdf.

a model) and of its "ontotypology," which he locates in metaphysics and specifically in Heidegger's "national-estheticism" (*Heidegger, Art and Politics: The Fiction of the Political*), whereas Nancy turned, in the wake of Bataille (*La Pensée dérobée* [Thought Stripped]) and Blanchot (*The Inoperative Community*, "The Compearance"), toward motifs that he himself describes as "ontological and community-oriented (or rather: born out of an ontological community)."[9] The "cum," the philosophy of the "with" that the Heideggerian *Mitsein* and *Mitdasein* left in abeyance, the question of being-in-common, thus significantly lies at the heart of his philosophy of writing, as we are about to see.

Nancy's meditation on literature has continued unabated since the 1970s, as evinced by *Expectation*, which I will turn to in a moment and which collects pieces written over a period of almost forty years. Literature occupies a decisive position in this philosophical body of work, often unexpectedly. Let us recall, for instance, Nancy's reformulation of *ex nihilo* creation in *The Creation of the World, or Globalization*. As Michel Lisse notes, "[i]nterestingly, Nancy does not consider artistic or poetic creation to be creation in the weak sense, but rather creation in the strongest sense," "taking the concept of creation understood as God's act of creation to be the least bad analogy for the process of literary writing."[10] Let us also recall his essays on Blanchot, which he inscribes at the heart of *Dis-Enclosure*'s frame [*dispositif*], the multiple quotes by Rimbaud, Faulkner, Lowry, and Coetzee that are featured scattered throughout *Adoration* or, more recently, *Sexistence* (2017), in which he revealingly resorts to literature once again, stating that he "will invoke, in counterpoint to [his] discussion, different texts, mostly literary, as witnesses to what discourse does not suffice to say"[11]:

> I take the occasion of this citation to note that literary or poetic inclusions and intrusions will crop up throughout my discussion as relays, allusions, or supplementary turns toward what discourse alone doesn't suffice to speak or rather to announce. Everything here hangs upon a desire to say what desire expresses or experiences beyond words.[12]

"[A] desire to say ... beyond words": that is already a definition of "literature," or of what this name entails for Nancy, who thus claims to bestow a name "less to something than to a beyond of all things":

> I name a sort of thing-in-itself or a Parousia, an absolute presence, a pleroma or plethora—plenitude, fullness, infinite reiteration, principle of unlimited pleasure.

---

[9] Nancy, "D'une '*mimesis* sans modèle,'" 109.
[10] Michel Lisse, "Literary Creation, Creation ex Nihilo," trans. John McKeane, in *Re-treating Religion: Deconstructing Christianity with Jean-Luc Nancy*, ed. Alena Alexandrova, Ignaas Devisch, Laurens ten Kate, and Aukje van Rooden (New York: Fordham University Press, 2012), 207–8.
[11] Nancy, *Sexistence*, trans. Steven Miller (New York: Fordham University Press, 2021), 127.
[12] Ibid., 124.

Pleasure is revealed in its plenitude of desire: it is less what charms and seduces than what flares up in pursuit, in ceaseless intensification.[13]

II

Before discussing *Expectation* and describing, in detail, the kind [*genre*] of fiction that fascinates Nancy by dint of its "excess of sense,"[14] I would like to briefly return to a fundamental volume of his, *The Literary Absolute*, where two separate aspects mark the concept of *Literatur* as elaborated by the Jena Romantics: the question of myth, on the one hand, and the notion of *poiesis*, on the other hand, namely an act that "gives itself a figure, a fashion," "[t]hat demands nothing, therefore, but to be said: to say what cannot be said but only done, and thus to do what cannot limit itself to being said, to saying-doing or doing-saying,"[15] as he also writes in *Sexistence* with reference to fiction. As Aukje van Rooden insightfully points out in *Re-treating Religion*, literature is thus for Nancy that which

> would displace mythology, or rather ... this displacement itself is literature. Literature and poetry mark, in other words, the retreat of an original foundational sense; they echo the interruption of myth. More specifically, literature and poetry do not provide a fixed and accomplished sense, a full presence, but are the expression of a creative and transgressive force, a force that resists presence. Following the early Romantics, Nancy thus proposes to understand literature or poetry not as a specific artistic genre but as the expression of the very act of creating: as *poiesis*.[16]

No less than the interruption of myth, the notion of *poiesis* is crucial if we wish to grasp the essential relationship between fiction and the world, not as its representation but rather as the *actual* creation of the world. In *Adoration*, Nancy makes explicit the importance of these two traits by tying them to the question of the "with" and of shared voices [*le partage des voix*]:

> This is also why our world is the world of literature: what this term designates in a dangerously insufficient, decorative, and idle way is nothing other than the opening of the voices of the "with." On the same site where what we call myth gave voice to the origin, literature tunes in to the innumerable voices of our sharing [*partage*]. We share the withdrawal of the origin, and literature speaks starting from the interruption of myth and in some way in that interruption: it is in that interruption that literature makes it possible for us to make sense.

---

[13] Ibid., 9.
[14] Ibid., 122: "excess of sense that we unendingly undergo and enjoy."
[15] Ibid., 114.
[16] Aukje van Rooden, "Intermezzo," in *Re-treating Religion*, 186.

> This sense is the sense of fiction: that is to say, neither mythical nor scientific, but giving itself in creation, in the fashioning (*fingo, fictum*) of forms that are themselves mobile, plastic, ductile, and according to which the "with" configures itself indefinitely.[17]

One cannot overstate the scope of this notion, for it is *poiesis* (and here I am quoting van Rooden again) that

> provides Nancy with a specific view not only of creation but also of community, of our being together in the world. According to Nancy, our idea of being together has always been characterized by a mythological search for a common figure or narrative with which we can identify. By contrast, Nancy tries to understand our being together as an act, a *praxis*, rather than as a fulfilled work or a closed figure ... This original co-existence of beings does not correspond to a common figure but is in itself figurative, or poetic. Our co-existence, in other words, can be conceived of as a form of co-*poiesis*.[18]

For obvious reasons, I cannot retrace here the birth of the concept of *Literatur* in the writings of the early German Romantics. I refer you to Cosmin Toma's *Neutraliser l'absolu. Blanchot, Beckett et la chose littéraire* (Neutralizing the Absolute: Blanchot, Beckett, and the *Res literaria*), in which he shows that literature henceforth presupposes a triple "sublation" (*relève*):[19]

> 1) insofar as it [literature] was devised by the Early German Romantics, it sublates (*aufhebt*) [*relève*] philosophy, overriding *logos* conceived as the highest bastion of reason; 2) it is predicated on [*relève de*] philosophy as a necessary condition or, to mime Kant's idiom, as a condition of possibility; 3) it sublates [*se relève*] itself by displacing its now obsolete sense of "culture" towards that of "progressive universal poetry"—the aim is thus no longer to *know* literature but to *make* it. In other words, there is no literature without culture and without philosophy, yet literature must nonetheless break with them in order to come into being: such is the seminal gesture of Jena Romanticism and more

---

[17] Nancy, *Adoration*, 41–42.
[18] van Rooden, "Intermezzo," 187.
[19] In French, the verb *relever* means to raise or lift up anew, but also to relieve, replace, or correct. Legally speaking, *relever de* is tantamount to "falling under the jurisdiction of something or someone." As such, the conventional rendering of *Aufhebung* as "sublation" in English does not do justice to the French *relève*, a translation that was initially suggested by Jacques Derrida (see "From Restricted to General Economy: A Hegelianism Without Reserve," in *Writing and Difference*, trans. Alan Bass [New York and London: Routledge Classics, 1978], 251–77), which is doubly "relevant" to the topic at hand due to his emphasis on *Aufhebung* as a translating/translated gesture. Likewise, the word *Literatur* in German, which is the earliest modern instance of what we call "literature" today, can itself be construed as a translation/*Aufhebung*/*relève* of the Latin *literatura*, which is to say as a porous boundary between languages no less than between art and philosophy.

specifically of what Philippe Lacoue-Labarthe and Jean-Luc Nancy call, after Friedrich Schlegel and Novalis, "the literary absolute."[20]

According to this Romantic conception, which Nancy inherits, "literature [is] held to be the essence of art," implying that henceforth "[i]t is the poetic intention that makes the Poem," which consequently does not limit itself to poetic *tékhnē*, "assumed to be basically ornamental."[21] Nancy, on the contrary, grants special attention to these prosodic and rhythmic matters (rhyme, meter, syncope), which rely on what Isabelle Alfandary calls "sensing" [*pré-sentir*] in her study of Nancy's *ars poetica*. Not entirely "reducible to Romantic presentiment nor to hyperbolic emotion," this "sensing" "dwells at the heart of the experience of poetry, of the experience that makes up poetry from the perspective of thought,"[22] and it is the path taken by Nancy's poetics—his poematics, to be more precise—as early as *The Muses* (1994), in which, as Alfandary notes, he exhibits an "acute sensibility" toward "'the sensitive essence' of the production of meaning" in poetry, a "tensional necessity"[23] that characterizes his poetic conception. To quote Alfandary again: "This analysis of the pro-duction of the meaning that is proper to poetry, this untenable protension of meaning between the touching and the touched, this 'for-wardness' between sensation and meaning, philosophically account for the sense-process that is at work in the poem."[24]

It is thus impossible to overestimate the theoretical legacy of German Romanticism for the *question* of literature in Nancy's work, along with his debt to Bataille, Blanchot, Benjamin, and Derrida when it comes to the "refusal to believe in a transparent and transitive language,"[25] to say nothing of the autonomy of the work of art and the calling into question of representation for the sake of presentation or *Darstellung*. As Walter Benjamin argued, "[o]nly since romanticism has the following view become predominant: that a *work* of art in and of itself, and without reference to theory or morality, can be understood in contemplation alone, and that the person contemplating it can do it justice."[26]

That is indeed what the Romantics have taught us, as Nancy argues: the work as "*opus operans*" (E, 67), as "incompletion" [*infinition*] (E, 66), "not its fulfillment but its operation, not its end but its infinity, not its entelechy but its energy as act of a dynamic that can't be absorbed into a product" (E, 67). This autonomist understanding of the literary absolute (as self-production and self-criticism) must not however overlook its counterpoint, which is dissolution (*absolvo* means "to complete" but it also means

---

[20] Cosmin Toma, *Neutraliser l'absolu. Blanchot, Beckett et la chose littéraire* (Paris: Hermann, 2019), 32.
[21] Alfandary, "'[L]'*ars poetica* en tant que tel*,*" 211.
[22] Ibid., 200.
[23] Ibid., 201.
[24] Ibid.
[25] Toma, *Neutraliser l'absolu*, 25.
[26] Walter Benjamin, "Letter to Gershom Scholem, 30 March 1918," in *The Correspondence of Walter Benjamin, 1910–1940*, ed. Gershom Scholem and Theodor W. Adorno, trans. Manfred R. Jacobson and Evelyn M. Jacobson (Chicago and London: The University of Chicago Press, 1994), 119.

"to separate, to detach"). Literature must thus become its own absolute even as it relinquishes it (gathering, totalization, completion).

Lastly, a final liminary remark: although in *The Literary Absolute* Lacoue-Labarthe and Nancy do not strip "the notion of 'absolute' of its latent mystery, thus recalling its complicity with theology,"[27] it is important to note that "Mystery in Literature," to borrow a title from Mallarmé, cannot for Nancy "be pursued through exclusively solitary means; it must necessarily set sail for the outside, consent to appearance and exteriorization,"[28] even to what he calls "compearance." Hence his insistence on writing as "the community of writing, the writing of community,"[29] to quote a chiasmus that once again evinces how much he owes to Blanchot.

III

By bringing together, in *Expectation*, Nancy's main theoretical writings on literature, as well as several essays in which he ponders the act of writing through the diversity of its genres (poetry, narrative, theatre, oratorio, dialogue, etc.), our aim was to make readable the entire spectrum of his thoughts on literature, chiefly grasped in its relationship with philosophy, but also, and more radically still, with language and sense. I say "*our* aim" because although this project was undertaken alongside the author (Nancy himself picked the title and the layout of the writings that I gathered and edited), this book is hardly his "doing" alone. A Brazilian writer, André Queiróz, gave this project its initial impetus in 2008 by asking me to prepare the volume. After a long developmental period, not one but two versions of the book were simultaneously published, in French by Galilée in 2015 and, for its Brazilian translation, by Editora da UFSC in January 2016 (it is the Galilée version that was translated into English as *Expectation* for Fordham University Press in 2017). As befits the author and his taste for musical variations, Nancy insisted that the two editions, Brazilian and French, would be different.[30] Even as he kept the same overall compositional layout, he made a few changes, moving chapters around from section to section, adding, for the French edition, a preface and "A Kind of Prologue: *Menstruum universale*. Literary Dissolution," as well as three more pieces: "Exergues" in the first section, "Sonate facile" ("Easy

---

[27] Toma, *Neutraliser l'absolu*, 52.
[28] Ibid., 120.
[29] Nancy, "The Inoperative Community," trans. Peter Connor, in *The Inoperative Community* (Minneapolis and Oxford: University of Minnesota Press, 1991), 42. See also this statement, which remains in a sense programmatic for Nancy's conception of poeticity: "the reasons for writing a book can be compared to the desire to modify the relations that exist between a man and his fellow men" (*E*, 42), as well as this most Mallarméan definition of the writer as narrator of the self, an own narrator of "the world of a mime who has no example to follow and will have no imitator": "This pure *poiesy* of the self in the pure community haunts but does not discontinue all of literature" (*E*, 37).
[30] This also applies to the American edition, from which five pieces were subtracted: "Making Poetry," "Taking Account of Poetry," "He Says," "Paean for Aphrodite," and "Vox Clamans in Deserto" are not included in the volume but are available in English in *Multiple Arts: The Muses II*.

Sonnet") and "'Let him kiss me with his mouth's kisses'" in the fourth. These shifts bear noting. In repositioning the "Coda" (which comes last in the Brazilian edition) at the beginning of the French edition, where it becomes a "true pre-preface, the book's antechamber," Nancy already draws our attention to "writing's antecedence" and "the circularity of saying,"[31] a *dispositio* that overlaps with an essential aspect of his poetics wherein the "end" is an ever-renewed beginning. Let us note that this circularity also plays itself out via the very placement of the words "literature" and "philosophy" in the subtitle, inverting them: on the cover, one reads "Literature and philosophy," whereas on the title page, the words "Philosophy, literature" are simply juxtaposed, without a conjunction. Likewise, in appending a poem on the kiss to the tail end of the French edition, Nancy further stresses this sensual-erotic resonance with his 1979 poem, "The Young Carp," and the internal circularity is this time part and parcel of the book.

I will now focus on *Demande* (a more complete edition than *Expectation*) in order to draw out a few propositions aimed at shedding light on Nancy's poetics of exscription. *Demande* consists of thirty-three diverse texts that nevertheless make up a highly coherent whole. Divided into four parts that delineate its articulations ("Literature," "Poetry," "Sense," and "Parodos"), the book allows us to hear a share of voices—timbres, modulations, phrasings, rhythm above all—that mark for Nancy the essential stakes of what we call by this ever-wanting name that is "literature" (and let us note from the outset that his attentiveness to rhythm does not limit itself to verse; it also, perhaps even especially, focuses on "words, the sounds they make, their countenance [*allure*],"[32] a term of which he is especially fond). Let us remark in this respect that he cites Mallarmé and Valéry with no less familiarity than Joyce, Borges and Sterne, Schlegel, Freud, and Celan, questioning the "cultural privilege assumed by the French language" as well as the "misunderstanding of the foreign that followed from this" (*E*, 11–12). Earlier I quoted Jean-Michel Rabaté, who speaks of a "*summa poetica*," but it is important to note that this is a closure-less, system-less totality, as Nancy suggests in his short "Preface to the English-Language Edition," in which he marks a sharp period: "But I have to stop here, for I'm beginning to rewrite the entire book… or a different one" (*E*, vii), thus demonstrating that his philosophy is ever willing to reopen the debate. This *summa*-like effect hinges not only on the fact that *Expectation* is a compilation of writings but also on the theoretical and philosophical aspects raised in the book (I am quoting Alfandary's description *in extenso*):

> In *Expectation*, Nancy seemingly seeks to embrace all of literature's dimensions, not just Literature with a capital L: from the book to the poem, from creation to reception, poetics and aesthetics are unwaveringly held together, traversed in their tracery, their overlaps, their infinite folds: the literary passion that is experienced here is inseparable from the desire to hear the expectation of literature itself, to embrace the multiple dimensions of the literary process, without neglecting

---

[31] Alfandary, "'[L]'*ars poetica* en tant que tel,'" 199.
[32] Nancy, "Pensée psalmodiée," VII.

those aspects that philosophy routinely dismisses, that are all too often relegated, abandoned to literary criticism, such as reading or prosody. Therein resides the singularity of Nancy's approach: delineating the event of literature as the event of its expectation.[33]

I will now pause for a moment and attend to the title and the "Coda" that opens the book. First, the title. Let us note that the word *demande*, which Nancy retained as the book's title in French, acts as both verb and noun, and can thus signify a commandment no less than a prayer (*prière*), already enacting, performatively speaking, the opening of sense that plays itself out in this address. In his "Preface" to *Expectation*, Nancy illuminatingly comments on the word's resonance for him: "In English, 'demand' resonates with much greater imperiousness or exigency than in French. A *demande* is a request and can even be a kind of prayer, supplication, or entreaty. Colored by psychoanalysis, it resonates like a 'demand for love,' which is quite distinct from both need and desire" (*E*, vii). He even analyzes it in such a way as to amend his "*Préface—*Coda" to the French edition:

> "Expectation" responds better to what "*Demande*" says to me in French. Philosophy and literature are in need of one another: not because they desire something of the other but as a "demand for love" or, at least, for encounter and sharing. Moreover, expectations are not symmetrical and in that sense I need to correct my introductory "Coda" somewhat. Philosophy expects more than literature because philosophy is experienced through suffering and is required to have a sense, whereas literature continues to defy sense. From this point of view, the "expectational" affect is much stronger in philosophy. On the other hand, literature expects to make sense while defying demonstrative and argumentative regimes. It doesn't want to be merely decorative or entertaining.
>
> (*E*, vii)

It would be interesting to further discuss this statement with regard to the difference in affect between philosophy and literature, as Nancy gives precedence to philosophy due to its "suffering," whereas literature seems to go beyond this demand for meaning, as if it were closer to desire or *jouissance* in its address without intention or finality, from the outset. In his "Coda," Nancy immediately insists on the reciprocity of philosophy and literature: "Philosophy ceaselessly expects that truth be realized (system, architectonic, certitude). Literature expects that it be pursued (recitative, recitation, recital)," at the risk of giving up on "the expectation of truth" (*E*, 3), thus harking back to Wisdom and Myth. He stresses what the two have in common, namely their relationship with the *outside*, a decisive notion in all of his writings ("This silent outside is what each of them does not forgo saying" [*E*, 1]). In the preface to *Expectation*, he instead emphasizes their asymmetry, as if to acknowledge Alfandary's objection.

---

[33] Alfandary, "'[L]'*ars poetica* en tant que tel,'" 206.

Indeed, she picks up on this contradiction in her study: "Literature and philosophy do not stand in a symmetrical relationship with reference to the expectation," she notes: "That which 'literature' expects is intransitive, does not have a bearing, properly speaking, on an object other than itself, assuming it can constitute itself as an object in the first place." As such, expectation "does not go without creating problems among them, for, as Nancy writes, while 'reason demands poetry,' poetry doesn't demand anything"; "What's more, poetry denies that sense can be accessed via a route other than its very own, which cannot be said for philosophy."[34]

The prologue appended to the French edition—recast in English as "A Kind of Prologue"—is equally important: in "*Menstruum universale*. Literary Dissolution," which dates from "April–May 1977"—written in close proximity, as the title, borrowed from Novalis, suggests, to *The Literary Absolute*—Nancy discusses *Witz* and thus that which, in literature, "is neither genre nor style, not even a rhetorical figure"; that which, even as it is not "a concept or a judgment or an argument" is "capable of playing all those roles, but mockingly" (*E*, 8). Within this notion that is simultaneously logical, semantic, philosophical, and pragmatic, Nancy already perceives the aporias of Early German Romantic theory regarding "the deliquescent union of these heterogeneities" that are literature and philosophy, the "mix of genres and prosodies," conceived here in terms of "literary dissolution, where 'literary' refers solely to the domain of text, of writing in general, the scriptural West" (*E*, 13). Although the *Witz* is, as Rabaté observes, "a witty knowledge that eschews the stale and systematic discursivity of Reason" (*E*, xv), it has long emblematized for Nancy a "double postulation, either dissolution or energy" that "can be combined—dissolution *and* energy," thus bringing it "closer to Maurice Blanchot's concept of 'unworking,' or 'undoing' (*désœuvrement*), also a manifestation of latent irony and parody" (*E*, xvi).

The volume's first section gathers texts Nancy wrote in the "beginnings," but their date of composition hardly matters since his entire philosophy, as we know, is fascinated with the birth of sense. Everything thus opens under the sign of the gods' withdrawal, as the first piece in this section, "'One day the gods withdraw…': (Literature/Philosophy: in-between)," suggests. In this incipient scene of mourning and desire, *mûthos* interrupts and opens itself, leaving in abeyance an interval, a rift where one can glimpse the trace of the divine's passage, a "vestige," Nancy says, that "at the same time remains the material and fading trace of a presence that is not worthwhile as sustenance, as being-present-there, stable and manifest, but which is worthwhile as passing, coming and going, arriving, occurring and departing" (*E*, 99). Nancy already posits, as he would later do in *Dis-Enclosure* and *Adoration*, the gods' absence as the shared condition of literature and philosophy, for both are "irreversibly atheological." It is this very absence "that legitimates them both": "they are responsible for nurturing the in-between: for keeping the body open, for allowing it the possibility of that opening" (*E*, 28). This in-between, both opening and gap, delineates the "singular body of absence on either side of which narration [literature] and the perspective of

---

[34] Ibid., 205–6.

truth [philosophy] touch": "One describes the forms of the body, the other inscribes its excavation," yet "[b]etween description and inscription," there remains what Nancy calls "an absent outside" (*E*, 27), "exscribed outside words" (*E*, 28).

In this first section still, "Reasons to Write" draws our attention to the question of rewriting and recitation. Already (in 1977, once again), this motif, which would later undergo a singular development in Nancy's philosophy of literature, is initially and decisively formulated, to borrow his wording, as "an appeal in one or more throats of writing" (*E*, 34):

> The repeated call always comes from him. It is the call of a solitude that predates any isolation, the invocation of a community that no society contains or heralds. How can the utterly different commonality of the book be released, someone asks, an ordinary writer, an *I* who is called?
>
> (*E*, 37)

Hence the attention lavished on the infinitely "renewed" voice, "clamor or murmur of a demand, an urgent appeal" (*E*, 34). Nancy unceasingly hears its resonance as it inspires or expires, most notably in the moving "He Says" or in the more ironic "Vox Clamans in Deserto," which stages this echo chamber. Is this reiterated call about "vocation, invocation, or advocation"? "Narrative, Narration, Recitative" suggests an answer to this question even as it is itself a privileged example of the aforementioned in-betweenness: between *aria* and *recitativo*, between melody and rhythm, language opens itself up to its other and lets through "a delicate balance ... a singsong effusiveness as well as a vocalized beat, one bordering the other" (*E*, 258n18). Aside from narrative, Nancy also examines, in this section, several fundamental categories of genre: the novel, where, as Schlegel put it, "[t]he theory of the novel would itself have to be a novel"; literary metalanguage, which is "immediately deprived of any claim to create metalanguage or metaliterature" (*E*, 58); the tensions that belabor the notions of author, work, and book, with Nancy stating that literature's "most telling mark"—whether it be narrative, prose, poem, or speech—dwells in this opening, this "antecedence both virginal and initiatory" where it "is always already present but always yet to come" (*E*, 62). Literature, in other words,

> begins and is continued outside itself; in fact, it is it-"self" nothing more than this antecedence and this unrealizable succession. We cannot complete meaning. At every moment, we assume we are positing a signification: meaning displaces them all and deposits them somewhere else, near an earlier and later exterior. Patiently, hopelessly, this elsewhere inscribes, exscribes its traces.[35]
>
> (*E*, 62)

---

[35] See also this excerpt from "Narrative, Narration, Recitative": "For that to arrive, it must also leave. It must first of all have gone—absent, not given, distant, lost even, nonexistent—for it to come or come back. Here, coming and coming back are the same, for coming always comes back from the same empty anteriority, coming comes back from nowhere, and returns there. (To come, coming, of course)" (*E*, 48).

Another capital aspect of Nancy's poetics is brought to light here, broaching temporality, or rather the "disjointing [*non-concordance*] of tenses"[36] of which the work is the locus. "The narrative will have begun before its narrator, who, however, must have preceded it: this is the lesson of literature—a lesson that philosophy rejects in principle, satisfying itself with the decision to be contemporary with its beginning" (*E*, 49). Here, literature hinges on the immemorial, the future perfect. In this regard, Alfandary sketches a generic hypothesis: "If the poem's saying is phenomenologically ahead of its being-said, fiction's narrative falls structurally behind its origin ... Indeed, it is proper to the structure of every narrative ... to assume antecedence and to pose itself as its sublation."[37] Literature, she continues, "does not idealize, does not essentialize, does not sacralize the original event that it nevertheless assumes,"[38] the "non-relationship with the origin"[39] that marks the privilege it maintains in its argument with philosophy.

The second part of *Expectation* focuses on poetry, as a matter of course [*comme de raison*], one is tempted to add, with reference to the title of the interview "Reason Demands Poetry." Meter, Nancy writes in "The Poet's Calculation," "is the divine: it is incommensurate in its strictly determined precision, the exactitude of the impossible" (*E*, 98). If meter itself inscribes—materially, he insists—"the passage of the gods" (*E*, 99), one readily grasps the importance of prosody, which is far more than just a "technical" matter. In these major theoretical writings, Nancy examines the modalities that touch on poetry's "doing," on calculation and excess, on the cuts and the scansion set to work by the poem. His study on the thinking poem is tightly woven into Hölderlin's poetics, which touches not only on compositional rules but also, bypassing them, on "an absolute point of exactitude" (*E*, 84) in the act of *saying*—and one cannot underestimate this word's scope in Nancy's thought. The poet thus affirms

> [t]he act that exactly calculates the moment—the instant, the weight, the passage— of the presence of the whole. The act that leaves nothing outside itself: not the background of an "intention," not the background of a "thing in itself." But the thing itself in presence of the gaze itself, in the very clarity—and the distance, the wide-eyedness of this "itselfness," its exact calculation.
>
> (*E*, 85)

The key features Nancy hails in Hölderlin's work—sobriety, concision, the work as "the place of an exact saying: no transition, intonation, flexion"—mark not only the force of the thinking poem per se but also the singular relationship with language that it represents for him: "I cannot insist too strongly on the fact that in them—language, prosody, rhythm—it is directly upon the words and song that the tone and tact of his poetics are arranged—that is, his thought, the outside of his thought, his thought outside thought" (*E*, 94). Some twenty years later, he comes back to Hölderlin in

---

[36] Alfandary, "'[L]*ars poetica* en tant que tel,'" 201.
[37] Ibid.
[38] Ibid., 202.
[39] Ibid., 203.

"Wozu Dichter" and gives a new reading of two well-known lines from "Brod und Wein" ("Why poets in a time of distress")—all too often wrongly commented upon in his estimation—divesting them of pathos so as to underscore the prosodic inflection, the poet's particular way of "doing," while remaining as close as possible to the German language's resources, "at his most intimate work of rhythm and song"[40] (*E*, 127).

Part III gathers pieces written in very different styles yet all of them invariably focus on the question of sense. In the wake, once again, of *The Literary Absolute*, the interview with Lacoue-Labarthe, "*Noli me frangere*," redeploys the Romantic *Gespräch* form even as it criticizes the limits of fragmentary writing in light of the then-recent publication of Blanchot's *The Writing of Disaster*. Via a variety of avenues—dialogue, "body-theatre," tragedy, the neuter according to Blanchot—Nancy translates the question of sense in terms of answer [*réponse*] and response [*répons*], of resonance, for meaning is conceived here in terms of reference [*renvoi*] and listening, music or speech on the brink of song. Resonance, that is also to say tension and expectation [*attente*], an access without violation [*atteinte*], a desire for the unheard-of point where literature and thought traverse and tune into each other before even so much as saying anything, in this singular extreme point of cutting and touching that is "the scansion of truth in sense" (*E*, 149). The philosopher then mingles his voice with that of the *aoidós*, a "sacred reciter" who is not an *I* but someone, *some one*: "The resonance leads us to understand: don't say what it is but make your saying be. This chiastic reversal is not a pirouette, it's the simplest outline, and the poorest, as well, of what creates resonance between poetry and philosophy, to say being or to be (to cause to be) the saying" (*E*, 112).

In "Responding for Sense," Nancy returns once again to the question of vocality, tuning into the voice somewhere between request, desire, clamor, supplication; into "the rustle of language," to quote Roland Barthes, and even "Exclamations," at the edge of articulate language. This turns out to be one of the most significant traits of Nancy's thought, as he has always shown a marked interest in infra-language, whether it be Derrida's rumblings or the spasms of the Mallarméan glottis. In *Sexistence*, Nancy incidentally notes that "[m]ore than on couches, it is in literature … that … speech makes itself sexual."[41] Tying desire to language, he further adds that "the one gives the other the élan of sense, which only takes place in the address, the appeal, the declaration, adoration, or exclamation"[42]: "They are two modes of address, sending, destination: sense. The relation between them forms nothing other than the play of sense, its opening, its space."[43]

The question of sense invariably calls upon those of writing and interpretation, and it is indeed a remarkable aspect of Nancy's poetics, whereby "[t]he 'relationship' between book and reader, a complex and asymmetrical one, a relationship based on

---

[40] In "Pensée psalmodiée," simultaneously calling upon Hölderlin and the spoken-sung recitation of *Sprechgesang*, Nancy reaffirms this essential aspect of his poetics by defining the poem as a "composition of sounds, assonances, cuts and beats that is simultaneously very clear, classic, and syncopated, quivering, with disjunctions as sharp as they are discreet." ("Pensée psalmodiée," VII.)

[41] Nancy, *Sexistence*, 40.

[42] Ibid., 26.

[43] Ibid., 28.

inclusion, is not indifferent to the poetic experience, nor to literature as an experience, even if it does not limit itself to it."[44] Toward the end of this section of *Expectation*, Nancy makes room for reading, describing it as an enigmatic gesture that "escapes" him "as form, essence, or definite property": the "only form of reading" that he foregrounds is "reading aloud," wherein "[o]ur voice takes over from the letter" and sense "finds itself pushed aside, not suppressed but distracted, pushed to the margin, postponed" (*E*, 197), indefinitely suspended. Once again, we see in this piece, no matter how brief, what the essential traits of reading rest on: no longer conceived in hermeneutic terms—as information, intelligibility, interpretation—it is instead envisioned from the point of view of orality and the body (lips, throat, tongue), of an experience of sense and meaning that is "sensible, sensitive, sensual"[45] (*E*, 197).

This question can only escape the scope of my chapter. For now, I will simply say that we must take stock of a certain experience of "Misreading," an experience that ought to be heard in more ways than one, as accomplished readers such as Philip Armstrong[46] and Isabelle Alfandary have seen, analyzing the occasionally disconcerting, even violent reading strategies Nancy employs vis-à-vis Derrida or Blanchot.[47] From Nancy's point of view, "misreading is not a reading that can be deemed a logical contradiction, nor a misinterpretation. Rather, it is a mode of reading that is not blind to its problematic condition—a reading against the tide, which is not unaware of itself as an act of reading subject to caution."[48] Nancy's approach therefore implies a kind of complex and somewhat distorting "(mis)reading" that brushes against the text with which it engages so as to expose it "to unforeseen contexts—to a high-risk to-come (*à-venir*)"; it "consists not in the application of a force that is extrinsic to reading, but rather a force within reading itself."[49]

Lastly, in the fourth and final section, entitled "Parodos," one finds several pieces written besides, perfectly besides … poetry. Nancy himself unpacks the word *parodos*, a homonym that refers "*to the song sung by the members of the choir as they made their way to the stage*" but that also apocryphally calls to mind *parōdia*, "*an overblown, comic song*" (*E*, 199). These essays are no mere "*hors d'oeuvres*." Rather, they are incursions that run the gamut from theory to experimentation, as evinced by "'Within my breast,

---

[44] Alfandary, "'[L]'*ars poetica* en tant que tel,'" 207.

[45] One could recall here the question of taste and its judgment, where taste now trumps criteria: "But what is taste in a world without rules? It's not nothing but what is it? To what 'universal,' as Kant remarked, can it claim? I'd like to be able to grasp this question," as Nancy says (*E*, 118). Reading is thus a "direct and immediate encounter" with the work: "An opportunity brings us together, no criterion has preceded us, and we try one another out … It's a form of pleasure, somewhat, a curiosity, a sensibility or, maybe a better way of putting it would be, susceptibility, an excitability" (*E*, 118–19).

[46] See Philip Armstrong, "Translator's Introduction," in Nancy, *The Disavowed Community*, trans. Ph. Armstrong (New York: Fordham University Press, 2016), 84: "Arguably one of the decisive factors in the reception of Nancy's *The Disavowed Community* will also be a question of (mis)reading."

[47] On Nancy's (mis)reading of Blanchot, see Leslie Hill, *Nancy, Blanchot: A Serious Controversy* (London and New York: Rowan & Littlefield International, 2018).

[48] Alfandary, "(Mis)Reading in *Dis-Enclosure*," trans. Priyanka Deshmukh, in *Nancy Now*, ed. Verena Andermatt Conley and Irving Goh (Cambridge: Polity, 2012), 129–30.

[49] Ibid., 139.

alas, two souls...,'" a Faustian recitative meant to accompany Claudio Parmiggiani's work, the suite entitled "City Moments" or the prose poem "Paean for Aphrodite" (which echoes "'One day the gods withdraw...'"). Among these pieces, two occupy a singular position: "Psyche," an allegory born of a posthumous note by Freud that Nancy repeatedly quotes and that Derrida analyses in *On Touching—Jean-Luc Nancy*, and "He Says," made up of elliptical "primitive scenes" about the relationship between literature and philosophy as Nancy conceives of it. "The Young Carp" also draws our attention, an early piece that "parodies" Valéry but is more than just a pastiche, already outlining a cardinal figure of Nancy's poetics, namely the mouth, present in his writings since "Le ventriloque" ("The Ventriloquist," in *Mimesis des articulations*, 1975) and *Ego Sum* (1979). Much like "*Sprung*," a philosophical poem or philosophy become poem, which also stresses the primordial figure of springing that is emblematic of Nancy's thought, this final poem on the kiss also foreshadows *Sexistence*, in which saying, conceived as a sexual gesture, occupies an essential place.

IV

What key elements may we foreground based on this survey? I will limit myself to three points. First, it must be said that Nancy's meditation lies under the conjoined sign—and it is not without its paradoxes—of a radical beginning and an original repetition. It is what he calls, alongside Blanchot, "the immemorial," which here does not mean the ancient, the primitive or the first, no more than the outside is the exterior (on the contrary, it is located within the heart of hearts, and comes "from within the cave, from its depths" [*E*, 112]). "Fiction" is thus for Nancy a figuration of the unfigurable: "Writing is devoted to considering the event that hasn't taken place or for which the taking-place can only be conjectured because it has withdrawn before any vestige, any trace one might discover" (*E*, 60). As such, writing does not consist for Nancy in "transcribing pre-existing givens—events, situations, objects, their significations—but in inscribing possibilities of meanings not given, not available, opened up by writing itself" (*E*, 59). Isabelle Alfandary is thus right to suggest that "[t]his critical statement isn't a statement among others: the singularity that writing signifies and enacts ... stems from a dislocation between literature and event, a disjunction between writing and occurring [*avoir-lieu*]."[50]

Second point: Nancy's writings are insistently shot through, as we've seen, with the motifs of orality,[51] of proclaiming/enunciating, of the "sharing of voices." This is hardly surprising. From the very beginning of his philosophical career, the notions of

---

[50] Alfandary, "'[L]'*ars poetica* en tant que tel,'" 203.
[51] For Nancy, orality is not reducible to phonation: "This latter [orality]—utterance, pronouncement, address—is far from being limited to the instrumentation of a phonatory apparatus. Orality is not phonation alone: it is the transmitting body, the body open to the outside as the transmitter of its 'inside,' which is only given in this transmission. Vocal production entails a resonance of the body through which inside and outside separate and respond to one another." Said "pronouncement" outwardly thrusts "the facilitation of meaning as it strives to escape" (*E*, 45–46).

interruption, of suspension, and of syncope revealed themselves to be essential (see his book, published in 1976, *Le Discours de la syncope* [*The Discourse of the Syncope*]). What's more, the Greek *sun* in "syncope" translates the Latin *cum*, the "with," that is to say: separation and conjunction, the disjunctive conjunction that unceasingly enacts itself [*s'opérer*], *opens* itself [*s'apérer*] in Nancy's philosophy as a whole. The "syncope" dis-closes every synthesis, as he argues in "Reason Demands Poetry." Let us recall that this "with," "constitutive of existents," is to be understood "in an existential rather than a categorial manner."[52] In *Sexistence*, Nancy specifies once again that "[t]he 'with' is never a thing, a substance, or a subject. It is the element of sense alone, in all of its senses—that is, in all the ways of sensing, of receiving, or of repulsing an outside, of not being 'inside' without this outside that comes and that distances itself."[53] This "with"— which may be called by many different names: in-between, coming, ab-sense—is inextricably tied to the question of the outside, which, in this poetics of exscription, turns out to be primordial. Indeed, whether in literature or poetry, what especially interests Nancy is the pair that comes "from far off" to "lift each other away, raise each other up far into the distance"[54]: "in order to present itself, presence must *come*. And in order to come it must be sent, addressed, expedited. This is what is called existence: the coming of everything to everything,"[55] as he states in *Sexistence*. What matters to him above all is thus this "sending—this liftoff, this raising up—[that] always expedites itself outside of itself."[56]

Third point: the interaction between sense and body. Relying on a conception of literature that is grounded (but is it a grounding?) in "the creative division of the speaker," "the demotion of the domineering Author," and "a newly enfranchised Reader" (*E*, xviii), literature, for Nancy, answers to no use or function: it is an exchange, passage, *trans*-formation of forms, without any prior given. Perhaps its specificity for him, like that of art, comes down to this statement: it produces not so much "meaning" as sense[57] (as long as we maintain the word itself between languages): "It is called sensation: such is sense's first guise."[58] Literature is what is sensitive to the possibility of sense; it "is always liable to 'make,' at the very least to suggest sense."[59] Sense, senses, and not sense as such; significance, signifiability rather than signification. Much like the question he raised early on regarding the *Witz*, "[t]he question that must be asked,

---

[52] Nancy, "Mit-Sinn," in *Mit-Sein*, ed. Elke Bippus, Jörg Huber, and Dorothee Richter (Zürich: Voldemeer, 2010), 21–32.
[53] Nancy, *Sexistence*, 29–30.
[54] Ibid., 28.
[55] Ibid., 29.
[56] Ibid., 51.
[57] See Jean-Michel Rabaté's remarks on this word: "Following Nancy's use, one should translate *sens* as 'sense,' for in recurrent phenomenological explorations that are not limited to poetry and include the substance of the world, Nancy insists upon the interaction between the body and meaning, between flesh and words." (*E*, xvii).
[58] Nancy, "Mit-Sinn," 3.
[59] Ibid., 2.

therefore, is extremely simple: how can the insignificant assume such importance and what does this operation entail?" (*E*, 9). In literature or art, what is indicated (or drawn) is not so much a "fullness of sense"[60] as the relationship with the thing itself. Literature is thus the site where the thing is approached, without any possible appropriation. It is "the approach of an unimaginable intimacy,"[61] which gives itself even as it withdraws, tangibly capturing the withdrawal wherein touching, the touch, can only come to pass as a gap, as spacing, as reference to the other. Literature—the poem, song, art, or any other nascent art form—clears a privileged access in that it makes "itself" sense in excess of sense, through glut and intensification. Nancy condenses what this *ars poetica* gives us to think/sense as a relationship with the world in the following terms:

> In feeling as we understand it (as affect, emotion, turmoil) ... there is nothing other than the development of this feeling [*sentiment*] of self that makes (up) the world: opening and receiving oneself from one's own opening like so many keys, indefinitely multiplied and relayed from thing to thing, from pressure to grasp, from sensor to reflector, action to reaction.[62]

It is thus no longer a matter, for this poetics of exscription, of acknowledging that the work of art interacts with the world; rather, the world comes about as shape. Better yet: as a shape that "replays and relaunches the ex nihilo that is [the] sharing"[63] of the world. Thus, literature is not "the answer to a question," to a demand, but "the response to a call" (*E*, 34).

V

In this, the final movement of my chapter, I would like to say something of poetry, for it bears out the sharpest point of our relationship with language,[64] consequently offering the greatest "resistance" according to Nancy. In an interview where he comments on the triple transformation now taking place ("capitalism, technology, democracy"), he argues that "although we don't know what it means to 'think,'"

---

[60] Ibid.
[61] Ibid., 3.
[62] Ibid., 5.
[63] Nancy, *Adoration*, 41.
[64] "Poematics," namely "the thought of poetry" (*E*, 91) rather than merely "a poetics of rules, genres, and examples" (*E*, 93). The word "poetry" does not refer here to a generic category but to that which spans all genres, fiction, narrative, and novel: "the word 'poetry' refers indiscriminately to a type of language, a particular artistic genre, and a quality that may be present elsewhere, and indeed may be absent from works of this type or genre altogether" (Nancy, *Multiple Arts*, 3). See also this passage on the novel: "I use the word 'novel' to express what for us subsumes or indeed represents the narrative in exemplary fashion. That is, not the narration of picturesque adventures and highly colored episodes (not the novelistic), but the thought that is held under the major sign of arrival, of arising and disappearance" (*E*, 47).

[w]e nonetheless know—or perhaps I should say we experience—something else: the same language [*parole*] that lays its fragile, worn out or emptied significations, yet continues to rekindle itself as call and exchange, exhortation or emotion, inextinguishable desire for sense and incessant passage on the brink of sense, or rather sense as a limit ... This resonates more clearly in poetry than in philosophy, but no culture, no configuration of humanity has ever been exempted from what the word "poetry" names so poorly and so well (it too torn apart like the infinite).[65]

If, then, "poetry," even as it inadequately names that to which it refers, continues to hold our attention, it is because it remains intimately bound to an "inextinguishable desire for sense."[66] But what exactly does "poetry" mean for Nancy? First and foremost, it is a matter of touching language, a nascent language or "intimating form"[67]: "poetry" (an obviously tricky word) is, for him, essentially sending [*envoi*], address, *tenue* and guise, the tone and timbre of a voice—of a highly singular voice, for it is neither that of the poet in his/her/their subjectivity, in the common sense of the word, nor even that of the poem, but that which emanates from language, "from language's becoming-voice,"[68] to quote Jean-Christophe Bailly's essay, *L'Élargissement du poème* (Broadening the Poem), which was published at the same time as *Demande*, and which is closely related to it. The voice's coming, whether dictating or reciting, ancient and unheard, hinges on saying rather than on what is said, on "a diction, a scansion, a recitation in which the most ancient has always already vanished ... arises and makes itself felt, lends itself to a *jouissance* that is neither of signification nor of satisfaction, but of touching and tact—a cadence of reading, and the unscathed face of the thousand-year-old friend,"[69] as Nancy writes with reference to Pascal Quignard.

These lines already express how "literature" interacts in a particular, perhaps even unique, manner with the question of myth. In *Proprement dit* (Properly Speaking), Nancy takes up this question anew and further complexifies it:

But let us return to the myth or rather to what might be left of it—since at bottom, the question is: what remains after the "interruption"? Or rather: what still makes itself heard? What continues to covertly traverse the partition that came to interrupt?

This leaves us with... literature (and the question of literature for/in philosophy).[70]

---

[65] Juan Manuel Garrido Wainer, "Phraser la mutation: entretien avec Jean-Luc Nancy," *Mediapart* (October 2015), online, accessed November 24, 2021: http://blogs.mediapart.fr/blog/juan-manuel-garrido-wainer/121015/phraser-la-mutation-entretien-avec-jean-luc-nancy; reprinted in *Les Cahiers philosophiques de Strasbourg*, no. 42 (2017): 119–25.
[66] On this issue, see Ben Lerner's essay, *The Hatred of Poetry* (New York: Farrar, Strauss & Giroux, 2016).
[67] Jean-Christophe Bailly, *L'Élargissement du poème* (Paris: Christian Bourgois éditeur, 2015), 109.
[68] Ibid., 58.
[69] Nancy, "Jadis, jamais, bientôt (l'amour)," in *Pascal Quignard, figures d'un lettré*, ed. Philippe Bonnefis and Dolorès Lyotard (Paris: Éditions Galilée, 2005), 384.
[70] Nancy, *Proprement dit. Entretien sur le mythe*, with Mathilde Girard (Paris: Lignes, 2015), 33.

This leaves us with literature, then, and with the poem as the "open," without a capital O, that "exceeds the sole question of its genre,"[71] broadening it and freeing it, extending it beyond itself: the open "as the generic name of that which does not close on itself, of that which unshackles itself from the impulse to enclose, which is still, despite all the efforts made to reduce it, absolutely dominant."[72]

The Nancean poem *par excellence* would thus be that which, far from "declamation or poetic prose in general,"[73] imposes itself through its *restraint*, "*just barely declaring itself as such. Nothing that touches on the emphasis this word suggests. Brief, fleeting, almost laconic envoys. Nothing that verges on hymn or even on what we call 'lyricism'.*"[74] He is especially attentive to a certain timbre, which is first and foremost that of "*a language that is spoken more than it is sung, rather brief, rapid, at times whispered, and thus addressed. Sonority comes through there, along with timbre and the rhythms of this parlando.*"[75] Such is the vocality that attracts Nancy in its "material truth,"[76] by way of lines that are "*measures of a breath of thought. Breaths that are more or less short, tense, held back, exhaled, breathed out. Phrases too: uttered, pronounced.*"[77] That is why the question of verse carries with it such vital stakes:

> What of verse when it is no longer entitled to be rounded up into a form, a figure, a round cadence commensurate with a great cosmological and theologico-lyrical harmony? What happens to verse when it is no longer poured, molded by an elevation of the soul or sublime passion—neither is it when enough to space out pure shards of language across the page?
>
> How, in other words, tune into a detuned world, or how find a breath without inspiration or expiration (apnea, as it were)?[78]

Verse thus impels a "necessary desubjectivation of poetry," and "to desubjectivate means: to recover the world's measure,"[79] no less. Such a definition single-handedly calls for a more serious examination of the poetic than we've been afforded so far, especially since, more readily than other forms of thought perhaps, it resists. But this salute to poetry is also for Nancy—it is important to stress this—a farewell:

---

[71] Bailly, *L'Élargissement du poème*, 8. This point deserves to be stressed further: for Nancy as for Bailly, it is never the question of genre or genres that matters so much as that of "modes or ways of singing," to quote Nancy on the recitative and its precipitates—psalmody, litany, threnody—"three poetic guises … bound to hymn but which also stood apart from it." (Nancy, "Pensée psalmodiée," VII.)
[72] Bailly, *L'Élargissement du poème*, 9.
[73] Nancy, "Deguy l'an neuf !," in *Le poète que je cherche à être. Cahier Michel Deguy*, ed. Yves Charnet (Paris: La Table Ronde and Éditions Belin, 1996), 168.
[74] Nancy, preface to Gérard Haller, *Météoriques* (Paris: Seghers, 2001), 10; italics original.
[75] Ibid.
[76] Nancy, "Vers endurci," afterword to Philippe Beck, *Dernière Mode familiale* (Paris: Flammarion, 2000), 210.
[77] Nancy, preface to G. Haller, *Météoriques*, 13.
[78] Nancy, "Vers endurci," 204–5.
[79] Ibid., 205.

It is possible that this farewell has yet to be uttered towards poetry ... Poetry, the elevation of hymn ... the sheer greatness of an access to *epos* and to the *lyre*: to a language of origin, to an accent of eternity. That is what we must take our leave from, insofar as we are unmoored from origin and eternity. This unmooring ... is not a decline, as we keep hearing. It is our drift in the *clinamen* that is named here. Saying goodbye means standing on a drifting boat and simultaneously looking at the image that draws away (myth, the originary scene) and at *the next one, which is still invisible*.

Saying goodbye means: knowing how to look at the invisible. Looking at it anew and looking at it new.

That is what the poem does: it moves away from the poem, eyes turned towards it, but turned also towards the invisible of a form to come, or perhaps only of a line [*trait*], of a beat. Poetry as the cadence of a coming rather than as the scansion of a cycle of origin and end.[80]

"[L]ooking at the image that draws away (myth, the originary scene) and at *the next one, which is still invisible*": is this the figure of a myth or of its dismissal, or is it a poem that begins to extend itself, to turn "towards the invisible of a form to come"? Tomb or birth? Mourning or desire? A beginning, an end? Both at once?[81] In "Pensée psalmodiée," Nancy recalls that "[t]he immanent poetics of languages [the wording is his] makes the words 'psalm' and 'spasm' resonate, as Paul Celan has so keenly used them," and although it is now impossible, for the poem, to settle for "lamentation," it must nevertheless find the means to "implore in a singular, bittersweet and stricken-vibrant song."[82]

Literature or "art" is thus worthwhile in that they exchange "sense outside of sense"[83]: they "do not signify: they carry significations away into another realm, where signs point [*renvoient*] to the infinite."[84] It is no accident that in *Adoration*, Nancy resorts to what he calls a "final cadence,"[85] quoting a brief erotic scene from Coetzee's *Elizabeth Costello* that outlines, perhaps better than any discourse might, what is at play in adoration itself. Literature is the trope of the infinite that gives access to a language without which "we could not enter into the sphere of sense, which is to say, above all into that of language."[86] These literary convocations go beyond reason, as

---

[80] Nancy, "Poème de l'adieu au poème: Bailly," *Po&sie*, no. 89 (1999): 61–62. In "Pensée psalmodiée," Nancy cites Bailly's essay on Hölderlin once again, pointing out "the inevitable consequence of the situation in which even Hölderlin is no longer possible: heroic and tragic elevation is not becoming of a world in which even the lament for the bygone divine is no longer possible. Furthermore, this impossibility is dual: on the one hand, we've run out of forms to sing in this register—the hymn has come to an end, like Jean-Christophe Bailly says; on the other hand, we cannot lament anymore—which always implies that we're hoping for a return, which Hölderlin indeed hoped for." (Nancy, "Pensée psalmodiée," VII.)

[81] On this myth, see Federico Ferrari and Jean-Luc Nancy, *La fin des fins. Scène en deux actes* (Nantes: Éditions nouvelles Cécile Defaut, 2015).

[82] Nancy, "Pensée psalmodiée," VII.

[83] Nancy, *Adoration*, 19.

[84] Ibid., 42.

[85] Ibid.

[86] Ibid., 60.

poetic speech allows "the very much elsewhere as elsewhere to come, all the while keeping it elsewhere."[87] Is this not what poetry does: return "once more from the further away, the more ancient, as the most ancient, the very much elsewhere, *here even elsewhere*"[88]?

It is in this sense that poetry becomes exscription. The poem attempts to extend, to broaden (the tenable, extension, tension, attention, expectation [*attente*], temptation: this lexical chain returns whenever literature is discussed in these pieces for a reason), it calls for overstepping boundaries, for an expansion, an escape from themselves, into the outside, into the world. What is sought in poetic saying is the world itself, never "objects," nor "subjects," for that matter, but "things: that is to say presences. Presences are mysterious, they evade approach, even as we may come into their proximity."[89] Such, then, is the force—a fragile, precarious, ever uncertain force—of these forms "wherein the text with its prosody, on the one hand, music with its colors, on the other, maintain their autonomy": poems "stress [*scandent*], they cadence a thought that neither conceives nor concludes, instead experiencing the world."[90]

Thus, what we call by the ancient yet ever-renewed name of "poetry" is no state of mind, nostalgia, or imprecation. If the poem matters, it is because it conforms to no "ideal precedence,"[91] to no given, it is attention to all that comes. If the poem survives and foils the myths of the origins and the ends, it is not because it is tantamount to evasion or a supplement of soul, but because it is an offer without expectation; it does not "fall" under the jurisdiction of meaning.

How, then, are we to think through this word, "literature" or "poetry"? Does it maintain some measure of relevance? The poem, to quote Nancy again, is an "inextinguishable desire for sense and incessant passage on the brink of sense, or rather on sense as a limit." This leaves us, yes, with the poem. In any case, it is on this question, phraseless once again, that the interview ends, as he asks whether we must not "[t]oday deliberately become poets again … what might this mean?":

> Each one of us is within reality [*le réel*], is only there… immersed in it, getting by in his or her own way with the opacity and the weight of the real…
>
> But of course, this requires that we speak of what is "real" once again, that we phrase it, name it, experience it and speak this experience. And so we recover the pinprick of an expectation of writing, of expression, of words in which reality may breathe [*respire*] or sweat [*transpirer*]…
>
> …
>
> Nothing I am able to name—but to know at least that we are in that element.[92]

---

[87] Nancy, "Deguy l'an neuf !," 168.
[88] Ibid., 169.
[89] Nancy, "Il fervore della parola," preface to *Narrazioni del fervore. Il desideria, il sapere, il fuoco*, trans. Alberto Panaro (Bergame: Moretti & Vitali, 2007), 9. I would like to thank Jean-Luc Nancy for granting me access to the French version of this essay.
[90] Nancy, "Pensée psalmodiée," VII.
[91] Bailly, *L'Élargissement du poème*, 102.
[92] Garrido Wainer, "Phraser la mutation."

I will leave the very last final word—even though there can be no such thing in these matters—to Nancy. In an email from two days ago to John Ricco, who was so kind as to share it with us, he writes: "We need poems more than philosophemes." Yet another way of rephrasing what "philoliterature" means for us now.

(Translated by Cosmin Toma)

(Keynote Lecture, Workshop "Reading with Nancy: Poetics of Exscription," co-organized by Philippe P. Haensler, Stefanie Heine, and John Paul Ricco, University of Toronto, Toronto, 14–September 15, 2018.)

2

Fort-Pflanzung: The Literary Absolute's Botanic Afterlife

Stefanie Heine

On the occasion of Johannes Kleinbeck's translation of *The Literary Absolute* into German, Nancy revisited the book he co-authored with Philippe Lacoue-Labarthe at an event organized by the Institute for Cultural Inquiry Berlin (ICI).[1] He began the discussion with Susanne Lüdemann by stressing the project's thoroughly collaborative nature: *The Literary Absolute* is a work written *à deux* that was originally conceived as an anthology of German Romantic theoretical texts, thus complicating the question of its authorship. In the blurb to the French original, Nancy and Lacoue-Labarthe write that their "primary ambition is ... to allow some of these texts to be read,"[2] that is, in France. Indeed, the twelve Romantic texts gathered in *The Literary Absolute* were translated into French for the first time by Lacoue-Labarthe and Nancy with the assistance of Anne-Marie Lang. Lacoue-Labarthe and Nancy's essays, which in the course of the book's reception became its center of attention (the English translation, for example, only consists of the essays), were, according to the "authors," merely added out of a necessity to "provide each of these texts with an accompaniment."[3] If we take this claim seriously, it becomes questionable whether Lacoue-Labarthe and Nancy *are* the book's sole, or primary, authors. Pointing this out is not so much a search for appropriate terminology (are the two names mentioned on the book's cover those of its authors, editors, translators?)[4] as it is a way of emphasizing the multiplicity or community of authorial voices contained therein. It is important to note that some of the Romantic

---

[1] Jean-Luc Nancy and Susanne Lüdemann, "The Literary Absolute," online, accessed November 25, 2021: https://www.ici-berlin.org/events/the-literary-absolute/.
[2] Philippe Lacoue-Labarthe and Jean-Luc Nancy, *L'Absolu littéraire. Théorie de la littérature du romantisme allemand* (Paris: Éditions du Seuil, 1978).
[3] Lacoue-Labarthe and Nancy, *The Literary Absolute: The Theory of Literature in German Romanticism*, trans. Philip Barnard and Cheryl Lester (Albany: State University of New York Press, 1988), xxii. Hereafter *LA*.
[4] While the translations, for example into English or German, present Lacoue-Labarthe and Nancy as authors by placing their names above the book's title, the original French, at least on the title page (though not on the cover), defines their role differently: "*L'Absolu littéraire. Théorie de la littérature du romantisme allemand*. Présenté par Philippe Lacoue-Labarthe et Jean-Luc Nancy avec la collaboration d'Anne-Marie Lang."

texts published in *The Literary Absolute* were themselves written collaboratively and that one of them, Friedrich Schlegel's "Dialogue on Poetry," presents us with a conversation carried out by multiple voices. This constellation is no coincidence given that one of Lacoue-Labarthe and Nancy's major interests in the German Romantics was their "desire for collective activity, for a certain 'community' life" (*LA*, 7) as well as the "collective writing" (*LA*, 9) that was practiced (whether tentatively or not) in the literary circle around the Schlegel brothers in Jena, especially through the short-lived journal *Athenaeum*.

Looking back on *The Literary Absolute* at the ICI Berlin, Nancy places the question of community at the center of his retrospective. Nancy points out that he and Lacoue-Labarthe were especially concerned with the difficult relation between the Romantics' philosophical and literary striving for unity and community. "How far can we follow the Romantic gesture towards unity without exposing ourselves to the danger of totality?,"[5] he asks. While a definitive answer is still pending, Lüdemann and Nancy both agree on the aspect of Romantic theory where this danger becomes most pronounced: in the "organic model," tying the autonomy of natural organisms to the dream of a *Gesamtkunstwerk* and of political totality. The "*ab-solute*, its isolation in its perfect closure upon itself (upon its own organicity), as in the well-known image of the hedgehog in *Athenaeum* fragment 206" (*LA*, 11), which self-reflexively states that the fragment "has to be … complete in itself like a hedgehog" (*LA*, 43), anticipates what Nancy diagnoses as the peril of a totalitarian "corps politique" prevailing in 1978, when *The Literary Absolute* was written.

Nancy's rejection of the "organic model" in his attempts to think a community beyond totality does not mean the Romantics' organic images no longer deserve critical attention. In fact, in the talk on *The Literary Absolute* which preceded her discussion with Nancy and served as its starting point, Lüdemann allows the famous hedgehog to move out of the totalizing framework by drawing attention to its complexity and ambiguity. Indeed, the "organic unity of the hedgehog" (*LA*, 50) collapses when we look at it from a different angle: *Igel* read backwards is *legi*, which Lüdemann interprets as "*J'ai lu*," pointing to a process of reading that always remains open.[6] Emphatically embracing how Lüdemann turns "the organic *Igel* into the inorganic *legi*,"[7] Nancy adds that such a rewriting of the hedgehog gets to the heart of Romantic equivocity, a double movement he and Lacoue-Labarthe observe in their essays and that "governs the entire question of 'literature' up to the present" (*LA*, 124): somewhere between self-enclosure, autonomy, and autogenesis, on the one hand, and the way in which, on the other hand, "something always resists—or escapes" (*LA*, 122) the totality that is "un-worked" (*LA*, 123) from within. What Phillip Barnard and Cheryl Lester translate as "unworking" is

---

[5] Nancy and Lüdemann, "The Literary Absolute." My translation throughout.
[6] The talk was subsequently published: Susanne Lüdemann, "Die Ko-Präsenz der Igel. Vom unendlichen Gespräch zum Literarisch-Absoluten, billet aller-retour," *Arcadia* 53, no. 1 (2018): 187–98.
[7] Nancy and Lüdemann, "The Literary Absolute."

a term borrowed from Maurice Blanchot, *désœuvrement*,[8] which Lacoue-Labarthe and Nancy reinterpret as the central countermovement that unsettles the totality embraced by the Romantics.

The Vegetal Literary Absolute in Romanticism

In this chapter, I would like to turn to a different set of biological images, which the Romantic texts draw upon when outlining poetry as an "organic Whole capable of engendering itself ... the absolute *Organon*" (*LA*, 91): plants and flowers.[9] Tracing vegetal imagery in *The Literary Absolute*, that is, both in Lacoue-Labarthe's and Nancy's essays and in the Romantic texts they compile, allows for a more detailed elaboration of a specific feature of Romantic equivocity: the peculiar meshing of the notion of an "organic Whole," its generation/auto-engenderment, and *désœuvrement*. Arguing that *The Literary Absolute* was not "an archival enterprise" (*LA*, 2), Lacoue-Labarthe and Nancy single out *historical afterlife*[10] as one of the book's main concerns: the "'literary absolute' ... continues, even today, to haunt our theoretical semisomnolence and our reveries of writing" (*LA*, xxii). In tracing this historical afterlife, especially with regard to organicism and botanic images, we find that the bio-aesthetic trajectories of the Romantic literary absolute lead us to the very heart of modernist poetics: to Bloomsbury aestheticism and one of the seminal and most representative figures of modernism, Virginia Woolf. In an autobiographical text, "A Sketch of the Past," we find the vegetal, botanic, and organic tensions of Romanticism reflected in considerations about "moments of being" and the nature of language and literature in their relation to being. Through a closer examination of Bloomsbury organicism and Woolf's own notion of being, we can complement the notion of Romantic equivocity with modernist equivocity.

Arguing that the *Athenaeum* "is our birthplace" (*LA*, 8) and that the early German Romantics inaugurate an idea of literature concerned with "its own engendering" (*LA*, xxii), Nancy and Lacoue-Labarthe describe the Romantic project in terms of *procreation*—what in German is subsumed under the word *Fortpflanzung*. As Jocelyn Holland has shown, *Fortpflanzung* became a defining term for a particular way of thinking procreation around 1800. In contrast to *Zeugung*, which "originates in the context of animal generation" and implies an individual who "is somehow indebted

---

[8] See Blanchot's essay on the early German Romantics, which was highly influential for *The Literary Absolute*: "Romanticism ... is, indeed, often unproductive—for it is the work of the absence of work, poetry affirmed in the purity of the poetic act ... freedom without realization." Maurice Blanchot, "The Athenaeum," trans. Deborah Esch and Ian Balfour, *Studies in Romanticism* 22, no. 2, "Des Allemagnes: Aspects of Romanticism in France" (Summer 1983): 163–72.

[9] For a broader investigation of plant imagery and organicism in Romanticism, see chapter VII of M. H. Abrams's seminal book *The Mirror and the Lamp: Romantic Theory and the Critical Tradition* (Oxford: Oxford University Press, 1953).

[10] For a study of this afterlife in the works of Maurice Blanchot and Samuel Beckett, see Cosmin Toma's book, *Neutraliser l'absolu. Blanchot, Beckett et la chose littéraire* (Paris: Hermann, 2019).

to its parent or creator," *Fortpflanzung* is more broadly determined "by duration and expansion,"[11] often corresponding to "*Erhaltung*, with its register of continuity, perpetuation and sustainment,"[12] thus "lend[ing] itself to narratives of production and generation that are less conditioned by biological concepts."[13] Importantly, this latter claim, confirmed by the occurrences of *Fortpflanzung* in the procreative discourses Holland investigates ca. 1800, marks a significant development in the word's use.

In 1781, Johann Christoph Adelung's first definition is rooted in the vegetal domain: "1) Weiter pflanzen, dem Orte nach. Ein Gewächs fortpflanzen, es von einem Orte wegpflanzen. [Plant to another place. Move a plant to another place.]"[14] The second definition, "Der Art oder Gattung nach vermehren, fortdauern machen eigentlich von Pflanzen, in figürlichem Verstande auch von Thieren, ja von fast allen Dingen [Propagate a species or genus, make it last, originally said of plants, figuratively also of animals, in fact of almost all things]"[15] shows a shift from the literal to a figural use: originally, *Fortpflanzung* referred to the reproduction of plants and the sustainment of their species or genus (*Gattung* or *Art*)[16]; in a *figural sense*, it is extended to animals and "almost all things." The increased presence of the word in "narratives of production and generation that are less conditioned by biological concepts"[17] is based on this later figural sense. When the Romantics employ vegetal imagery in order to address art's "auto-engendering" (*LA*, 16), especially the emergence of a unified poetic *Gattung* (genre)—an "organic Whole capable of engendering itself" (*LA*, 91)—the concept of *Fortzplanzung* is thus at the same time metaphorized and re-literalized; the organic plant, which often disappeared in the broader use of the term around 1800 returns figuratively. In other words, the *Pflanze* in *Forpflanzung* is involved in a dynamics of presence and absence, a *fort-da* game.

Lacoue-Labarthe's and Nancy's discussion of "the absolute *Organon*," the "organic Whole capable of engendering itself," in the essay "The Poem: A Nameless Art," is to a large extent based on a passage from Friedrich Schlegel's *Dialogue on Poetry*, reproduced in *L'Absolu littéraire* after the essay:

> It is not necessary for anyone to sustain and propagate [*fortzupflanzen*] poetry through clever speeches and precepts, or, especially, to try to produce it, invent it, establish it, and impose upon it restrictive laws as the theory of poetics would like to. Just as the core of the earth adorned itself with formations and growths

---

[11] Jocelyn Holland, "*Zeugung / Fortpflanzung*: Distinctions of Medium in the Discourse on Procreation around 1800," in *Reproduction, Race, and Gender in Philosophy and the Early Life Sciences*, ed. Susanne Lettow (Albany: State University of New York Press, 2014), 84.
[12] Ibid., 88.
[13] Ibid., 84.
[14] Johann Christoph Adelung, *Grammatisch-kritisches Wörterbuch der Hochdeutschen Mundart*. Zehnter Theil (Leipzig: Breitkopf und Sohn, 1796), 257.
[15] Ibid.
[16] The complex differentiation between *Gattung* (genus) and *Art* (species) is not addressed in Adelung's definition.
[17] Holland, "*Zeugung / Fortpflanzung*," 84.

[*Gewächsen*], just as life sprang forth of itself from the deep and everything was filled with beings merrily multiplying; even so, poetry bursts forth [*blüht*, i.e., blooms] spontaneously from the invisible primordial power of mankind when the warming ray of the divine sun shines on it and fertilizes it. Only through form and color can man recreate his own creation, and thus one cannot really speak of poetry except in the language of poetry.[18]

Lacoue-Labarthe and Nancy do not cite this paragraph in their essay, even as they cite other passages from the *Dialogue* that focus on vegetal images and autopoiesis, as well as from the *Athenaeum* fragments and Schelling's *Philosophy of Art*. Moreover, in their French translation of Schlegel's *Dialogue, fortzupflanzen* becomes *répandre* (to spill or spread) (*LA*, 290). This double disappearance of the concept in *The Literary Absolute*, on the most basic material-textual level, already reveals a crucial gesture: the "fort," or absence, of *Fortpflanzung* pervades the book's negotiation of one of its central themes, engenderment, through botanic imagery. Concerning the latter, Schlegel's use of the language of propagation is representative. Starting with the figural, non-botanic meaning of *fortpflanzen*, he proclaims that poetry is not dependent on someone to propagate, sustain, create, or invent it. He then draws a comparison between poetry and the vegetal world, whose "life sprang forth by itself," creating the impression that the *Pflanze* in *Fortpflanzung* "grows" out of the word into which it is embedded, liberating itself from the idea of being sustained by someone and taking on an autonomous life. This then culminates in the metaphor of poetry "blooming" on its own ("blüht … von selbst"). Schlegel thus performatively demonstrates his claim that "one cannot really speak of poetry except in the language of poetry": through the metaphoric bloom, poetry's central feature is presented in poetic language.

In the course of unpacking the various aspects of the "literary absolute" from different angles—following the essays' layout, which moves from the subject to the fragment to the idea to the poem, and then to criticism—Lacoue-Labarthe and Nancy repeatedly emphasize the importance of "*Darstellung* (the presentation, the figuration, the staging …)" (*LA*, 31). As Philip Barnard and Cheryl Lester argue in their introduction to the English translation, the "analysis and elaboration of this more adequate form of presentation as it appears in the romantic theory of literature is the subject of *The Literary Absolute*" (*LA*, ix). In "the romantic theory of literature," *Darstellung* is not merely an embellishment; the way the theoretical texts present ideas about poetry is precisely how these ideas come closest to realization, as Lacoue-Labarthe and Nancy argue. Accordingly, Schlegel's *metaphor* of poetry blooming by itself enacts the literary self-engenderment described. At the same time, it becomes what Lacoue-Labarthe and Nancy define as a "*Darstellung* of impossible auto-constitution," "the admission of the

---

[18] Friedrich Schlegel, *Dialogue on Poetry and Literary Aphorisms*, trans. Ernst Behler and Roman Struc (University Park: Pennsylvania State University Press, 1968), 54. The German original is cited from Philippe Lacoue-Labarthe and Jean-Luc Nancy, *Das Literarisch-Absolute. Texte und Theorie der Jenaer Frühromantik*, trans. Johannes Kleinbeck (Vienna: Turia + Kant, 2016), 345.

failure and insufficiency of the work, if not the index—perhaps—of its 'unworking'" (*LA*, 90). This "romantic equivocity"—a fantasy of literature's self-sufficiency, unity, and autopoiesis, indebted to idealism and simultaneous pervaded by *désœuvrement*—is strikingly articulated in Schlegel's floral metaphor for poetry. The claimed *organicism* of poetry's auto-engenderment is a *linguistic* product, its autonomous bloom a *Setzung* (positing/planting) in language. This linguistic *Setzung* corresponds to what Lacoue-Labarthe and Nancy describe as a "*Darstellung* of impossible auto-constitution": it requires a *Setzung* that does not operate all "by itself." In other words, poetry's self-blossoming is grounded in what Schlegel's argument vehemently denies: it has to be *fortgepflanzt* by an external agent. In contrast to the idea of spontaneous self-engenderment, and parallel to Adelung's definition ("Weiter pflanzen, dem Orte nach. Ein Gewächs fortpflanzen, es von einem Orte wegpflanzen"), the *Pflanze* undergoes various transplantations in the course of Schlegel's text: stemming from the word *fortpflanzen*, it is first understood literally, in reference to vegetal beings, only to become a metaphor for poetry.

Thus, the organic model of poetry presented in this vegetal image ceases to be biologically founded. Through its metaphorical constitution, poetry's blooming flower turns out to be absent: trans-posed or *fort-gepflanzt* from the vegetal domain to the domain of language, the plant is "fort" as an organism of the natural world and turned into a sterile thing of print. The linguistic domain of flower-ideas is precisely what enables Schlegel's argument for an "original" and "unconscious poetry that stirs in the plant … without which there would be no poetry of the word" (*Dialogue on Poetry*, 53–54; cited in *LA*, 92–93). The human creators of the "poetry of the word" are themselves "part and flower" of "the poem of the Godhead" (*LA*, 93) that is, of nature. As Lacoue-Labarthe and Nancy argue, this "hyperbolic movement" that

> dissolve[s] the concept of poetry in the idea of a "natural poetry," which is nothing other than nature itself … proceeds from nothing other than the literalization of the organic metaphor. Or more precisely … the hyperbolization of poetry, the poetic dissolution is the very effectuation of the idea of *organon*—or of the *organon* as Idea.
>
> (*LA*, 92–93)

The "idea" of "organon" and "natural poetry" depends on mediation through language, or, to be more precise, a poetic use of language, which involves a double movement: paradoxically, in Schlegel's *Darstellung*, "original poetry," that is, nature—"the unconscious poetry that stirs in the plant … without which there would be no poetry of the word"—can only be effectuated as idea by rendering the natural world absent through words. At the same time, the idea presented by Schlegel is based on a "*literalization* of the organic metaphor": the plants and flowers thereby addressed have to be taken literally (as opposed to figuratively or metaphorically) in order to amount to the notion of natural poetry. This tension reveals how the organico-poetic wholeness embraced is "un-worked" from within in the early German Romantics' writings.

Immediately following their discussion of Schlegel's passage on original vegetal poetry, Lacoue-Labarthe and Nancy move to an excerpt from Schelling's *Philosophy of Art*, which also focuses on plants: what Lacoue-Labarthe and Nancy describe as "the hyperbolization of poetry" reaches its peak when Schelling inverts Schlegel's comparison of a superior original "poetry that stirs in the plant" with the "artificial works" of poetry and prioritizes the "more highly organized and complexly interwoven plant called the work of art" over "the intricacies of a plant or of an organic being in general" (*Philosophie der Kunst*, 378; cited in *LA*, 93). Lacoue-Labarthe and Nancy argue that Schelling's claim of "artistic organicity" being purportedly "superior to natural organicity" follows from "the literalization of the organic metaphor" that effectuates "the idea of *organon*" (*LA*, 93). They thus touch upon a double movement enacted by literary-poetic language, as would later be illustrated by Mallarmé in his remark on the verbalization of a flower: literary language makes the real-life referent disappear and thus enables the emergence of the thing—the flower—as idea. For Schelling, the idea becomes ideal: the "more highly organized and complexly interwoven plant called the work of art," or, in Lacoue-Labarthe's and Nancy's terms, "poetry as absolute work" (*LA*, 93).

Their comments on Schlegel's and Schelling's vegetal imagery are embedded in a discussion of genre/*Gattung*, the very concept that constitutes "poetry as absolute work" within the Romantic framework. Rather than attempting to distinguish different genres from one another in order to define them, the Romantic project embraces the idea of unifying all genres into the genre of "Literature (or Poetry)" (*LA*, 92). This unified "literary Genre" is precisely what Lacoue-Labarthe and Nancy call "the *Literary Absolute*." Equated "with totality (with the absolute) in the dissolution of all limits," genre coincides with generation and thus with the idea of an "organic Whole capable of engendering itself … organicity itself or the process of auto-formation." Organicity here exceeds the notion of a biological organism. As Jochen A. Bär pointed out in his study of language-reflection in German Romanticism, the word "organic," which harks back to the Greek ὄργανον (*organon*: instrument, tool),[19] did not only mean "biological" or "animate" but was often used in the sense of inner structures, organized according to inner laws or regularities.[20] This sense predominates in the passage from Schlegel's "On the Combinatory Spirit," which Lacoue-Labarthe and Nancy cite in their description of the Romantic genre as "the absolute *Organon*": not "this or that genre … but rather literature itself that would be a great, thoroughly connected and organized Whole, comprehending many worlds of art in its unity, and being at the same time a unitary work of art" (*LA*, 91). In Schlegel's image of the "highly organized and complexly interwoven plant called the work of art," the notion of organism as an "organized Whole" and of an autonomous living being is interwoven.

The very idea that Romantic poetry seeks to "mix and sometimes fuse … the poetry of art [*Kunstpoesie*] and the poetry of nature [*Naturpoesie*]" (*Athenaeum* fragment

---

[19] Jochen A. Bär, *Sprachreflexion der deutschen Frühromantik. Konzepte zwischen Universalpoesie und Grammatischem Kosmopolitismus* (Berlin: De Gruyter, 1999), 420.
[20] Ibid., 213.

116; cited in *LA*, 91) is rooted in a conception of *Gattung* determined by mixture and union. Outlining the "word's etymological filiation" (*LA*, 91), Lacoue-Labarthe and Nancy gesture toward a biological implication of *Gattung* in German without further commenting on it.

> *Gattung* is not unrelated to assemblage in general, or to union and even marriage. But the process of generation ... obviously supposes interpenetration and confusion. Or in other words, *mixture* (*gattieren* means "to mix"). It could be said that this is precisely what the romantics envisage as the very essence of literature: the union ... of poetry and philosophy, the confusion of all the genres arbitrarily delimited by ancient poetics.
>
> (*LA*, 91)

And in a footnote, they add:

> The *ghedh-* root reappears in *gatten* (to unite oneself to or come together) or the couple *Gatte/Gattin* (husband/wife), and refers to the idea of jointure or connection.
>
> (*LA*, 144)

What is not made explicit in these elucidations is that the references to marriage and the union of husband and wife also involve *Fortpflanzung* in the sense of procreation: one meaning of *gatten* and *sich gatten* is *sich paaren* as sexual union, copulation.[21] When Lacoue-Labarthe and Nancy identify "the very essence" of the Romantics' notion of literature as *Gattung*, they to a certain extent neglect the organic and biological dimension of genre in German, *Fortpflanzung*, as well as its heteronormative and androcentric premises (which, according to their argument, would be the very premises of Romantic literature).

One key text in which the etymological kinship between genre, gender, and procreation is highlighted and presented through vegetal imagery is Friedrich Schlegel's *Lucinde*, which, as Lacoue-Labarthe and Nancy argue, "would seem to qualify" for an appropriate *Darstellung* of the Romantic theory of genre: a *literary* work "containing its own reflection and ... comprehending the theory of its 'genre' (or the law of its own engendering, which amounts to the same thing)" (*LA*, 90). The passage in question is part of "A Dithyrambic Fantasy on the Loveliest Situation in the World," a "novel in miniature"[22] embedded within the book, which stages a gender-crossing erotic-aesthetic fantasy emerging from Lucinde's absence: "A large tear falls on this sacred page that I've found here in place of you."[23] In the piece of writing—"this sacred

---

[21] "Gattung," in *Deutsches Wörterbuch von Jacob und Wilhelm Grimm*, Band 4 (Leipzig: Hirzel, 1978), 1512.

[22] Eleanor Ter Horst, "The Classical Aesthetics of Schlegel's *Lucinde*," *Goethe Yearbook* 23 (2016): 129.

[23] Friedrich Schlegel, *Lucinde and the Fragments*, trans. Peter Firchow (Minneapolis: University of Minnesota Press, 1971), 46.

page," a placeholder for Lucinde herself—Julius conjures up a vision of unity, of the absolute as totality and dissolution, on several levels: sexual union approaching the "farthest reaches of unbridled lust,"[24] "marriage, the timeless union and conjunction of our spirits,"[25] an image of humankind as a whole in the persons of Julius and Lucinde, etc. In this context, Lucinde briefly transcends gender boundaries, entering an undivided state of wholeness: "You're untouched by the faults that custom or caprice call female ... You feel completely and infinitely; you know no separations; your being is one and infinitely."[26] As Eleanor Ter Horst observes, *Lucinde* becomes a site where Schlegel "does advance an aesthetics based on the mixing of what are considered to be the established characteristics of each gender, just as he advocates the mixing of genres in his aesthetic theory."[27]

When Schlegel employs an "organic" floral "metaphor" in this context, the evoked unity of a *Pflanze* conjoining the lover's minds meets *Fortpflanzung* in the sense of procreation:

> There will come a time when the two of us will perceive in a single spirit that we are blossoms of a single plant or petals of a single flower ...
>
> Do you still remember how the first seed of this idea grew in my soul, and how it immediately took root in yours as well? So is it that the religion of love weaves our love ever more closely and tightly together, just as the child, echolike, redoubles the happiness of its tender parents.[28]

The floral fantasy of wholeness, claimed to be the result of a thought's spontaneous engenderment, "perfect in itself ... unique and indivisible,"[29] which in the process of emerging within two souls simultaneously unites them, culminates in a comparison featuring the child, the product of the sexual union of *Gatte* and *Gattin*. Schlegel thus locates the process of engenderment in the past or present, while the outcome is projected into the future. The reproductive parts of the plant, "blossoms" or "flower," are yet to be encountered; the still pending flower provides the metaphorical basis for the narrative of its generation: a "seed" has sprouted and already taken root. In a further twist of figural language, this scenario becomes the basis for a comparison: the "happiness [*Lust*] of its happy [*zärtlichen*] parents"[30] is claimed to be doubled in the unborn child. The account of spontaneous creation is thus increasingly poeticized and the "organic" realization of the imagined wholeness deferred. In other words, the logic of vegetally conceived procreation turns out to be a logic of incompletion: a *Fort-Pflanzung* determined by endless continuation

---

[24] Ibid., 47.
[25] Ibid., 48.
[26] Ibid., 47.
[27] Ter Horst, "The Classical Aesthetics of Schlegel's *Lucinde*," 130.
[28] Schlegel, *Lucinde*, 48–49.
[29] Ibid., 48.
[30] The German original is cited from *Lucinde. Ein Roman* (Jena: Eugen Diedrichs, 1907), 26.

as much as by the absence of engenderment that is at stake here. This logic repeats itself on another level: the "incompletion of *Lucinde*" (*LA*, 90) as a novel is central to Lacoue-Labarthe's and Nancy's attempt to reveal how "unworking" pervades the Romantic ideal of genre. "It would not be difficult to demonstrate that *Lucinde* is constructed on the principle of auto-engenderment, although the important thing is still, perhaps, that the book should never have been completed or, if you will, that once begun, it should have been aborted" (*LA*, 143). The "failure and insufficiency" of Schlegel's novel as realization of the Romantic genre amount to a "*Darstellung* of impossible auto-constitution" (*LA*, 90).

In their discussion of the Romantic fragment, Lacoue-Labarthe and Nancy explicitly address the overlap between organic procreation and the generation of art. The starting point of this observation, which goes hand in hand with the second moment where they engage with plant imagery, is the claim that the literary absolute as envisioned by the Romantics is essentially based on non-actualization and incompletion: "The actuality of romanticism, as is well known, is never *there* ... But it is indeed in this not being there, this never yet being there, that romanticism and the fragment *are*, absolutely. *Work in progress* henceforth becomes the infinite truth of the work" (*LA*, 48[31]). Consequently, questions of (literary) production become the major focus of attention: "Thus it is also necessary to grasp ... the dialectical unity of artificial production (of art) and of natural production: of procreation, germination, and birth" (*LA*, 49). As an example, Lacoue-Labarthe and Nancy turn to a scenario of literary *Fort-Pflanzung par excellence*:

> the fragment is as yet no more than germinating [*en germe*] because it is not yet fully completed ... And according to the last of Novalis' *Grains of Pollen*, the fragment is indeed a germ or seed [*semence*]: "Fragments of this kind are literary seeds: certainly, there may be many sterile grains among them, but this is unimportant if only a few of them take root!" ... Fragmentation is not, then, a dissemination, but is rather the dispersal that leads to fertilization and future harvests. The genre of the fragment is the genre of generation.
>
> (*LA*, 49)

Nancy and Lacoue-Labarthe add a footnote on dissemination: "In the 'sense' Jacques Derrida gives the word in *La Dissemination* [sic] ... of a sterile dispersion of seed [*la semence*] and of the semic [*le sémique*] in general; in other words, of sign and sense" (*LA*, 135). The argument that the fragmentation Novalis has in mind is *not* "a dissemination" in Derrida's sense rests on the premise that it marks a movement of language, of "sign and sense." Despite "*playing* on the fortuitous resemblance, the purely simulated common parentage of *seme* and *semen*,"[32] dissemination remains "sterile." The reference to procreation conveyed by an inorganic signifier "produces a

---

[31] Italics original throughout unless otherwise noted.
[32] Jacques Derrida, *Positions*, trans. Alan Bass (Chicago: University of Chicago Press, 1981), 45.

kind of *semantic* mirage: the deviance of *meaning*."³³ Such a deviance of two different signifieds is precisely what produces the movement referred to by "dissemination": an opening and a dispersion of meaning. Insofar as Novalis's fragment self-reflexively identifies itself as a "literary seed" and consists of language that metaphorically evokes vegetal fertilization, it is, in fact, "a sterile dispersion of seed [*la semence*] of the semic [*le sémique*] ... of sign and sense."

This, in fact, holds true for any textual or literary product; it is, apart from contiguous vocabulary, not *specific* to Novalis's fragment. When Lacoue-Labarthe and Nancy argue that "[f]ragmentation is not, then, a dissemination, but is rather the dispersal that leads to fertilization and future harvests," they allude to additional qualities of dissemination and thus point to the characteristics of a *specifically Romantic* genre. Derrida locates dissemination, a process that resists closure,³⁴ outside of "teleological and totalizing dialectics."³⁵ The Romantic fragment, as outlined in *The Literary Absolute* and later spelled out by Nancy in "Art, a Fragment," involves precisely such teleological and totalizing tendencies, as well as closure: it "retracts its frayed and fragile borders back onto its own consciousness of being a fragment, and onto a new type of autonomy."³⁶

> [D]ispersion and fracturing absolutize their erratic contingency: they *absolve themselves* of their fractal character.
> When Friedrich Schlegel compares the fragment to a hedgehog, he confers on it all the autonomy, finish, and aura of the "little work of art."
> ...
> The fragment becomes at once an *end* (limit, fracture) and a *finish* (annulment of the fracture), the torn borders folded back into the sweetness of microcosmic self-enclosure.³⁷

Through this reference to the hedgehog, we may differentiate two modes of organic absoluteness: the hedgehog is held up as an image of the fragment's detachment, autonomy, and self-enclosure. Novalis's seeds illustrate a completion that is teleologically conceived yet always pending in actuality. Even though Novalis hopes that some of these literary seeds will "take root," become fertilized, and lead to harvest, they are, as Lacoue-Labarthe and Nancy note, "no more than germinating because [they are] not yet fully completed"—and never will be. Like Romantic poetry, Novalis's literary seed "is still becoming; that is its real essence, that it should forever be becoming and never be perfected" (*Athenaeum* fragment 116; cited in *LA*, 43).

---

[33] Ibid., 46. Emphasis mine.
[34] Ibid.
[35] Ibid., 45.
[36] Nancy, "Art, a Fragment," in *The Sense of the World*, trans. Jeffrey S. Librett (Minneapolis and London: University of Minnesota Press, 1997), 124.
[37] Ibid., 125.

This is precisely what accounts for the Romantic fragment's absolute character; the endless deferral of actual completion makes it infinite. The vegetal absolute is pervaded by unworking as "incalculable and uncontrollable incompletion" (*LA*, 59). In Novalis's fragment, *Fort-Pflanzung* unfolds its inherent ambiguity: planting on and planting away. The *Gattung* that is imagined to be propagated and perpetuated ("Der Art oder Gattung nach vermehren, fortdauern machen") by the seed's fertilization and procreation is a literary one that will never be actualized and whose works are necessarily absent. Novalis's vegetal image is less concerned with the idea of a work in progress than with the act of *Setzung* (planting/positing) itself, which the fragment itself embodies—a *Setzung* in language that exhausts itself in the *Darstellung* of future fertility.

The fragment, moreover, depicts the "invention" of a *Gattung* without *Begattung*: the vegetal image evokes an engenderment that escapes the notion of heteronormative biological procreation. In contrast to *Lucinde*, where the "blossoming of a *single* plant or petals of a *single* flower," the "seed" of an idea that "took root" in the two lovers' minds, almost simultaneously represents a vision of their unity, the plant reproduction envisioned in Novalis's fragment hinges on the dispersion of multiple seeds. The literary products depicted through vegetal imagery do not follow the logic of human procreation; rather, they suggest a notion of *Fort-Pflanzung* that is shot through with Romantic equivocity. In *Lucinde*, human procreation ultimately gives way to *Fort-Pflanzung* when *Begattung* (the union of heterosexual lovers) is alluded to via the extended floral metaphor. Both modes of aesthetic *Fort-Pflanzung* remain sterile, bearing neither fruit nor children, thus embodying the literary absolute as "absent Work" (*LA*, 50). The Work is "transformed in an almost imperceptible manner into the 'work of the absence of work', as Blanchot has put it." Lacoue-Labarthe and Nancy go on to argue that "Novalis' seminal dispersion exceeds or extenuates the generation within it and disseminates it. Within the romantic work, there is interruption and dissemination of the romantic work, and this in fact is not readable in the work itself … it is readable in the *unworking* [*désœuvrement*]"; "what is involved here is a minute displacement or interval that is undoubtedly the most romantic aspect—or the most modern, beyond all modernity—of romanticism" (*LA*, 57).

Afterlife: Woolf's Fractured Flower

This quintessential—and "most modern"—aspect of Romantic poetics is strikingly reflected in a central text of modernist poetics, Virginia Woolf's memoir "A Sketch of the Past." There, amidst a description of "moments of being," she develops a kind of floral *désœuvrement*. In contrast to the "nondescript cotton wool" of everyday life, determined by "moments of non-being,"[38] "moments of being" erupt as "a sudden

---

[38] Virginia Woolf, "A Sketch of the Past," in *Moments of Being*, ed. Jeanne Schulkind (New York: Harcourt, Harvest Books, 1985), 70.

violent shock."[39] One of the examples Woolf gives for such moments of being is the observation of a flower in St. Ives:

> I was looking at the flower bed by the front door; "That is the whole," I said. I was looking at a plant with a spread of leaves; and it seemed suddenly plain that the flower itself was a part of the earth; that a ring enclosed what was the flower; and that was the real flower; part earth; part flower.[40]

"When I said about the flower 'That is the whole,' I felt that I had made a discovery,"[41] Woolf adds, a discovery that turns out to be the very core of her poetics: "I go on to suppose that the shock-receiving capacity is what makes me a writer."[42]

> I hazard the explanation that a shock is at once in my case followed by the desire to explain it. I feel that I have had a blow ... it is or will become a revelation of some order; it is a token of some real thing behind appearances; and I make it real by putting it into words. It is only by putting it into words that I make it whole.[43]

First, Woolf expands on the observation that the "real" or "whole" flower is the flower unified with the earth out of which it grows by resorting to Platonic vocabulary: the shock or blow reveals "some real thing behind appearances."

This "real thing" is, second, exposed as one "made" by literary language rather than a timeless and unchanging preexisting idea. It is precisely through this twisting of Platonic ideas that Woolf "reach[es]" what she "might call a philosophy"[44]—a philosophy which draws on the legacy of Romanticism and represents a modernist variation on the literary absolute:

> behind the cotton wool is hidden a pattern; that we—I mean all human beings—are connected with this; that the whole world is a work of art; that we are parts of the work of art. *Hamlet* or a Beethoven quartet is the truth about this vast mass that we call the world. But there is no Shakespeare, there is no Beethoven; certainly and emphatically there is no God; we are the words; we are the music; we are the thing itself. And I see this when I have a shock.[45]

We may recall that Lacoue-Labarthe and Nancy—in the context of Schlegel's and Schelling's plant images—discuss the Romantic genre as "the absolute *Organon*," not "this or that genre ... but rather literature itself that would be a great, thoroughly

---

[39] Ibid., 71.
[40] Ibid.
[41] Ibid.
[42] Ibid., 72.
[43] Ibid.
[44] Ibid.
[45] Ibid.

connected and organized Whole, comprehending many worlds of art in its unity, and being at the same time a unitary work of art" (*LA*, 91). In Schelling's *Philosophy of Art*, the "thoroughly connected and organized Whole" parallels art and nature: "art" is indeed "just as unified, organic, and in all its parts necessary a whole" as is "nature."[46] This amounts to mixing vocabulary from both domains in the image, "this highly organized and complexly interwoven plant called a work of art." The "absolute work" (*LA*, 91), Lacoue-Labarthe and Nancy conclude, involves the "*organon* as Idea," which in Schlegel's *Darstellung* articulates itself through a "literalization of the organic metaphor" (*LA*, 93).

In contrast to the vegetal literary absolute—an organic whole presented via plant metaphors, as outlined by Lacoue-Labarthe and Nancy with regard to the Romantics—Woolf's "philosophy" of aesthetic wholeness is rooted, in her *Darstellung*, in the observation of an actual plant. In Woolf's text, this plant is subject to a *Fort-Pflanzung* within language: it engenders the very reflection on writing and art into which it disappears and is supplanted by an idiom imbued with a philosophical and aesthetic meaning (e.g., "some real thing behind appearances"; "the thing itself"). Woolf adopted this terminology from an aesthetic discourse to which she was exposed via the Bloomsbury group, especially Clive Bell and Roger Fry's ideas of a new aestheticism/formalism that they saw at work in contemporary post-impressionist art, influenced by the Kantian notion of disinterestedness and G. E. Moore's principle of organic unity. The resonances between Woolf's "philosophy" and Roger Fry's essays on aesthetics are particularly noticeable; in fact, Woolf wrote "A Sketch of the Past" while working on Roger Fry's biography in 1939. Reading the two texts side by side reveals that Woolf transplants words and terms from one to the other. In *Roger Fry: A Biography*, she cites Fry's introduction to the catalogue of the second Post-Impressionist Exhibition in October 1912:

> these artists ... do not seek to give what can, after all, be but a pale reflex of *actual appearance*, but to arouse the conviction of a *new and definite reality*. They do not seek to imitate form, but to create form, not to imitate life, but to find an equivalent for life. By that I mean that they wish to make images which by the clearness of their logical structure, and by their closely-knit unity of texture, shall appeal to our disinterested and contemplative imagination with something of the same vividness as the things of actual life appeal to our practical activities. In fact they aim not at illusion but at *reality*.[47]

Woolf immediately afterwards adds "Once more the public exposed themselves to the *shock* of reality."[48] Yet on closer inspection, the integration of Fry's terminology into her

---

[46] Friedrich Wilhelm Joseph Schelling, *The Philosophy of Art*, ed. and trans. Douglas W. Stott (Minneapolis: University of Minnesota Press, 1989), 9.
[47] Fry cited in Virginia Woolf, *Roger Fry: A Biography* (New York and London: Harcourt Brace Jovanovich, 1940), 177–78. Emphasis mine.
[48] Woolf, *Roger Fry: A Biography*, 178. Emphasis mine.

own text (e.g., "some real thing behind appearances") and the application of her own term "shock" to his notion of "reality" reveal more contrast than continuity between their aesthetics.

Fry's conception of "organic unity in a work of art"[49] corresponds to the Romantic notion of the "*ab-solute*, its isolation in its perfect closure upon itself" (*LA*, 11). The "new and definite reality" created by art is not only thought as non-secondary in relation to factual reality—i.e., a mere imitation of it—but is radically detached from it, precisely through its "closely-knit unity," which completes it in itself. Because of a "re-establishment of purely aesthetic criteria" and "new indifference to representation,"[50] Fry's ideal artwork evokes a disinterested "unity emotion"[51] in those who behold it: "the mind is held in delighted equilibrium by the contemplation of the inevitable relation of all the parts in the whole, so that no need exists to make reference to what is outside the unity, and this becomes for the time being a universe."[52] In contrast to this idea of a self-contained work that withdraws from the world, echoing Schelling, for whom art is "as unified [Kunst als ein *geschlossenes*, which is also to say: as something *closed* (my emphasis)], organic, and in all its parts necessary a whole"[53] as nature, Woolf's aesthetic unity is "whole" precisely because the boundaries that tend to keep things apart, enabling their enclosure and autonomy, are shattered. The "revelation" of aesthetic wholeness emerges as a "sudden violent shock." What Woolf describes as the "sledgehammer force of the blow" ab-solves or loosens a system that keeps categorical differentiations intact so that flower and earth, as well as world, humans, and art, interpenetrate. The flower responsible for triggering the vision of wholeness that Woolf subsequently turns into a "philosophy of art" is not a closed organism: "I was looking at a plant with a spread of leaves." "Spread" here does not only mean "extension" or "expansion" but also "diffusion" and "dissemination."[54] What Woolf claims to see during the shattering "violent shock" is indeed a "dissemination" in the Derridean sense: "an irreducible and generative multiplicity,"[55] a flower that *becomes* earth.

Bearing Lacoue-Labarthe's and Nancy's argument about Romanticism in mind, we can now pinpoint a specifically modernist equivocity: the "poetic dissolution" Woolf outlines is a shattering vision of wholeness—an ab-solute unworked through a *Darstellung* that in Nancy's terms may best be called "presentation as fragmentation."[56] Woolf neither formulates a theory of the fragment, nor can her writing be situated in the genre of the fragment; her thoroughly modernist aesthetics, however, is an art of *frangere*, of breaking. Also in line with modernist aesthetics, Woolf's moments of

---

[49] Roger Fry, "The Grafton Gallery: An Apologia," in *A Roger Fry Reader*, ed. Christopher Reed (Chicago: The University of Chicago Press, 1996), 113.
[50] Fry, *Vision and Design* (London: Chatto & Windus, 1920), 8.
[51] Ibid., 55.
[52] Ibid., 53–54.
[53] German original cited from Lacoue-Labarthe and Nancy, *Das Literarisch-Absolute*, 466.
[54] "spread, v.," in *OED* Online, accessed June 8, 2020.
[55] Derrida, *Positions*, 45.
[56] Nancy, "Art, a Fragment," 126.

being, the "sudden violent shock[s]," are epiphanic and fleeting; they are bursts of presence in the sense Nancy theorizes it when he distinguishes between two kinds of fragmentation in "Art, a Fragment": "fractality," *frayage* and its birth to presence, in opposition to "romantic fragmentation," where "dispersion and fracturing … *absolve themselves* of their fractal character." "Thus, there are two different forms of extreme fragmentation: on the one hand, exhaustion and finish, and on the other hand, event and presentation."[57] As Nancy elucidates, the "event" in the latter form of fragmentation "is not a 'taking-place': it is the incommensurability of coming to all taking-place."[58] Coming into presence, or birth to presence is not "a given, accomplished, 'finished' presence … it is *presentation itself*, distinguished this time from what would be the 'presentness' [*la présentité*] of a presence."[59]

In Woolf's text, the "revelation" of wholeness coincides with its literary presentation. Woolf stresses that "[i]t is only by putting it into words that I make it whole." The way she puts the scene into words—her *Darstellung*/presentation—is highly significant: "it seemed suddenly plain that the flower itself was a part of the earth; that a ring enclosed what was the flower; and that was the real flower; part earth; part flower." The description's relative inconsistency—undermining Fry's notion of "structural design and harmony"[60]—is indeed remarkable. Woolf seems to equate three things: the *ring enclosing* the flower, the real flower, and "part earth; part flower." In her rendering, the enclosing ring is fractured into a staccato of words cut apart by punctuation: "part earth; part flower." As we can see in the typescript of "A Sketch of the Past"[61] this effect is deliberately created when she cuts the end of the sentence (see Figure 2.1). The chopped rhythm of "part earth; part flower" echoes in the conclusion of Woolf's argument that "all human beings" are "connected with" a "pattern," and that "the whole world is a work of art": "we are the words; we are the music; we are the thing itself." Also in this case, the rhythm is consciously composed, as evinced by the addition of semicolons in the typescript (see Figure 2.2).

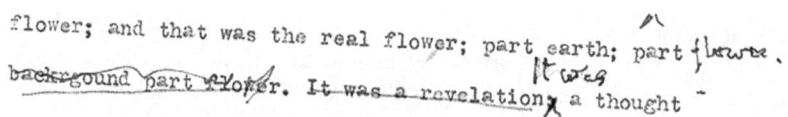

Figure 2.1 Woolf, *Typescript*, 12.

---

[57] Ibid.
[58] Ibid.
[59] Ibid.
[60] Fry, *Vision and Design*, 8.
[61] Woolf, "Typescript. A Sketch of the Past," *Woolf Online*, ed. Pamela L. Caughie, Nick Hayward, Mark Hussey, Peter Shillingsburg, and George K. Thiruvathukal, online, accessed November 25, 2021: http://www.woolfonline.com. The images are reproduced with the kind permission of The Society of Authors as the Literary Representative of the Estate of Virginia Woolf.

The effect created is an overlap of experience and rendering: the "shock" described takes effect by destabilizing and shattering Woolf's language. One change Woolf made in the typescript especially gives a sense of how deliberately "event" and "presentation," that is, *Darstellung* through words, are merged (see Figure 2.3). By deleting "and I suddenly saw a whole compose itself," Woolf erases the notion of any perception of the "whole" preceding its articulation in words. Thus, the vision of wholeness becomes a pure speech act: "'That is the whole,' I said." "*That*," in a self-referential gesture pointing to the utterance itself, to the very words on the page, and *only that*, "is the whole." At this moment in Woolf's *Darstellung*, deixis accounts for the "in-finity of a coming into presence":[62] "That," referring to what Woolf "said," to what she wrote, and to what we read now, *is*, in all these instances, the very "event"—and it is an event that at the same time keeps unworking its "taking place." Significantly, Woolf erases another sentence in the typescript: "It was a revelation." The revelation never "was," never took place as actual experience or perception of a wholeness composing itself. Consequently, "the plant with a spread of leaves" also takes leave, *pflanzt sich fort*. Woolf corrects "a ring enclosed the flower" to "a ring enclosed *what was* the flower": the whole or "real

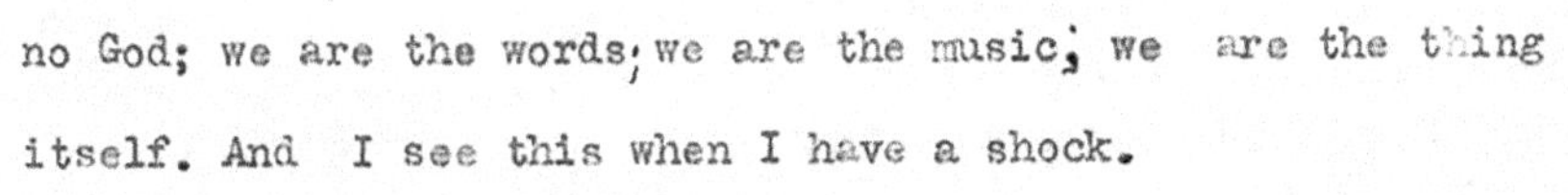

```
no God; we are the words; we are the music; we are the thing
itself. And I see this when I have a shock.
```

Figure 2.2 Woolf, *Typescript*, 15.

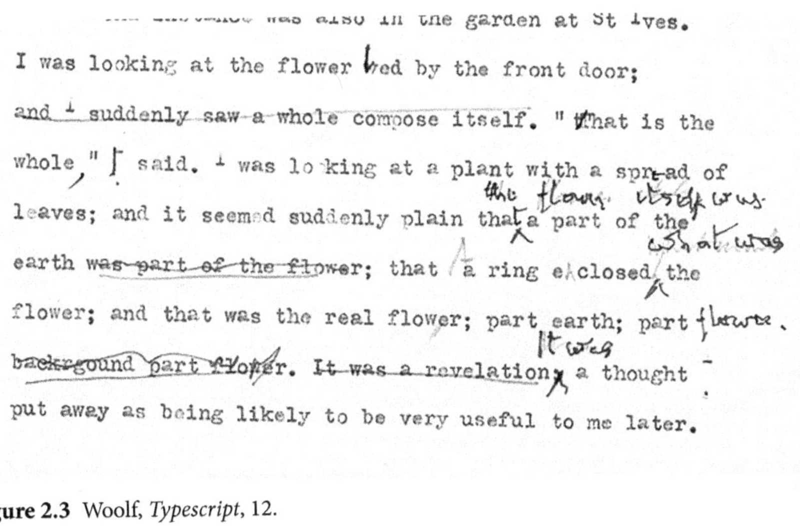

```
----- ------ was also in the garden at St Ives.
I was looking at the flower bed by the front door;
and I suddenly saw a whole compose itself. "What is the
whole," I said. I was looking at a plant with a spread of
leaves; and it seemed suddenly plain that a part of the
earth was part of the flower; that a ring enclosed the
flower; and that was the real flower; part earth; part flower.
background part flower. It was a revelation; a thought
put away as being likely to be very useful to me later.
```

Figure 2.3 Woolf, *Typescript*, 12.

[62] Nancy, "Art, a Fragment," 126.

flower" is an absent one, a flower that no longer *is*—that has dissolved into a modernist presentation/*Darstellung* of organic unity.

When Nancy distinguishes between the "absolute" Romantic fragment and what we may be tempted to call "modernist" fractality, he notes that the "two gestures are not contradictory," and that works cannot "be simply classified into one category or the other."[63] Tracing vegetal images in Romantic outlines of an organic absolute and its afterlife/*Fort-Pflanzung* in modernism, however, allows for more distinct differentiations. As Lacoue-Labarthe and Nancy argue, the Romantic ideal of literature is determined by incompletion and eternal becoming: its realization in actual literary works or *Gattung* is projected into a future that cannot take place but that exhausts itself in the *Darstellung* of the philosophical texts. As we have seen in the discussion of Novalis's fragment, the idea of future accomplishment, the literary seed's "fruit," is *suspended* rather than dismissed; the Romantic notion of becoming is thus directed toward an end. Here, we can put our finger on the difference between the Romantics' anticipation of a literary *Gattung* springing forth from the asexual coupling of philosophy and poetry, and Nancy's *birth* to presence, described as a "'coming and going' … which nowhere exceeds the world *in the direction of a Principle or an End*."[64] "Presence itself is birth, the coming that effaces itself," a "nativeness" that radically *abandons* offspring or fruit: "*Presentia frui*. But at present it is a question of what has no 'fruition,' nor any 'fruit.'"[65] Rather than being concerned with a future fruition (the Romantic tendency), or the process of *coming/generation* as such (Nancy's birth to presence), Woolf's floral epiphany is a "unity of the whole … grasped in passing, as passage."[66] *As passage*: only through its presentation in the textual passage, *in* passing *by* already passing *away*—a spread of leaves.

---

[63] Ibid.
[64] Nancy, *The Birth to Presence*, trans. Brian Holmes et al. (Stanford: Stanford University Press, 1994), 5. Emphasis mine.
[65] Ibid.
[66] Nancy, *Expectation: Philosophy, Literature*, ed. with the assistance of Ginette Michaud, trans. Robert Bononno (New York: Fordham University Press, 2018), 92.

3

Back to *The Muses*: A Di-versation on the World(s) and the Plurality of Arts

Nicholas Cotton

One day the Nine appeared to [Hesiod] and they told him, "We know how to speak false things that seem true, but we know, when we will, to utter true things."
— Edith Hamilton, *Mythology*[1]

The technical out-of-workness [désœuvrement] *incessantly forces the fine arts, dislodges them endlessly from aestheticizing repose. This is also why art is always coming to its end. The "end of art" is always the beginning of its plurality.*
— Jean-Luc Nancy, *The Muses*[2]

A piece such as this one could or should begin by backtracking or marking a break. When I first picked its title, long before I began writing it, I pictured the road ahead as a return, a rereading, a *going to* or *toward*, *back to* this edited volume, which is itself a collection of broken pieces, of thoughts scattered and gathered. What in French we call a *recueil* (to pick again, *re-cueillir*) bespeaks this most academic act of gathering and bringing together, but also a singularization of the multiple, the act of picking up, of seeking out, of choosing and keeping, as well as a *recueillement* (contemplation, recollection, openness). I envisioned a path that takes us *back to* this highly significant title, significant for the study of art, for the art of talking *about* works of art, as well as for the entirety of Nancy's writings and, in his wake, for modernism as a whole. Yet this process of backtracking or rewinding quickly took on unexpected proportions; indeed, it assumed the guise of a reversal or, perhaps, a turnaround—not so much a "back to…" as a "back from…" How do we get back from here? How do we get out? And in what state?

***

---

[1] Edith Hamilton, *Mythology* (New York: Back Bay Books, 1998), 40.
[2] Jean-Luc Nancy, *The Muses*, trans. Peggy Kamuf (Stanford: Stanford University Press, 1996), 37. Hereafter *M*. Italics original throughout unless otherwise noted. *Multiple Arts: The Muses II*, a 2006 volume edited by Simon Sparks, which gathers various uncollected writings by Nancy in English, will not be discussed here despite its subtitle.

Near the very outset of *The Muses*, Nancy suggests that "what we moderns mean by 'art' seems to have little to do with technics [*la technique*]." Yet our understanding of the relationship between the two, the historical significance we ascribe to *la technique*, "could in its own way condense the enigma of our time" (*M*, 5). First postulate. Second postulate: "Why are there several arts and not just one?," a leading question one is tempted to answer by stating, as Nancy does, that "the arts come about against each other."[3] In fact, the scope of these two postulates exceeds the aforementioned chapters, which organize the book's definitive French edition. But what are the historical and philosophical conjunctures that made these questions possible in the first place? In contrast to the "art"—singular, with inverted commas—of the moderns and the Romantics, Nancy posits the Muses, who concurrently foil and reiterate binary oppositions, within a single—singular yet plural—gesture. Here, Nancy inaugurates a meditation that will later be taken up in his essays on the visual arts (*Le Regard du Portrait* [The Portrait's Gaze], *Allitérations*, *The Pleasure in Drawing*, etc.) while simultaneously expanding on his understanding of modernity, sketched out in *The Literary Absolute* and *The Inoperative Community*. As for the Muses themselves, whose voices resound indivisibly yet apart, the present essay will attempt to think together the questions Nancy raises in his book, which is to say: think them *with* and *against* each other. Chief among these questions: the arts' plurality, their "interpenetration," the meaning (*sens*) of art's relationship with the "world," technics/technique, art as vestige, the experience of being on the threshold, etc. For what is "art" (singular) if not a promise foreshadowed and disappointed by modernity? To what extent, as Nancy might say, is "[t]he *singular plural* ... the law and the problem of 'art,' as it is of 'sense' or of the sense of the senses"?[4]

Why Are There Several Muses and Not Just One?

The fate of the Muses is inseparable from poetry and harmony. Long before there were nine, the three Muses of Mount Helicon (Melete, Menene, Aoide), already plural to begin with, symbolized poetic activity: "The first designates mental exercise, concentration, and attention. The second bears the name of memory, that psychological function without which there is neither recitation nor improvisation. The third refers to the completed poem, the product of Melete and Mneme." As daughters of Zeus and Mnemosyne (memory), the Muses, thanks to their ability to embrace the past, present, and future at the same time, and hence "to know the totality of things in one glance,"[5] play an important part in the upkeep of cosmic order. Thus, the Nine—Calliope (epic poetry), Clio (history), Erato (song), Euterpe (music), Melpomene (tragedy),

---

[3] Nancy, "Les arts se font les uns contre les autres," in *Les Muses* (Paris: Galilée, 2001), 161–74. [Translator's note: my translation throughout unless otherwise noted.]
[4] Nancy, *The Muses*, 13–14.
[5] Jeannie Carlier, "The Muses and Mnemosyne," trans. Gerard Honigsblum, in *Greek and Egyptian Mythologies*, ed. Yves Bonnefoy (Chicago and London: The University of Chicago Press, 1992), 192.

Polyhymnia (rhetoric), Terpsichore (dance), Thalia (comedy), Urania (astronomy)—all point toward the singular (artistic and literary) dispositions that the poet, a mere mortal, derives from the gods. Yet, as Jacques Lacarrière reminds us, Apollo entrusted Aristaeus to the Muses not so much that they might teach him music and dance but rather to sharpen his mastery of "technique": proper shepherding, ewe-milking, beekeeping, and honey extraction: "Upon reaching adulthood, Aristaeus hastened to teach men what he himself had learned from the Muses."[6] The Muses, as guardians of memory and harmony, are thus the custodians of technique in general. Moreover, they are always called the Muses, in the plural, even in retellings where there are but three of them. One never speaks of *the* Muse, one views them as a group, a chorus that speaks with a single voice, always measured and soothing, yet composed of distinct timbres. As a matter of course, this uncanny "singular plural" has not escaped Jean-Luc Nancy's notice, for it lies at the heart of his approach to the question of (the) art(s). In Hesiod, for example, the Muses are presented as indistinct: "nine daughters—girls of but one thought, whose hearts' sole care / Was song."[7] Indeed, the Muses, unlike Pan and Athena with their flutes or Hermes and Orpheus with their strings, have no instrument with which to beguile or unsettle us; they can only draw on the nonpareil retinue of their voices to resolve conflicts.

Of course, one cannot discuss the Muses without mentioning museums. Claude Foucart stresses this kinship in his reading of Paul Valéry's "The Problem of Museums" (1923): "traditional museums bring together 'incomparable' works; thus, they 'vie for our gaze,' which is incapable of simultaneously perceiving such a diversity of unequal riches."[8] For Valéry, the aim is obviously to "define the principles which must lead to the creation of a museum that is adapted to the modern world's expectations," and hence to bring back the Muses' *singular plural*, "to apprehend a 'harmonious order' at last, to re-endow the gaze with the ability to feel the exceptional value of what the poet calls 'units of pleasure.'"[9] Indeed, from the very first lines of Nancy's own *Muses*, a more enigmatic title than first meets the eye, this is what is at stake: both the singular *and* the plural, such that the relationship between the two, far from indicating mere opposition, drives the world of art as a whole. A tension is at play here—indeed, the relationless relation of Nancy's "singular plural" is precisely what makes it possible to conjoin without a conjunction—a tension that hinges on whether the two interminable terms are involved in one another, calling and tending toward each other, like the Muses themselves, who speak with a single voice and out of a single—singular plural—choral heart.

---

[6] Jacques Lacarrière, *Au cœur des mythologies* (Paris: Gallimard, 1998), 304.
[7] Hesiod, *Theogony* and *Works and Days*, trans. Catherine M. Schlegel and Henry Weinfield (Ann Arbor: The University of Michigan Press, 2006), 25.
[8] Claude Foucart, "Musées," in *Dictionnaire des mythes d'aujourd'hui*, ed. Pierre Brunel (Paris: Éditions du Rocher, 1999), 529. See Paul Valéry, "Le problème des musées [1923]," in *Œuvres*, II, ed. Jean Hytier (Paris: Gallimard, 1960), 1290–91.
[9] Ibid.

Indeed, tension is what drives this essay in its entirety. The questions raised by Nancy aim to make apparent the necessary tensions between the singular and the plural, of course, but also between *technique/technics* and *the sublime, product* and *production, doing* and *knowing*—eternal modalities of art and philosophy. What is at play here is the very nature of the tension between the parts that make up the choir and the fundamental unity it represents, or, better yet, what puts it in tension—understood here as a motor—thus setting it to work: "The Muse animates, stirs up, excites, arouses ... she keeps watch forcefully over the form" (*M*, 1). And within tension, be it as fundamental as that which drives the singularity of art and the diversity of the arts, there is always pleasure: "The pleasure of quenching one's thirst differs from the pleasure of tasting a delectable drink—in the first case, a tension is overcome, while in the second a tension is preserved and promises to return."[10]

"Why Are There Several Arts and Not Just One?" (subtitled "Conversation on the Plurality of Worlds," an explicit reference to Fontenelle) is the title of the first of five essays gathered in 1994 under the title *Les Muses*. At the time of its publication, *The Literary Absolute* (1978) was approximately fifteen years old, Nancy had already written "Sharing Voices" (1982) and *The Inoperative Community* (1986), while *Corpus* (1992) had just been published. Two short paragraphs kick off this opening chapter and may thus be read as symbolizing *The Muses* as a whole. Indeed, everything here bespeaks—speaks volumes about—what will soon unfold in the pages they foreshadow:

> The Muses get their name from a root that indicates ardor, the quick-tempered tension that leaps out in impatience, desire, or anger, the sort of tension that aches to know and to do. In a milder version, one speaks of the "movements of the spirit." (*Mens* is from the same root.) The Muse animates, stirs up, excites, arouses. She keeps watch less over the form than over the force. Or more precisely: she keeps watch forcefully over the form.
>
> But this force springs up in the plural. It is given, from the first, in multiple forms. There are Muses and not the Muse. Their number may have varied, as well as their attributes, but the Muses will always have been several. It is this multiple origin that must interest us, and it is also the reason why the Muses, as such, are not the subject here; they are merely lending their name, this name that is multiplied from the first, so that we may give a title to this question: Why are there several arts and not just one?

(M, 1)

"[T]he Muses, as such, are not the subject here." And yet... an essay on *The Muses*, or the chapter of a volume on Nancy that would attend to it, could easily be conceived as the commentary of these inaugural paragraphs alone. More than

---

[10] Nancy, *The Pleasure in Drawing*, trans. Philip Armstrong (New York: Fordham University Press, 2013), 68.

one seminar could be disseminated therein, to riff on Jacques Derrida. The first of these two paragraphs, devoted to the "tempered tension that leaps out in impatience, desire, or anger," thus gives way to the second, which stems from it: "There are Muses and not the Muse." Already the (hi)story's beginning is *preceded*, there is a before, the (hi)story that begins here has already begun, and this beginning unfolds against the backdrop of a coexistence of versions: the *strong* version and the *milder* version. But this (hi)story is interrupted as soon as it has begun (again). From the false start, whose form and content will linger on, arises its counterfeit: never just the Muse, always the Muse*s*. It is in the tension between these two (hi)stories that another (hi)story will be thought up: ours, perhaps that of what we call *modernity*, since the Muses only lend their (singular) name and therefore their form, which may well be nothing other than their multiplicity. After all, the question of the multiple is what is being discussed here—especially the question the multiple asks of us, that we think *it* in *its* multiplicity, always in a singular manner—and it is the very question that drives Nancy, that puts him *in tension*, by way of an essay that promises to leave no stone unturned as regards this other, impossible question: "Why are there several arts and not just one?" Standing on the threshold, as though the Muses' shadows, these two short paragraphs appear to foretell or recapitulate the perspective of a crossing or traversal in reverse. And, as we shall see, a true traversal is only possible to the extent that it is impossible, which is to say: ever promised, in abeyance. The piece Nancy chose to place on the threshold of his book thus opens onto these questions, so to speak, or rather opens these questions up—questions which, like the Muses, will arise in each of the pieces that make up this collection.

Why are there several arts and not just one? We have seen that the Muses have always been several, that they are meaningfully bound to each other, and that they derive their *unity* from their diversity, so to speak. In *Cosa volante*, her book on the relationship between thinking and the arts in the work of Jean-Luc Nancy, Ginette Michaud invokes the eloquent image of a *round dance* of sleeping Muses "whose intertwined yet distinct bodies lean against each other, touching but not conjoining."[11] This image deserves credit for drawing on the modern myth of art (in the singular) while simultaneously highlighting the arts' essential plurality and, beyond the opposition between the two, their oblique allure. Sandrine Israël-Jost, in her own contribution to *Figures du dehors* (Figures of the Outside), a significant edited volume, which collects the papers presented at the eponymous conference that took place in Paris in 2009, retraces the "philosophical constraints" that, since Kant, Schelling, and Hegel, have been instrumental in "subsum[ing] the plurality of the arts under an essential unity."[12] Several years after the initial publication of *The Muses*, Nancy himself revisited their figures in an interview with Véronique Fabbri, published in *Rue Descartes*, the journal

---

[11] Ginette Michaud, *Cosa volante. Le désir des arts dans la pensée de Jean-Luc Nancy* (Paris: Hermann, 2013), 205.

[12] Sandrine Israël-Jost, "La *mimesis* comme synesthésie," in *Figures du dehors. Autour de Jean-Luc Nancy*, ed. Gisèle Berkman and Danielle Cohen-Levinas (Nantes: Cécile Defaut, 2012), 245.

of the Collège International de Philosophie. Echoing the argument laid out in the first chapter of *The Muses*, Nancy says that

> the arts exclude each other yet they all touch each other, and Benjamin, in a quote of which I was not aware when I first published *The Muses*, speaks of this. There is a very beautiful quote by Benjamin where he says: "the proper name of art is nothing but the plural name of the Muses." The word art in the singular simply means the Muses. I think this is extremely important, and it also implies that the arts all drive each other away even as they are drawn to one another, and each art also carries something that passes through [*traverse*] all the others.[13]

This "first postulate"—that of the "differential plurality of the arts, as well as of their complete mutual impermeability"[14]—is likewise analyzed in *Cosa volante*, where Ginette Michaud reminds us that it is intimately tied to the broader question of the senses. Taking up Hegel's classification of the arts according to the materiality of the senses, Nancy reroutes the question (or turns it around): "At this point, the question of the difference between the arts ought to be transformed into the question of the difference between the senses. Perhaps in fact they are the same question. But how is one to understand this identity?" (*M*, 10). This illusory and ultimately impossible symmetry is conceivable only if we disregard various obstacles, which Nancy calls "determinant reasons": the heterogeneity of the senses is not homothetic to that of the arts; the heterogeneity of sense is itself unfixable; any perception is unsatisfactory and calls for a kind of "sensorial integration" (*M*, 12). Thus, for Nancy it is a matter of deconstructing relations of difference and similarity (implicit and current) between *the* arts and *the* senses, between sense and sense, between the arts *and* the senses: "Their identity and their difference contain no less than the structure and the stakes of the *sense* and/or the *senses* of what is called, perhaps too quickly, 'art'" (*M*, 10).

On the Plurality of Worlds

The Muses thus make up a collection of writings on art, on the modern idea of art and its deconstruction, at least on the in-depth *mise en abyme* of this idea. The English version consists of five chapters whereas the French version features seven, as "Les arts se font les uns contre les autres" (2000) and "*Praesens*" (2001) were added to Galilée's "augmented" 2001 edition. In "On the Threshold," a lecture given at the Louvre Museum, before Caravaggio's *Death of the Virgin*, Nancy undertakes a lengthy dual meditation on art and death, one reiterated time and again whenever the topic of Christian painting comes up in his work (see also: *Visitation* and *Noli me tangere* in

---

[13] Jean-Luc Nancy and Véronique Fabbri, "Entretien avec Jean-Luc Nancy," *Rue Descartes*, no. 44 (2004): 67.
[14] Michaud, *Cosa volante*, 205.

particular). Before the *Death of the Virgin*, Nancy suggests that art, no less than death, can only be apprehended from the vantage point of a threshold. That this lecture was given in 1992 bears recalling, since it was an important year for Nancy, pivotal in more ways than one, as it is the year he received his second heart, whose graft would become a philosophical topic for him in works such as *Corpus* (1992) and, later, *The Intruder* (2000). His reading of Caravaggio's painting, which is also an insightful reading of the question of death, unfolds according to a logic of entanglement: what is said of the artwork, of the work as inexorably forbidding, may also be said of death: "At what are we thus present or to what are we presented? To what are we exposed? Everything shows us that it is death" (*M*, 58).

This piece, perhaps among the most beautiful and most powerful that Jean-Luc Nancy has given us, resonates differently since his own death in August 2021. What the experience of mourning *and* Caravaggio's painting have both taught us is that we are indeed "on the threshold," if not "on the edge": "Death: we are never there, we are always there. Inside and outside, at once, but without communication between inside and outside, without mixture, without mediation, and without crossing" (*M*, 60). Somehow, there is neither a *back to* nor a *back from* here, there is no "crossing"; it is always happening as we speak, and we cannot reach the other side, which is why we cannot go back without a *to* or a *from*. What is lacking here are shores to welcome the one who stands on the threshold. And *there will be none*—such is the implacable lesson of art and death—there will be no crossing: "Perhaps that is what we have access to here, as to that which is absolutely inaccessible. Perhaps it is to this that we ourselves are the access, we mortals. Perhaps that is the water, the light, and the stuff of this visibility. The very thing, the threshold that we are, we the living." It is in this sense that, for Nancy, we stand neither *before* nor *in* the work, much as we stand neither *before* nor quite *in* the world. Likewise, there is no such thing as "death itself," and "neither is there before nor beyond [*ni en-deçà ni au-delà*]" (*M*, 60). Yet it is in this sense that art grants us access to the world, to the sense of the world—like an *ekphrasis*, it is meant to be performed. Indeed, art takes us back to the dual idea that "[t]he sense of the world must lie outside the world,"[15] to quote Wittgenstein, but also that this "opens *within* the world an *outside* that is not a beyond-the-world,"[16] as Nancy argues. The work, like death, and death, like the world, are not pure representation. As Ginette Michaud puts it, "[t]hat there is not only the 'world of art,' but that art makes a world or, better yet: that it is the art of world-making—this is what we must think alongside Nancy."[17] On the threshold, one who does not quite stand *before* (even less so *in*) the painting thus brings the world about at least as much as they present it.

This characteristic gesture is indeed a dive *into* the work, an entry, a penetration, yet it upholds what Nancy calls *touching*, which entails a gap, and hence spacing,

---

[15] Ludwig Wittgenstein, *Tractatus Logico-Philosophicus*, trans. Frank P. Ramsey and Charles Kay Ogden (London: Kegan Paul, Trench, Trubner & Co., 1922), 87.

[16] Nancy, *Dis-Enclosure (The Deconstruction of Christianity)*, trans. Bettina Bergo (New York: Fordham University Press, 2008), 79.

[17] Michaud, *Cosa volante*, 122.

distance. Nancy's philosophy of art thus harks back to one of philosophy's most profound concerns, later developed in *What's These Worlds Coming To?* (2011), namely the shattered singularity of the world when it is understood as *cosmos*. If we touch Caravaggio's painting, it is through a "real touch,"[18] a touch that settles nothing, appropriates nothing, conveying the absence or the departure of presence, much as the painter's own real or true touch consists "of a living withdrawal of the hand that sets it down."[19] We stand neither in nor before the painting any longer, but on the threshold, neither in nor before the world, neither in nor before sense, for "'the world' withdraws and transports in a spiraling manner the consistency of its reality 'in itself.'"[20] Therein lies the whole question of (post-)modernity: "perhaps we do not live in a world or in several worlds. Perhaps it is rather that the world or worlds unfold, diverge, or intersect in us and through us."[21] To stand on the threshold is therefore to draw and withdraw, both at the same time, to push back at the very moment one advances. This is precisely the gesture (or *movement* or *touch*—one no longer knows what to call it) Derrida highlights in *On Touching* when he points out that "Nancy always pairs 'touching one another' and 'distancing oneself,' coupling and placing them side by side and putting them in contact or contiguity."[22] Unlike Derrida, however, Nancy steps into the melee of the work. His point of view on the threshold is paradoxically that of one who has already stepped inside: "Here, (the) painting is our access to the fact that we do not accede—either to the inside or to the outside of ourselves. Thus we exist. Thus painting paints the threshold of existence" (*M*, 61).

Once again, it is a matter of tension, as Nancy stresses via his study of hands in Caravaggio's painting: "There is neither resurrection nor assumption. [We must remember that the painting depicts the death of the Virgin Mary and, at her bedside, a whole retinue of living weepers.] There is more and less than a negotiation or a philosophy of death" (*M*, 65). There is always "more" and "less"—strictly speaking, a perpetual "tension"—as though the more and the less (the "inside" and the "outside") were drawn toward each other in a desperate attempt to signify, widening the gap between them, and hence perhaps the illusory idea of a threshold, which is also to say a *starting point* or, better yet, a *point de départ* (in French, this expression marks both the place where it starts and its negation). Thus, there is "neither abyss, nor ecstasy, nor salvation." Nancy goes on: "There is pleasure and pain, which touch each other without joining, are opposed without tearing each other apart. All the hands here [the survivors' hands, which abound in the painting's chiaroscuro], held, held out, laid on, like light feeling its way about in multiple ways" (*M*, 65). Indeed, Caravaggio's painting,

---

[18] Nancy, *Noli me tangere: On the Raising of the Body*, trans. Sarah Clift, Pascale-Anne Brault, and Michael Naas (New York: Fordham University Press, 2008), 50.
[19] Ibid., 51.
[20] Jean-Luc Nancy and Aurélien Barrau, *What's These Worlds Coming To?*, trans. Travis Holloway and Flor Méchain (New York: Fordham University Press, 2015), 4.
[21] Ibid., 6.
[22] Jacques Derrida, *On Touching—Jean-Luc Nancy*, trans. Christine Irizarry (Stanford: Stanford University Press, 2005), 221.

which draws us in even in the absence of an inviting gaze, shows nothing other than what the painter and the painting itself are doing. It splits its sense and its gesture in half. It exposes without representing. It is a "presentation of presentation," as Nancy writes in *The Muses*' opening chapter:

> Art exposes this. Which does not mean that art *represents* originary patency ... The presentation of presentation is not a representation: it does not relate presentation to a subject for which or in which it would take place. The presentation of presentation relates it to itself.
>
> (*M*, 34)

On the threshold of the *Death of the Virgin*, Nancy reminds us that

> [b]y a device which is far from being unique in painting, but which here finds one of its chosen places, the canvas signals to us, makes us this sign: Enter and look. Come and see. Exhaust your looks until your eyes close, until your hands are raised over them, until your faces fall upon your knees. See the invisible.
>
> (*M*, 59)

With Derrida, one had to *think not to see*. Nancy, by contrast, suggests thinking not to *lay hold*. Seeing the invisible, yes, but only to let go of what is being seen, without yielding to the temptation of shaping the invisible: "Here, (the) painting is our access to the fact that we do not accede" (*M*, 61), for Nancy invites us to reflect neither *within* nor *without*. Neither touching nor laying hold, marking a preference for the ambiguity of the Greek *háptou* (touching/laying hold) over the univocal Latin *tangere*. And Nancy incidentally identifies this same tension between touching and grasping another of art history's scenes, which also happens to be biblical, laying the groundwork for an ulterior piece, entitled *Noli me tangere*. In this "Essay on the Raising of the Body" (per its original subtitle), he picks up his conjoined work on the deconstruction of the arts and Christianity where he left it off, analyzing several "versions" of the scene representing the resurrected Christ appearing as a gardener to Mary Magdalene. He shows that the image presents absence-as-departure, in the strong sense of a re-presentation that is no longer merely the presentation of an absence but rather the intensification of "the presence of an absence as absence."[23] One may see in this essay that death as an experience of the threshold is once again bound up with Nancy's meditation on art—indeed, something here insists on this intimate connection—for everything in this scene is a "presentation of presentation," from the tomb on whose threshold the figures are standing and which, in its emptiness, "un-limits death in the departing of the dead," to the figure of the resurrected Christ whose very presence is disappearance:

---

[23] Nancy, Noli me tangere, 51.

Do not touch me [both he who is risen and the painting we *absolutely* must not touch seem to be saying the same thing], *do not hold me back, do not think to seize or reach toward me for I am going to the Father* [and the Father, writes Nancy, is "none other than the absent" here] ... *I am only in this departure; I am the parting of this departure. My being consists in it and my word is this: "I, the Truth, am going away."*[24]

To see the invisible, yet from the absence that lies beyond the visible, in its evanescent emergence, such is "the ordinary command or demand of painting: very simple, very humble, even derisory" (*M*, 59). This is also what Caravaggio's painting may be saying if we envision it as an image beholden neither to the relation between the figurative and the proper nor to the relation between representation and reality (*mimesis*) but rather to an experience of seeing that *takes part* in the image (*methexis*)—after all, "no *mimesis* occurs without *methexis*."[25] Much like the portrait, which is truth *itself* rather than truth represented, the life of Jesus as depicted in the parable "is precisely the truth that appears [*se présente*] in being represented [*se représentant*]."[26] Truth is not distinct from the image or the parable; it is quite *rightly* what is betokened through them. And what is said here of death and art also holds true for sense and the world. What we call "art"—in its modern acceptation, at least—is precisely the coming of sense as it departs, a convocation that is neither an interpellation nor an inspection [*arraisonnement*], but more like a circulation. Art reminds us that sense is possible, that it is circulating, in movement, that we can't stop it, that we weren't even invited to it, and that it only takes place through us regardless. Nancy's commentary of the *Death of the Virgin* is in this sense a remarkable lesson on the ever-roving gaze, which opens works of art and quickens their senses. And it is also a remarkable lesson on reading, for to "be on the threshold" is perhaps the sole experience one may rightly expect of a text. The experience of the text as such. Of any text.

Methexis and Modernism

Art in the singular is thus a Romantic and modern idea. Understanding this most singular plurality means understanding modernism as much as it means understanding Nancy. In "Why Are There Several Arts...?," Nancy clearly formulates the idea that the age kicked off by modernity (by the Romantics, at least) may well be ending or, at least, that a kind of "duty for art to put an end to 'art'" (*M*, 38) is involved here. Put simply, modernity marks the moment when art thinks itself absolutely, *as such*, when art becomes Art. With regard to this point, Christophe Bident specifies that "if, 'indeed, the arts pass through each other,' it is not so much by way of 'practices

---

[24] Ibid., 16.
[25] Nancy, "The Image: Mimesis and Methexis," trans. Adrienne Janus, in *Nancy and Visual Culture*, ed. Carrie Giunta and A. Janus (Edinburgh: Edinburgh University Press, 2016), 74.
[26] Nancy, *Noli me tangere*, 4.

that mix or synthesize'"; rather, "the plurality of the arts is to be found in the unity of each."[27] It is in this sense that Nancy calls for the end of a certain conception of modernity while simultaneously steering clear of an *ethics of aesthetics* ("this duty does not, in some puritan mode, erect an 'ethics' against an 'aesthetics'" [*M*, 38]). It is thus a matter of knowing which "modernity" we are talking about here and, in this respect, the two texts that follow, "Painting in the Grotto" and "The Vestige of Art," are both quite helpful. Each in its own way prolongs Nancy's meditation on art by attending to the problems of (art's) beginnings and ends.

"Painting in the Grotto" deals with the "self outside of self" of which painting is presumed to be the reiterated discovery, each time, in the manner of a surprise: "Painting paints this surprise. This surprise is painting" (*M*, 69). According to Erich Hörl, this piece must more specifically be read "as a discussion of the question of technics/technique and of its relevance to a philosophy of openness."[28] Nancy stresses that the pleasure we derive from mimesis is one of re-cognition, and hence a dual movement of spacing and resumption: "The pleasure men take in *mimēsis* is made up of the troubling feeling that comes over them in the face of recognizable strangeness, or in the excitement that comes from a recognition that one would have to say is *estranged*" (*M*, 69–70). Art thus reveals itself to be coextensive with the conscience of being. It lies in the beginning, and it is effectively *the* beginning. Being and art both begin with a single gesture, which consists of sketching an idea of self and other on a wall—they begin with this *self outside of self*. Indeed, the cave paintings of the Paleolithic, such as those at Lascaux, gesture toward the very beginning of being, as Nancy observes. What we call *art* (or *ars* or *tékhnē*), knowledge and know-how, is in fact the beginning of a conscience: "fascination with the monster of presence exited from presence." "Man" is an *animal monstrans*, as Nancy writes, "for 'to show' [*montrer*] is nothing other than to set aside, to set at a distance of presentation, to exit from pure presence, to make absent and thus to absolutize" (*M*, 70). In "Why Are There Several Arts...?," Nancy had already shown that "[t]echnique means knowing how to go about producing what does not produce itself by itself," (*M*, 25), and here he seeks to show that *la technique* understood as the birth of a form is simultaneously an interruption of being and the advent of its conscience. It is because the "continuity of being was interrupted" (*M*, 74) that being has become detached from itself. And this detachment, this *necessary* distance, this start—in every sense of the term—is the very condition of self-conception, the condition without which being remains caught in its own continuity. Let us also recall that, as regards *methexis*, "[t]he participation of sight in the visible and, in turn, the participation of the visible in the invisible is nothing other than seeing itself," hence his claim that "[b]etween the image and sight, then, there is not imitation but participation and penetration."[29]

Nancy's claim that the human is a *homo monstrans* underpins the postulate that every drawing bears the trace of something inaugural. This time, what is at stake is

---

[27] Christophe Bident, "Jean-Luc Nancy et le théâtre," in *Figures du dehors*, 303.
[28] Erich Hörl, "Nancy et la technologie," in *Figures du dehors*, 276.
[29] Nancy, Noli me tangere, 7.

the tension between *form* and *formlessness*, since the line [*trait*] keeps an open trace of this absolute strangeness. The figure thus traced, which takes shape by means of what is already *technique*, marks "the spacing by which man is brought into the world, and by which the world itself is a world" (*M*, 70). Hence the idea, developed in *The Pleasure in Drawing*, according to which there is something of the line, of sketching and therefore of drawing, in *all* of the arts: "What was only design [*dessein*] becomes drawing [*dessin*] for the first time—in other words, it leaves intention or aim in order to enter into the tension of the gesture alone and its abandon, its way of running a risk."[30] This dual movement is always involved—self-conscience is only possible when it is borne out of a conscience of self outside of self. Here, Nancy envisions the arts as traces of formlessness, with the proviso that modernity merely accentuates the idea according to which the Muses unveil themselves without a prior form, at the very limit where this form dissolves and disseminates itself—like a mirage that, for one moment (always too late), we would like to touch, or that we have glimpsed out of the corner of our eye. Thus, in *The Pleasure in Drawing* again, Nancy stresses that

> [t]he practice of forms only applies insofar as it is extended toward something like an excess or exuberance, an expansion that cannot know its limit a priori because it must always be in order to begin and (in reproduction [*génération*] and death) finish with a relation to the excess of form [*l'outre-forme*]. In such a relation, on the one hand, one could say that the form tames the formless and makes it visible, but, on the other hand it does not do so without touching its own limit, and thus opening onto the invisible itself.[31]

As for Erich Hörl, he further stresses the importance of the question of technics/technique, which Nancy deploys to think through the tension that sets the form/formlessness coupling in motion. This deployment is marked with the seal of ambivalence:

> Nancy defines [technics/technique] in *The Muses* as "exteriority to self" and as "exposition to a lack of ground or foundation," in the sense of a generalized philosophy of the prosthetic and of prostheses. Technics is understood in this text—in an utterly ambivalent manner—as "the obsolescence of the origin and end" and as "withdrawal of the 'ground,'" and more specifically as that which historically prepares and propagates the withdrawal of the ground even as it occasionally conceals it. It appears, moreover—this is its exact position in history—as the essential protagonist of a heterogenetic turn that paves the way for, and even impels, a philosophy of multiplicity and of the heterogeneity of worlds.[32]

---

[30] Nancy, *The Pleasure in Drawing*, 99.
[31] Ibid., 75.
[32] Hörl, "Nancy et la technologie," 275.

In this sense, then, the question of technics/technique is once again inexorably tied to modernity, which Nancy and Philippe Lacoue-Labarthe had already discussed in *The Literary Absolute* before Nancy expanded on it in "Why Are There Several Arts…?":

> "Technique" is a rule for an end. When the end is in-finite, the rule must conform. In a sense, this is a summary of thinking about art since romanticism—since the infinitization of the ends of man. The romanticism of "art"—of absolute or total art—consists in hypostasizing the Infinite End (Poetry, Fragment, or *Gesamtkunstwerk*). With that, technique dissolves into the form of the "genius." To overcome romanticism is to think rigorously the in-finite, which is to say, its finite, plural, heterogeneous constitution. Finitude is not the deprivation but the in-finite affirmation of what incessantly *touches* on its end: another *sense* of existence and, by the same token, another sense of "technique."
>
> (*M*, 37)[33]

As in "The Girl Who Succeeds the Muses," the final piece featured in the English edition, "The Vestige of Art," is less interested in the foundational archetypes that drive modernism than in those we occasionally experience in the nostalgic manner of a loss. The thesis defended in "The Girl Who Succeeds the Muses," namely that art steps onto the scene when the gods withdraw, would also be developed a few years later in a small book entitled *Visitation*, where Nancy not only shows that Christian painting can be understood as the catalyst for a self-deconstructing Christianity but, more importantly still, that the art of painting bears within itself the entire history of Christianity's (self-) deconstruction. "The Vestige of Art," on the other hand, proceeds by means of remarks (ten in all) on the subject of a "vanishing point in the *being* of art" (*M*, 82). With each gesture, in any case, art tackles the question of its being: "it quests after its own trace. Perhaps it always has with itself a relation of vestige—and of investigation" (*M*, 83). Thus, modernity is but a reiteration of art conceived as a vestige—a key moment indeed, yet a moment among others nonetheless, which orients us toward art as a remainder, or art as the *rest*, and thus also as that which *resists*. If we assume that art now seems to require a quest for sense or meaning, one bound for its own essence or for the "manifest enigma of its own vestige," Nancy replaces this quest, which is coextensive with art itself, in a long sequence of "tensions" that some would simply call its *history*: "This is not the first time: perhaps the whole history of art is made up of tensions and torsions toward its own enigma." So, what now? One could say that "[t]he tension and the torsion seem to have reached their high point today" (*M*, 86). Such an art gives form to formlessness—a syncope where, for a split second, one catches a glimpse of sense—and hence to a conception of art as the sensible presentation of the Idea (Hegel). Nancy deconstructs this as well, and makes a point of showing that "all of modernity that speaks of the invisible or the unpresentable is always at least on the

---

[33] See Philippe Lacoue-Labarthe and Jean-Luc Nancy, *The Literary Absolute: The Theory of Literature in German Romanticism*, trans. Philip Barnard and Cheryl Lester (Albany: State University of New York Press, 1988).

verge of renewing this motif" (*M*, 89). What is more, Nancy, for whom art lacks an *origin* and an *end*, contrasts this vision with an *art-vestige* inspired by Thomas Aquinas ("vestige is an effect that 'represents only the causality of the cause, but not its form'" [*M*, 95]), undermining the Hegelian conception of art no less than that of modernity:

> In these conditions, what I am setting down here—which, I believe, has been expressly proposed since Hegel—is that art is smoke without fire, vestige without God, and not presentation of the Idea. End of image-art, birth of vestige-art, or rather, coming into the light of day of this: that art has always been vestige (and that it has therefore always been removed from the ontotheological principle).
>
> (*M*, 96)[34]

That art has always been vestigial brings us back to the space opened by "Painting in the Grotto" and to the question of technics/technique. Here, Nancy writes that "[t]he vestigial is not an essence—and no doubt this is what puts us on the track of the 'essence of art.'" And what it ultimately presents is this: "That art is today its own vestige, this is what opens us to it. It is not a degraded presentation of the Idea, nor the presentation of a degraded Idea; it presents what is not 'Idea': motion, coming, passage, the going-on of coming-to-presence" (*M*, 98). Gisèle Berkman is thus right to note that *The Muses* are haunted by the motif of insufficiency, specifically that of the phenomenological method: "the discretion of a background that withdraws and retraces itself as forms cannot be matched by the *sole* theme of appearance."[35] One should thus see in *The Muses* an exhortation to *carve* a path through the—essential yet obsolete—categories that are ontology and experience. This is what Berkman underscores: everything "words itself at least twice" in the interminable question of art as recast by Nancy, ontologically and phenomenologically, yet "these two times are but one if we consider that, in Nancy's thought, being is without essence, appearing and slipping away in the flash of existence, in the light instant of this commutation where the infinite plays (itself) upon finitude."[36]

* * *

There is no going back. If aesthetic modernity appears to affirm itself on a tense note; if, as we have seen, "the whole history of art is made up of tensions and torsions toward its own enigma" (*M*, 86), then the tension that must be thought here, itself singular plural, is perhaps nothing other than the reiterated or paleonymous name of a passage—inevitable and interminable—from "self to self." In *Cosa volante*, Ginette Michaud cites an unpublished letter Nancy wrote to the Italian artist Claudio Parmiggiani.

---

[34] See Thomas Aquinas, *Summa Theologiae*, la, q. 45, art. 7. Nancy also refers to Georges Didi-Huberman's *Fra Angelico: Dissemblance and Figuration*, trans. Jane Marie Todd (Chicago: The University of Chicago Press, 1995).
[35] Gisèle Berkman, "La 'chose-dehors' de la pensée," in *Figures du dehors*, 448.
[36] Ibid.

This letter is about *The Muses* and, more specifically, about art as the "experience of a crossing infinitely begun again with every gesture,"[37] as Michaud writes. It is, to quote Nancy, a "passage from self to self, from border to border [*de bord à bord*] and hence within borderlessness, across a space-time where there is no guarantee that the other shore will be found: for it is perhaps this crossing itself that opens the borders and therefore spaces them ever more as it crosses."[38] *The Muses*' composition, perhaps like all of Nancy's body of thought, mirrors this passage which opens the borders even as it spaces them out whenever we move across them, and this is of course because sense is at stake. Yet art—or, better yet, the arts—is never for Nancy a mere question of sense or even of the senses. Indeed, the sense of the world, the very possibility of a world, is always involved—perhaps the sole possibility "to be 'represented,' that is to say … presented to our senses … in such a manner as to make sensible what lies between us and that can make 'us' be 'with.'"[39] In *The Muses*, we thus follow movements of *différance* between the arts and, for *each* art, movements that give sense to the world. In this case, the word *sens* in French is not only felicitous due to its polysemy (a trait it shares with other languages) but also because it "leaves the plural and the singular undiscerned," as Nancy himself reminds us in "Les arts se font les uns contre les autres."[40] A work of art can thus be understood as the gift of its giving, the presentation of its presentation, the "thing grasped as though found—at the crossroads between the fateful and the *rendez-vous*."[41] In "*Praesens*," the final chapter of *Les Muses* initially published as part of the catalogue of an exposition that took place at the Palazzo delle Papesse de Sienne (2001), he takes this idea all the way, and it is on these words, or very nearly, that the final version of *The Muses* ends:

> Our positive and analytic modernity denies itself the all-too hazy charms of "inspiration" or "secrets." In so doing, it further quickens the surprise that remains proper to the gift. If I consider as coldly as possible an artist who paints, placing no halo on their head and attributing them no divine inspirer, then I am thrust even further ahead of their hand's gesture, of this self-assuredness which is only partly proper to the art, and which is only ever assured of the fact that, for all intents and purposes, it remains naked, exposed, risky, never sure of itself.[42]

And so of this essay, of this series of musings that reflectively lose themselves in one another, and whose criss-crossing keeps all shores at bay. Their movement of thought is perhaps to be understood in the Hegelian sense of art's reincarnation on the threshold of its dissolution, of its *Aufhebung*. The image is alluring. Yet, in "The Girl Who Succeeds the Muses," Nancy questions this very movement: "Several indications

---

[37] Michaud, *Cosa volante*, 122.
[38] Nancy, "Lettre inédite à Claudio Parmiggiani" (May 4, 2006), cited in Michaud, *Cosa volante*, 122.
[39] Nancy, "Entretien avec Michel Gaillot," in *Jean-Luc Nancy* (Paris: ADFP Ministère des Affaires étrangères), 7.
[40] Nancy, *Les Muses*, 170.
[41] Ibid., 180–81.
[42] Ibid., 180.

converge, therefore, to suggest that art is … reincarnated as it were at the very limit of its own dissolution, and that in 'reincarnating' itself, it again grants a place to the set of 'particularizations' that are essential to it" (*M*, 43). It is thus not a crossing from one end to the other, but from ends to ends with no possibility of a *back to* or *back from*—merely the departure of a *revenance*, since "something … of art absolutely resists absorption by the dialectical spiral" (*M*, 41–42). The aim here will thus not have been to put forth a definition, for *The Muses* are neither a "determination" of art nor a "description" of the arts: "We are seeking merely a fashion of not leaving this diversity behind, a fashion not of 'saying' but of *articulating* something of 'art,' singular plural, right at its inorganic plurality and without synthesis or without system" (*M*, 36–37). In *The Muses*, the aim is never to define (or to redefine) art—nor, for that matter, to put an end to it—on the basis of its plurality; rather, it is not to leave art behind, as though this tension, which is also a resistance, were itself irresistible.

(Translated by Cosmin Toma)

4

After *Listening*: Music, Musicians, and Modernity

Sarah Hickmott

And there lies, one more time, a little privilege of music: music ends visibly, ostensibly, always with a call, which always calls for the end of music … The property of the fading of musical sound is similar to the infinitely delicate end, little by little receding, in increasing paleness, of a pencil trace.

— Jean-Luc Nancy, "Variations on the Reprise"[1]

In the opening paragraph of Nancy's short text, "Listening,"[2] we are presented with a simple question to which no similarly straightforward answer can be found: "Is listening something of which philosophy is capable?"[3] Nancy continues by outlining the fundamental tensions that underpin this problematic: the intra-philosophical dualisms between, for example, the audible and the intelligible, the sensuous and the signifying/symbolic, or the sonorous and the logical. Indeed, as he suggests, "figure and idea, theater and theory, spectacle and speculation suit each other better, superimpose themselves on each other, even can be substituted for each other" (*L*, 2). In one sense, *Listening* simply evidences the way in which Nancy, along with many of his contemporaries, is engaged in a critique—at once poetic, political, and philosophical—of the values and biases that have sustained Western metaphysics and which constitute the very terms of its operation as a coherent system; and, in another, it offers an affirmative answer that reimagines a philosophy that is attentive to meaning not merely as *logos*, but also to the passing of sounds always yet to come. At first blush, then, readers who are familiar with Nancy's larger oeuvre will quickly recognize motifs that are central to his project when leafing through this short volume; it unambiguously offers a sonorous counterpoint to his broader ontological project, not least through a sustained meditation on role of resonance and the *corps sonore* (sonorous body).

---

[1] Jean-Luc Nancy, "Variations on the Reprise," trans. Irving Goh, *CR: The New Centennial Review* 18, no. 2 (2018): 238. Hereafter *VR*.

[2] Originally published in French as *À l'écoute* (Paris: Galilée, 2002). The English translation, *Listening*, comprises the original essay "Listening," and two others not included in the original French edition.

[3] Nancy, *Listening*, trans. Charlotte Mandell (New York: Fordham University Press, 2007), 1. Hereafter *L*.

Indeed, given both the emphasis Nancy places on the sensuous presentation of the world on sense *as* meaningful rather than *having* meaning that needs to be located "elsewhere" and the obviously auditory nature of sensuous lived existence, it seems prudent to offer an acoustemological[4] complement to his other work on the sensuous subject.

But what, then, of music, musicians, and modernity, in this text that appears to be primarily concerned with philosophy and its limits—even if this is approached through a probing of philosophy's constitutive forgetting or repression of the sonorous or the audible? Though it is often advanced that Nancy's primary aesthetic focus is the visual,[5] it is certainly the case that it is not only—or merely—sound (or the sonorous or the resonant) that is theorized in *Listening*, but something that pertains to the specifically musical, even if that potential distinction is simultaneously problematized. Further still, this chapter would like to make the case that even if *Listening* may well assume a fundamental role in any Nancean philosophy of sound and/or music, it is music, specifically, that assumes an increasingly important role in Nancy's output thereafter. It marks something of a turning point, or at the very least the tensions explored in *Listening* continue to reverberate long after: the original text, *À l'écoute*, was published in 2002; the English translation in 2007, to which two additional essays, "March in Spirit in Our Ranks" and "How Music Listens to Itself," were appended; in 2008 "La scène mondiale du rock" ("The International Rock Scene") appears; followed by a dialogue with musicologist Danielle Cohen-Levinas, *Inventions à deux voix* in 2015; "Variations on the Reprise" arrives in 2018 (though based on a transcript of two seminars from 2006/7, and originally published in French in 2010); and, most recently, "*Galant* Music" was published in 2020.[6] In these more recent texts, some of the productive tensions found in *Listening* are further explored, and greater clarity emerges, particularly in relation to the two intertwined poles or "faces"[7] of music: for want of a better denomination, the musical and the musicianly, whereby music is shown to be, as Naomi Waltham-Smith describes, "an irreducible mixture of freedom and technicity."[8] Moreover, for Nancy, these elements appear to stand not only in an essential relation to the modern problematic of the subject, but are also figured in relation to an explicitly ethical or political questioning of European modernity, one which insists on "the intrinsic membership of fascisms (in general, of totalitarianisms) in the history of Europe and consequently in its essence or its truth"

---

[4] First coined by Steven Field, the term "acoustemology" denotes the epistemology of sound as such and hence listening as a way of knowing.

[5] See, for example, Rodolphe Burger, in *VR*, 218.

[6] Though the content is not explicitly musical, Nancy's short coda to a special issue of *Angelaki*, published shortly before his death in 2021, is framed as "An Accordion Tune." Music, it seems, was both the first and final breath for Nancy. See Jean-Luc Nancy, Marie Chabbert, and Nikolaas Deketelaere, "An Accordion Tune," trans. Marie Chabbert, *Angelaki* 26, nos. 3–4 (2021): 239–42.

[7] Nancy, "*Galant* Music," trans. Naomi Waltham-Smith, in *The Oxford Handbook of Western Music and Philosophy*, ed. Tomás McAuley, Nanette Nielsen, and Jerrold Levinson, with Ariana Phillips-Hutton (Oxford: Oxford University Press, 2020), 1023.

[8] Ibid., 1021. See also Jean-Luc Nancy and Danielle Cohen-Levinas, *Inventions à deux voix. Entretiens* (Paris: Le Félin, 2015), 59.

(*L*, 54). Consequently, this chapter will offer an assessment of what Nancy's thinking contributes to a philosophical understanding of music "after" *Listening* in three senses: first, and above all, what comes after our engagement with Nancy's essay, "Listening"— its philosophical demands or consequences for our thinking about music and sound; second, in the sense of the two essays that come after the English translation of the text; and third, albeit in a rather more cursory fashion, in the sense of the ongoing resonance of these ideas in the texts that Nancy has written on music since the publication of *Listening*. As we will see, Nancy—the self-professed "philosophe non-rocker"[9]—has thus made a rather larger contribution to musico-philosophical thinking than has hitherto been appreciated.

The Possibility of Listening: After "Listening"

As noted above, in "Listening," Nancy questions philosophy's capacity for listening. This is proposed as an auricular mode that is of quite a different order to *hearing*— the subtle sense of this distinction is lost in translation, however, because *entendre* connotes not only hearing but also understanding (as well as expectation, intention, and agreement). In order to pursue his philosophy of *listening*, rather than *hearing*, he posits that the auditory pairing subsists in a privileged relationship to intellectual or intelligible sense; in short, while *entendre* preserves the dichotomy between a perceiving subject and a perceptible object, Nancy's philosophy of listening demands that "sense not be content to make sense (or to be *logos*), but that it want also to resound" (*L*, 6). This allows him to challenge the traditional philosophical pursuit of "truth," or the "hidden" meaning of sense (as *making* sense or *logos*), and instead to pursue a dynamic, resonant philosophy that subsists in the space of the return [*renvoi*]; in sound that exists only as a *resounding*. Nancy clearly states that "[m]y whole proposal will revolve around such a fundamental resonance, even around a resonance as a foundation, as a first or last profundity of 'sense' itself (or of truth)" (*L*, 6). While it may appear that the *renvoi* reinstates a kind of fundamental ground or essence toward which we can turn, the emphasis on the "re" negates any claims of foundationalism; any sounding is always already a *resounding*, with no recourse to an originary or "pure" sounding, and indeed this should be kept in mind throughout, especially when considering the "foundational" nature of resonance.

In particular, the auditory articulation of a sonorous *renvoi* allows Nancy to (re)theorize in ontological terms the ocularcentric aspects of the oppositional pairing of subject-object; indeed, Adrienne Janus even goes so far as to position *À l'écoute* at a "culminating moment" of a broader "anti-ocular" turn.[10] Nancy's subject, described

---

[9] Jean-Luc Nancy, "La scène mondiale du rock," *Rue Descartes* 60, no. 2 (2008): 76.
[10] Adrienne Janus, "Listening: Jean-Luc Nancy and the 'Anti-Ocular' Turn in Continental Philosophy and Critical Theory," *Comparative Literature* 63 (2011): 182. See also Martin Jay, *Downcast Eyes: The Denigration of Vision in Twentieth-Century French Thought* (Berkeley: University of California Press, 1993).

as "a diapason," is one which is "[t]uned to self" but is nonetheless a "'self'" without substance; it is only a "self" insofar as it exists in the sonorous *renvoi* itself (*L*, 16–17). Only through this "return" can the self be said to come into being; through feeling oneself feel ("*se-sentir-sentir*" [*L*, 8]) the self feels itself, and is only a self in this feeling. As Nancy emphatically states—insisting on the non-metaphorical nature of this sonorous ontology—listening is theorized "not as a metaphor for access to self, but as the reality of this access, a reality consequently indissociably 'mine' and 'other,' 'singular' and 'plural'" (*L*, 12). Nancy also develops his account of subjectivity through his conceptualization of the sonorous or resounding body (*corps sonore*), where both the object and the subject of listening resonate: "Which is always at once the body that resounds and my body as a listener where that resounds, or that resounds with it" (*L*, 70n11). The remarkable corollary of this, as Adrienne Janus has noted, is that "all objects, insofar as they resonate" are able, therefore, to be listening *subjects*; this has the consequent (and no doubt intentional) effect of making Nancy's "human" subject less properly "'subject'-like, less human."[11] Finally, then, despite the essentially rhythmic constitution—the resonance created by the fundamental *renvoi*—of the *corps sonore* that might lead us to think of it in purely temporal terms, Nancy's *corps sonore* also opens onto a spatiality; "it spreads in space" (*L*, 7). This temporal movement even seems to constitute, be a pre-condition of, or afford the *manifestation*—which Nancy has been keen to insist on as an inherently *visual* domain—of a spatial dimension, and thus to a relation with others. Or, as Wagner's Gurnemanz, cited by Nancy, sings in *Parsifal*: "Here, time becomes space" (*L*, 14).

Nancy's affirmative rehabilitation of philosophy's (failed) repression of the sonorous thus offers some enthralling possibilities for our thinking about music—at least if we take music to be the (set of) techniques that most explicitly explores, assembles, or even problematizes the potentials of sound or the sonorous. At the very least, as Roger Matthew Grant states, it is "new and provocative" for its "turn to the sonic as a solution, rather than as the basis of the problem"[12]; Nancy therefore also invites the possibility of rethinking the historically difficult relationship between music and meaning: through the sonorous return (*renvoi*) music (and its fundamentally non-signifying—or *beyond*-signifying—resonance) is understood as essentially meaningful—not as/through representation but simply by virtue of its sensuous presentation in and of the world. The corollary of this is that we are also offered a way of thinking about music beyond inherited binaries; Michael Gallope has gone so far as to suggest that, at least in theory, *Listening* offers a "completely different philosophy of music," one that has the potential to transcend the dualism of approaches focused on either the "immateriality of sonorous structure ... [or the] materiality of practice and context"[13]—given the central importance that Nancy places on the co-valence of sense as both sensuousness and

---

[11] Janus, "Listening," 194.
[12] Roger Mathew Grant, "Review: *Listening* by Jean-Luc Nancy," *Journal of the American Musicological Society* 62, no. 3 (2009): 751.
[13] Michael Gallope, "Review: Jean-Luc Nancy. 2007. *Listening*. Translated by Charlotte Mandell," *Current Musicology* 86 (2008): 157.

meaning. Instead, the audible appears affirmatively as the perpetual flux of a shared, sonorous world. In short, Nancy's position suggests a potentially radical avenue beyond a dualism that has often seen music considered in either wholly immaterial terms—the closed, positivist approach to score-based analysis or "purely" formal procedures—or as a mere product of a particular socio-cultural context, with no specificity of its own. Nancy either refuses or exceeds this distinction, and instead positions music as a shared space of resonance; as the auditory distribution of sense (*sens*), which is "a simultaneous listening to a 'self' and to a 'world' that are both in resonance" (*L*, 43).

Before we turn to the short essays appended to the text in its English translation, I think it is worth a moment to briefly highlight some of my reservations about *Listening*. Although it is incontestable that Nancy's contribution productively challenges some of our musico-philosophical assumptions and has the potential to bring about new ways of engaging with music, it is also the case that some of Nancy's suggestions depend on associations that I find contentious or problematic. Readers of the English translation will no doubt have noticed immediately the image which graces the cover, Titian's *Venus with an Organist and Cupid*, which Nancy also comments on in his meditation on listening, and which is reproduced as part of the short coda that ends the essay. In brief, the musical tableau depicts an organist gazing at a nude Venus; she appears to pay him no attention, instead attending to Cupid who is embracing her. Behind these figures we can see out to the modestly landscaped garden of the villa in which the musical scene presumably takes place; the pipes of the organ in the upper left blend almost seamlessly with the lines of trees outside which demarcate the limits of the garden. In effect, Nancy's short oto-iconographical analysis allows for a more lucid recapitulation of the key claims of the short but dense text: above all, that sound is always already a re-sounding that folds into itself any distinction between subject/object and inside/outside, and that sound subsists as a kind of opening or sharing, and in a privileged relation to all the resonances of *sens* (as perception, intelligibility, and direction). In the organist's sensuous gazing at the naked Venus, we learn how "[t]he ear opens onto the belly, or the ear even opens up the belly" (*L*, 45). The resonant chamber of Venus' belly is both, Nancy claims, "the very place where his music comes to resound" (*L*, 45) and where the inside and outside open up to one another, itself echoed in the externality of the garden scene in the background of an otherwise intimate indoors scene. As I have suggested elsewhere, I think we ought to pause in order to question why Nancy requires the naked body of a woman—and Venus, as the archetypal image of feminine sexuality, no less—to propound his musical theorizations.[14] Moreover, it seems to play into a trope that describes or understands music in reference to an uncritically "fixed" conception of the (maternal) feminine, that ultimately serves to send both women and music—or at least the essentially musical—to a pre-cultural and ahistorical beyond of signification—a gesture which relentlessly aligns women with the subordinate term

---

[14] See "(En) corps sonore: Jean-Luc Nancy's 'Sonotropism,'" *French Studies* 69, no. 4 (2015): 479–93 for more on this specifically, and *Music, Philosophy and Gender in Nancy, Lacoue-Labarthe, Badiou* (Edinburgh: Edinburgh University Press, 2020) for how this relates to broader contemporary and historical tendencies in this regard.

in the list of oppositions while erasing the lived presence of women in the signifying, symbolic, and linguistic domain. As Robin James has compellingly shown, rather than disrupting a more fundamental binary, the male philosopher is simply able to appropriate "feminized experiences of being affected by or acted upon while avoiding the denigration and marginalization that go with these experiences *when they are attributed to women*."[15] Though it remains difficult to resolve the specifically gendered aspect of this critique, in what follows I hope to show that some of the related tensions, most evidently between an essential or prior "musicality" and a "music" proper—one which emerges in specific historical, social, and cultural contexts, and which depends on a changeable repository of techniques, instruments, traditions, institutions, styles, and so on: its "conditions … *the condition of its resonance*" (*L*, 11[16])—are developed in productive ways in the texts that post-date *Listening*.

After "Listening": Hearing Fascism; Listening (to Music Listening to Music…)

The short essay, "March in Spirit in Our Ranks," which is appended to the English translation of "Listening," is bold and provocative. In a mere eleven pages, it offers a contribution to the Wagner question, but framed in terms of Nancy's specific philosophical interests: sense, signification, resonance, and so on.[17] It also pushes at a number of the distinctions found in *Listening*, such as the differentiation between listening (*écouter*) and hearing (*entendre*), as well as probing at the relation already established between (musical) "resonance as a foundation" (*L*, 6)—though again it must be noted that any sounding is always already a *re*sounding, with no recourse to an originary or pure sounding—and the *conditions* that allow for the perversion of this fundamental resonance, stifling or quashing it in the service of a myth and culminating in a music that cannot be listened to, even though it must be heard. In short, it is Nancy's contention that by subjecting music to a logic of signification (rather than resonance), National Socialism (and its musics) was not entirely "foreign to the musical possibilities awakened long before Nazism" (*L*, 55). Rather, Nazism "benefited from an encounter, which was not a chance one, with a certain new condition … [with] something [that] had already been preparing itself for a long time—something that did not as such prefigure the Third Reich, but that offered it a choice space" (*L*, 50–51). This damning critique—not only of Wagner, as adduced already by Nietzsche, but of European

---

[15] Robin James, "Affective Resonances: On the Uses and Abuses of Music in and for Philosophy," *PhaenEx* 7, no. 2 (2012): 68.
[16] Italics original throughout.
[17] Badiou has suggested that the Wagner question has become a specific genre for philosophy, one which "created a new situation with respect to the relationship between music and philosophy" and that therefore Wagner has become a necessary "subject" for any philosopher to approach. See *Five Lessons on Wagner*, trans. Susan Spitzer (London and New York: Verso, 2010), especially, 56.

musical modernity at large—presents many angles to which the contemporary reader/listener may wish to "stretch" their ear ("*tendre l'oreille*") (*L*, 5).

There are a number of elements that are worth staking out more clearly, however. First, and above all, the specific ways in which Nancy's claims pertain to the affective or emotive dimension of music. Nancy makes it quite plain that the idea that music, perhaps even uniquely, "harbors a force of communication and participation" (*L*, 52) is nothing new; since Plato, music (or more broadly, and more accurately, *mousikē*) has been understood in terms of a psychagogical model, whereby it plays a central role in shaping, molding, and training the psyche (in order to achieve psychical, social, and even cosmic harmony). Indeed, the claim is not that the Nazis and their ideologues invented music's ability to affect or effect, to mobilize and manipulate subjects, but it is rather a question of locating, within a longer continuity, "the turning point of a shift or of a specific perversion" (*L*, 55). For Nancy, this turning point is figured as a reversal: it is "no longer a question so much of letting a fundamental affect come to expression but of shaping such an affect, of forming it and conforming it to a measure not yet registered in nature or in history" (*L*, 55). In short, though philosophy has long attested to, and been convinced by, the pathetic or affective dimension of music—even if the mechanisms that underpin this capacity remain unclear and, at the very least, contested—according to Nancy, "[t]his expressive, communicative, pulse-shaping, disseminating power ... acquired an entirely new consideration in the age of subjectivity" (*L*, 52).

Second, this is all fundamentally connected to some key distinctions that are more evidently Nancean, and which also make claims as to the mechanism by which this fascist perversion of musical resonance can take place. While resonance has been conceptualized throughout "Listening" as being "beyond-significance [*outre-signifiance*]" (*L*, 58), in "March in the Spirit in Our Ranks," (Wagnerian) music is identified as being aligned instead with an *oversignification*.[18] Music's sensuousness, its resonance, is co-opted to a signifying logic, and it becomes "indexed to a mode of signification and not to a mode of sensibility" (*L*, 57). It is a "signifying imposition" that refuses any resonance or dissonance (i.e., sense rather than *meaning*) precisely because it is the sensuous *representation of* a signified ideal; the form is therefore also indistinguishably the (spiritual) content and "[t]hus *feeling* manages to be identified all at once as signified and signifier of realities, images, or concepts like 'people,' 'community,' 'destiny,' 'mission' and so on" (*L*, 57, 58). This is, as Michael Gallope has so lucidly described, because "there is no spacing. Like two nervous systems fused together, or a dialectic that has conquered its internal differences, freezing the singularity of its motion, music has ceased to resonate between us. The consequence is an affective solidarity."[19] It is thus not music's supposed ineffability—its

---

[18] Nancy's long-time friend, colleague and collaborator, Philippe Lacoue-Labarthe has also written about this, and similarly described it in terms of a *surcodification* (overcodification). See *Pour n'en pas finir: écrits sur la musique*, ed. Aristide Bianchi and Leonid Kharlamov (Paris: Christian Bourgois éditeur, 2015), 68.

[19] Gallope, "Review: Jean-Luc Nancy. 2007. *Listening*," 163.

"beyond-signifiance [*outre-signifiance*]"—that is on trial, but the Romantic obliteration of the "*distance* between sound and sense, a distance without which sonority would cease to be what it is" and which paves the way for the *over-signifying* proto-fascism of Wagner (*L*, 58). As Gallope, again, has questioned, however, there remains a large question mark about what this means in practice: "how could we have a *kind* of music on the side of *entendre*, a mythical kind of music that has been saddled with horrible signifying content that 'disfigures,' 'obliterates,' and 'stifles' resonance?"[20] In many respects, this leads us to more questions than answers, the most pressing of which seem to be whether or how we could know when we are faced with a kind of music (a genre? a composer? a performance or recording? a whole tradition?) that is "on the side of *entendre*"? How would we identify it or know it as such? And given that Nancy has suggested at the very beginning of "Listening," that *écouter* (listening) and *entendre* (hearing/understanding) are "two paces [*allures*] of the *same* … [that] one cannot, in the long run, do without the other" (*L*, 2), can we nonetheless resist it by choosing, despite all, to *listen*?

Finally, the remaining point worth clarifying is that we are not talking about a straightforward or given causality here. One of the major claims of this brief essay is that Western musical-aesthetic practices—*ergo*, we are not only or merely speaking of Wagner—in nascent form from the early seventeenth century and amplified by Romanticism at the beginning of the nineteenth century have embedded within them if not the promise, then at least the possibility of totalitarianism and fascism. Nancy insists "stubbornly, on the intrinsic membership of fascisms … in the history of Europe and consequently in its essence or its truth" (*L*, 54). This is truth not in a timeless or universal sense, but as the constituting essence or kernel of a particular historical construction, the implication thus being that—assuming music is not cleanly severable from the society whence it emerges—music is co-constituted or relates in some fundamental way to the historical epoch from which it comes. Thus, for Nancy, though we miss something crucial if we consider this to be only a question about Wagner, National Socialism, the "Horst-Wessel-Lied," and so on, especially if viewed as some kind of unique aberration or deviation (a "demonic accident" [*L*, 54]), this is not the same as insisting on a straightforward "mechanical causality" (*L*, 53). Rather, though the literate European musical tradition has the possibility of fascism inherent in its structures and practices—as Nancy clearly says, "that fascism and Nazism could … arise from it—that is … beyond argument" (*L*, 53)—this does not confer any kind of inevitability; simply, we are not dealing with something "purely foreign to the musical possibilities awakened long before Nazism" (*L*, 55).

In the second, even shorter, essay adjoined to the English translation, "How Music Listens to Itself," we are treated to a rich and evocative meditation on musical listening. This is less about how we (could/should) listen *to* music—a concern which would return us to all the dualisms that Nancy has provocatively challenged throughout, such as any straightforward sense of listening subjects and musical objects—and more about

---

[20] Ibid.

"the opening of a world in resonance" (*L*, 67); about the musical art of making the infinite return of resonance not only resound, but something to which we can listen. We also find, unusually, a couple of quasi-definitions of music: according to Nancy, music is both "the art of the hope for resonance: a sense that does not make sense except because of its resounding in itself" and it is also "the art of making the outside of time return to every time, making return to every moment the beginning that listens to itself beginning and beginning again" (*L*, 67). Although these definitions—and especially the latter—seem somewhat opaque, they evidently connect both to Nancy's emphasis on the primacy of resonance (as opening and infinite return of this opening) and to his desire to steer us beyond "structural" or technical listening and, relatedly, beyond our (Eurocentric) assumption of a bound or closed musical work—a musical object. Indeed, much of this concise but deceptively thorough text condenses around the problematic of the work, and specifically of

> the distance between what links a work to its means, conditions, and regulated contexts, and what makes it exist as such, in its indivisible unity (which is, moreover, nothing but the indivisible unity of a whole and of the discrete units, all just as indivisible, of its parts, moments, components, aspects…).
>
> What makes the work is nothing but this: what makes it in its totality and as its "whole" is present nowhere but in its parts or elements … What we are calling "work" is much less the completed production than this very movement, which does not "produce" but opens and continually holds the work open—or, more precisely, maintains the work as this opening that it essentially is, all the way to its conclusion, even if this conclusion takes shape from what music calls resolution.
>
> (*L*, 64–65)

Above all, in this fleeting reflection on musical listening Nancy is pushing at the question of *how* "the musicianly [*musicien*] and the musical [are] shared or intermingled," or of the relation between the "compositional and the sensory" (*L*, 64). These are questions which are not only largely unaddressed in the primary essay, "Listening," which focuses far more on resonance as a foundation for a sonorous ontology, but which are also developed further in the texts published after *Listening,* as we will briefly consider in the final section of this chapter. On one end of the spectrum we have resonance, even "pure resonance," which is explicitly not a metaphor or figure for the understanding of ontology, but rather its pre-condition or possibility, a first principle and "the very beginning and opening up of sense" (*L*, 31). On the other, we have music proper—a technical assemblage which is irreducibly social, historical, cultural, and so on, but which nonetheless speaks or grants passage to the infinite return (to self) of resonance. Somewhere—it is not clear where—between these poles (though it is of course inaccurate to think of them as straightforward oppositions), there is something identified as "musical." At points this seems to be closer to (pure) resonance, and at others it appears to play a (technical) role closer to "music," as when

Nancy describes resonance as being "placed in the condition ... of the musical sense" (*L*, 37), or as an amplification or "intensification of the sonorous" (*VR*, 211).

Consequently, there is a fundamental question underpinning the issues at stake here: do we believe that there is a timeless, placeless, universal essence of music? Can we speak of such a thing as an "essence" of music, something that precedes any manifestation of "actual" music (however loosely defined)? Music as we know it and live it often has a specific origin, at a specific point in time, that we can identify (e.g., opera and the Florentine camerata at the beginning of the 1600s; rock in 1950s USA; grime in London in the early 2000s). Or, to paraphrase Derrida, do these specific points of musical origin, that musics emerge in particular times and places, mean that the very opposite is true, and there is no essence of music?[21] Nancy, I think, leaves this question open. Though, as a broadly anti-foundational thinker, we might well expect him to reject such a proposition—after all, it is key to Nancy's ontology that sense/meaning (*sens*) does not need to *make sense* (*logos*) or be located elsewhere and subjected to (and available to us only as) an impoverished re-presentation. Furthermore, Nancy's interest in the distribution, or the (re)routing of the senses—especially in the arts—disrupts this very opposition, giving heft to a broadly materialist position that refuses to locate in music (and in "great art" more generally) any kind of transcendental reserve (of spirit, will, etc.) that neutralizes the cultural and historical implications or ramifications—the situatedness—of these aesthetic "objects." And yet, something about music, its intimate relation to resonance, and the way it eclipses or evades not only philosophy's (phallog) ocularcentric schema, but also attempts to unsettle that same regime, leaves Nancy noncommittal. In short, it seems that no matter which way we approach music, an "infinitely fragile but resistant kernel of obscurity [remains] still intact" (*L*, 64).

In sum, Nancy does not deny the contextual or the historically situated aspects of musical works—far from it—but locates specifically musical listening not in the technical apprehension of these elements (formal, instrumental, compositional, and so on—though these remain, are necessary and indeed constitutive of the musical whole) but in the capacity of music for "the presencing activity of listening itself."[22] What Nancy offers most compellingly here is a radically egalitarian philosophy of (musical) listening, one which refuses to validate (good/correct) listening as would be grounded by some kind of training or expertise, whether musicological or otherwise. It is not that these technically oriented modes of listening are illegitimate—though Michael Gallope does raise the intriguing and compelling possibility that they may in some cases lead us to err on the side of *hearing*[23]—but that listening, being always already technical anyway (there is no "pure" listening freed of all relation—quite the opposite), is musical in its indeterminate openness, in its "sonorous presentation of presentation."[24] Nancy wrenches us from our inherited assumption that specifically

---

[21] Derrida says this about literature in his interview with Derek Attridge, "This Strange Institution Called Literature," trans. Geoffrey Bennington and Rachel Bowlby, in *Acts of Literature*, ed. D. Attridge (Abingdon: Routledge, 1992), 41.
[22] Gallope, "Review: Jean-Luc Nancy. 2007. Listening," 161.
[23] Ibid., 164.
[24] Ibid., 161.

musical listening entails listening *to* something quantifiable—form, structure, gesture, dynamics, pitch, style, and so on—and emphasizes a listening that any of us (trained or otherwise) who have touched, or "[been] touched by," music have already sensed. A listening that touches "the work in each part" (*L*, 65)—that is to say, it moves freely between techniques—that makes "the outside of time return to every time" (*L*, 67); at once a presenting of the flux of the present, and ceaselessly deferred.

(*Renvoi*) After *Listening*: The (Modern?) Problem of Music and Philosophy

In this final section, I simply want to bring to the fore some of the thematics that emerge in the texts that appear after the publication of *Listening*. There is far more in this collection of texts than can be considered in a few pages, but they return frequently enough to a relatively small number of concerns that it seems pertinent to bring these more explicitly to the surface. To begin, then, with the most recent text, "*Galant* Music," which appears in *The Oxford Handbook of Western Music and Philosophy* (2020), and which continues to probe at a number of the problematics already considered.[25] Key among the ideas we find returning, as imperfect echoes of claims already advanced in *Listening*, is the primacy of resonance in relation to the senses and, as its corollary, the special status granted to music amongst the arts. Waltham-Smith describes "[t]he exemplary status accorded to music and sound ... as what deconstructionists would call a quasi-transcendental."[26] This seems to chime very well with where we left our musings on "How Music Listens to Itself," and is certainly not the only point of contact. Just as "How Music Listens to Itself" seems to validate amateur, naïve, or even ignorant listening as potentially musical, "*Galant* Music" offers a provocative defense of gallantry, conceived largely as a rebuttal or refusal of "a gravity or emphasis that easily hovers around 'serious' music."[27] His use of "gallantry" therefore extends far beyond its usual historical specificity and is mobilized instead to demand our attention be turned more widely to music's gaiety and frivolity, the play(fulness) of playing music, and to forgo "learned counterpoint" in order "to musick ... to let oneself be carried away by a gallantry."[28] In turn this is linked to freedom, articulated again in terms of

---

[25] This is an unusual piece, which consists of a translator's introduction by Naomi Waltham-Smith, the short essay on "*Galant* Music" by Nancy, followed by an afterword, which is prefaced with another short note from the translators, and which is itself a response to his friend and fellow philosopher Marie-Louise Mallet's response to his text!

[26] Waltham-Smith, in "*Galant* Music," 1020.

[27] Nancy, in "*Galant* Music," 1026.

[28] Nancy, in "*Galant* Music," 1022. The translators Naomi Waltham-Smith and Jerrold Levinson have, with good reason, chosen to use "musick"; I take this to be a reference to Christopher Small who coined this verb to denote all kinds of musical activity, from composition, performance, and listening (whether live or recorded) through to singing in the shower. See *Musicking: The Meanings of Performing and Listening* (Hanover: University Press of New England, 1998).

the two "faces" of music, this time the "technical and calculated" (the "musicianly"?) on one side and the "free and the *galant*" (the musical?) on the other; the two "faces" are characterized as being mutually dependent, and in their intermingling is offered the possibility of a virtuosity that sets music apart, or has no "exact equivalent in other disciplines."[29]

Above all, Nancy's provocation of a musical *galanterie*—far above and beyond its historical remit—speaks not only to "music's capacity to touch the real or truth but also [of] the relation between music and philosophy."[30] As Waltham-Smith continues, drawing on Derrida, "that there is no 'the' meaning of music does not mean that there is no meaning whatsoever—that music is ineffable madness."[31] What Nancy tries to carve out here is a philosophy of music that refuses to decide, tugging instead at oppositions that are then shown to be illusory or untenable in an absolute sense, but which also refuse to be extinguished entirely, ceaselessly bouncing back while continuously evading one's grasp: musical *galanterie* is rather "the delicacy of brushing against (*effleurer*) the truth without pretending to master it."[32] Nancy's music therefore seems to be content, perhaps even *galante* and free in these vacillations; it is both material and immaterial, mediated and autonomous, real and ideal, utterly mundane, yet also beguilingly (quasi-)transcendental. As a consequence, music is constantly and necessarily held in suspense between these poles; it is neither given over nor reduced to finite technicity nor lost to the infinitude of unshaped or undistributed sense, though something in this equivocation is precisely what allows music, as Nancy claims elsewhere, to "*[dispense] a certain truth*" (VR, 219).

Another of Nancy's texts that brings together the musical and the philosophical in interesting, and perhaps unexpected ways, is a lecture given at the *Cité de la musique* in 2004, entitled "La scène mondiale du rock." It strikes me as especially worthy of comment, not only because of the ways it draws links between music and philosophy, but also as a welcome deviation from *musique savante* in a philosophical tradition that rarely takes much else to be (philosophically) significant. In it, Nancy neither disparages rock—which he understands less as a specific genre than as a broader movement that encompasses a swathe of subgenres, such as techno, pop, rap, and so on—as merely popular, mass culture entertainment, nor idealizes it—it is simply a "bearer of sense [*sens*],"[33] though he does grant it a significant status *as* a philosophical phenomenon in itself, a "philosophical phenomenon in the largest sense, which is to say a form of thought, of the representation of the world, of values, even of meaning."[34] Throughout the text, rock is characterized as something that both influences society and is influenced by society (or at least "external" factors); in this respect rock is

---

[29] Nancy, in "*Galant* Music," 1023.
[30] Waltham-Smith, in "*Galant* Music," 1021.
[31] Ibid.
[32] Nancy, in "*Galant* Music," 1026.
[33] *Sens* also connotes "meaning," and both are at play here and throughout. Nancy, "La scène mondiale du rock," 77. All translations my own.
[34] Ibid., 76.

considered as both a subject-like form of affective agency and an object-like repository that resounds with contemporary values, meanings, identities, and politics. For Nancy, rock played a crucial role in socio-political events such as the fall of the Berlin wall; indeed, he suggests that there are few "cultural phenomena which might be able to claim such capacity for propagation, for contamination, for contagion"; rock, he claims, is "a call to remake the world."[35]

Alongside this conception of rock as a musical force that is able to act on the world, it also appears to reflect prevailing philosophical concerns and discourses in its narrative and aesthetic innovations. Nancy explicitly parallels the emergence of rock in the middle of the twentieth century with the concurrent "end of metaphysics" in philosophy. Just as this philosophical trajectory is described as "the passage from an era where philosophy consisted of a vision of the world or a system of truth, to one where philosophy has ceased to consider itself as knowledge or the construction of systems of thought," rock is understood as a composite genre (rather than a self-authorizing musical system) that "entirely puts back into play the whole question of meaning."[36] Furthermore, one of the novelties—or so Nancy claims—that "rock, like jazz" (and subsequent genres such as techno) attests to is the centrality of the body through its co-instantiation as both music and dance.[37] I want to both insist on and *desist* from this narrative: though it is welcome and necessary to admit the body "into" musical ontology (again, *contra* a longer history of structural or technical listening), this is not because "all the musical innovations of our history [classical music] were not accompanied by innovations in dance"[38] (what about *Le Sacre du printemps*?) or because *musique savante* doesn't co-instantiate a vast repertoire of bodily techniques: indeed, "[w]ho would deny," as Benjamin Piekut so eloquently describes, "the agency of a training regimen that develops fine motor skill in the hands" or the "corporeal protocols that discipline the performing body"[39]—not to mention the composite bodily practices (seated stillness, silence, applause at appropriate moments) that are demanded by idealized and reverent concert hall listening. Indeed, the radical indistinction between subject and object (and so on) found elsewhere in Nancy's sonorous philosophy may very well allow us to move beyond such superficial oppositions and to better articulate not only the affective but also the embodied dimension of music not as a "natural" unidirectional effect of an object on a (bodily) subject, but as something that is created in relation—that even our ideas about distinctions between subjects and objects, minds and bodies, are co-instantiated in this way. Indeed, at its best, a Nancean philosophy of

---

[35] Ibid., 78, 84.
[36] Ibid., 77–78, 83.
[37] Ibid., 79. Nancy has also written on techno, in dialogue with Michael Gaillot; this is perhaps Nancy's earliest text dealing specifically with music. Although it pre-dates our considerations here, many of the ideas discussed we find echoed in *Listening* and subsequent texts. See Michel Gaillot, Jean-Luc Nancy, and Michel Maffesoli, *Sens multiple : la techno, un laboratoire artistique et politique du présent* (Paris: Dis voir, 1998).
[38] Nancy, "La scène mondiale du rock," 79.
[39] Benjamin Piekut, "Actor-Networks in Music History: Clarifications and Critiques," *Twentieth-Century Music* 11, no. 2 (2014): 202, 191.

music demands that there are no naturally occurring subjects and objects (of music); music is instead one of the modalities through which the *sens* of this distinction is technically and affectively (re)routed.

Nonetheless, we are returned not only to the vexed relationship between musical aesthetics and an explicitly political or ethical world-making, as well as to the way in which philosophy has long struggled to navigate the contours of this connection. In "Variations on the Reprise," which is mostly a dialogue between Nancy and Rodolphe Burger (described by Nancy as a "philosopher turned rocker"[40]), published in English in 2018, though transcribed from seminars during Burger's residency at the Strasbourg Conservatory in 2006–7, we find a set of variations on most of the themes already covered in this chapter, such as the primacy or fundamental opening that is resonance, and music's special power to shape, forge, or arouse. As ever, this is not unique to music—all arts have this capacity to some degree—but music is more powerful in this regard because of "a sensible property of music that distinguishes it from all that is visual" (*VR*, 220). Consequently, music is able to fashion not only the soul but also the body; and, seemingly at odds with some of the claims in "La scène mondiale du rock," Nancy even contends that "all music makes us dance, even that of Schoenberg" (*VR*, 220). Developing further this exemplary or privileged status of music in comparison to the other arts, we also find more extended variations on the themes already posed concerning an intimate and fundamental triangulation of relations between music, resonance, and the subject. Recalling Nancy's oto-iconographical analysis of the Titian painting in "Listening," we have a return to the uterine environment and the birth of the infant, with the first breath or cry figured—though this is perhaps not quite the right word, there is no figuring or imaging here—as the first relation to the world, the establishment of resonance—or of the subject which "is first a body that resonates" (*VR*, 209). The links between the privileging of resonance amongst the senses, and of music in comparison to the other arts, are staked out more clearly in this piece, and more explicitly resonate also with music's special relationship to the (modern) problematic of the subject: we are told explicitly that "music … behaves like a subject … it is in relation with itself" (*VR*, 221). Again, therefore, we find a recapitulation of the idea that "music … listens to itself," and this is grounded in music's fundamental sonority—indeed, Nancy reminds us that even "the silence of Cage resonates" (*VR*, 236)—because "the fundamental phenomenon of resonance … [is] the phenomenon of sound itself" (*VR*, 221). It seems that even if music "proper" is "fashioned by great ensembles of affective values" (*VR*, 213), it can never be severed entirely from the more fundamental question of resonance or from the fluxional processes of being(-with).

Accordingly, it is this intimate link to the sensible that is also staked out as affording music's complicated relation with philosophy, for reasons that are both independent to philosophy—resonance precedes the philosophical schema—and also indissolubly connected to the history of (Western) philosophy. In response to the question of "Why does the history of philosophy (the history of philosophy, the history of politics),

---

[40] Nancy, "La scène mondiale du rock," 76.

which is no less the history of Western civilization, begin with this strange philosophy/music vacillation?" (*VR*, 219). Nancy suggests that it connects to "the effort of a whole new world to relate itself to the world that has become strange" (*VR*, 205). A world which previously made sense, or rather, was made sensible by the dominating presences of the gods, was faced with this loss of sensibility, and thus Nancy conceives of philosophy as a symptom or response to the monumental changing of a world. The "loss" of the sensible world leads to a questioning of the sensible, and ultimately to Plato "posit[ing] the intelligible against the sensible" (*VR*, 206). All in the same breath, in a society (*polis*) that has found itself "deprived of its own founding" (*VR*, 206), politics emerges—again, symptomatically. For philosophy, then, music is less a mere problem to be solved than a fundamental condition or founding question, "because one senses it by an interpellation of the sensible" (*VR*, 208), and all of this in spite of the constitutive loss of the sensible to which Nancy attributes both the emergence of (Western) philosophy and politics. One powerful conclusion we are led to through an engagement with Nancy's resonant philosophy is that we are simply not able to think (philosophically) about the musically sensible without engaging also with politics; that the two are indissociably intertwined in Western philosophy and culture. Secondly, and above and beyond this founding "philosophy/music vacillation," it is only in the modern period that the question of music rises to philosophical prominence, most evidently following the introduction of Kantian aesthetics. In short, Nancy states that we can "fairly say that the overture of philosophy to music is tardy" (*VR*, 205). Again, this is linked to the becoming strange of the world, this time the "crisis of the subject" that develops progressively as the autonomous self-constituting unity bequeathed to us by Descartes is "revealed to be untenable" (*VR*, 208). The most intriguing—if underdeveloped—suggestion, however, is that we are now in the wake of another crisis, one which Nancy explicitly parallels with the becoming strange of the ancient world and the founding of philosophy: "It was a phenomenon similar to that which is happening in contemporary philosophy via-à-vis politics" (*VR*, 206). Though Nancy describes not only the coming of music (as aesthetics) to philosophy as tardy, but also his own coming to resonance (this "has come to me tardily in my philosophical life," he says), it might be more apt to consider it as timely, and utterly apace with what Nancy describes as a third and "completely contemporary reopening to it [music]" (*VR*, 205)—or even, as Kara Keeling and Josh Kun have noted, with a sonorous or auditory turn in the humanities more generally.[41] We are left wondering, then, exactly which of our many current philosophical-political crises this third wave of melomania might well be a response? And whether, much like the music Nancy resonantly theorizes, the answer to that might remain *à venir*.

---

[41] In their "Introduction," Keeling and Kun describe us as being at "a moment [in the humanities] when the study of sound and listening is suddenly more ubiquitous than ever." See *Sound Clash: Listening to American Studies*, ed. K. Keeling and J. Kun (Baltimore: Johns Hopkins University Press, 2012), 2.

5

Fabula, Bucca, Humanitas: On *Ego Sum*

Andrea Gyenge

In his preface to the English translation of *Ego Sum* (1979), Jean-Luc Nancy declares his commitment to the mouth: "Since I wrote this book, the mouth is the other motif that never leaves me, even if I have not written much more about it, as if I was waiting (but who, 'I'?) for a special occasion, the sudden discovery of the opportunity for an epic of the mouth."[1] Seemingly prompted by his own declaration, Nancy offers a series of starts for such an epic but each time he names the mouth, he proposes a different entry, as it were, to this heterogeneous space at once fleshy and ephemeral. Using the grammar of the colon, the text passes across breath and voice, food and digestion, speech and song in a remarkable homage to the organ. Not the organ of daily practice and familiar labors (i.e., a mouth we might recognize as our own) but rather an unmasterable hole unmoored from its personified axis. By identifying the mouth through its anonymous, general actions—never *our* mouth, *your* mouth, *my* mouth—Nancy thus refuses its traditional fusion with selfhood, that is, the mouth as the figural locus of a Subject who speaks and therefore knows, the Subject who masters the universe with its tongue. An epic of the mouth is decidedly *not* an epic of the Subject. Even the act of saying "I" appears only as one action among many and a tenuous, fragile one at that: "The mouth: this jetty that says 'I,' sometimes shouting it and other times stifling it" (*ES*, xi). And when the echoes of this "I" fade away, we are left with a mouth that has no name, a mouth that swallows language, a mouth that speaks nothing but its proliferating, abundant difference: "The mouth: the orifice the elastic pulped edge of which draws the mobile contours of the opening of a sense that is each time other, singular, thrown and suspended in various ways, interrupted, without accomplishment, so that it can better retain in suspense the force of its impulse" (*ES*, xi).

Thinking such a mouth is the essence of Nancy's project in *Ego Sum*, a mouth that comes before the Subject, but which paradoxically lies at the heart of the Cartesian project, the discourse of the Subject *par excellence*. In pursuing this "other" mouth as a foundational disruption of Cartesian thought, *Ego Sum* is both a fearless reckoning with Descartes's legacy and a singular philosophy of the mouth. Moreover, Nancy's return

---

[1] Jean-Luc Nancy, *Ego Sum: Corpus, Anima, Fabula*, trans. Marie-Ève Morin (New York: Fordham University Press, 2016), x. Hereafter *ES*. The title of my essay is a play on the English title—it is my sense that these three words are equally possible, which is to say, equally important as a subtitle.

to Cartesian philosophy inaugurates a critique of its unique position as the founding logic of modern philosophy, one that grounds the very possibility of philosophical discourse itself, including Nancy's own: "Descartes imprints the mark of certainty onto three centuries of modernity. We are still there." To address this *"terra firma"* (*ES*, 12), Nancy's project thus proceeds with a certain methodological irony: how can one question Descartes's *cogito* and its legacy of certitude without reaffirming the *cogito* itself? How can such a philosophy be written, if to write philosophy is already to fall into the eminently modern trap of Cartesian epistemology?[2] *Ego Sum* will answer: in the language of the mouth, a language unlike any other, but one which Descartes alone makes possible. To hear the mouth that "calls *us*"[3] (*ES*, 12) from within Descartes's philosophy is thus to hear that which in Descartes *continuously* speaks otherwise. It is a future that arises out of the making-different of Descartes—that which "in Descartes's thought, in the thought of the Subject, *has already started to bring* the metaphysics of the Subject *to an end*" (*ES*, 16). The mouth is thus less a concept than the trace of an infinite disruption, a textual event that defines *Ego Sum*'s impossible, dizzying contact with Cartesian philosophy, and our own—whether that be a direct interrogation of Descartes or the gestures of thinking that define the terrain of critical discourse. Any contemporary account of Nancy's thought, therefore, must pass through *Ego Sum*, not only because it marks a particularly important moment in postwar French thought, but also because its method continuously provokes a contestation with the very work of critical praxis itself.

That a philosophy of the mouth appears at its center, however, is perhaps surprising to those who are better acquainted with Nancy as a thinker of touch or as a political philosopher whose theory of inoperativity has now borne the reputation of his name for several decades. Nor do we associate Descartes himself—famed author of the *Optics*—with any distinctive thought of the mouth, let alone a thought of the mouth that might threaten the edifice of philosophical certainty. Even within Nancy's oeuvre, *Ego Sum* suffers from a sort of peripheral status, marked perhaps by its late translation to English relative to the speed with which his texts have met English readership. That *Ego Sum* has been relegated too often to the margins leaves Nancy's critique of the Subject open to contemporary readings that might have proceeded differently, if *Ego Sum*, and its tarrying with Descartes had been considered. I am thinking, for example, of a recent special issue of *Cultural Critique* titled "What Comes after the Subject?" Citing the original title of Nancy's special issue of *Topoi* in 1988—"Who Comes after the Subject?"—in which Nancy's question was posed to several prominent thinkers in France, editors Christian P. Haines and Sean Grattan orient their intervention toward a critique of Nancy's slippery attachment to a *who* in the original grammar of his

---

[2] In her introductory comments to *Ego Sum*, Marie-Ève Morin observes the same idea at work in Foucault and Derrida's discussion of Descartes, albeit in a slightly different fashion: "The first question, then, is: In what language can the mad speak about his or her madness? If *logos* or reason is to be excluded from the discourse on madness, then only a mad discourse can be adequate to madness" (*ES*, xvii).
[3] Italics original throughout unless otherwise stated.

provocation.[4] By "insisting on a *who* of subjectivity," Haines and Grattan argue that Nancy risks "a submission in advance to the placeholder that Nancy designates as *some one*,"[5] an accidental clearing of a place for a renewed and revived Subject. In replacing the *who* with a *what* (a lineage they trace from Hannah Arendt to contemporary biopolitical philosophy), Haines and Grattan aim instead to "investigate the alternative organizations of thought, agency, and practice that appear when one suspends the *who* and lingers in the *what*."[6] Such a shift to the *what* "entails a reclaiming of the present as a fecund time for politics, as a time in which productive struggles can occur over what it means to be, over who/what counts, and over how matter comes to matter."[7] They thus propose a timely question of their own: "Is this to say, then, that after the subject comes life?"[8] In doing so, they identify the *what* as taking place "in the interval that opens up between, on the one hand, 'the subject'—understood as the product of technologies of power ... —and, on the other, the excess of life, affects, and political, and social conducts that refuse grounding in a *sub-jectum*," to which they add: "One could speak, here, of a subjectivity without a subject or of forms of life that do not conform to the desire for mastery."[9] But while Haines and Grattan position Nancy as the original provocateur and thus the instigator of their project, he is nevertheless afforded only the honor of an inaugurating negation, which is to say, Haines and Grattan assign Nancy to having authored—if inadvertently—the possibility of a new logic of the Subject, a "latent anthropocentrism"[10] that must be contested by the *what* they propose as an alternative. In the same vein, they critique his question (via Rancière) as bearing the signs of "a melancholy tone of privilege in which to think—*to truly think*—means recognizing the unbearableness of the subject, its impropriety, its status as *démodé*."[11] To escape this melancholia of the philosopher "in the know" and his [Nancy's] purported tendency toward an "apocalyptic mood," Haines and Grattan propose that we might instead pursue a "praxis" that would be "conflictual, pragmatic, nonexceptional, and radically open to alterity."[12]

Yet strangely enough, not only does one recognize the character of Nancy's thought in their description—experimental, affirmative, even joyous—but already in 1979, *Ego Sum* clearly warned against the very dangers that Haines and Grattan here ascribe to Nancy's *who*, which, if not necessarily dispelling the problematics of its grammar, at least put to test what they deem to be the irreconcilable impasses of a renewed

---

[4] For more information on the origins of the *Topoi* issue, see Eduardo Cadava and Peter Connor's introduction to the English edition of *Who Comes after the Subject?* (New York: Routledge, 1991), 1–8.

[5] Christian Haines and Sean Grattan, "Introduction," *What Comes after the Subject? Cultural Critique* 96 (2017): 1.

[6] Ibid., 3.

[7] Ibid.

[8] Ibid., 13.

[9] Ibid., 15.

[10] Ibid., 2.

[11] Ibid.

[12] Ibid., 3.

thought of the Subject as risked by Nancy's provocation. In fact, as Marie-Ève Morin emphasizes in her introduction, *Ego Sum* specifically questions the claim that one can proceed with a thought of a "subjectivity without a subject or ... forms of life that do not conform to the desire for mastery."[13] For Morin, Nancy's "lesson is that any theoretical discourse, no matter how subversive, always produces a subject: the subject of the discourse," and that "no matter how split or mad the subject of discourse is, this discourse on such a subject itself presupposes a master subject, a subject who is certain of himself and is master of the meaning of this split or mad subject."[14] After all, even those systems of thought (e.g., psychoanalysis) that attempted a critique of the Subject succeeded only in reasserting the *cogito*'s essential functioning: "Any operation of identification of a subject, even if it leads to an identity that is purely negative, critical, dissociative, or chaotic, is in the end itself *the* Subject, the true substratum" (*ES*, 14). It is for this reason that Nancy casts his return to Descartes in the language of Heidegger, that is, the *forgetting* of the metaphysics of the Subject, while also flagging the danger of solving this metaphysics by simply reassigning the *I* (who) to an *it* (what): "in recent years thought has come to a standstill ... by heavily insisting upon this: 'not *I* think, but *it* thinks,'" thus harking back to Nietzsche, who, "after having substituted 'it thinks' for 'I think'" in *Beyond Good and Evil*, "adds: 'In fact, there is already too much packed into the "it thinks": even the "it" contains an *interpretation* of the process, and does not belong to the process itself'" (*ES*, 14–15). Nancy's canny warning here sounds all the more imperative in light of the recent turn to materialism, especially object-oriented ontology, as a way of once more attempting to dislodge the "anthropological subject"[15] (*ES*, 5). As Morin reflects, *Ego Sum*'s English publication confirms that its core concern, "the problematic return of the Subject, remains very much our own today."[16]

What remains at stake, then, is not just the grammar of the *who* but the very metaphysical edifice of thought itself in which a knowing subject is assumed and which retains its efficacy even in the very moment that it announces having gone "beyond" the *who* to the *what*. In other words, it's not the *who* of Nancy's question that risks reinstalling the hegemony of the Subject. It is already risked in the mode of analysis offered by Haines and Grattan; indeed, risked as soon as their text masterfully announces its difficulty with Nancy's *who*. Moreover, Nancy is too hastily reduced to this proposition—one not afforded the generosity of a reading within his oeuvre. If Nancy is guilty here of a dangerous "grammar," so too do they risk a totalizing gesture that reduces his philosophy to the same "who" of his proposition, that is, the subject of a thought with no other valence or difference than his rehearsal of a troubling idea.[17] In raising questions about their reading of Nancy, however, I mean to do more here than point out the slippages in an otherwise compelling account of contemporary politics,

---

[13] Ibid., 15.
[14] Morin, "Translator's Introduction," in *Ego Sum*, xvi.
[15] See also Haines and Grattan on the significance of new materialism in contemporary discourse ("Introduction," 3).
[16] Morin, "Translator's Introduction," xv.
[17] Haines and Grattan, "Introduction," 5.

one that also offers a vigorous justification for renewed thought in what feels like an impoverished and desperate moment. Rather, if Haines and Grattan seem to offer no other place for Nancy but the confines of the *who* (even as they dedicate an issue to the provocations of his thought), one is left with the sense that deconstruction (and by extension, Nancy) is an uncertain and ambivalent presence, one whose legacy (if we can call it that) is expressed only in the repeated references to "affirmative" critique.[18] But one does not have to go far to find examples of Derrida's impassioned insistence that deconstruction is the hermeneutics of a wild and generous affirmation, an affirmation that must be separated from the infallible philosophical certainty inherited from Descartes; indeed, separated from the Subject that philosophy perpetually reproduces. In fact, if one wanted to venture an accusation of nihilism, one would be correct to locate it in the fetish for certitude, which renders a stale death to both life and politics. There is a politics of utopia here, of course, insofar as such a hermeneutics would also gesture toward something like hope—what Haines and Grattan call "affirmations of possibility"—that would nevertheless stand against the naïve pursuit of the "new" that is endemic to capitalism.[19]

What then does such affirmation mean if that *which* (or that *who?*) would do the affirming is no longer the locus of such an action, if affirmation rests now on something neither lacking nor negated but living in the interstices between matter and thought? In his conclusion to *Ego Sum*, Nancy offers a name for this interstice, and it is the name of the *mouth*:

> *Unum quid*, a something that is neither soul-nor-body, opens its mouth and pronounces or conceives: *ego sum*. Besides, this is still saying too much. *Unum quid* does not *have* a mouth that it could manipulate and open, no more than it has an intellect it could exert to reflect upon itself. But something—*unum quid*—opens (it would therefore have the appearance or shape of a mouth) and this opening articulates itself (it would therefore have the appearance of discourse, hence of thought), and this articulated opening, in an extreme contraction, forms: *I*.
>
> (*ES*, 107)

In proposing *ego* as a mouth before all other mouths that is no more a subject than it is a body, Nancy offers something still yet different from the *what* of Haines and Grattan, something that would not be answerable or reducible to the distinction between a *who* and a *what*. The question that he would engage later (i.e., "who comes after the subject?") is thus understood here as a matter of discerning what comes "before" the Cartesian Subject. It is only insofar as we answer the latter question that the former has any meaning. As such, I read *Ego Sum* as Nancy's answer to their troubling of his question, an answer that came a decade ahead of the *Topoi* collection but which returns to the scene of contemporary thought with renewed force and interest. That Nancy's

---

[18] Ibid., 4.
[19] Ibid., 4, 6.

own reflection identifies the mouth as its crucial motif likewise instructs us to treat the mouth as more than an idiosyncratic theme put forth by a young philosopher, or a peripheral organ worthy only of psychoanalytic fetish or speculation. Despite Nancy's own assessment of his oeuvre, *Ego Sum* marks the first of many texts that pass through the mouth, texts that amount to a clandestine corpus of buccal gestures. Indeed, it is in the later *Corpus* (1990–2), for example, where Nancy calls for a dictionary of the body's infinite points of access: "We need a corpus of *entries* into the body: dictionary entries, language entries, encyclopedia entries, all the body's introductory *topoi*, registers for all its articles, an index for all its places, postures, planes, and recesses. A corpus would be the registration of this long discontinuity of entries (*or exits: the doors always swing both ways*)."[20] A decade later, Nancy would write a short essay on Claire Denis's horror film *Trouble Every Day* (2001), where a set of tooth marks on skin (an "icon of fury") provokes a meditation on cinema's "taste for blood."[21] Themes of devouring and corporeality sink their teeth into an ontology of film violence: the image and the mouth touch at the threshold between death, desire, and the rending force of the visual. Other essays get wildly drunk (*Intoxication*), circle the mouth in painting (*Portraits*), send lips to taste the nude (*Being Nude*), and open in ecstasy (*Coming*). Despite the plethora of other mouths, however, *Ego Sum* is the text most intimately bound to the mouth's power—it is where its philosophical weight is given force and history. In fact, that the mouth even has a place in the history of philosophy is perhaps the extraordinary event of *Ego Sum*, what Derrida called "an experience, an experiment, and an abyssal 'provocation' of what is called the mouth."[22] If *Ego Sum* still calls us to thought today, it is in this "provocation" toward a buccal philosophy, a philosophy that also shapes, if silently, the political verve of Nancy's writing. It is my intention, therefore, to make a case for reading *Ego Sum* as an enduringly contemporary text, most especially if we return to the oral motif that Nancy identifies as essential to its movement.

Fabula

While *Ego Sum* is undoubtedly a book "about" Descartes, it is also an extraordinarily idiosyncratic reading of a philosopher whose weighty name seems almost defiant of new interpretations. Despite the many critiques leveled against his philosophy, Descartes's self-proclaimed preference for vision as the supreme sense remains central to contemporary readings of his legacy. In tandem with Cartesian dualism, this is the story we tell so often about Descartes that it seems hardly possible to read him without its baggage. Even critical reflections on the accepted story of philosophical modernity come via optical metaphors: "Blinded by the historical import of the impulses that

---

[20] Nancy, *Corpus*, trans. Richard A. Rand (New York: Fordham University Press, 2008), 55.
[21] Nancy, "Icon of Fury: Claire Denis's *Trouble Every Day*," trans. Douglas Morrey, *Film-Philosophy* 12, no. 1 (2008): 1, 6.
[22] Jacques Derrida, *On Touching—Jean-Luc Nancy*, trans. Christine Irizarry (Stanford: Stanford University Press, 2005), 25.

have come to be associated with these luminaries, we are barely able to return with an unbiased eye to the epoch [that of the Enlightenment]."²³ While *Ego Sum* eventually displaces the priority of the eye for the mouth, Nancy, too, first renders Descartes's legacy in the language of illumination: "His name, his portrait, the phrase *cogito ergo sum* cling to the whole of our philosophical memory as a kind of emblem to which only a few are equal. There is something striking, decisive, and luminous (blinding even) about this emblem, which makes of it both a banner and a prerequisite for thought" (*ES*, xi–xii). In contrast to Descartes's other readers, however, Nancy does not rehearse the accepted story of Descartes's philosophy of vision as the essence of the Cartesian project nor indeed the fetish of the *cogito* as the terminal point of his ocularcentrism. On the contrary, *Ego Sum* returns to Cartesian philosophy to show that its own thought already bears a critique of the metaphysics of the Subject within it—one that we must attune ourselves to hearing (*ES*, 16). In returning to the moment of its founding, Nancy's opening gesture is thus to question the *cogito* as the destiny of modern philosophy, even as he simultaneously acknowledges its extraordinary powers of capture. What follows in the subsequent chapters amounts to a Descartes slowly shedding the skin of his philosophical clichés toward a future in which the Cartesian tradition no longer drives the theoretical scene to inevitable ruin. By the time we reach the end of *Ego Sum*, therefore, Nancy has so radically destabilized the terrain that it is a Descartes we barely recognize. Much of this is shaped by Nancy's distinctively literary, even modernist, reading of Descartes, which transforms *Ego Sum* into a kind of unholy Cartesian experiment where the reader is as often plunged into poetics as often as they are into "proper" philosophical exegesis. As Ian James notes, *Ego Sum* produces a "discourse which is not quite philosophy and not quite theory, but which is figural and affirms itself as a kind of fictionality or ficticity."²⁴ Chapter 2, for example, is written from the private vantage of Descartes's inner monologue as he writes *Rules for the Direction of the Mind* (*ES*, 20). We are thus constantly placed both inside and outside the vertigo of Cartesian philosophy—witnesses both to its birth and to its radical transformation. Above all, the literary gestures of *Ego Sum* serve to underscore its key intervention in the accepted Cartesian doxa: that Cartesian philosophy is a thought of the *fable*. Not the Enlightenment science we have edified, or an immovable dualism, or the *cogito* of an enduring epoch of a strict philosophy, but indeed a *literature*. Even as Nancy insists that the literature he means should not be confused with the ordinary methods and interests of basic poetic analysis, Nancy's reading of philosophical modernity nevertheless orients itself toward an account of the literary (*ES*, 68–69). This is another way of saying that Descartes is responsible not only for the discourse of the Subject but also for a distinctively modern form of reading, which positions hermeneutic truth within a field of the fictive. By doing so, Nancy brings Descartes closer to Nietzsche, perhaps, than anyone might have previously imagined, given the

---

[23] Peter Sloterdijk, "Descartes," in *Philosophical Temperaments: From Plato to Foucault*, trans. Thomas Dunlap (New York: Columbia University Press, 2013), 27.

[24] Ian James, *The Fragmentary Demand: An Introduction to the Philosophy of Jean-Luc Nancy* (Stanford: Stanford University Press, 2006), 51.

former's propensity for rationalism[25] (*ES*, 16). Nancy thus offers a reading of Descartes that reveals not only a profoundly poetic philosopher in gesture and practice but also the philosopher to be the modern author of a new literary ontology.

In fact, philosophy-as-fiction turns out to be the essence of Cartesian method for Nancy, which shapes two of Descartes's most decisive texts: *The World* (1633) and *Discourse on the Method* (1637). In particular, Nancy cites a passage from *The World*, where Descartes pauses to reassure the reader that his analysis of the elements will not continue to dull the reader: "Many other things remain for me to explain here ... But so as to make this long discourse less boring for you, I want to wrap up part of it in the guise of a *fable*."[26] After remarking on the need for a fable, Descartes begins narrating a mythical account of creation as if it were God making a world again. While Descartes ostensibly proposes only to entertain his reader with this fable, perhaps one more accustomed to literary artifice than sober philosophical discourse, Nancy treats these asides on the fable as the privileged example of the structural analogy governing Cartesian science; indeed, the structural analogy that births the Cartesian *cogito*. For the very moment that Descartes announces his transition from writing philosophy to writing a fable, Descartes too becomes a God of a world: "The fable of the World is then less the instrument of an exposition than *the organ of an equivalent of creation* (equivalent to *the* Creation)." Descartes's literary gesture thus positions him as mimetically equivalent to God because just like God, he produces something out of nothing. Even if what Descartes produces is representation (i.e., not the world but a fable of a world), it is his power to *make* that renders him parallel to divine creation. Like God, he has endowed a world with being: "In *inventing* this fable, I make—I make and I feign, I fiction, I fashion—a world ... The inventor of the fable is the God of a world that, even though it is not the world itself, is nevertheless *another true world*, and it is so *because it is invented* ... The subject of true knowledge must be the inventor of his own fable" (*ES*, 70). Or, put differently, it is by inventing his own fable that the subject of true knowledge comes into being:

> The subject takes place insofar as he says *I feign*, insofar as he says *I fabulate* ... and insofar as he says this at such an extremity that he brings himself to the fable's origin, which also means that he transports the *fable* itself, withdrawn from fiction as well as truth, to the point where it illuminates its own etymology: *fari*, to speak, to say.
>
> (*ES*, 84)

To write a fable is then to say—at the level of the utterance—that *I feign* and because *I feign*, I perform my being into being. I *am* the fable that I create and in creating myself

---

[25] Nietzsche's importance to *Ego Sum* cannot be understated and would require a separate essay of its own, especially given Nancy's explicit comment on the lineage between Heidegger, Nietzsche, and Descartes. See pp. 15–16 of *Ego Sum*. See also pp. 51–54 in Ian James's *The Fragmentary Demand*.

[26] René Descartes, *The World and Other Writings*, trans. Stephen Gaukroger (Cambridge: Cambridge University Press, 1998), 21.

as a fable, I become true. The Subject's ontology is thus bound to the truth of its own fiction. And like all literary gestures, its most powerful truth thus appears in the very moment when it is most fabricated. It depends on nothing else. Not God. Not history. Not proof. The Subject *is* because it *says* it is. And insofar as it speaks itself into being, the Cartesian Subject cannot thus *be* a subject since at its origin, it *is* its own self-invention: "I pronounce, I am. I pronounce I, I *am* pronouncing I" (*ES*, 84). Revising Benveniste's theory of performative enunciation, Nancy thus rejects the Cartesian Subject as concept of human consciousness, that is, the idea of an inner self that apprehends itself apprehending: "The truth that Cartesian mathesis erects as the certainty of the subject is at the same time determined [*décidée*] as the self-conception of this subject, or as the self-conception that this subject *is*. The ontology of subjectivity is not that of a subjective 'interiority' or a consciousness; it is the ontology of the self-conception of being" (*ES*, 58).

At this point in his argument, however, Nancy appears to posit the Cartesian *cogito* as the absolute we have long suspected it to be. The *cogito* now seems an edifice so powerful and elusive that only one future appears on the horizon: the hegemony of the Subject. Anticipating the objection, Nancy instructs the reader not to misunderstand the *cogito* as taking place "*at* the extremity of the feint, as if it were its absolute exteriority of truth" (*ES*, 79). In other words, if the fable of the subject passes into truth because it is created, it is not to be understood as the moment in which the fable *ceases* to be fictive and the *cogito* therefore becomes its truthful and final "outside." Rather, the *cogito* is the "extremity" of an undecidability, that is, the "limit" point of a dialectic in which both truth and fiction simultaneously appear and "withdraw" from each other in a performative event that both *is* and *is not* at the same time: "[w]ithin the *uttering*, the subject loses all finish, all finition of figure: it is not, definitely not, infinite, yet it is not finite either. In-finite, it *is* not" (*ES*, 85). In contrast to the Subject proper, then, this "other" being (or event) exists as the *retreat* between both sides of a fold—being and not-being: it "posits itself, imposes itself … through the convulsion in which it tears itself apart and binds itself together … in a spasm that articulates and dismembers it, that articulates it only in dismembering it" (*ES*, 103–4). The *cogito* is thus without a ground since its existence *is* the vanishing point of the chiasm between truth and fiction, saying and not-saying: "the extremity of the Cartesian Subject, his extreme *nature*, strips him once and for all of any property of 'principle,' 'ground,' 'last foundation,' and instead of 'positing' him, only *ex-poses* him as the becoming-extreme of extremity" (*ES*, 80). In returning to the Cartesian Subject at its founding origins to identify this essential convulsion, Nancy is careful to show that he is not performing a philosophical reverse sleight of hand (i.e., showing us that there is nothing where we saw something). This would suggest that the Subject is nothing more than a philosophical phantasm in need of a dose of rationalism that would then deliver us over—in secret—to the Subject's mastery. Nor should this convulsion be taken as the sign of some kind of mournful, nihilistic philosophy thinking at the edge of an annihilation—the "apocalyptic mood" that Haines and Grattan fear Nancy indulges.[27] Confronting the specter of nihilism

---

[27] Haines and Grattan, "Introduction," 3.

hovering over his work, Nancy addresses the problem in his "Introduction" to the *Topoi* issue and diagnoses nihilism as part of the metaphysics to resist: "There is nothing nihilistic in recognizing that the *subject*—the property of the self—is the thought that reabsorbs or exhausts all possibility of *being-in-the-world* (all possibility of *existence*, all existence as being delivered to the possible)."[28] For Nancy, a critique of the Subject is thus a gesture *against* nihilism, which is to say, such a critique identifies the Subject itself as the form of consuming negativity *par excellence*—a consuming negativity that is *opposed* to the convulsion described above.

In this sense, *Ego Sum* aims—as do Haines and Grattan—to restore the differential potential of being or what they term "the possibilities of forms of life beyond or beside the subject."[29] By contrast, however, Nancy is rather more cautious about what "beyond or beside the subject" might produce by way of a new figure (or figures) of worship (*ES*, 4). Noting that such replacements inevitably force a renewed hegemony of the Subject, Nancy identifies his exhaustion with idols of difference—"those so-called *self*-saying nonsubjects"—charged with the duty of clearing the metaphysical toxins from our collective air: "we have despaired of their theoretical and aesthetic, practical and political virtues" (*ES*, 15). In contrast to such hastily declared victories and the reactionary programs they provoke, Nancy proposes "to show how the anthropological profusion of the subject covers over and muffles the question ... of someone: this someone, neither a subject nor the Subject, will not be named, but this book would like to let it call itself: *ego*" (*ES*, 3). Not a resuscitation of the Subject in different clothes yet still more than the "nothing" of a terminal nihilism, *ego* is the promise of the Cartesian legacy. *Ego* is what strains to be heard over the incessant discourse of the Cartesian Subject—"the uttering from which a whisper comes out or seeps out, always untimely and inactual—and which calls *us*" (*ES*, 12). Given the trajectory of *Ego Sum*, a trajectory that directly attempts to think something *other* than "subject" or "Subject," it is rather surprising that Haines and Grattan make no reference to its influence on the *Topoi* material, which makes explicit reference to the quotation above (*ES*, 3). Without considering *Ego Sum*, Haines and Grattan do not recognize—indeed, fail to read—the deconstructive gesture of Nancy's original *Topoi* question:

> Everything seems, however, to point to the necessity, not of a "return to the subject" (proclaimed by those who would like to think that nothing has happened, and that there is nothing new to be thought, except maybe variations or modifications of the subject), but on the contrary, a move forward toward someone [*quelqu'un*]— *some one* [quelque un]—else in its place (this last expression is obviously a mere convenience: the "place" could not be the same).[30]

As Nancy explains here, "some one" is not a subject nor the Subject. In fact, the metaphysics of the Subject occludes this "some one." As such, it is decidedly not the

---

[28] Nancy, "Introduction," 4.
[29] Haines and Grattan, "Introduction," 4.
[30] Nancy, "Introduction," 5.

Subject that Haines and Grattan fear Nancy has resurrected but rather that *ego* to which Nancy dedicates the entirety of *Ego Sum*. In the introduction to the published collection *Who Comes after the Subject?* Nancy reflects on his original invitation and notes—quite clearly—that this "some one" is exactly the *who* that he meant to think when he proposed the original question. This *who* is definitively not the Subject of metaphysics:

> Not only are we not relieved of thinking this some *one* [*quelque un*]—this some *one* that the subject has perhaps always pointed towards or looked for, and that brings us back to the same figures: the individual, a people, the state, history, production, style, man, woman, as well as "myself" and "ourselves" ... —but it is precisely something like this thought that henceforth comes toward us and calls us forth.[31]

Who or what is this "some one"? None other than the object of Nancy's encounter with Descartes in *Ego Sum*, where the term first appears.[32] While Nancy does not yet use "some one" [quelque un] but rather "someone" [quelqu'un] in *Ego Sum*, *Ego Sum*'s meditation on *ego* is clearly the origin of Nancy's return to these themes. In revisiting the terms of *Ego Sum*, Nancy also offers further clarification regarding the "nature" of *ego*. As he explains in the following quotation, *ego* is not a subject at all but rather takes the form of a "singular existent."[33] I repeat here the beginning of the quotation, which I cited earlier, for clarity:

> There is nothing nihilistic in recognizing that the *subject*—the property of the *self*—is the thought that reabsorbs or exhausts all possibility of *being in the world* ... *and* that this same thought, never simple, never closed upon itself without remainder, designates and delivers an entirely different thought: that of the *one* [*d'un* un] and that of the some *one* [*quelque* un], of the singular existent that the subject announces, promises, and at the same time, conceals.[34]

As Nancy explains here again, "some one" is not at all the self-same Subject of a dangerous anthropology but rather what he calls here a "singular existent," a term that sounds almost identical to the "singular entities"[35] that Haines and Grattan wish to think *en route* to a new politics, a politics they mistakenly *oppose* to Nancy's original question. This misreading is especially noticeable once Nancy begins meditating on the nature of this "singular existent" in a series of paragraphs on the problem of the *who* and the *what*, paragraphs that Haines and Grattan either miss or deem unimportant. And yet it is here that Nancy most explicitly takes up their objections to his use of the *who*:

---

[31] Ibid.
[32] The introduction of the hyphen into "some-one" is the addition of the translator.
[33] Nancy, "Introduction," 4.
[34] Ibid.
[35] Haines and Grattan, "Introduction," 4.

But what existence? It is not an essence, it is the essence whose essence it is to exist, actually and in fact, in experience, "hic et nunc." It is the *existent* (and not the existence *of* the existent). With this in mind, the question asks "who?" Which means that the question of essence—"What, existence?"—calls forth a "who" in response. The question was therefore a response to the question of existence, of its "being" or its meaning, nothing more and nothing less.[36]

Reflecting further on the *Topoi* question, Nancy clarifies that he does not intend to establish the "who" as an essence or self-same identity. He is not asking after the "existence" of someone (i.e., to whom that existence would belong) that would arrive after the Subject. The *who* refers to the singularity of the *what*: "every 'what' that exists is a 'who,' if 'who' means: *that* actual, existent 'what,' as it exists—a factual (even) material punctuation of Being."[37] In other words, the *who* refers to the difference of the *what*—to the matter of its *thatness*. In this sense, the *who* asks after the matter or material of being, that is, the *what* of its infinite expressions. In this sense, anything can be a *who*. This is perhaps another way of saying for Nancy, being is always a *what* that cannot be separated from the *who*. If we do not stage this question—if we do not ask after the *who*—then we are left only with bare life: crude, irrelevant, without purchase and eminently destroyable. Asking after the "who" is thus a gesture of affirmation insofar as it affirms that being is that which takes up space—not just as an object or a thing—but as that which forces us to reckon with the sheer excess of its being *here* and being here in *this* way, what Nancy calls "a spacing that allows that something *come* into presence, in a unique time that engenders itself in this point in space."[38] In fact, Nancy says so directly: "'Before/after the subject': *who*. This is first all an *affirmation*: the being is *who*."[39] Isn't this the exact "affirmation" that Haines and Grattan imagine for their theoretical turn to the *what*? They write: "We have less in mind connotations of 'falsifiability' or of a scientific method than an openness to radical otherness conceived in a positive manner, or, more generally, an affirmative stance: a thinking that maps emergent forms of life, or singular entities, through the analysis of transformations in the *whatness* of contemporary subjectivities."[40] In short, it is clear that Nancy has been thinking of the exact problematics that Haines and Grattan suggest he has neglected or forgotten. In fact, one might say that he has thought of nothing else since the publication of *Ego Sum*, not at the risk of exclusion, but rather as an infinite call.

---

[36] Nancy, "Introduction," 6–7.
[37] Ibid., 7.
[38] Ibid.
[39] Ibid. Second emphasis mine.
[40] Haines and Grattan, "Introduction," 4. I do not have the space to develop it but one important point of difference here would be their invocation of "life" instead of "being." Even so, I would argue that Nancy's concept of being here is not necessarily opposed to a thinking of life. It is certainly a materialist ontology of sorts.

Bucca

At this point in my reading of *Ego Sum*, readers would be right to wonder about Nancy's retrospective declaration that "since I wrote this book, the mouth is the other motif that never leaves me" (*ES*, x). How is it that Nancy's reading of Descartes will lead us to such different waters from what a traditional encounter with *the philosopher of vision* might suggest? Up until the final paragraph of "Mundus Est Fabula," the motifs of fiction and fabulation are more powerful and persuasive. That *Ego Sum* is a philosophy of the mouth appears erroneous even up to most of the last chapter, "Unum Quid," until it takes a sudden, axiomatic turn in the final pages: "The mouth is the opening of *Ego*, *Ego* is the opening of the mouth" (*ES*, 112). From a strictly hermeneutic standpoint, there is little to support the claim that Descartes is the author of a radical orality. The Cartesian texts themselves take no wild turn, offer no open embrace of a strange, unthinking mouth. There is nothing necessarily in the *Meditations on First Philosophy* that freely establishes an obvious oral theme. It is only as Nancy passes through the Cartesian proofs for the union of the soul and the body that he finds a mouth opening at the heart of Descartes's thought. Nancy's reading is too complex to summarize here but his conclusion once again intervenes in the accepted Cartesian doxa. Despite its infamous ability to snare both modern and contemporary readers, Cartesian dualism or "the distinction between the soul and the body plays [only] a functional—or supporting—role in Cartesian theory, whereas the ontology to which it refers would be the ontology of *ego* insofar as it distinguishes *itself* while uttering itself, and hence insofar as it 'posits' itself as distinct from the distinction between substances" (*ES*, 101). What mouth, then, if *ego* is neither subject nor existence and *prior* to the question of substance (e.g., thought or extension)? Nancy will answer that the mouth he means is a "faceless mouth," not of someone (who) or something (what), but rather that which opens itself *as* it fabulates an I. Indeed, *ego*

> does not *have* a mouth that it could manipulate and open, no more than it has an intellect that it could exert to reflect upon itself. But something ... opens (it would therefore have the appearance or shape of a mouth) ... and this opening articulates itself (it would therefore have the appearance of discourse, hence of thought), and this articulated opening, in an extreme contraction, forms: *I*.
>
> ...
>
> Imagine a faceless mouth [*une bouche sans visage*] ... forming the ring of its contracture around the noise: *I*.
>
> (*ES*, 107)

This invocation to "imagine a faceless mouth" would seem rather abstract and speculative were it not for Nancy's reference to a forgotten taxonomy in Latin. The taxonomy separates the mouth into two distinct modalities—one mouth for speech (*os*) and one for everything else not related to speech, including all its animal and organic movements (*bucca*):

Bucca, a more recent and more trivial term, is not *os*. *Os, oris*, oral mouth, is the face itself taken metonymically for this mouth that it surrounds, carries, and makes visible, this mouth that is the passageway for all kinds of substances, first of all of this aerial substance of a discourse. *Bucca*, on the other hand, is the puffed cheeks, the movement, the contraction/distention of breathing, eating, spitting, or speaking. Buccality is more primitive than orality.

(*ES*, 111)

In his late work, *On Touching—Jean-Luc Nancy*, Derrida was the first to identify the importance of this "subtle but firm distinction" for *Ego Sum*.[41] The distinction rests on a discovery that "[t]he mouth *speaks* but it does so *among other things*. It can also breathe, eat, spit. It has 'not always been speaking,' not always been an *oral* agency."[42] Nonetheless, the mouth's subjection to speech is a powerful one—so powerful, in fact, that even the mouth's more organic modalities risk assimilation to a signifying logic. The hegemony of the *os* is rooted in its structuring relationship to the face, which undergirds the discourse of the Subject. Not only that the face determines the mouth, that is, gives it contour and ground, but the mouth reciprocally signifies the face by eternally producing meaning, even if it is doing something else other than speaking (e.g., vomiting, screaming, etc.). The speaking mouth thus anchors the face as *the* image of a reasoning, willful consciousness, even if the mouth is in the throes of abjection. As Sara Guyer notes in her essay "Buccality," in the oral mouth "all activities (including eating, crying, spitting, etc.) are metonymies of speaking."[43] And insofar as the mouth speaks and produces meaning, it secures the foundation of a self-same Subject, who masters the world in language. Moreover, for Guyer, the adherence to the face has profound consequences for a philosophy of ethics, which rests on the inherent humanism of the face, especially in the wake of Emmanuel Levinas. While Nancy does not reference Levinas in *Ego Sum*, he nevertheless devotes substantial pages to thinking Descartes's ironic reliance on the mask and portraiture as so many feints against a discourse of the face, especially as the elementary gestalt of a discourse of philosophical knowing. Deleuze and Guattari, nearly a decade later, would echo this intervention with their account of "facialization," and its strangulation of the "strange true becomings"[44] of a face without system or structure. Nancy's intervention, however, is singular for its attention to the buccal mouth as an alternative opening that undoes the face and its adherence to systemization. In Guyer's account, Nancy's interest in

---

[41] Derrida, *On Touching*, 20.
[42] Ibid. This split has an ancient history, which Derrida does not discuss, but which a longer paper would need to consider. See, for example, the section of Plato's *Timaeus* dialogue, where Socrates discusses the distinction between the eating and speaking mouth. There, Socrates develops a hierarchy between eating, which is in service of the "necessary," and speaking, which is in service of the "best." The former is only tolerated because of its production of the latter.
[43] Sara Guyer, "Buccality," in *Derrida, Deleuze, Psychoanalysis*, ed. Gabriele Schwab (New York: Columbia University Press, 2007), 90.
[44] Gilles Deleuze and Félix Guattari. "Year Zero: Faciality," in *A Thousand Plateaus*, trans. Brian Massumi (Minneapolis: University of Minnesota Press, 1987), 171.

buccality opens the possibility for a "defacing of ethics"[45] that might exclude any notion of figurality or rhetoric as the origin for ethical responsibility. The mouth is no longer the figure of human dignity, difference, or value, but rather that which *undoes* the very relationship between ethics and figurality. The buccal mouth thus opens the possibility of a "fundamentally ethical account of the subject that coincides with a nonfigural rhetoric."[46] For in contrast to the *os*, the buccal mouth is neither a mouth that one *has* (face) nor a mouth that one *is* (self). The buccal mouth is an "opening of a mouth that belongs to no one" or put differently, *bucca* is "a mouth in the opening of a one who—opened, disfigured—has no face."[47] The buccal mouth is defined by anonymous gestures, which are the actions of an elemental opening of a mouth without a Subject: "*ego* does not want to say anything, *ego* only opens this cavity" (*ES*, 111).

Even though this "a-figural" cavity is strictly unrepresentable, Nancy is fond of a photograph by Jacques-André Boiffard that depicts the buccal mouth in its potent, anonymous elasticity.[48] Shot in black and white, a grotesque close-up of a mouth (a woman's perhaps, but nothing is verified) takes up the center of the image. The photograph is cropped such that little remains of the face but two retreating, faint nostrils at the top edge—a set of tiny mouths or tunnels. The open cavern of the mouth operates as both abyss and border: something wet, fleshy, and gelatinous is caught moving back, or forward—it resembles a tongue, but the shape is too irregular, too deformed. The erotic is distinctly, even texturally present. The longer we look, the more we see that this hole is aggressively organic: we go to live there; we would not be surprised to die. The opening has anal contours, also vaginal, clearly digestive too. Still other holes resonate, pass through, appear and disappear. None dominate but none retreat: all entries are possible. It is a mouth, yes, but no mouth we have seen, no mouth we know, not a mouth at all. And yet it opens. It *opens* an opening—infinite lines toward the interior and the exterior. Figuration is thus evaded, even as the mouth is suggested.[49] Moreover, for Nancy, the buccal mouth is an ontological event, not just an evocative image of a disrupting, scandalous organ. In *Ego Sum*, ego is not a mouth that any *thing* opens nor a mouth that represents anything by association or phobic concealment. There is nothing under it or behind it or inside of it. And yet each time it opens, it opens as *itself*—as a radical singular being that comes from nothing but arrives

---

[45] Guyer, "Buccality," 80.
[46] Ibid., 91.
[47] Ibid., 88, 90.
[48] This photograph is not referenced in *Ego Sum*. Jean-Luc sent this photograph to me and my colleague in conversation. It was originally published in Georges Bataille's *Documents*.
[49] Drawing on Nancy's references to the photographic in *Ego Sum*, Philip Armstrong's analysis of Ann Hamilton's work—"Buccal Exscriptions: Ann Hamilton's *Face to Face* Photographs," *Parallax* 26, no. 4 (2020): 366–83—further argues that the mouth and the photograph both enter the world at the same time—as a material event of being (ibid., 370). In Hamilton's work, the camera is placed in the mouth and so the existence of the photograph literally coincides with the opening of the mouth. The body, and so by extension the history and repertoire of photography, becomes an indefinite series of orifices open to the world (ibid., 376). For Armstrong, if *ego* had an image, it would perhaps by necessity be a photographic one, but one that is thus disconnected from all humanist associations (ibid., 378).

on the scene as more than the triumph over chaos. It is the thrill of being as it erupts with life. As such, even as Nancy links the performative saying of *ego* to the action of the buccal mouth, he moves away from any account of *ego* that would conceive of it as a form of linguistic orality, which would only fold it back into the machinations of the *os*. Despite his interest in Benveniste's theory of performative enunciation, Nancy ultimately departs from his conclusion that "the basis of subjectivity is in the exercise of language."[50] *Bucca* is thus a mouth that disrupts every association with the *who* of a subject born of grammar (i.e., that subject also targeted by Haines and Grattan) or the *I* of a thinking substance, or even ultimately, the corporeal force of a purely physical cavity (*ES*, 112).

That the buccal mouth exists "before" the mouth of speech, however, suggests a subtle allegiance to a psychoanalytic understanding of the oral drive, that is, that the mouth of animal actions and erotic practices belongs to another, more primordial history of the subject. Nancy's inevitable reference to Freud is thus brief but declarative. He turns to Freud only to correct a misunderstanding: that the oral stage is merely a part of a developmental sequence in psychic life, easily overcome and necessarily replaced.[51] For Nancy, Freud's great philosophical innovation was his recognition of the buccal mouth as the origin of being.

> The Freudian child (I will not say subject) is not initiated into an "oral stage." He first opens himself as a mouth, the open mouth of the cry, but also the mouth closed upon the breast to which the child is attached in an identification more ancient than any identification with a figure, as well as the slightly open mouth, detaching itself from the breast, in a first smile or a first facial expression, the future of which is thinking.
>
> (*ES*, 111–12)

As Nancy explains here, the child is not prior to the mouth—it doesn't open it as a conscious action. Rather, a child *is* the opening of a mouth. The Freudian child is thus a landscape, a geography of buccal gestures that inaugurates everything to come: thinking, being, acting. In other words, we come into the world—announce our contact with it (and the other)—as an event of the mouth. Possibility and potential generate their force from this opening, a space which is not any space we know, but which nevertheless organizes both our finitude and our tenderness with the world. While for Guyer, Nancy's turn to Freud "revises the history of subjectivity" and "the possibility and impossibility of an autobiography of the mouth,"[52] I would argue that his turn to Freud also has profound consequences for the final pages of *Ego Sum*, which connect

---

[50] Émile Benveniste, "Subjectivity in Language," in *Problems in General Linguistics*, trans. Mary Elizabeth Meek (Coral Gables: University of Miami Press, 1971), 226.

[51] *Ego Sum* makes two references to Freud—the first is a reference to Freud's comment that "Psyche is extended, knows nothing about it" (*ES*, 110). Derrida uses this line as the opening provocation for his reading of *Ego Sum* in *On Touching—Jean-Luc Nancy*.

[52] Guyer, "Buccality," 91.

the buccal mouth to the political questions provoked by Descartes's philosophy. As Nancy begins this turn, he extends his reading of Freud with a reference to Heidegger, who further guides the way to understanding the ontological force of the mouth as a "spacing" that exposes us to the world:

> The mouth is the opening of *Ego*, *Ego* is the opening of the mouth. What comes to pass there is that ego spaces itself out there. "Clearing-away [*Räumen, espacer,* spacing] brings forth what is free, the open for human's settling and dwelling." But the human being is that which spaces itself out, and which perhaps only ever dwells in this spacing, in the *areality* of his mouth.[53]
>
> (*ES*, 112)

If, for Heidegger, clearing-away is what opens the possibility for human beings to "dwell" in the space of the free, Nancy argues via Freud that human beings rather *are* this spacing. If the human dwells here, it is because the human is understood only as an experience of *ego*—a provisional and finite event of a *temporary* saying of "I." This event never properly takes place: it neither has the contours of phenomenal reality nor the material structure of space: "The term [areality] suggests both a lack of reality (which is not an absence and makes it impossible to carry out a negative egology in the fashion of negative theology) and area—*area* in Latin—the quality of space and extension prior to any spatiality" (*ES*, 19). The buccal mouth is thus where the human "happens" but it happens only as that which never stops tarrying with its radical incompleteness. It is where "*ego* utters itself" as the "primordial spatiality of a true *outline* in which, and only in which, *ego* may come forth, trace itself out, and think itself" (*ES*, 112). The space of the mouth, therefore, is neither an absence nor a plentitude but an oscillating opening that ecstatically expresses being without positing this opening as either its essence or its ground. This is the mouth that Nancy "hears" in Cartesian philosophy, even if it is muffled and distant.

As if to provide a final, determining example, Nancy once again makes recourse to a literary gesture. Without any commentary, Nancy immediately follows his revision of Freud and Heidegger with an extended citation of Paul Valéry's "Bouche" poem. It appears in italics—almost as if in another language. Like the Boiffard photograph, it serves to illustrate by encounter. Ignorant of its philosophical context, Valéry's poem declares, almost polemically: "The buccal space. One of the oddest inventions of the organism." As the poem continues, the architectural metaphors arrive quickly: the mouth is a gulf, a temple, a theater, a "hell-gate of the Ancients." Both marvelous and monstrous, it is populated by more than just tongue or tooth: "Multipurpose machinery. There are fountains and furniture." In fact, the buccal mouth is so impossible an organ that descriptions of its practices bring us, once again, to the doorstep of fantasy and fiction: "If one were to describe without naming names this cavern, ingress of matter, what a tall tale!" Even speech is a force arriving from beyond the body, a body

---

[53] Nancy is citing Heidegger's "Art and Space." See *ES*, 138n50.

convulsed by sweeping organic movements, more materially volcanic or oceanic than personal and human: "And finally Speech ... That huge phenomenon of the deep, with its shakings, rollings, explosions, rhythmical mutations ..."[54] For Valéry, the mouth is precisely that which is inhuman in us—that anonymous force of potential and bodily event. All mouth actions are ultimately uncanny and distant, sovereigns of the strange and wordless. To use the language of Haines and Grattan, it is a *what* that engenders, at times, a *who*—but only ever as a temporary event, always finite. Neither animal nor human exactly, the mouth is the terrain of a limit—there where all things (human, animal, and mineral) open themselves toward an otherwise. This is perhaps not yet a posthumanism but it moves toward a resolutely modern and political decentering of the human—a recognition that the mouth's volatile organic truth is already a trace of a non-human difference. As if to speak back to Valéry, Nancy adds his own defining line: "The subject ruins itself and collapses into this abyss" (*ES*, 112). If the subject "ruins itself" here, it is because there is no mastery of this inhuman space, no signification adequate, no representation possible. Never itself, always other, the mouth is exposed, infinitely, to the outside.[55] That this outside is given as poetry, however, tells us that *Ego Sum* does not accomplish a theoretical intervention as a closed work. On the contrary, *Ego Sum* writes the exposure of being as an ecstasy of the mouth by opening itself to poetry as a generous promise for thought to come. It is a literary ontology of Descartes and an "attempt to pass, slowly, gently, almost insidiously, to this other thought that is not a representation but the experience of the mouth: speech, address, and why not song, and kiss?" (*ES*, xi).

Humanitas

In proposing that the buccal mouth undoes the binding logics of the face, Nancy ultimately offers the buccal mouth as a critique of the metaphysical legacies born of Descartes's *cogito* while also compelling us beyond the humanism we associate with his name. For Nancy, it is through Descartes that the human being *has* a future, even if Nancy calls it "the least improper" one (*ES*, 112). The striking conclusion of *Ego Sum*, therefore, is that Descartes (yes, Descartes) ultimately makes another *humanitas* possible and so too another politics:

> Descartes is the founder neither of humanism nor of anthropology or the so-called human sciences. He made their general program possible only at the cost of a misunderstanding—inevitable, no doubt, and inscribed everywhere within his discourse as well—of the impossible experience of the human being that the thinking of the Subject is compelled to reach, but which it cannot face.

---

[54] Paul Valéry, *Collected Works, Vol. 2: Poems in the Rough*, trans. Hilary Corke (New Jersey: Princeton University Press, 1969), 50. Quoted in *ES*, 112.

[55] Nancy, "The Inoperative Community," trans. Peter Connor, in *The Inoperative Community*, ed. P. Connor (Minneapolis and Oxford: University of Minnesota Press, 1991), 31.

> ...
> In the thinking of the Subject and by means of a convulsive thought, a *humanitas* was thought that remains exorbitant for this humanism to which we still belong, even if against our own *body*.
>
> (*ES*, 109–10)

It is a compelling, powerful diagnosis. Not only is Descartes *not* responsible for the ills so often associated with his name throughout the history of modern philosophy, he is the author of a different thought, one he himself perhaps would not have endorsed, nor even understood, but which "convulses" his philosophy nonetheless: "It is this thought—*ego, unum quid*—that alone can find out that it does not give rise to any recognition of its subject, of the human being" (*ES*, 112). What, then, is this other *humanitas* that Descartes makes possible, a *humanitas* that is *not* the human being of a universal essence? Nancy takes his cue from Heidegger's "Letter on Humanism," where the term first appears: "Humanism is opposed because it does not set the *humanitas* of man high enough."[56] For Heidegger, the failure of humanism is rooted in its metaphysical baggage, which cannot think the relation between human beings and the question of Being. If humans have an essence, argues Heidegger, it is in this relation to Being, which is singular but not transcendent (i.e., not given by God, or posited as an eternal concept). It thus separates humans from animals, but "without elevating man to the center of beings."[57] For Nancy, insofar as *ego* is a mouth—a mouth that is neither the Subject nor the Human—then it *is* this *humanitas*, even if its ontology is fragile, provisional, and always opening onto the chaos of areality. Moreover, Nancy's ontology implicates the question of the common at every turn. If this "other" *humanitas* is what Descartes leaves as his political legacy, then we are left with a concept of human community without essence, a way of being human that joins us neither in a universal nature nor in a subjective consciousness. And if the mouth is that which infinitely rends itself open as the impossible "event" of the human, then it is already that which is inoperative—by definition. As Marie-Ève Morin notes, Nancy's thinking of the mouth as an "areality" indeed comes to shape his political philosophy: "Interestingly, a few years after the publication of *Ego Sum* and before coming back to the areality of the body ... Nancy will use the logic of arealization to describe the 'being' of the community."[58] It's odd, then, that Haines and Grattan, in their hope for new theories of collectivity, did not recognize Nancy's thought as contemporary to others in his generation deemed to be authors of a "renaissance of theories of subjectivity."[59] As they write, these thinkers (e.g., Badiou,

---

[56] Martin Heidegger, "Letter on Humanism," trans. Frank A. Capuzzi and J. Glenn Gray, in *Basic Writings*, ed. David Farrell Krell (New York: HarperCollins, 1977), 210. In his essay, Heidegger makes direct reference to Sartre's "Existentialism is a Humanism," which is another important text for *Ego Sum*. Nancy does not cite the text directly but Sartre's explicit recourse to Descartes as the foundation for his thinking of existence and action seems implicated in Nancy's critique.
[57] Ibid., 255.
[58] Morin, "Translator's Introduction," xix.
[59] Haines and Grattan, "Introduction," 16.

Žižek, Rancière) allow us to see that "[t]he subject is, if not utopian, then at least an atopian excess that traverses the order of things and promises the reconstitution of the world."[60] That Nancy went to Descartes for this exact imaginary already in 1979 demonstrates his timely and ongoing intervention in the discourses of our moment. By the time he publishes *The Inoperative Community* (1986), however, little remains of the oral motif, with the exception of one particularly provocative paragraph in his commentary on Bataille: the open mouth "exposes to the 'outside' an 'inside' that, without this exposition, would not exist ... The speaking mouth does not transmit, does not inform, does not effect any bond; it is—perhaps, though taken *at its limit*, as with the kiss—the beating of a singular site against other singular sites."[61] Despite its brevity, Nancy teaches us here again that the mouth is *not* the foundation of a humanism rooted in language, social communication, and linguistic bonds. If the mouth is bound up in the question of the common, it is precisely because it opens as a singular event of being that gives itself as infinitely exposed to the world. Each of us, insofar as we are this mouth, stands in relation to each other only ever *as* this opening, which is the opposite of a work, or a practice, or even a gesture. Staging philosophy in the "faceless mouth" is thus always to write in darkness but there where a politics—feral and unbound—keeps its vigil (*ES*, 107).

Afterword

That these questions remained of great importance to Nancy is more than a speculative or hermeneutic proposition. In January 2020, I proposed to my colleague, John Paul Ricco, that we approach Jean-Luc about themes of the mouth in his work, most especially as they have shaped the texts that followed *Ego Sum*. More specifically, I wanted to ask Nancy about the comment that so struck me—that the mouth was the other motif that has never left him. It was my sense that this might very well be the last opportunity to ask him, or rather, that there was no reason to wait. When we wrote to him, we had hoped he would give us the time for an extended written interview. What we received has left us still in wonder and surprise. In response to our question about his interest in writing an "epic of the mouth," he told us he could only answer such a question in the form of the epic itself. Days later, we received an extraordinary poem, titled "Stoma: A Hymn," which offers an homage to the buccal cavity in a manner not unlike Valéry. Like so many of his readers, we were moved by his incredible generosity, if not also the speed with which he wrote a new text in reference to a book he wrote several decades ago. And like so many of his readers, we quickly realized the importance of the work and sought to find a proper home. We are very pleased to say that "Stoma: Hymn" will be published in *Corpus III* with

---

[60] Ibid.
[61] Nancy, "The Inoperative Community," 30–31.

Fordham University Press with context given for its creation, so that his readers know something about what we asked and why. We knew then (as we know now) that Nancy is *the* preeminent philosopher of the mouth—a description we hope will shape the many interpretations and homages to come. Most importantly, I want to extend my sincere thanks to him: *Merci*, Jean-Luc, for the poem and for trusting us as its readers in life and now in death.

6

From *Dis-Enclosure* to *Adoration*: Literature and the Deconstruction of Christianity

Schalk Gerber

Jean-Luc Nancy's engagement with theology is most prominently apparent in a two-volume work entitled *The Deconstruction of Christianity*, which consists of *Dis-Enclosure* and *Adoration*.[1] Together, they make up a collection of essays written over several decades and which cannot be said to mark a sudden break from his earlier work or within his corpus to form a standalone venture. Rather, one needs to situate it within the broader trajectory of his thought. Indeed, Nancy's interest in themes and concepts pertaining to Christianity can be traced at least as far back as *The Inoperative Community*, which deals with politico-religious myths,[2] although his first direct mention and formulation of the project as such appear in a footnote to *The Sense of the World*. Nancy, moreover, paved the way for *The Deconstruction of Christianity* by exploring its themes across various disparate writings prior to the publication of *Dis-Enclosure*.[3] Apart from the religious motifs he revisits in these texts, Nancy also offers his own reading of the West's historical development, arguing that it is intrinsically bound up with Christianity, from the rise of monotheism and its turn away from mythology to our current, globalized world. Furthermore,

---

[1] Jean-Luc Nancy, *Dis-Enclosure (The Deconstruction of Christianity)*, trans. Bettina Bergo, Gabriel Malenfant, and Michael B. Smith (New York: Fordham University Press, 2007) and *Adoration (The Deconstruction of Christianity II)*, trans. John McKeane (New York: Fordham University Press, 2013). Hereafter *DE* and *A*, respectively.

[2] See also Philippe Lacoue-Labarthe and Jean-Luc Nancy, "The Nazi Myth," trans. Brian Holmes, *Critical Inquiry* 16, no. 2 (1990): 291–312.

[3] These include *The Muses*, trans. Peggy Kamuf (Stanford: Stanford University Press, 1996); *Being Singular Plural*, trans. Robert D. Richardson and Anne E. O'Byrne (Stanford: Stanford University Press, 2000); *The Creation of the World, or Globalization*, trans. François Raffoul and David Pettigrew (Albany: State University of New York Press, 2007), where Nancy explores the deconstruction of Christianity with regard to modernity; and the essays gathered under the title *Multiple Arts: The Muses II*, trans. Simon Sparks (Stanford: Stanford University Press, 2006). After the publication of *Dis-Enclosure*, Nancy also expanded the project in other works such as *Noli me tangere: On the Raising of the Body*, trans. Sarah Clift, Pascale-Anne Brault, and Michael Naas (New York: Fordham University Press, 2008) and *God, Justice, Love and Beauty: Four Little Dialogues*, trans. Sarah Clift (New York: Fordham University Press, 2011).

commentary on Nancy's project—especially within the English-speaking academic world—has burgeoned since Nancy first published the programmatic essay entitled "The Deconstruction of Christianity" in 1998, which was later included in the diptych's first volume and discussed by Jacques Derrida in *On Touching—Jean Luc Nancy*, leading to an important exchange between the two philosophers.[4] The task of analyzing Nancy's project is therefore enormous.

I will thus limit my focus here to the (self-)deconstruction of Christianity as it was initially laid out in *The Creation of the World, or Globalization* in order to explore Nancy's treatment of modern literature in both volumes of *The Deconstruction of Christianity*. More specifically, I will concentrate on *Dis-Enclosure*'s approach to the literary with reference to two of Nancy's essays on Maurice Blanchot. I will begin by delving into what Nancy means by the deconstruction of Christianity, and how it relates to the question of secularization. Thereafter, I will turn to the notions of "dis-enclosure" and "adoration" so as to elucidate how the literary (via Blanchot) figures in Nancy's understanding of Christian theology, as well as within the modern dis-enclosure of metaphysics as such.

Modernity and the Self-Deconstruction of Christianity

To understand what Jean-Luc Nancy means by the (self-)deconstruction of Christianity, it is important to unpack the multiple notions that are directly and indirectly conveyed by this phrase and how Nancy deploys them—or not. Let us begin, then, with what Nancy does *not* wish to achieve by means of this project. One can be certain that Nancy is not interested in a universal theory of religion (i.e., defining religion anew), in the influence of religion on the formation of modernity per se (his emphasis is rather on our fluctuating understanding of the relationship between religion and deconstruction), or in carrying out a cross-cultural analysis of religious history.[5] Nor does Nancy seek to attack Christianity or to redeem it in any way, shape, or form, as is so often the case when "the return to religion" is invoked. Although Nancy acknowledges this to be an observable phenomenon, it is not his chief preoccupation, since he neither advocates for a return to religion that would manifest itself as the restoration of religious experience nor does he engage in a renewed critique of religion. A third distinction to be made here concerns the so-called "theological turn" in French phenomenology (first suggested by Dominique Janicaud), as well as other late twentieth- and early

---

[4] In this regard, see especially Alena Alexandrova, Ignaas Devisch, Laurens ten Kate, and Aukje van Rooden, *Re-treating Religion: Deconstructing Christianity with Jean-Luc Nancy* (New York: Fordham University Press, 2012). Ian James's essay in this collection addresses the question of deconstruction in Derrida and Nancy. See also Jacques Derrida, *On Touching—Jean-Luc Nancy*, trans. Christine Irizarry (Stanford: Stanford University Press, 2005).

[5] See Tenzan Eaghll, "Jean-Luc Nancy and the 'Exit from Religion,'" *Religion Compass* 11 (2017): 1–11 for an interpretation of Nancy's project of the deconstruction of Christianity in terms of the "flight of the gods," that is, the exit from the ancient polytheistic religions and the world of myth.

twenty-first-century philosophical ventures that aim for a revitalization of religion.[6] Indeed, Nancy does not walk in the footsteps of thinkers such as Michel Henry, Jean-Luc Marion, and Jean-Louis Chrétien (or, more subtly, Emmanuel Levinas and Paul Ricœur), all of whom aim to impel a turn toward the non-apparent, which would purportedly allow for the rehabilitation of religious experiences and practices within the realm of phenomenality.[7] Fourth, Nancy is likewise critical of what Jürgen Habermas calls "the post-secular," a line of inquiry which implies a linear trajectory that goes from the pre-secular to the secular and beyond, thus setting up a general program for the return to religion.[8]

In short, Nancy cannot be situated in either an atheist, a theological or, for that matter, a post-secular paradigm. Nor is he looking for a purely aesthetic figure, along the lines of nineteenth-century philosophers and writers, to fill the gap left behind by God's abandonment, as though it were the sole possible corrective to nihilism. His divergence from these movements is best summarized in his own words: "It is not a question of reviving religion ... It is not a question of overcoming some deficiency in reason ... It is not our concern to save religion, even less to return to it" (*DE*, 1). Instead, one might say that he reckons with what we have come to know as "the death of God," attempting to understand how this came about from within the Christian-philosophical complex as such. For Nancy, Christianity "understands itself in a way that is less and less religious in the sense in which religion implies a mythology (a narrative, a representation of divine actions and persons)," thereby deconstructing itself from within as it "de-composes what we have agreed to call, in our culture, 'religions'" (*DE*, 37, 43). In other words, what is at stake here is the deconstruction of modernity as the process of Christianity overcoming itself, thus opening up to a sense beyond the religious and otherworldly—to a sense of the world as *sens*.

Rethinking Secularism

In outlining what Nancy does not mean by "the deconstruction of Christianity" thus far, we have noted that, in his view, modernity is not to be understood as the mere overriding of Christianity, as if one epoch were merely supplanted by the next in linear fashion, from without. Indeed, Nancy offers an alternative reading of secularism

---

[6] See Dominique Janicaud, "The Theological Turn of French Phenomenology," in *French Phenomenology and the "Theological Turn*," trans. Bernard G. Prusak (New York: Fordham University Press, 2000), 16–107; Christopher Watkin, *Difficult Atheism: Post-Theological Thinking in Alain Badiou, Jean-Luc Nancy and Quentin Meillassoux* (Edinburgh: Edinburgh University Press, 2011); and Richard Rorty and Gianni Vattimo, *The Future of Religion*, trans. William McCuaig (New York: Columbia University Press, 2005).

[7] See Alexandrova, Devisch, ten Kate, and van Rooden, "Re-opening the Question of Religion: Dis-Enclosure of Religion and Modernity in the Philosophy of Jean-Luc Nancy," in *Re-treating Religion*, 35–36.

[8] See ibid., 33; Jürgen Habermas, "Faith and Knowledge," in *The Future of Human Nature*, trans. Hella Beister and Max Pensky (Cambridge: Polity Press, 2003), 101–15. Habermas himself ultimately argues that the secular state must be upheld yet reconciled with religion—especially in the face of a plurality of worldviews.

that challenges the traditional model according to which emancipation from religion has been achieved by way of science and reason. In *Dis-Enclosure*, he writes that the withdrawal of Christianity is too easily "assumed to be the effect of the modern transition toward a rationalized, secularized, and materialized society. So it is said, but without having any idea why that society has become what it is ... unless that is because it has turned away from Christianity, which merely repeats the problem, since the defined has thereby been placed within the definition" (*DE*, 143). He goes so far as to describe this conventional view as "doubtless the most tenacious and insidious illusion ever to be concealed in the nooks of our many discourses" (*DE*, 7). Here, Nancy comes close to other twentieth-century philosophers who have also challenged this ubiquitous interpretation of Western history, thus demonstrating that the origins of modernity are instead to be found in the different ways it relates to its Christian-philosophical provenance. Most notable among this group of thinkers are the German philosophers Karl Löwith and Hans Blumenberg, each of whom respectively asserts that we lose sight of what is truly "new" about modernity if we deem it to be a history of secularization and liberation, and nothing else.[9]

Löwith argues that modernity is the continuation of Christianity under a different guise.[10] Blumenberg in turn posits that modernity, endowed with a life and a singularity of its own, is neither a mere product of Christianity nor a radical offshoot of scientific reason's resistance to it.[11] Another important figure, the Canadian philosopher Charles Taylor, likewise suggests that the modern secular age developed out of the Jewish and Christian traditions, thus coming close to Nancy's view insofar as he believes these traditions to have slowly but surely impelled the gradual retreat of religion from the public sphere.[12] Most significant for Nancy, however, is the work of Marcel Gauchet, one of many contemporary thinkers who evince a renewed interest in the theologico-political constellation as it manifests itself today.[13] Gauchet argues that something like a "disenchantment of the world" developed out of the monotheistic tradition, wherein the divine "enchantment" of existence progressively faded as God become absent from the world, leaving behind an empty place.[14] Faced with the vacancy brought about by the absence of God, humans have variously attempted to fill the void through a

---

[9] See Alexandrova, Devisch, ten Kate, and van Rooden, "Re-opening the Question of Religion: Dis-Enclosure of Religion and Modernity in the Philosophy of Jean-Luc Nancy," 31.

[10] See Karl Löwith, *Meaning in History: The Theological Implications of the Philosophy of History* (Chicago: The University of Chicago Press, 1949).

[11] See Hans Blumenberg, *The Legitimacy of the Modern Age*, trans. Robert M. Wallace (Cambridge: MIT Press, 1983).

[12] Charles Taylor, *A Secular Age* (Cambridge: Harvard University Press, 2007), 15.

[13] See *DE*, 142, where Nancy mentions his "overwhelming agreement with the work by Marcel Gauchet, *Le Désenchantement du monde*." Whereas Carl Schmitt famously held that modernity consists of the translation of theological concepts into a secular vocabulary understood in terms of what he called "political theology," Nancy distinguishes between Schmitt's use of political theology and the *theologico-political*—rejecting the former for a post-Bataillian, "atheological" reading of politics to which we will return below (see *DE*, 175).

[14] See Marcel Gauchet, *The Disenchantment of the World: A Political History of Religion*, trans. Oscar Burge (Princeton: Princeton University Press, 1999), 130–44.

secularized form of sovereignty and a resolutely modern quest for transcendence. It is this notion of the absence of God as empty space—or, better yet, as *spacing*—that plays an important role in Nancy's thought from the early 1980s onward, especially in terms of its relation to the question of the political.

Nancy may at first glance appear to be closer to Löwith's contention that modernity is a mere extension of Christianity, even though Nancy never cites him per se. But Nancy also raises, alongside Blumenberg, the question of what grounds modernity as such, since it opens onto something quite different if we assume that it is required to legitimize itself autonomously rather than as a secularized version of divine transcendence (which is what Carl Schmitt argues in his political theology, for example).[15] It is this interleaving or neutralization, beyond both Löwith and Blumenberg, that distinguishes Nancy's trajectory, since the self-deconstruction of Christianity opens onto something that lies beyond itself—a principle that is in fact characteristic of Christianity from the outset. This position is most explicitly advocated by Gauchet, whom Nancy echoes when he writes that "Christianity is inseparable from the West. It is not some accident that befell it (for better or worse), nor is it transcendent to it. It is coextensive with the West qua West, that is, with a certain process of Westernization consisting in a form of self-resorption or self-surpassing" (*DE*, 142). And it is this reading, which arises out of the West's own self-reflexive and deconstructive unravelling, that sets Nancy apart from the majority of his contemporaries.[16]

The (Self-)Deconstruction of Christianity

We may now turn to the notion of deconstruction in Nancy's thought in order to better understand how it relates to Christianity. It is clear that Nancy conceives of it as a process internal to Christianity proper, thus rejecting claims according to which deconstruction is a form of secularist destruction that happens to religion from without. In *Dis-Enclosure*, Nancy offers the following definition: "The deconstruction of Christianity comes down to this: an operation of disassembling, focusing on the origin or the sense of deconstruction—a sense that does not belong to deconstruction, that makes it possible but does not belong to it, like an empty slot that makes the structure work" (*DE*, 149). Of note here is Nancy's poststructuralist understanding of deconstruction as predicated on an empty slot—a spacing.

"Deconstruction" was, of course, made famous by Jacques Derrida. But Derrida coined this term as he was translating Martin Heidegger's own *Destruktion*, which was borrowed from Martin Luther's *destructio*, inspired in turn by the Book of Isaiah.[17] In short, the history and use of the term stretch back over several centuries to the very roots of the modern Western tradition. Derrida chose to translate Heidegger's *Destruktion* or *Abbau* as *déconstruction* in order to avoid the negative reduction and

---

[15] See Nancy, "Entzug der Göttlichkeit: Zur Dekonstruktion und Selbstüberwindung des Christentums," *Lettre International* 76 (2002): 76–80.
[16] Eaghll, *Exit from Religion*, 7.
[17] See Derrida, *On Touching*, 54; Isaiah 29:14.

demolition implied by the French *destruction*. *Déconstruction* hence came closest, as it "conveyed a bearing on the structure or traditional architecture of the fundamental concepts of ontology or of Western metaphysics."[18] Yet Derrida further indicates that what is at stake here is a kind of *self-*deconstruction, beyond the work of deconstruction as a hermeneutic methodology, which is how it was typically perceived in the United States at the time. Indeed, deconstruction is not a mere tool waiting to be picked up and used by the modern subject. "Deconstruction takes place, it is an event that does not await the deliberation, consciousness, or organization of a subject, or even of modernity. It deconstructs itself."[19]

What is being deconstructed here? Put simply, Western metaphysics. As Nancy argues, "[w]hat must be set in motion can only be effected by way of a mutual *dis-enclosure* of the dual heritages of religion and philosophy. Dis-enclosure denotes the opening of an enclosure, the raising of a barrier. And the closure that should interest us is that which has been designated as 'the closure of metaphysics'" (*DE*, 6; emphasis original). Yet even though Nancy borrows Derrida's understanding of deconstruction as a dissembling of the structure of Western metaphysics, he recasts it as the dis-enclosure of the very closure of metaphysics, thus extending the idea of self-deconstruction further.[20]

Let us more closely consider the structure of Western metaphysics—which for Nancy is co-extensive with the West as such—that is being deconstructed and dis-enclosed here. In effect, this concerns not just the ontological but the *ontotheological* constitution of metaphysics, as analyzed by Heidegger in particular, which has come to form a confined, enclosed worldview—one that needs to be rethought. In describing Western metaphysics as "ontotheology," Heidegger was specifically referring to the structure that seeks to ground reality in a first principle.[21] The first principle, as developed by Aristotle and later adopted by the scholastic Christian tradition, provides a dual grounding for reality: first, as the principle of being, *óntos*, that grounds all beings, and second, as the highest ground or cause—the divine *theós*. For Aristotle and the subsequent scholastic tradition that tied Christian scripture to metaphysics—for instance, by incorporating the notion of *creation ex nihilo* into philosophy—the primary being is "God," conceived by Aristotle as the unmoved mover and, later, by the scholastics, as the creator. Heidegger, although inspired by Luther and Saint Paul, sought to reverse Aristotle's conflation of Being with a Deity or divine entity as part of his attempt to overcome the reduction of Being to beings or to merely present things. As Nancy puts it,

---

[18] Derrida, "Letter to a Japanese Friend," trans. Andrew Benjamin and David Wood, in *Derrida and Différance*, ed. David Wood and Robert Bernasconi (Warwick: Parousia, 1985), 3.

[19] Ibid.

[20] There are also notable differences between Nancy and Derrida as regards deconstruction's relationship with Christianity. See Derrida's comments on Nancy's "The Deconstruction of Christianity" throughout *On Touching*. For an overview of these differences, see Ian James, "Incarnation and Infinity," in *Re-treating Religion*, 257–59.

[21] See Martin Heidegger, *Identity and Difference*, trans. Joan Stambaugh (Chicago: University of Chicago Press, 2002).

metaphysics sets a founding, warranting presence beyond the world (viz., the Idea, *Summum Ens*, the Subject, the Will). This setup stabilizes beings, enclosing them in their own beingness [*étantité*]. Everything—properly and precisely *everything*—is played out in the mutual referral of these two regimes of beings or presence: the "immanent" and the "transcendent"; the "here-below" and the "beyond"; the "sensuous" and the "intelligible"; "appearance" and "reality." Closure is the completion of this totality that conceives itself to be fulfilled in its self-referentiality.

(*DE*, 6; emphasis original)

Heidegger called for the de(con)struction of Western metaphysics in order to sketch out an alternative understanding of being in terms of *Dasein*. In other words, his aim was to free the question of being from the ontotheological structure that had enclosed it. Taking his cues from Heidegger, Derrida further developed this critique of the *arché* of Western metaphysics in order to loosen and dislodge the fixed sense of the world imposed by its strictures. Derrida, however, went beyond Heidegger in laying out the political and ethical elements of this enclosure, which Nancy takes up in turn. In another one of his definitions of deconstruction, which mirrors Derrida's, he notes that the deconstructive gesture seeks to lay bare "the assembled structure in order to give some play to the possibility from which it emerged but which, qua assembled structure, it hides" (*DE*, 148). And inasmuch as the structure of Western metaphysics is inseparable from Christianity for Nancy, deconstruction is necessarily the deconstruction of Christianity.

God's Absenting and *ex nihilo* Creation

In the very first definition cited above, we may recall that Nancy included a second element: an empty slot that is not part of deconstruction per se but that makes it possible in the first place. To understand what Nancy means by the *self*-deconstruction of Christianity, we may consider this empty slot in relation to Nancy's reading of the notion of *creatio ex nihilo*. More precisely, what is at stake here is God's becoming absent from the world as the world is created, as well as the introduction of this monotheistic postulate into metaphysics during the scholastic period, deconstructing it from within, as it were, and giving rise to our modern philosophical concern with the world as such in the process.

We begin with the transition from the world of myth or polytheism to ontotheology or the suspension of myth. The world of myth, according to Nancy, "is the world of given presupposition," whereas ontotheology is "the order of posited presupposition: actively posited as the affirmation of the unique God and/or as thesis of Being."[22] Insofar as the presupposition of ontotheology is no longer given but posited, "the presupposition also contains the principle of its own deposition, since it cannot presuppose anything like a cause (nor therefore like an end) or like a production, without also extending,

[22] Nancy, *The Creation of the World*, 71.

correlatively, the limits of the world."[23] If one raises the question of what produced Aristotle's unmoved mover, for instance, or of how God came into existence, presupposition points toward an infinite absence, which is ultimately tantamount to nihilism. And it is this very principle of self-deposition that makes up the "historical" movement of the deconstruction of metaphysics according to Nancy.

One may draw a brief line from Aristotle to modernity to illustrate this point. In rejecting the Greek religious myths of his time in favor of a rational engagement with the world, Aristotle famously argued that for there to be a science of being, different understandings of the verb "to be" must be subsumed under a homogenous concept of being. The concept could thus not be synonymous, which would nullify any difference, but it could not be equivocal either, since that would undermine logico-scientific rigor. In other words, an equivocal sense of being would inadvertently trigger the self-deposition of Aristotle's own metaphysics. Accordingly, he argues for a paronymic relation between the different senses of being as they relate to a primary sense of being, defined as substance, much like the different senses of being "healthy" refer to the primary sense of "health." Here we may pinpoint the very *óntos* of ontotheology. But, insofar as beings are finite, there must be an eternal being that caused the movement of all other beings, that may be the subject of universal knowledge and the science of being. A primary being is thus posited—this is the *theós* of ontotheology. The relation between the primary eternal being and finite beings is, again, one of paronymy, which implies a sense of univocity in the notion of being that paradoxically presupposes difference. Indeed, the prime mover "moves" from within an already existing universe and is part of that eternal universe with no beginning or end, and hence nothing before or after it.

Christian theology, from Saint Augustine onwards, holds that God created the world out of nothing, *ex nihilo*. Several centuries later, Aquinas famously sought to synthesize Christian dogma with Aristotelian metaphysics since the postulate of a Creator God—existing outside of his creation, in another world, transcending this form of existence *in absentia*—runs counter to Aristotle's first principle, forcing both ontotheological constructions to face their limits. Indeed, existence is given to beings and guaranteed by the Christian God, but the existence of said beings is of a different nature than that of God. An equivocal sense of being has now slipped into the equation, problematizing ontotheology's structure, and deconstructing it from within.

This self-contradiction drew the attention of various Christian thinkers such as Duns Scotus and—more importantly for Nancy—Descartes, Spinoza, Malebranche, and Leibniz.[24] Each in his own way rejects God's purported otherworldliness in order to advocate for a more immanent and worldly conception of God that we may begin, from Kant onwards, envisioning a world rid of its theological trappings. Nancy specifically frames this process as the *kenosis* of the God of ontotheology, "progressively stripped of the divine attributes of an independent existence," having "only retained those of the existence of the world considered in its immanence."[25] In short, modernity

---

[23] Ibid.
[24] See, for instance, Nancy, *Being Singular Plural*, 15.
[25] Nancy, *The Creation of the World*, 44.

theorizes the "absenting" or *kenosis* of God, who does not vanish or dissolve into another world, but rather into this one: "The God of onto-theology has produced itself (or deconstructed itself) as subject of the world, that is, as world-subject. In doing so, it suppressed itself as God-Supreme-Being and transformed itself, losing itself therein, in the existence for-itself of the world without an outside (neither outside of the world nor a world from the outside)."[26]

Moreover, Nancy warns that we should be wary of closing off the space opened by God's withdrawal. He thus shows us how Kant himself fell into this trap by filling the void with the modern subject, perpetuating the very tradition he was keen on deconstructing *avant la lettre*:

> a world "viewed," a represented world, is a world dependent on the gaze of a subject of the world [*sujet du monde*]. A subject of the world ... cannot itself be within the world [*être dans le monde*]. Even without a religious representation, such a subject, implicit or explicit, perpetuates the position of the creating, organizing, and addressing God (if not the addressee) of the world.[27]

This also points to the political stakes at play here, as the space left open by the absence of God has also historically been filled with figures such as "race" or "national identity," echoing the question of community, which occupied Nancy throughout the 1980s in particular.[28]

What remains, then, is the philosophical question of the world, as its own "subject," as well as the task of understanding what it means to be in the world (*au monde*) rather than within the world (*dans le monde*), which implies being inside something endowed with an outside. This absence of a fixed or stable sense—the world devoid of author, producer, creator—compels us to consider the world as *sense*, a new starting point that emerges from nothing and creates itself each time anew. Here, Nancy further deconstructs and rethinks the notion of *ex nihilo*: "The *ex nihilo* contains nothing more, but nothing less, than the ex- of *existence* that is neither produced nor constructed but only existing [*étante*] (or if one prefers, *étée*, 'made' from the making of constituted by the transitivity of being). ... *ex nihilo* means that it is the *nihil* that opens and disposes itself as the space of all presence."[29] Moreover, it is the question of the world that still occupies us today, reframed by Heidegger as the question of what it means to live in the world as *Dasein*, which Nancy rethinks as the question of *Mitsein*, of what it means to live in the world *with* others.

---

[26] Ibid.
[27] Ibid., 40.
[28] See, for instance, Lacoue-Labarthe and Nancy, *Retreating the Political*, ed. Simon Sparks (Abingdon: Routledge, 1997); and Nancy, *The Inoperative Community*, ed. Peter Connor, trans. P. Connor, Lisa Garbus, Michael Holland, and Simona Sawhney (Minneapolis and Oxford: University of Minnesota Press, 1991).
[29] Nancy, *The Creation of the World*, 71.

Dis-enclosure and Literature as the Absenting of Fixed Sense

Blanchot, the Name of God, and Writing

Much like his project pertaining to the deconstruction of Christianity, Nancy's dialogue with Maurice Blanchot stretches at least as far back as *The Inoperative Community*,[30] attesting to a certain degree of continuity in his oeuvre. In *Dis-Enclosure*, Nancy first revisits the work of his predecessor in "The Name *God* in Blanchot."[31] He then further explores Christian concepts by reflecting on death and dying in terms of "Blanchot's Resurrection."[32] In both these texts, Nancy engages with Blanchot's experimental novel *Thomas the Obscure*, published in 1941 and significantly revised in 1950. Bridging the gap with theory, Nancy analyzes this facet of Blanchot's novel in relation to other philosophically charged titles of his, such as *The Space of Literature*, *The Infinite Conversation*, and *The Writing of the Disaster*.

In "The Name *God* in Blanchot," Nancy continues to lay bare the self-deconstruction of monotheism and especially of Christianity through the theme of God's emptying out into the world, which opens the possibility of *creatio ex nihilo*. Put differently, he aims to show that there can be no "return to religion" in Blanchot's use of the name "God." Indeed, Nancy argues that the name "God" as it is inscribed here is not the name *of* God nor, for that matter, the philosophical question of God as such. Hence, the choice of wording in the title already indicates that the name "God" does not name anything specific here; it is a name bereft of the concept it points toward, signifying (almost) nothing, as there is no prefixed meaning that one may call upon. Nor is the question of God's existence or nonexistence what is at stake here. Instead, the name "God" is very nearly nothing, opening up the space of our finite existences. Nancy illustrates this by discussing Blanchot's understanding of atheism by way of what he calls "absentheism," before showing how this sense of absence—the absence of a fixed sense—figures in the name "God" itself. In keeping with what Blanchot calls "the neuter" (*le neutre*), "absentheism" accordingly dismisses atheism and theism alike.[33] Nancy and Blanchot thus deploy a similar strategy in rejecting two regimes of metaphysical thought—characterized by themes such as transcendence and immanence, the finite and the infinite, etc.—in order to show how, in each case, the two seemingly binary notions are intertwined.[34] Nancy describes Blanchot's (and his own) rejection of both atheism and theism, which are two sides of the same coin, as follows:

---

[30] For an overview of the exchange between Nancy and Blanchot, see Leslie Hill, *Nancy, Blanchot: A Serious Controversy* (Lanham: Rowman & Littlefield, 2018).

[31] First published a few months after Blanchot's death in a special issue dedicated to his work, "Le nom de Dieu chez Blanchot," *Le Nouveau Magazine littéraire* 10 (2003): 66–69.

[32] On this topic, see also Nancy, *Noli me tangere*.

[33] See also Nancy, "Deconstruction of Monotheism," in *DE*, 29–41, where he argues that monotheism and atheism are two sides of the same coin, with monotheism revealing itself to be a hidden atheism through the absenting of God.

[34] See Laurens ten Kate, "Humanism's Cry: On Infinity in Religion, and Absence in Atheism—A Dialogue with Blanchot and Nancy," in *Words: Religious Language Matters*, ed. Ernst van den Hemel and Asja Szafraniec (New York: Fordham University Press, 2016), 181–98.

> To reject in the same gesture both atheism and theism means to consider first and foremost the point that the atheism of the West (or the double atheism of monotheism: the one it causes and the one it secretly bears within itself) has thus far never pitted against or set in the place of God anything other than a different figure, instance, or Idea of the Supreme punctuation of a sense: an end, a good, a parousia—that is, an accomplished presence, especially that of man.
>
> (*DE*, 85–86)

Here, Nancy brings to bear both his historical understanding of the self-deconstruction of Christianity and his critique of the ontotheological constitution of metaphysics. Instead of a mere repetition of this tradition, what is at stake for Blanchot, according to Nancy, is "the displacement of atheism in the direction of an absenting of sense, of which, it is true, so far no notable atheistic figure has been capable." More specifically, Blanchot does this by tying atheism to writing, which undermines the traditional opposition between presence and absence.[35] Nancy highlights Blanchot's use of the expression "absent sense," which "does not designate a sense whose essence or truth is to be found in its absence," but rather "makes sense in and by its very absenting, in such a way that, in sum, it never stops not 'making sense.'" Sense is thus not to be found in a fixed signifier or even, counterintuitively, in nihilism, but rather in the exposure to the "absenting" of sense, to an opening. Writing for Blanchot, Nancy notes, therefore designates "the movement of exposure to the flight of sense that withdraws signification from 'sense' in order to give it the very sense of that flight" (*DE*, 86).

More importantly, Nancy argues that this absenting sense takes place within the very name "God" as employed by Blanchot. Noting that Blanchot's text is devoid of any overt thematic interest in religion, Nancy nonetheless remarks that the name "God" is not absent from it.[36] Indeed, the name "God" stands in the very place of sense's absenting, "because this name does not involve an existence but precisely the nomination (and this is neither designation nor signification) of that absenting" (*DE*, 86–87). This is not a matter of negating God's existence; rather, the name itself lacks a concept, being a name that escapes nomination—it is an *absentheism*. Nancy concludes the chapter by further outlining the implications of the absenting of sense, stressing Blanchot's association between humanism and the cry (*le cri*), which is embedded in writing (*écriture*) as such: "The humanism of the cry would be a humanism that abandons all idolatry of man and all anthropo-theology. If it is not exactly in the register of writing, it is not in that of discourse either—but it cries out: Precisely, it 'cries out in the desert,' Blanchot writes" (*DE*, 88), in a turn-of-phrase that emphasizes the Judeo-Christian provenance of this "absenting."

---

[35] See Maurice Blanchot, "Atheism and Writing: Humanism and the Cry," in *The Infinite Conversation*, trans. Susan Hanson (Minneapolis: University of Minnesota Press, 1992), 252–53.

[36] Nancy suggests "a rapid re-reading of *Thomas the Obscure* [first and second versions], *The Infinite Conversation*, and *The Writing of Disaster* or *The Last to Speak*, to verify at least from a formal point of view the presence of the word God—even if at times only latently—and the manifestly diverse, complex, or even enigmatic modalities of its role or tenor" (*DE*, 86).

Blanchot, Resurrection, and Literature

The second of the two essays devoted to Blanchot in *Dis-Enclosure* is entitled "Blanchot's Resurrection." At first glance, the theme of resurrection, as Nancy points out from the outset, does not appear to play a major role in Blanchot's oeuvre, yet it is ultimately inseparable from the quintessentially Blanchotian themes of death and dying. Nancy goes on: "And if the phenomenon of dying is, in turn, not only indissociable from literature or writing but consubstantial with them, that is only to the degree that it is engaged in resurrection and does nothing but espouse its movement" (*DE*, 89). As such, death and literature are to be thought alongside a certain form of resurrection, which unexpectedly makes up the very movement of the literary work, as well as of its unworking or *désœuvrement*. Here we may recall that, in "The Name *God* in Blanchot," writing was understood as the movement of the absenting of sense. Hence, if we read the two essays—which were published and presented only a couple of months apart—together, we may argue that death is synonymous with the absenting of sense, and that writing is the movement of its resurrection. What's more, Nancy strengthens the underlying connection between these two essays by having the latter explicitly refer to the former (*DE*, 93).

In the second essay, Nancy makes plain that his aim is to inquire into the movement of resurrection as such. As ever, Nancy begins by spelling out what resurrection is *not* in this particular context: "The resurrection in question does not escape death, nor recover from it, nor dialecticize it." Indeed, resurrection "constitutes the extremity and the truth of the phenomenon of dying. It goes into death not to pass through it but, sinking irremissibly into it, to resuscitate death itself" (*DE*, 89). It is thus, somewhat counterintuitively, the resurrection of death rather than that of the dead, as Nancy makes clear. In drawing this distinction, he thus explicitly distances himself from the Christian source, emphasizing its deconstructive (un)working.

In his analysis of the movement of resurrection, Nancy undertakes a close reading of *Thomas the Obscure*. More specifically, he delves into the alterations that occur between its first and second versions. The passage in question marks the only moment when Blanchot mentions the resurrection motif, by way of the expression "death resurrected," as well as the name "Lazarus," the man from Bethany whom Jesus resurrects according to the Gospel of John. Nancy remarks that, although the second version of the novel is much shorter than the first one, the exact phrase which refers to Lazarus's resurrection is maintained almost word for word. The sole notable difference concerns the two lines before and after it: "He [Thomas] walked, the only true Lazarus, whose very death was resurrected."[37] Nancy also points to another significant modification that occurs six lines earlier, which in the second version reads as follows: "he appeared at the narrow gate of his sepulcher, not resurrected, but dead and having the certainty of being torn

---

[37] Maurice Blanchot, *Thomas the Obscure*, trans. Robert Lamberton, in *The Station Hill Blanchot Reader* (Barrytown, NY: Station Hill Press, 1988), 74. Nancy is referring to the two French versions of *Thomas l'Obscur* (Paris: Gallimard, 1941 [first version], and 1950 [second version]). The passage in question is found on p. 49 of the first edition and p. 42 of the second edition.

away at once from death and from life." This sentence was "lightened" two-fold: first, through a reversal of the word order in the first version, which read: "from life and from death"; second, by modifying the modal clause, whose original version was "having suddenly, through the most pitiless of sudden blows, the feeling that he was torn away." In other words, the "feeling" of commotion was turned into a "certainty" in the new version. Nancy then notes that these "micrological specifications" are highly instructive for our understanding of Blanchot's deconstruction of resurrection: "From a sort of commotion we have moved toward the affirmation of a certainty—which is never, in a general sense, very far removed from the order of a Cartesian *ego sum*. From an overwhelming impression, Thomas has moved to a kind of dead *cogito*, in or of death" (*DE*, 91).

Let us explore in more detail the significance of this passage by returning to the cross-references between Nancy's two essays on Blanchot. In the first essay on the name "God," Nancy equates the absenting of sense in the name "God" with the name "Thomas": "The same may be said, no doubt, of this name and of the name *Thomas*, who might be called the eponymous hero of Blanchot's writing" (*DE*, 87). In other words, God's withdrawal and the death of the ego are, in a sense, synonymous, referring to the space left open in the ontotheological structure of metaphysics by the absenting of God no less than that of the Cartesian subject, thus making room for something else entirely: "Death is the subject: the subject is not, or is no longer, its own subject. Such are the stakes of resurrection: neither subjectivation nor objectivation. Neither 'the resurrected' nor the dead body—but 'death resurrected'" (*DE*, 91). Nancy is thus describing the death of the subject in Blanchot's *Thomas the Obscure* as the absenting of a transcendental entity, which takes itself as its subject and objectifies the world. He subsequently confirms this reading when he associates the two pieces a second time in the essay on resurrection, referring to the relationship between the *space* of resurrection and the name "God" in Blanchot.[38] Nancy goes on to describe the absenting of the subject and the resurrection of death in the following terms: "death no longer befalls me as the cutting off inflicted on 'me' but becomes the common and anonymous fate that it cannot help but be, and, in a corollary way, death resurrected, absenting me from myself and from sense, exposing me not only to the truth but exposing me at last as myself the truth," and, even more directly: "the infinitely simple—and by that very fact indefinitely renewed, indefinitely reinscribable in us—experience of being without essence and thus of dying" (*DE*, 94, 96).

Nancy not only illustrates how Blanchot's work partakes in the self-deconstruction of Christianity through dying (*le mourir*), but also how it helps formulate the role modern literature plays in the movement of the absenting of fixed sense, thus dis-enclosing the stranglehold of metaphysics so as to allow sense to better resonate with our finite existence. Nancy sums it up as follows:

> If consent, or resurrection—the raising that erects death within death like a living death—obtains within writing, or literature, that means that literature can stand

[38] See *DE*, 93.

the cessation or the dissipation of sense. "Literature," here, does not mean the "literary genre," but any sort of saying, shouting, praying, laughing, or sobbing that holds—as one holds a note or a chord—that infinite suspension of sense. It is understandable that this holding or sustaining has more to do with ethics than aesthetics—but in the end it eludes and undoes these categories as well.

(*DE*, 97)

Writing Our Shared Existence: Adoration and Literature

We have seen how Christianity is of paramount importance to deconstruction according to Nancy. Indeed, "Christianity is at the heart of the dis-enclosure just as it is at the center of the enclosure [*clôture*]" (*DE*, 10). This centrality implies a double function, that is, the possibility of not only deconstructing Christianity—the movement whereby it dismantles its own closure—but also of grasping it in the very act of its (self-)deconstruction. The movement of deconstruction thus simultaneously accounts for its dis-enclosure and its accompanying "eclosure" (*éclosion*), the opening or hatching of something new. Nancy also refers to this movement as a "gaze" directed toward the "no-thing": the opening, the absence, the void. In the second volume of *The Deconstruction of Christianity*, Nancy goes on to name this gaze "adoration," which "simply means: attention to the movement of sense, to the possibility of an address that would be utterly new, neither philosophical nor religious, neither practical nor political nor loving—but attentive" (*A*, 20). Thus, to adore—a verb which residually presupposes language by dint of its etymon—is to be attentive to the movement of dis-enclosure that exposes us to the no-thing of our existence. It is "the movement and the joy of recognizing ourselves as existents in the world" (*A*, 62). We have, moreover, noted that Nancy calls this movement of deconstruction (and/or dis-enclosure) literature *qua* writing in his chapters on Blanchot. Such, then, is the writerly movement of the absenting of sense as it dismantles the myth of the origin, thus opening up our existence into an ek-istence that is always shared—being-in-the-world as being-*with* others. Nancy reiterates this claim in *Adoration*:

> This is also why our world is the world of literature: what this term designates in a dangerously insufficient, decorative, and idle way is nothing other than the opening of the voices of the "with." On the same site where what we call myth gave voice to the origin, literature tunes in to the innumerable voices of our sharing [*partage*]. We share the withdrawal of the origin, and literature speaks starting from the interruption of myth and in some way in that interruption: it is in that interruption that literature makes it possible for us to make sense. This sense is the sense of fiction: that is to say, neither mythical nor scientific, but giving itself in creation, in the fashioning (*fingo, fictum*) of forms that are themselves mobile, plastic, ductile, and according to which the "with" configures itself indefinitely.

(*A*, 41)

In closing, it is important to note that the absenting of God and the death of the subject as they take place in modernity as the self-deconstruction of Christianity do not lead to nihilism for Nancy. Rather, this movement dis-encloses an opening that allows for the adoration of our shared existence in the world. And it is modern literature, writ large, that gives us the voice whereby we adore this existence—literature as saying, shouting, praying, laughing, or sobbing—thus holding us in the infinite tension of the continuous creation of our shared finite existence.

Part Two

Nancy and Modernity

7

Before the Abyss

Jean-Luc Nancy

Ever since what is known as "the death of God," we—we Westerners, or Western planetary civilization—find ourselves before an abyss [*Abgrund*]. And this is true in a very precise sense. For the "god" who has "died" was nothing other than "ground" [*Grund*] itself. To be the ground of the existence of the world and of every existing being in the world is to be not just the essence of that world, but also its cause and its goal, to be its ground and obviously *our ground* and to belong to the realm of sense.

For us, to belong to this realm of sense (and of the senses) means also and above all to inquire about the ground of all things, in order to find an explanation, a meaning, and a use for our presence here.

I

God was somehow (including outside of religion, for example through the divinization of man himself, who has been considered as the ground and purpose of the world for almost three centuries)—God was the answer to what thanks to Leibniz had been named the "Principle of Ground" or "principle of sufficient reason" [*Satz vom Grund*]. Which means: everything must have a sufficient ground (*principium rationis sufficientis*).

But it was precisely in Leibniz's time that the principle of ground both emerged as such *and* retained its status as an "ought" [*sollen*]. (In fact we are dealing with a mixture of "ought" and "must"—the Must of a causality and the Ought of an intelligibility, of a signifying capacity [*Sinnfähigkeit*] without which everything descends into absurdity).

This Must-Ought, this claim to a ground—which is an intellectual claim as much as an existential one—is always present for us. We need it absolutely in order to know that human life is worth living.

… Or might it rather be the case that it is we who are needed because of this claim? Could we be / are we perhaps the victims of a demand that belongs solely to our own model of rationality? We need grounds—*ratio* or *logos*, *causa* or *intentio*—because we are needed by the notion of grounds. But we are well aware that love or art, sport or dance, cookery or perfume are without ground. So we say they are "for fun"—but how can fun ever provide a truly serious ground?

Today for example we can read in a magazine: why do we experience different types of excitement—both joyful and sad? We are then given a neuroscientific explanation in terms of the brain, neurons, nerves, etc. But this brings us no closer to excitement itself. Such science [*Wissenschaft*] provides us with knowledge [*Wissen*] about causalities that have nothing to do with anxiety, joy, fun, or unease.

And so we remain before the abyss. The ground of an excitement can also be explained in psychic terms, but the way a particular psyche reacts is part of an idiosyncratic whole—a somehow fundamentally personal disposition [*ur-eignen Verfassung*], which can never be grasped [*die nie zu fassen ist*], which is never constantly one and the same, and which always eludes the search for it—as Freud himself understood.

The abyss does not only remain permanent therefore, it keeps growing larger or deeper. When things get too difficult—too sad or too enjoyable—we turn once again to… God or to a substitute, an "ineffable." (Think of what can be said today about what happened before the Big Bang. Naturally, more will be known about it later on, at least until a point is reached where it is no longer be possible to speak of a "before," or where there will simply be a never-ending "before." In fact Kant already knew this, which is why he was already searching, within the limits imposed by his time, for another way of thinking about the deity.)

II

This means that the situation we are in today was already known about or felt long before now—and so before the "death" of God. In the seventeenth century, Angelus Silesius wrote these well-known words:

> The Rose is without Why
> It blooms because it blooms.
> It pays no attention to itself,
> Asks not, if any can see it.[1]

Silesius had no knowledge of today's floral science. He was aware however that there was already considerable interest in causality in his own time (he had read Descartes). Why and for what purpose?, people said, in precisely the modern sense where it is less a matter of the power of custom and the drive toward a goal, than of a calculable series of phenomena—such that, as Kant will establish, the series is endless. And this endlessness of the causal chain needs either to have a first cause as *causa sui* (as God was for Descartes or Spinoza)—or to remain endless.

A goal is therefore also required, which can either be seen as a definitive totality (like Substance for Spinoza or Total Man for Marx—at least according to certain interpretations of this thinker) or as endless increase in production.

---

[1] Angelus Silesius, *Cherubinischer Wandersmann* (1675).

Production must of course be understood as the key notion here: producing something from something else, a "plus" in every dimension (size, power; speed and even productivity: production produces itself, causality causes itself [*die Kausalität verursacht sich selber*]). This self-production was called progress for as long as it led to the improvement or the development of human life.

Today, however, we are discovering at the same time that production is without purpose, and that this purposelessness can even become detrimental to human life and even to life in general. Every "improvement" brings with it a deterioration. Or—and this comes to the same—we no longer know what a "good life" should be—at least when our own life isn't so bad, as bad as it is for thousands of millions of the "underdeveloped"; they need a life that is acceptable; but those who are "developed" understand that development itself is not at all "acceptable," but rather superfluous and without purpose—unless money and power can be considered a purpose.

III

Hence for us a ground no longer exists—and yet we do not know how we could understand or experience ourselves as "without why," how we could view and appreciate ourselves and life as a whole as if we were Silesius's rose.

The alternative which confronts us is precisely this: either find a god again or find a way of thinking the abyss—the "without why." But the era of the gods is past, even though many people believe in gods today. Because between gods and self-production there is an incompatibility—at least when the gods are thought of as grounds. For then it is necessary to understand how the ground can ground self-production—and autonomy itself. The gods are essentially *others*—that is, they are *alloi*, the opposite of *auto* (as when we speak of an allochthon, of allogamy or allomorphism: namely, what is truly foreign, unknown, and not just different as is the case between *homo* and *hetero*).

The abyss is alterity as such. What is unknown and unknowable. It is this alterity that we must think—must and ought to, once again. That is to say, think the other in its absolute otherness. The other that should [*darf*] not be reduced to the self.

It may be that the gods have always represented something of the sort. But such a representation [*Darstellung*] or conception [*Vorstellung*] is plainly a way of making alterity knowable—even when it claims that God has neither form nor name. For even when we just say "God" we are still using a name for what is nameless, as is the case with Allah or with the unpronounceable tetragram of the Jews (when as a substitute the name "Hachem" is used, it means "he who bears the name").

Through the name, something is "known" and because for us, "knowing" always involves to some extent the knowledge of an object, for us the gods can become mere objects, that is to say: idols. Consequently, the abyss of the death of God is an abyss of nameability. Hence of language. The language that is ours today is unable to speak the unsayable [to express / to promise the unsayable]. Yet it is precisely that which we say poetry can do.

As we can read in Paul Celan:

Speak—
But do not separate the no from the yes.
Give your saying also meaning:
give it its shadow.

Give it enough shadow,
give it as much
as you know to be parceled out between
midnight and midday and midnight.[2]

But then this means that it is less a question of naming than of meeting. It is likely that the gods were to be found more in meeting than in naming or unnaming. Meeting at least signifies that what is met with is not an object.

The abyss is not an object. It does not stand before us [*ist nicht gegen-ständig*]: it is ourselves. We are our abyss. We never reach a definitive state because we are forever going further. That is why we may find the abyss fascinating—the way a ravine is fascinating. Man and with him the world are not something objective. They are not "before" us but "in" us, or more precisely, we are ourselves abyssal. Our current state thus reveals to us that our self-production leads to an allo-outlook in us. To the acknowledgment of a demand, of a desire whose opening out is revealed by the abyss. A desire for an encounter with alterity.

Münster, Jan. 2021

(*Translated by Michael Holland*)

---

[2] Paul Celan, "Speak, You Too," trans. Pierre Joris, in *Selections*, ed. P. Joris (Berkeley, Los Angeles, and London: University of California Press, 2005), 54.

8

Noli me operare: Reading Nancy (Re-)Reading Blanchot

Aukje van Rooden and Andreas Noyer

Nancy's Rethinking of Community Beyond the Work

In our times, Jean-Luc Nancy is undoubtedly among the most profound and original thinkers of community. Urged on, like many of his contemporaries, by the crisis of communism and the rise of individualist liberal thought in the 1980s, Nancy asks whether a thinking of community is at all possible.[1] The "stumbling block" to "communitarian" thinking—communist or otherwise—lies, Nancy alleges, in its basic presupposition of an "essence of humanness" and of community's being the "effectuation" of this essence (*IC*, 3, 8). Community, in other words, is taken to be the ultimate form of auto- or self-production, the association "of beings producing in essence their own essence as their work, and furthermore producing precisely this essence *as community*" (*IC*, 2).[2] Nancy terms this logic of absolute auto-production "immanentist," and dismisses it because it ignores what he takes to be precisely the essence of being-in-common: the *relation* or *clinamen*, the "inclining from one toward the other, of one by the other, or from one to the other" (*IC*, 3). This *relationality*, Nancy holds, cannot but thwart the immanentism of communitarian models of community because the "relation tears and forces open, from within and from without at the same time, and from an outside that is nothing other than the rejection of an impossible interiority, the 'without relation' from which the absolute would constitute itself" (*IC*, 4). Our relationality, in other words, disrupts the immanence presupposed in views that assume community to be "a productive or operative [*opératoire*] project" (*IC*, 15).

To present a thinking of the *inoperativity* (*désœuvrement*) of community, then, is the main aim of the essay "The Inoperative Community" ("La communauté désœuvrée") that Nancy wrote, at the invitation of Jean-Christophe Bailly, for a February 1983 issue

---

[1] Jean-Luc Nancy, *The Inoperative Community*, ed. Peter Connor, trans. P. Connor, Lisa Garbus, Michael Holland, and Simona Sawhney (Minneapolis and Oxford: University of Minnesota Press, 1991). Hereafter *IC*. This book is part of a much wider reflection on community taking place in the 1980s, especially in France and Italy.
[2] Italics original throughout unless otherwise noted.

of *Aléa*. Three years later, this essay was republished in a revised version as the first part of the book *The Inoperative Community*, which was to become Nancy's most seminal early work, establishing him as a contemporary thinker of community.[3]

Georges Bataille is an important starting point for Nancy in rethinking community from the perspective of an inoperative relationality, since Bataille was "the one who experienced first, or most acutely, the modern experience of community as neither a work to be produced, nor a lost communion, but rather as space itself, and the spacing of the experience of the outside, of the outside-of-self" (*IC*, 19). As Nancy stresses, community for Bataille is never a matter of self-sufficiency, but rather, in and through exposition to the other, a matter of an irretrievable *excess*, where what is shared, communicated, or "put to work" in community is, as Bataille famously contends, in fact "NOTHING"—only the ecstasy (*ekstasis*), the incommensurable standing-outside-oneself, which ultimately makes "each one [ecstasy and community] the locus of the other" (*IC*, 18, 20).[4] This "atopical topology" is the reason community cannot, according to Nancy, be understood as a work or through its works; after all, such works "would presuppose that the common being, as such, be objectifiable and producible (in sites, persons, buildings, discourses, institutions, symbols: in short, in subjects)" (*IC*, 20, 31).

In thinking community's resistance toward its own production as or in a "subject," Nancy argues that Bataille led the way, but also that we must "know it in part against him," since Bataille allowed excessive exposition to the outside, "at least up to a certain point ... to relate back to a subject, or to institute *itself* as subject" (*IC*, 23–24)—a stance exemplified, according to Nancy, by Bataille's prewar fascination with primitive religious or orgiastic social forms (e.g., as part of the Acéphale project) and his postwar attachment to the "community of lovers," representing "in many respects the figure of a communion, or of a subject that ... ends up being engulfed alone in its own ecstasy," thereby making itself "inaccessible" for the inoperative relationality of community (*IC*, 36). Even though his thinking does not repeat the "*immense failure*" of communitarian projects, Bataille "must have sensed" that these projects would lead to a similar impasse, and so, according to Nancy, "having sensed it he secretly, discretely, and even without knowing it himself, gave up the task of thinking community in the proper sense" (*IC*, 23–25).

In a way, Maurice Blanchot is put forward in *The Inoperative Community* to recalibrate the thinking of community opened up by Bataille. As is already clear from the title, Blanchot's signature word "*désœuvrement*" (inoperativity, worklessness, unworking) serves as the cue for Nancy to rethink Bataille's ecstatic community: "Community necessarily takes place in what Blanchot has called 'unworking,' referring to that which, before or beyond the work, withdraws from the work, and which, no longer having to

---

[3] The volume titled *The Inoperative Community* is rounded off by two essays ("Myth Interrupted" and "'Literary Communism'"). Blanchot's *The Unavowable Community* is a response to the earlier version of "The Inoperative Community" in *Aléa*, not to the revised version included in the 1986 book.

[4] Nancy is mainly referring to Bataille's *Œuvres complètes*, vols. V–VIII, that is, to the "projects" of the *Somme athéologique* and *The Accursed Share*.

do either with production or with completion, encounters interruption, fragmentation, suspension" (*IC*, 31). The literary context whence this Blanchotian notion stems is likewise adopted by Nancy. Shared, each time singularly and differently, by us and between us, community does not demand a figure or a model, nor perhaps even a "word" or "concept," as Nancy alleges. Rather, it "obliges us to adopt another *praxis* of discourse and community" (*IC*, 25–26), a praxis that Nancy, like Blanchot, identifies with literature, with that "unworked 'communication'" that, per Nancy, "would be the inverse of lovers' discourse such as Bataille presents it" (*IC*, 39) because it does not seek a place or duration for their joy, being nothing but the "sharing of community in and by its writing" (*IC*, 26).

Although he would later abandon this notion, Nancy suggests that it is preferable to speak of a "literary communism" or, to phrase it in a more Blanchotian manner, a "literary experience of community," to highlight this specific praxis of community (*IC*, 39, 64).[5] In so doing, however, "literature" itself also needs to be construed beyond models and genres, as an "*inscription* of the communitarian exposition" (*IC*, 39). For Nancy, then, "literature," taken in its most basic sense, is to be understood ontologically, as a synonym for the unworking exposition, the mutual inscription, of being-in-common as such. *The Inoperative Community*'s attempt to think community beyond the immanentism of operative communitarian models thus boils down to considering our shared existence as what is already there, a praxis "before or beyond the work." In the book's second essay, "Myth Interrupted," Nancy formulates this conclusion even more forcefully: "what 'literature' will have to designate is *this being itself ... in itself*" (*IC*, 64; emphasis ours; ellipsis in the original). The immense failures of operative models of community should thus be countered by what, in a later key work, *Being Singular Plural*, Nancy ambitiously calls a "redoing [of] the whole of 'first philosophy' by giving the 'singular plural' of Being as its foundation,"[6] that is, by a new *ontological* approach to community, along the lines of a specific thinking of the inoperativity of the singular plural.

The Conversation with Blanchot

Insofar as Nancy critically grafts the notion of *désœuvrement* onto the intellectual heritage of Blanchot's close friend Bataille, it comes as no surprise that "The Inoperative Community" should have aroused Blanchot's vivid interest. Within only a few months' time, Blanchot penned *The Unavowable Community* (1983), a slim volume consisting of two parts: "The Negative Community," written, as Blanchot states, "[i]n the wake of an important text ['The Inoperative Community'] by Jean-Luc Nancy,"[7] paired with the

---

[5] See also the essays "Myth Interrupted" and especially "'Literary Communism'" in the same volume.
[6] Nancy, *Being Singular Plural*, trans. Robert D. Richardson and Anne E. O'Byrne (Stanford: Stanford University Press, 2000), xv.
[7] Maurice Blanchot, *The Unavowable Community*, trans. Pierre Joris (Barrytown, NY: Station Hill Press, 1988), 1. Hereafter *UC*.

republication of an essay written earlier that year on Marguerite Duras' most recent *récit*, *The Malady of Death*, entitled "The Community of Lovers."

Blanchot's response to Nancy's essay is, on the whole, more tacit than explicit, but—so much is clear—not altogether favorable. Although not unwilling to endorse Nancy's key arguments against "immanentist" views of community, Blanchot clearly disapproves of Nancy's approach to Bataille's "communitarian" projects of the late 1930s, such as Acéphale, and to his work on the community of lovers in his postwar years. While Nancy views these projects as blind alleys, abandoned because Bataille would have presumably sensed, "secretly, discretely," that they were bound to lead to just another form of immanentism, Blanchot firmly states that Bataille, in each of these cases, "*excludes*... 'fusional fulfillment in some collective hypostasis' (Jean-Luc Nancy). It is something he is deeply averse to" (*UC*, 7).[8] For Bataille, it would be impossible, Blanchot goes on to emphasize, for a subject (individual or collective) alone, "locked in his immanence," to reach an experience of community—which is why Blanchot stresses what he terms Bataille's "principle of incompleteness [*incomplétude*]," quoting (from memory) the latter's dictum that "[t]here exists a principle of insufficiency at the root of each being..." (*UC*, 7, 5).[9]

Similarly, Blanchot seems reluctant to endorse Nancy's use of his notion of *désœuvrement*. Even though he fully agrees with Nancy that community "does not allow itself to create a work and has no production value as aim" (*UC*, 11), Blanchot, on a number of occasions in his book, hints that "unworking" for him does not exactly take place "*before* or *beyond* the work" (*IC*, 31). Nor is it *withdrawn from* the work, as Nancy would have it; rather, it is engaged in a more subtle dynamic with the work. "[T]he absence of a work [*l'absence d'œuvre*]," according to Blanchot, "*needs and presupposes works* so as to let them write themselves under the charm of unworking" (*UC*, 20; emphasis ours).

Blanchot's intervention, both generous and cautious, inaugurates what is no doubt one of the most intriguing and remarkable intellectual conversations in contemporary French thought, not least because it is largely conducted by Nancy *after* Blanchot's death in 2003. Indeed, only eighteen years after their first public exchange, in 2001, did Nancy reply to Blanchot's response by way of an extensive preface, published in French as *La communauté affrontée* ("The Confronted Community"), to the Italian translation of Blanchot's *The Unavowable Community*. In this preface Nancy finally announces that he will "revisit an episode entailing stakes which I [Nancy] had failed to accurately assess at the time."[10] The reason for this long interval, Nancy confesses, was that he never felt "either capable ... or authorised to" react to Blanchot's impalpable text, which

---

[8] Cf. *IC*, 14.
[9] Cf. *UC*, 8, which refers to Georges Bataille, *Inner Experience*, trans. Stuart Kendall (Albany: State University of New York Press, 2014), 85: "There exists a principle of insufficiency at the base of human life."
[10] Nancy, "The Confronted Community," trans. Amanda Macdonald, *Postcolonial Studies* 6, no. 1 (2003): 27.

he read "simultaneously [as] an echo, an amplification and a riposte, a reservation, and, for that matter, in some ways a reproach."[11]

Although a sense of intimidation prevented Nancy from completely clarifying Blanchot's reserve or reproach, "either in a text or for [him]self, and not in correspondence with Blanchot either,"[12] in the years to follow Nancy will have repeatedly done just that, starting with "The Confronted Community" (albeit by deliberately *not* rereading their respective writings of the 1980s[13]), then further in 2011, after Blanchot's death, by way of another preface, to *Maurice Blanchot. Passion politique*, and, more extensively still, in *The Disavowed Community* (2014).[14] This repeated return to Blanchot's response shows the difficulty in identifying what exactly is at stake in their exchange. A similar puzzlement can likewise be discerned, at least until 2011, in the scholarly reception of this debate. Where some critics note an unbridgeable disagreement between Nancy's and Blanchot's positions, positions they take to be "strongly" divergent or even "hard alternatives" revealing "significant differences,"[15] others, by contrast, emphasize that their disagreement is largely "rhetorical" and that they are "trying to say the same thing in different terms," aiming to stress a more fundamental agreement where both are "perplexingly ... close."[16]

This reception shifts after 2011, when Nancy radically changes his earlier interpretation of Blanchot, as evidenced by the publication, under the title of *Maurice Blanchot, passion politique*, of a letter of Blanchot's to Roger Laporte, dealing with the former's political commitments in the 1930s and written in December 1984—not long after *The Unavowable Community*. In his lengthy preface to the 2011 book, Nancy makes it clear that he won't be commenting on the letter itself. This does not prevent him, however, from commenting on Blanchot's thinking of community and politics, that is, on an aspect of *The Unavowable Community* that has "almost not been commented upon," even by Nancy himself in "The Confronted Community." The reason, he now

---

[11] Ibid., 30.
[12] Ibid.
[13] Ibid., 29: "rereading would make me rewrite history."
[14] Apart from these publications, there are a number of other occasions where Nancy, sometimes only in passing, returns to his debate with Blanchot—see, e.g., "Un commencement," in L'"Allégorie" suivi de *Un commencement*, ed. Philippe Lacoue-Labarthe (Paris: Galilée, 2006); "Reste inavouable," interview with Mathilde Girard, *Lignes* 43 (March 2014): 153–76; "Quand le sens ne fait plus monde," interview with Michaël Fœssel, Olivier Mongin, and Jean-Loup Thébaud, *Esprit* 403, nos. 3–4 (March–April 2014): 27–46; Étienne Balibar and Jean-Luc Nancy, "Discussion entre Étienne Balibar et Jean-Luc Nancy," *Cahiers Maurice Blanchot* 3 (Fall 2014): 9–28; Mathilde Girard and Jean-Luc Nancy, *Proprement dit. Entretien sur le mythe* (Paris: Lignes, 2015); Jérôme Lèbre, "Entretien avec Jean-Luc Nancy sur *La Communauté désavouée*," *Cahiers Maurice Blanchot* 4 (Winter 2015/2016): 91–104.
[15] Lars Iyer, "Our Responsibility: Blanchot's Communism," *Contretemps* 2 (May 2001): 72n31; Robert Bernasconi, "On Deconstructing Nostalgia for Community Within the West: The Debate Between Nancy and Blanchot," *Research in Phenomenology* 23 (1993): 7; Stella Gaon, "Communities in Question: Sociality and Solidarity in Nancy and Blanchot," *Journal for Cultural Research* 9, no. 4 (October 2005): 389.
[16] Ian James, "Naming the Nothing: Nancy and Blanchot on Community," *Culture, Theory and Critique* 51, no. 2 (2010): 177; Gregory Bird, "Community Beyond Hypostasis: Nancy Responds to Blanchot," *Angelaki: Journal of the Theoretical Humanities* 13, no. 1 (April 2008): 22.

notes, is that Blanchot "took [the meditation on 'community'] in a direction—removed from, if not opposed to, mine [Nancy's]—which made a 'communion' of several faces (erotic, Christic, literary) arise within the obscure ground of community."[17] With this critical reassessment, which also implies a rather striking revision of the crucial role that Nancy had attributed to Blanchot in his deconstruction of Christianity, and thus in rethinking modernity,[18] Nancy tentatively sketches the main point of his book to come, *The Disavowed Community*. There, he extensively addresses Blanchot's views on community by taking into account the latter's view on politics, and this time by explicitly responding to *The Unavowable Community* to the letter.

Tentative and non-unanimous until 2011, the reception of the exchange between Nancy and Blanchot becomes less hesitant in the wake of Nancy's latest contributions. Generally disapproving of what is taken to be an uncharitable and even ill-informed reading of Blanchot on Nancy's part, most critics assume the task of defending Blanchot against Nancy's accusations. Among them, Leslie Hill is no doubt the most fervent. In his richly documented and in many respects acute book, *Nancy, Blanchot: A Serious Controversy* (2018), Hill goes so far as to speak of "Nancy's interpretative violence with regard to Blanchot's writing."[19]

On this occasion, we will not try to endorse or counter these accusations of Nancy's work, nor will we unravel his debate with Blanchot in detail. Instead, we will single out what we take to be the dominant thread of their debate and situate it within the larger context of their respective works in an attempt to understand *why*, despite many of their shared assumptions with regard to the reconceptualization of community, Nancy and Blanchot cannot but disagree. This dominant thread is the theme of "unworking" and the "neutral" (*le neutre*) in relation to community and writing. In the end, we suggest, their disagreement does not rest on differing political views or sentiments, as suggested by Nancy and others, but rather on different conceptions of *ontology* and their ensuing consequences for (the work of) literature and community. Indeed, although it is advanced only half-seriously by Nancy in a note to *The Disavowed Community*, it seems as if their disagreement largely boils down to a matter of diverging "professions" in which the modernist *writer* Blanchot and the *philosopher* Nancy are testing the limits not only of each other's thinking and writing, but also those of thinking and writing as such. In this note Nancy comments on Blanchot's marked decision to dedicate half of *The Unavowable Community* to the literary work of Duras and thereby to direct more

---

[17] Nancy, *Maurice Blanchot, passion politique. Lettre-récit de 1984 suivie d'une lettre de Dionys Mascolo* (Paris: Galilée, 2011), 30–31. Our translation.

[18] See Nancy, *Dis-Enclosure (The Deconstruction of Christianity)*, trans. Bettina Bergo, Gabriel Malenfant, and Michael B. Smith (New York: Fordham University Press, 2008).

[19] Leslie Hill, *Nancy, Blanchot: A Serious Controversy* (London and New York: Rowman & Littlefield International, 2018), 242. See also his *Blanchot politique. Sur une réflexion jamais interrompue* (Geneva: Furor, 2020). Other attempts, often no less critical, to defend Blanchot against Nancy's accusations can be found in the *Cahiers Maurice Blanchot*, such as Jonathan Degenève, "À partir de quels modèles Nancy et Blanchot comprennent-ils la communauté ?," *Cahiers Maurice Blanchot* 3 (Fall 2014): 40–49; and particularly 4 (Winter 2015/2016). Cf. also Kevin Hart, "The Aggrieved Community: Nancy and Blanchot in Dialogue," *Journal for Continental Philosophy of Religion* 1, no. 1 (April 2019): 27–42.

firmly their conversation toward the domain of literature proper. "Without seeking to justify myself too much," Nancy comments,

> I would nevertheless say that I was certainly thinking of literary works but that I was more concerned with communicating their force and forms to everyone than the work of the writer where these forces and forms are created. In more than one respect, no doubt, Blanchot was saying to me: "You are not a writer, you are a philosopher." He also makes heard: "Bataille was desperate as a writer and philosopher," and "Duras and I, one through the other and one in the other, we are writing the unavowable."[20]

It is, we could argue, this playfully evoked difference between the work of the writer and the work of the philosopher that can be taken as the key impetus in assessing the notoriously difficult but intriguing debate between Nancy and Blanchot.

Work and Operation

In Nancy's entire exchange with Blanchot, the notion of *désœuvrement* seems to be what initially drew them together, but also what eventually caused them to drift apart. What this calls for, then, is an investigation into this *désœuvrement* (inoperativity, worklessness, unworking), the Blanchotian notion that served as the original description of community in Nancy.

For Nancy, *désœuvrement* is, as we saw, "before or beyond the work, [and] withdraws from the work" (*IC*, 31). This does not mean that workless community is *inactive*; community is not the *accomplishment* of a project for Nancy, but is marked, rather, by incompletion as "a workless and inoperative [*désœuvrée, et désœuvrante*] activity" (*IC*, 35; emphasis ours).[21] It is this workless activity that Nancy suggests casting as an ontological matter: *désœuvrement* is itself a "singular ontological quality that *gives* being *in* common" for Nancy. The praxis of community that Nancy would cast under the name of "literature," then, is this "being *in* common that *is* literary" (*IC*, 64). While such *désœuvrement* takes place in the "non-place" of what he once called "literary communism," this non-place is in no way an unchangeable outside or mythical space for Nancy; it is, he stresses, but the *passage*, the *sharing*, of being-in-common, a literary ontology of exposition without return.

While in *The Inoperative Community* Nancy quite explicitly develops this interpretation of literary unworking by invoking Blanchot, the latter, as we have seen, is reluctant to endorse the way in which Nancy distances unworking from the *works* from which, for Blanchot, it cannot be detached.[22] Indeed, in contrast to Nancy, whose

---

[20] Nancy, *The Disavowed Community*, trans. Philip Armstrong (New York: Fordham University Press, 2016), 97n 2. Hereafter *DC*.

[21] Nancy calls this incompletion (*inachèvement*) community's "principle" (ibid.).

[22] And already in the 1986 addition "Myth Interrupted," Nancy in turn begins to distance his view of literature from Blanchot's, for whom "'unworking' would be attained and presented by works" (*IC*, 65).

version of unworking resists or withdraws from the work, Blanchot would rather stress that work and unworking are not to be disentangled, that their entanglement is the work's impossible status. Already in *The Infinite Conversation* (1969), Blanchot had stressed—slowly coming to substitute "the absence of the work" (*l'absence d'œuvre*) for *désœuvrement*—that in writing one *passes through* the "book" (which concerns production, dialectics, a completed product) to the "absence of the book": "the passage of an infinite movement that goes from writing as an *operation* to writing as worklessness."²³ As such, for Blanchot, too, unworking has an "active sense" (an active sense tending toward passivity), even though its operation is only a *pseudo-operation*, an "inoperative"²⁴ operation, much like, as we shall see, the affirmation of the neutral, which "is not really affirmative or operative," and knows only "pseudo-work," while writing (the writing of *works*), in the absence of the book, passes from being an operation to being the "*insane game*" known as unworking.²⁵

It is in this sense that Blanchot stresses in *The Unavowable Community* that the passage to worklessness requires some kind of work, invoking the inextricable and complex relation "between what we call work, *oeuvre*, and what we call unworking, *désoeuvrement*" (*UC*, 56) at its close. For Blanchot, then, it is in *writing*—this doing of "not-doing" (*UC*, 23)²⁶—in *works* (be it Bataille's *Inner Experience* or *Madame Edwarda*, or *The Unavowable Community* itself), that the unavowable community is avowed, or tentatively avowed.

In his 2001 preface to *The Unavowable Community*, Nancy acknowledges this intimation of Blanchot's, writing that

> at the point where I claimed to reveal the "work" of community as society's *death sentence* and, as a corollary, to establish the need for a community refusing to

---

²³ Blanchot, *The Infinite Conversation*, trans. Susan Hanson (Minneapolis and London: University of Minnesota Press, 1993), 424; emphasis ours.
²⁴ Ibid., 424, 303.
²⁵ Blanchot, *The Step Not Beyond*, trans. Lycette Nelson (Albany: State University of New York Press, 1992), 75. Jacques Derrida notes that *opération*, in its French Hegelian usage, including that of Bataille, was the then-current translation of *Tun* ("From Restricted to General Economy: A Hegelianism Without Reserve," in *Writing and Difference*, trans. Alan Bass [London and New York: Routledge, 2001], 321). This also brings us to *sovereignty*—that which for Bataille is the outside of utility, labor, production, which is "NOTHING" and is "unavowable" (Georges Bataille, *The Accursed Share: An Essay on General Economy*, vol. II: *The History of Eroticism* and vol. III: *Sovereignty*, trans. Robert Hurley (New York: Zone Books, 1991), 197–98, 256, 430; "Method of Meditation," in *Inner Experience*, 171)—or rather to what Bataille paradoxically called the "sovereign operation," which is another name for inner experience, and which is marked by refusal, contestation, the same kind of "expiation" of its own authority as that which Blanchot is to have said to Bataille about inner experience ("Method of Meditation," 198; cf. *Inner Experience*, 14, 19, 58). A more apt name, notes Bataille, would have been "*comical operation*" ("Method of Meditation," 194), and precisely what is comical is this term, "operation," just like the text whence it is derived, that "method" of "meditation," with its "principles"; like the communitarian *project* of Acéphale, which, writes Blanchot, "would have renounced its renunciation of creating a *work* [*faire œuvre*]" (*UC*, 14), and like the writing of a book, a *work*, such as *Inner Experience*, but whose principle is "to get out through a project of the realm of the project" (*Inner Experience*, 52), so Bataille cannot but commit to a paradoxical *operation* that expiates its authority and its operativity.
²⁶ Cf. Hill, *Nancy, Blanchot*, 158.

constitute a work [*faire œuvre*] ... Blanchot informs me of or rather indicates to me the *unavowable*. Apposed but opposed to the *inoperative* or *unworked* of my title, this adjective proposes to think that beneath unworking there is still the work, an unavowable work.²⁷

Indeed, what he now seems to detect in Blanchot is that there is

> already, always already, a "work" of community [*"œuvre" de communauté*], an operation of sharing [*opération de partage*] that will always have gone before any singular or generic existence, a communication and a contagion without which it would be unthinkable to have, in an absolutely general manner, any *presence* or any *world*.²⁸

Blanchotian unworking is thus reinterpreted ontologically by Nancy as the *operation of sharing* existence, as a "work" (between quotation marks) of community, which can thereby be incorporated into his own view. In sum, the unavowable community, according to Nancy, is not "worked" (*œuvrée*) but "operated" (*opérée*).²⁹ It is important to note that, in Nancy's exchange with Blanchot, several meanings of "work" and "operation" are now juxtaposed: while for Blanchot unworking stands in a fundamental, albeit elusive, relationship to the work, ruining the work's self-presence, which passes through and thus *differs* from writing as an *operation*, Nancy now seems to treat the "work" of community, its unworking, and the operation of sharing nearly synonymously.

Why this sudden distinction, which Nancy leaves unexplained, between community as *work* and as *operation*?³⁰ This terminological change might be due to the fact that Nancy's commitment to an interpretation of unworking as the community's resistance to "its own setting to work [*mise en œuvre*]" (*IC*, 76) would not allow a (non-unworked) *work* to be retained favorably, while, in prefacing *The Unavowable Community*, Nancy does want to acknowledge a dynamics in Blanchot that could be compatible with his own conception of being-in-common. Nancy's substitution would appear, then, to "correct" a risky notion in Blanchot, insisting that what is always already presupposed for there to be unworking is not works but rather an operation—the *clinamen*, the *with* as the exposition of singularities in and as an operation of sharing. In attempting to bridge their different vocabularies by linking operation to unworking, Nancy consequently changes the view held in *The Inoperative Community*, namely, that the notion of operation is linked to the work and to organic totality, which would have "the operation as means and ... the work as end" (*IC*, 76).³¹

---

²⁷ Nancy, "The Confronted Community," 30–31; translation modified.
²⁸ Ibid., 32; translation modified.
²⁹ Ibid.; translation modified.
³⁰ Cf. Hill, *Nancy, Blanchot*, 117.
³¹ Instead, the community's totality is "a whole of articulated singularities." Cf. *The Unavowable Community*, 72–73: "the work in the community and the work of the community ... do not have their truth in the completion of their operation, nor in the substance and unity of their *opus*. What is exposed in the work, or through the works, begins and ends infinitely before and beyond the work—before and beyond the operative [*opératoire*] concentration of the work"; translation modified.

The operation of sharing—ontological, non-organic, *non-workly*—that Nancy now speaks of is rather that which is articulated, exposed, in common, which is visible in the "fuller," ontological sense that he gives to literature (which includes all kinds of communication, ontological exposure, sharing of voices, music, etc.).

Although one may wonder whether Blanchot would agree with Nancy's reconceptualization, Nancy's attempt in "The Confronted Community" largely seeks a common ground between their respective views of community. At the same time, however, he also conveys a distance between Blanchot and himself, anticipating his next return to their "exchange," starting in 2011; from then on, Nancy will no longer try to smooth over the possible differences between his interpretation of *The Unavowable Community* and Blanchot's, but will stress them all the more. As such, Nancy no longer describes the Blanchotian unavowable work as an ontological operation of sharing—i.e., as the activity of unworking (in Nancy's sense)—but rather as a "sacred" or "mythical" *work* that, in its central inaccessibility, cannot be shared, and that Nancy quite clearly links to Blanchot's earlier political preferences (*DC*, 37, 63–64).

The shift from interpreting unworking in terms of a "literary experience of community" to interpreting it in a more political vein is thus instigated, Nancy asserts, by two events: first, his (re)reading of Blanchot's "Intellectuals Under Scrutiny," written almost concurrently with *The Unavowable Community*, and, second, Nancy's editing process surrounding the publication (in *Maurice Blanchot, passion politique*) of Blanchot's letter to Laporte, written in 1984 just as attempts to edit a special issue of the *Cahiers de L'Herne* on Blanchot's political past came to naught. What rereading *The Unavowable Community* in light of these two texts reveals, according to Nancy, is that there is in Blanchot, despite his emphasis on unworking, not so much an "unworked work" as a *prior* work "devoted to its unworking" (*DC*, 74), or, as Hill puts it, a "transcendent secrecy or secret transcendence of the work."[32] If this secret, mythical work is not the communitarian work (*l'œuvre communautaire*) critiqued since *The Inoperative Community*—that which is made, completed, a project—it is because, per Nancy, it is even more anterior, constitutive, and occulted.

Admittedly, for Nancy to write that, for Blanchot, "there is only unworking from out of a work" is not inherently a criticism of Blanchot, for Blanchot himself affirms, as we saw, that there must be a work if it is to be "haunted" by unworking (*DC*, 72; *UC*, 20); nor is Nancy accusing Blanchot of a positive dialectics aimed at the completion of the communitarian work (that both Nancy and Blanchot would reject). Rather, since for Blanchot it is a matter of work "and" unworking, in a "relation without relation," instead of an "unworked" work, Nancy detects some presupposed nameless, unavowable work therein—indeed, "the work of relation without relation" (*DC*, 74) or a "motif of *sans rapport*"[33]—which, withdrawn in secrecy, not only takes on a kind

---

[32] Hill, *Nancy, Blanchot*, 171n113 (cf. 110, 116). Hill firmly rejects this view.

[33] Nancy in Lèbre, "Entretien avec Jean-Luc Nancy sur *La Communauté désavouée*." For Hill, Nancy's "reappropriation" of unworking, when discussing Blanchot, consists in "subordinat[ing] it to a teleological dialectic or, at the very least, treat[ing] it as a negative property or attribute belonging, so to speak, to the work" (*Nancy, Blanchot*, 110).

of negative-dialectical relation, but nearly reverses his earlier assessment of Blanchot's relationship of work and unworking, such that this hidden, unavowable work is now what ultimately counts rather than its unworking.

Neutralizing the Neutral

It is this presupposition of a work of relation without relation—associated, as we'll see, with another, notably less political, theme in Blanchot's work, namely, that of the neutral or neuter (*le neutre*)—beyond the reach of any instance of sharing, that is not only objectionable but also plainly unthinkable for Nancy. As we announced earlier, it might therefore be argued that the disagreement between Nancy and Blanchot, in the end, does not hinge on a difference in political views, as Nancy and most critics after him suggest, but rather from an underlying disagreement concerning ontology and its consequences for (the work of) literature and community. Rather than understanding Nancy's rereading of Blanchot's *The Unavowable Community* within the context of the renewed attention afforded to Blanchot's "politics,"[34] we will focus on this other theme of the *neutral*.[35] Indeed, in the same year as *Maurice Blanchot, passion politique*, Nancy also published "The Neutral, Neutralization of the Neutral," a short article on the neutral in Blanchot, referring to *The Step Not Beyond* and *The Infinite Conversation*, without mention of community or politics, and without polemics, arguing that "[i]t would be no exaggeration to say that everything in [Blanchot's] thinking is related to the 'neutral' as its point of condensation, incandescence, and vanishing, all at the same time."[36]

Although he does not make mention of community, Nancy continues to underline two characteristics in Blanchot which he takes to be central to inoperative community: its incessant need to write or expose itself and its "non-place":

> With Blanchot, we must begin with writing: with literature to the extent that it forms the ever renewed play and continual dwelling on "*the need to write*." This need means that what "does not take place" is repeated, that the non-place or non-presence of all origin, substance, subject is affirmed in the only way possible: in a "*nomadic affirmation*."[37]

---

[34] Philip Armstrong, "Translator's Introduction," in *The Disavowed Community*, xx. Nancy took part in this by publishing Blanchot's letter to Laporte, occasioned by the preparations for the *Cahier de L'Herne*, and by contributing to a special issue on the politics of Blanchot in *Lignes* 43 (March 2014).

[35] Although most critics follow Nancy in his political take on their disagreement, some indeed mention, like we do, the neutral as the heart of contention. Cf. Danielle Cohen-Levinas, "Notes et contre notes sur *La Communauté désavouée*" (105–12), and Gisèle Berkman, "Blanchot, après-coup" (116–22), both in *Cahiers Maurice Blanchot* 4 (Winter 2015/2016).

[36] Nancy, "The Neutral, Neutralization of the Neutral," in *Expectation: Philosophy, Literature*, trans. Robert Bononno, ed. with the assistance of Ginette Michaud (New York: Fordham University Press, 2018), 186.

[37] Ibid.; quoting Blanchot, *The Step Not Beyond*, 32–33.

Yet, despite the resonances with Nancy's earlier affirmative account of Blanchot in *The Inoperative Community*, here too we see a tension emerge between Nancy and Blanchot, one that does not rest on the notion of community; it may in fact be the other way around: that their disagreement on community rests on *it*.

For Blanchot, the neutral is first and foremost a way of thinking beyond the traditional ontological conceptions of being. Its relation without relation is what Blanchot also calls the "relation of the third kind," being *neither* an immanent relation of the Same *nor* a relation of "*mystical fusion*" of the Self with a transcendent Other—a communion of "coincidence and participation" where they "lose themselves in one another"[38]—quite in line so far with Nancy's vision of inoperative community. In Blanchot, however, this third kind of relation is not one of being-with or sharing, but tends toward the other—*autrui*—outside of the order of both the one and the other, that is, toward the other as "a being without being [*être sans être*], a presence without a present," whose relation to "us" can only be one of "*strangeness*," an interruption of relation that is still relation.[39] This has consequences for the way Blanchot sees the ontological status of relation: despite the substantive form (of "the" neutral), it is not some supra-ontological force, but a force that *marks* and *re-marks* being. As Blanchot, or rather, a voice in an *entretien* of his, utters, it "*places being in parentheses and in some sense precedes it, having always already neutralized it less by a nihilating operation than by an operation that is inoperative* [non opérante]."[40]

We can see how the neutral informs Blanchot's idea of the operation of writing as the passage to worklessness. If Blanchot had "intimated" to Nancy not to focus only on unworking because there is still a work, this is not to give way to a transcendent work beyond being, but rather to hint at a more complex relation between work and unworking, being and its bracketing, with neither the one nor the other taking on the emphasis, in contrast to Nancy's treatment of unworking in *The Inoperative Community* as withdrawn from the work. Indeed, in Blanchot it is not so much a question of the "non-workly" operation of the sharing of being as it is of work and unworking in the non-operative relation of the neutral. Put in terms of writing, and in contrast to Nancy's literary ontology, for Blanchot writing, literary language, "gives me the being, but it gives it to me deprived of being"—a marking that unmarks "the brilliance of being."[41]

The aim of Nancy's article on the neutral is to sketch the risk that the neutral as a work of worklessness would entail. The neutral, this "nameless name," as Nancy puts it, "dissipates mythical powers"—"[b]ut the difficulty increases when we realize the power this dissipation assumes in spite of everything. As long as 'the Neutral' or 'the neuter' function in a discourse that provides its predicates and describes it, a secret recourse

---

[38] Blanchot, *The Infinite Conversation*, 66, 73–74.
[39] Ibid., 67–69 (cf. 385). See also J. Degenève, "À partir de quels modèles Nancy et Blanchot comprennent-ils la communauté?" 44–45.
[40] Blanchot, *The Infinite Conversation*, 303.
[41] Blanchot, "Literature and the Right to Death," trans. Lydia Davis, in *The Work of Fire*, trans. Charlotte Mandell (Stanford: Stanford University Press, 1995), 322; *The Step Not Beyond*, 76.

to a supranominal power can be suspected."⁴² In a 2014 interview with *Esprit*, held at the time *The Disavowed Community* was published, Nancy repeats this view, stating that this purported supranominal power of the neutral may carry the name of "myth," linking the retention of an unnamable neutral, as *the* neutral, to Blanchot's supposed unavowable work of a mythical communion which Nancy discusses in *The Disavowed Community*.⁴³ For Nancy, in other words, the risk involved in the thought of the neutral is that the non-place of writing, initially introduced by Blanchot and endorsed by Nancy as *interrupting* mythical thought, itself becomes something mythical. It does so, Nancy alleges, because it "does not allow the 'real' to be separate from the 'imaginary'" and can therefore communicate or express nothing but itself, "like a declarative mystery—just as it is a declaration that accepts the truth of the Eucharist" (*DC*, 63–64).⁴⁴ The unavowable *neither/nor* of Blanchot's neutral, according to Nancy, thus ends up being mythical—in aesthetic terms one would say "autonomous"—i.e., *tautegorical*: expressing only itself by itself (*IC*, 49). In the *Esprit* interview Nancy advances a similar point, claiming that Blanchot, to his mind, did not go far enough in his dismantling of mythical thought, since in Blanchot literary discourse "ended up taking on the appearance of a kind of prophetic and sacred authority."⁴⁵

Tellingly, this mythical or eucharistic register of literature in Blanchot ensues, according to Nancy, in a *refusal of narrative*—a refusal Nancy is firmly opposed to:

> I don't like Blanchot's *récits*, not in the sense that they are not to my taste, but because they constantly display a refusal of narrative [*récit*]—which is Blanchot's big thing—and because narrative involves something contingent, accidental, or transformative, whereas Blanchot's non-narrative thinks it can show full presence.⁴⁶

We now see how the workless activity or operation highlighted earlier by Nancy here takes the form of a plea for the contingency and transformativity of literary *narratives* as opposed to the modernist Blanchotian "non-narratives," considered sterile and inert by Nancy. Where the literary praxis of community for Nancy is the non-workly passaging of ex-istence, it is for Blanchot, according to Nancy, rather a passage to workless inertia where nothing passes anymore. It is, furthermore, this refusal of narrative that Nancy, in the same interview and following Uri Eisenzweig's *Naissance littéraire du fascisme* (Literary Birth of Fascism) (2013), links with "the origins of fascism in literature."⁴⁷ The problem with Blanchot's literature is thus,

---

[42] Nancy, "The Neutral, Neutralization of the Neutral," 188.
[43] Nancy, "Quand le sens ne fait plus monde," 39.
[44] On this Christian motif, see Hart, "The Aggrieved Community."
[45] Nancy, "Quand le sens ne fait plus monde," 39. A last reiteration of this point can be found in Nancy's response or "echo" to Leslie Hill's "The Fragility of Thinking," *Angelaki: Journal of the Theoretical Humanities* 26, nos. 3–4, special issue "The Pulse of Sense: Encounters with Jean-Luc Nancy" (July 2021): 54–55.
[46] Nancy, "Quand le sens ne fait plus monde," 39; trans. and quoted in Hill, *Nancy, Blanchot*, 133.
[47] Nancy, "Quand le sens ne fait plus monde," 40; cf. *DC*, 101n29.

according to Nancy, that it is not only workless, but also no longer *operates*, moves—and is therefore in fact reduced to *nothing*.

It is, in our view, in this same vein that Nancy interprets Blanchot's central notion of the neutral, such that, neither the one nor the other, "[t]he non-place or out-of-place toward which the need to write moves is nothing, no place *toward* which one could make a move."[48] In order to avoid this, Blanchot's nominative or substantive use of *the* "neutral," this "excess word," therefore ought itself to be *neutralized* according to Nancy, lest it be transcendent, if not mythical.

When Nancy returns to this question in *The Disavowed Community*, now interpreted in terms of political sovereignty, this leads him to argue that Blanchot's view of the neutral "turn[s] away" from the "NOTHING" of Batallean sovereignty that, as Nancy would have it, "perform[s] … itself through its own negation," and instead wants "to bring into existence something like a sovereignty … raised above society though refusing to reign over it," as if sovereignty had a place elsewhere, outside community—a position Nancy associates with an "aristocratic" or "right-wing anarchism" (*DC*, 18, 58–60).[49] It is thus that Nancy discerns a negative "dialectical mobilization" in Blanchot's *The Unavowable Community*, with the community of lovers as described by both Bataille and Duras being a kind of *Aufhebung* or *relève* of the negative community without reconciliation. Instead, Nancy contends that Blanchot "mostly proceeds by a negation of negation (for which the 'neuter' becomes the form?) that has the traits of the dialectical *Aufhebung* while subtracting the moment of 'synthesis'" (*DC*, 19, 15, 35).[50]

Nancy admits that to speak, like a negation of negation, of a "neutralization of the neutral," risks being a "dialectical contortion," and that Blanchot would have been suspicious of this.[51] Indeed, the neutral for Blanchot, which is neither affirmation nor negation (in a positive, productive sense), "does not answer to ontology any more than to the dialectic";[52] it "evokes" *Aufhebung*, but "retains only the movement of suspending." Yet, while this neutral suspension (*parenthetically*) "neutralizes, neutralizes (itself)," for Nancy it ultimately denies the power to neutralize the *neutral*, and veritably negate the sovereign nothing.[53]

---

[48] Nancy, "The Neutral, Neutralization of the Neutral," 188.

[49] Nancy's use of the term "aristocratic anarchism," which appears largely polemical here, is thus paired with the right and ambiguously contrasted with the "'left' or democracy" (*DC*, 57). Cf. also "Entretien avec Jean-Luc Nancy sur *La Communauté désavouée*." For more or less opposed interpretations of Blanchot's "anti-democratic" tendencies, see Juan Manuel Garrido and Aïcha Liviana Messina, "Politique au-delà du politique. Le cœur et la loi de l'exigence communautaire chez Nancy et Blanchot," and Jérémie Majorel, "Parler en son nom propre – *La Communauté désavouée* (2014) de Jean-Luc Nancy," both in *Cahiers Maurice Blanchot* 4 (Winter 2015/2016).

[50] Nancy thus repeats what Jean-Paul Sartre had written about Bataille, namely, that "of the Hegelian trinity, he suppresses the moment of synthesis" ("Un nouveau mystique," quoted in Derrida, "From Restricted to General Economy," 437n16).

[51] Nancy, "The Neutral, Neutralization of the Neutral," 189.

[52] Blanchot, *The Infinite Conversation*, 209.

[53] Blanchot, *The Step Not Beyond*, 75. Blanchot will go on to write more explicitly that "the neutral … always neutralizes itself and," furthermore, "has about it nothing sovereign that has not already surrendered in advance" (*The Writing of the Disaster*, trans. Ann Smock [Lincoln and London: University of Nebraska Press, 1995], 131). As it stands, we have seen that its neutralization is not that of a "nihilating operation," a labor like that of the negative, but is rather "non-operative."

"[T]his whole constellation of the nothing," then, despite the "considerable role" it has played, is what one ought to be wary of according to Nancy. He thus speaks, in his 2014 interview with *Esprit*, of "the exigency to have done with the nothing" (without "putting something or someone in the place of this nothing"), to the extent one cannot see the *positivity* of this constellation, that is, that the nothing for Nancy is *not* nothing, that "the first sense of the word is positive, which one still finds in the expression '*il s'en faut d'un rien*.' A 'nothing' is a very little something."[54]

So too does Nancy see in the *neither/nor* of Blanchot's neutral not "simply [the] positing [of] a nothing between the two" (as nothing), but rather a "movement of their simultaneous conjunction and disjunction—*coincidentia oppositorum*" (*DC*, 35). This interpretation of the neutral as non-identical coincidence or juxtaposition, making this *neither/nor* at once decisively a *both/and*, is due to Nancy's own view of ontology, which cannot but consider things as coincidence, that is, the incidence which is always already a co-incidence pertaining to beings or singularities, *in common*. This would be, in turn, Nancy's *coincidentia*, which Blanchot, in Nancy's reading, "only envisages as eluded [*en échappée*]," only envisages *negatively* without neutralizing this "neutral" into the superior *coincidentia* of both "the encounter (if not the relation) [and] evasion ... the alliance of coincidence and distance [*écart*], touching and withdrawal" (*DC*, 72). It is this relation, where singularities touch and repel, that Nancy again likens to the Lucretian *clinamen*, the swerve of atoms in the void, a "void" which is thus always full, where there is, always anew, the sharing and exposition of being-in-common or being-with; and it is this relation—relation as such for Nancy—that is "always already present," "operative," and anterior, "preced[ing], constitut[ing], and accompan[ying] singularities" (*DC*, 75). As such, the in-common (if not community) never completely disappears or is lost; it is the being that is shared in the touching of bodies in the world (*DC*, 72).[55]

***

In the end, then, Nancy and Blanchot, instead of expressing a similar view in different vocabularies, have developed different views of relation and ontology, which, coming from quite different places, eventually could not but miss each other. Blanchot's relation of the neutral cannot be grasped from the point of view of Nancy's *being*-in-common, his coincident *clinamen*, save as an "aristocratic," negative-dialectical disavowal of community, which would hold on to some mythico-communial secret refusing to "neutralize" itself. Conversely, if we take the perspective of Blanchot's neutral and the relation without relation it implies, then its "work of worklessness" can never answer to ontology, because its "ontology" marks being *deprived* of being (deprived of being-in-common, being-with). While for Blanchot such marking shows the importance of an anterior neutral relationality and passes, in writing, toward a non-operative unworking, it is a non-workly operation that carries anterior weight for Nancy, namely,

---

[54] Nancy, "Quand le sens ne fait plus monde," 38–39.
[55] Cf. *IC*, 35.

one of sharing, of relation *tout court*, or, so to speak, relation *with* relation, if not simply "with" (the preference for which, instead of any nominalization, Nancy once described as being "dry and neutral"[56]). The "reality" of literature, of literary "works," then, is for Nancy not their working or their completion, but their operation, their dynamism, "[their] tension, [their] vibration, and—why not say it?—[their] life."[57]

---

[56] Nancy, "The Confronted Community," 32.
[57] Nancy, "On the Work and Works," in *Expectation*, 67.

9

"Close Relations": Nancy and the Question of Psychoanalysis

Jean-Michel Rabaté

In his work, first with Lacoue-Labarthe, then on his own, Nancy has provided one of the most powerful and comprehensive critiques of psychoanalysis, a critique that also aims to be a new foundation. From the early 1970s until recently, Nancy has touched eloquently and creatively on the discourse of psychoanalysis; he has revisited its crucial concepts by engaging in an ever-deeper conversation with Freud and Lacan, the two major interlocutors. Given the complexity and subtlety of Nancy's writings, I will proceed chronologically in order to stay as close as possible to the spiraling evolution under discussion. Some points are well known: Nancy began by dismantling Lacan's system, which he saw predicated on an unstable synthesis of Freud, Heidegger, and Saussure, whereas his late work provides its own dynamic combination of Freud and Heidegger, as one sees in *Sexistence* (2017), an important book summing up many previous analyses.

All the while, Nancy sustains another dialogue with Derrida, first through his critique of Freud's "speculations" and of Lacan's Hegelianism, up to the more recent questioning of Heidegger via the issue of sexual difference in several essays entitled *"Geschlecht."* One could argue that psychoanalysis, as with Derrida, is both everywhere and nowhere in Nancy's thinking. While psychoanalytic issues are disseminated in various contexts, what looms larger still is the question of sexuality. Symptomatically, an excellent *Nancy Dictionary* had announced an entry on *jouissance*.[1] However, the reader finds nothing between the two entries "Presentation" and "Relation." One has to look at the latter to be sent to "Sexual Relation": the term provides a fitting introduction to Nancy's groundbreaking revisionist thinking about sexuality.[2]

---

[1] Peter Gratton, "Jouissance," in *The Nancy Dictionary*, ed. P. Gratton and Marie-Ève Morin (Edinburgh: Edinburgh University Press, 2015), 126.
[2] Gratton, "Sexual Relation," in *The Nancy Dictionary*, 215–17.

Dismantling Lacanian Theory

Nancy and his close friend Lacoue-Labarthe began their careers with a fanfare. In 1973, barely in their thirties, they jointly published *The Title of the Letter: A Reading of Lacan*,[3] which presented itself modestly as a close reading of a 1957 essay by Lacan, "The Instance of the Letter in the Unconscious, or Reason Since Freud." This foundational essay was taken from the then recently published *Écrits*. In fact, a whole war machine had been deployed to promote the Lacanian version of psychoanalysis. Lacoue-Labarthe and Nancy were scrutinizing the theoretical program of Lacanian psychoanalysis by focusing on a text published at a tumultuous moment in its founder's career. Lacan had been caught between two "excommunications" and had launched the first Lacanian journal, *La Psychanalyse*, where the piece was published. His ambitious *écrit* is dense, highly allusive, and testifies to huge new claims for psychoanalysis. Freud remains the main reference point, since Lacan offers a formalization of condensation and displacement as poetic metaphor, illustrated by poetic examples, and metonymy. Saussure intervenes with his formula for the sign as made up of a signifier and a signified. After a detour through André Gide, it is Heidegger who then looms large in this essay-manifesto, as Lacan makes use of a bold and arresting sentence: "When I speak of Heidegger, or rather when I translate him, I strive to preserve the sovereign significance (*signifiance*) of the speech he proffers."[4] He was alluding to his friendship with Heidegger, and his translation of the latter's essay on Heraclitus and "Logos" for the first issue of *La Psychanalyse*.

No sooner was *The Title of the Letter* published than it was seen as a debunking, a severe attack on Lacanian doctrine coming from the school of Derrida. Lacan voiced his ambivalent reaction to the publication in his seminar. Conceding that here was an example of good reading, that none of his students had been able to read him as thoroughly and carefully, he added that the authors were motivated by the worst intentions. Lacan refused to name either Lacoue-Labarthe or Nancy: they were *sous-fifres* (underlings, minions, peons, subalterns), disciples acting at the behest of their leader, whose name likewise remained unmentioned, even though everyone knew Lacan was alluding to Derrida. Nancy and Lacoue-Labarthe were the goon squad of deconstruction applied to psychoanalysis.

Their strict commitment to reading Lacan at his word, word for word, patiently, philosophically, and rigorously, could not but attest to a certain love, but as Lacan quipped, such love was the flipside of hatred. Even though he recognized that the *Title of the Letter* had performed an extraordinary task, Lacan refused to credit the analyses of this text to its authors. Even though the conclusions sounded inconsiderate, Lacan recommended that everyone in the audience should buy the book, read it, and decide

---

[3] Philippe Lacoue-Labarthe and Jean-Luc Nancy, *The Title of the Letter: A Reading of Lacan*, trans. François Raffoul and David Pettigrew (Albany: State University of New York Press, 1992). Hereafter *TL*.

[4] Jacques Lacan, *Écrits: The First Complete Edition in English*, trans. Bruce Fink (New York: Norton, 2006), 438; translation modified. Hereafter *EC*.

whether its authors were right to assert that it was a hopeless task to combine Saussure's linguistics of the sign, Freud's Unconscious and Heideggerian truth as unconcealment. Lacan did not hesitate to compliment his anonymous readers, whose prescience he praised: they had anticipated, he claimed, that he planned to bring up the Aristotelian concept of *enstasis* in relation to his "formulas of sexuation." Lacan states:

> they even discover the ἔνστασις, the Aristotelian logical obstacle that I had reserved for the end. It is true that they do not see the relationship [*rapport*]. But they are so used to working well, especially when something motivates them—the desire, for example, to obtain their Master's, a truly serendipitous term here—that they even mention that in the footnote on pages 28 and 29.[5]

I will highlight the loaded term *rapport* later. The insinuation that the authors were mere MA students parroting the discourse of the Master, a.k.a. Derrida, is not justified when we read the note on Aristotle. Nancy and Lacoue-Labarthe were discussing the key term of "instance," which Lacan uses in the title of the essay, by alluding first to Émile Benveniste, who had suggested the term "*instance of discourse*" in 1956 to describe the insertion of the speaker in speech, then to Jakobson and his *shifters*, and finally by finding an older model via a term provided by Aristotle. The end of their footnote in the first edition was rendered obscure by the permutation of two lines, which may have given Lacan a hard time. Lacan may have argued that Nancy and Lacoue-Labarthe did not "see the rapport" based on this typographical error. Here is a part of the footnote (or endnote in the English translation):

> But one will not forget that for Aristotle, ἔνστᾰσις (*enstasis*), in the theory of refutation, designates the *obstacle* which one opposes to the reasoning of an adversary (*Rhetoric* II, 25, 1402a); cf. *Prior Analytics* II, 26, *Topics*, VIII, 2, 157ab. This "agency" is, in particular, what the exception opposes to a universal prediction. An example of this *topos* happens to be the following, to be appreciated according to its most "proper" meaning: "it is honorable in some places to sacrifice one's father, for example amongst the Triballi, but it is not honorable in an absolute sense" [*Topics* II, 11, 115b ...].
>
> (TL, 24n4[6])

Nancy and Lacoue-Labarthe managed to find in Aristotle a surprising anticipation of the Freudian murder of the Father, a point that resonates with their remarks, which parallel Lacan's subversive readings of Hegel and Aristotle with those of Georges Bataille. In any event, their note's content and its tone could hardly trigger the accusation that they "do not see the relationship." Lacan was afraid that Lacoue-Labarthe and Nancy

---

[5] Lacan, *On Feminine Sexuality, the Limits of Love and Knowledge, 1972–1973* (*Encore: The Seminar of Jacques Lacan*, Book XX), trans. Bruce Fink, ed. Jacques-Alain Miller (New York: Norton, 1998), 69; translation modified. Hereafter S 20.
[6] Italics original throughout.

had recognized, before he did, the concept of *enstasis* that runs through Aristotle's *Analytics*, *Rhetoric*, and *Topics*, and that this provided a key to his theory of sexuation. Indeed, the term of *enstasis*, literally the obstacle opposed to an argument, leads to the idea of an exception to a universal predicate. It allows one to navigate the logical couple composed of "exception" and "universal," a logical couple allowing Lacan to set in place the mechanism through which he establishes that "there is no sexual relationship."

Lacan continues his acid praise, guiding his audience toward the same passages in Aristotle's *Rhetoric* and *Topics*. He announces that *enstasis* will usher in his formula of sexual difference in terms of "all" and "not-all" (S 20, 70–72). Curiously, when he then lays out his formulas and begins to unpack the four formulas of sexuation in the following meeting (S 20, 78), and even though he mentions the *Nicomachean Ethics* (S 20, 70), Lacan does not bring up the concept of *enstasis* again. If the concept had played a role for him, it is muted. Here, then, is a silent admission of the impact of Nancy's and Lacoue-Labarthe's reading, an impact that reverberated forty years later in the many texts Nancy has since then devoted to sexual enjoyment. One should not reduce Lacoue-Labarthe's and Nancy's book to an attack mounted by two professional philosophers aimed at redressing the conceptual mistakes of Lacanian theory. One of the effects of their multifaceted reading reminds us that it is far from simple to articulate, in peaceful theoretical coexistence, the splicing of a post-Saussurean linguistics of the signifier, Freud's dream theory, and Heideggerian ontology. Even when the latter ushers in the negative theology of absent being, reduced to a "hole" of *jouissance*, *The Title of the Letter* proves that mixing Saussure and Heidegger cannot produce a good Freudian cocktail.

By showing how Lacan was torn between flaunting his scientific credentials and his ultimate philosophical goals, his commentators save Lacanian doctrine from closing itself into an all too rigid system. They acknowledge Lacan's power for poetic creation, for they see a saving grace in the very inconsistencies and contradictions of his theory. To do so, they have to go beyond the textual limits they had fixed, as a passage states: "the formulas of 'congruence' which *The Instance* gives for metaphor and metonymy, as well as the entire algorithmic process and all the calculations it may engender, are to be taken between the game and the feint, Lacan himself forbidding that one be taken in by them" (*TL*, 119; translation modified). It is nevertheless true that Nancy and Lacoue-Labarthe fault Lacan for his misguided attempt at blending structuralist linguistics and Heidegger's ontology of language. At the end of "The Instance of the Letter in the Unconscious," Lacan had concluded with a facile pun linking the letter (*la lettre*) and Being (*l'Être*) in the title of the last section, "The Letter, Being, and the Other" (*EC*, 435). This is where he mentions his translation of Heidegger, rejecting imputations that he suffers from "Heideggerianism" or "neo-Heideggerianism" (*EC*, 438). Lacoue-Labarthe and Nancy, however, merely wonder how Heidegger's Being can climb up the tree of the signifier without disrupting the circular logic of the letter. They also witness Heidegger's "Logos" turning into a *"master-word"* (*TL*, 134), which would echo Lacan's wish to a master Truth of his own. They remind us that Heidegger's "Logos" was mostly devoted to translation, even as it demonstrated that a word like *logos* remains untranslatable (*TL*, 135).

Heidegger took *logos* as an untranslatable Greek word for what ought to have placed Being in Language and ended up confining it within Reason instead. Historically, *logos* replaced Myth but also retroactively constituted a Myth that was opposed to Reason. Myth would be on the side of poetry, *Logos* on the side of abstract reasoning aiming at Truth. One of the sharpest insights brought to bear by Lacoue-Labarthe and Nancy was to read Heidegger's "Logos" text not as proposing a definition of Truth as *aletheia* but rather as an essay on translation (*TL*, 135–36)—not so much a translation of Greek into German, but of Greek into Greek and of German into German. Such an operation has something to do with Freud's idea that any dream interpretation is a translation (*TL*, 135). To keep translating means to be aware as language understood as a condition for the birth of subjectivity; this insight should have guided Lacan's interpretation of Freud via Heidegger.

If *logos* defines the Being-of-Language, Heidegger interprets truth as *aletheia*, an un-forgetting deployment of meaning struggling between withdrawing and appearing, since only language can reveal the un-concealment of Being. Heidegger's meditation on *a-lethe-ia* concludes that Truth does not bring objects into the light of Reason, a light in which we compare and produce perfect equations, for this movement "withdraw[s] itself from representation" (*TL*, 142). Heidegger's insistence on reading the history of metaphysics in terms of its unthought thought does not suggest a repressed unconscious in a history that could be described in a Freudian manner. There is no repressed content remaining hidden under appearances, for it "will 'always' have been caught in the homoiotical interpretation" (*TL*, 143), or reason as founded on the equation of similar objects for thought.

Lacan, in Lacoue-Labarthe's and Nancy's spirited reading, had been obliged to follow the same dialectical movement of concealment and un-concealment that underpins Heidegger's thought. This struggle sustains his effort at unhooking the superposition of signifier and signified in the classical formula of the sign by insisting on the slippage of the signifier. If this led Lacan to subvert the Cartesian cogito in the name of the Unconscious, he could not avoid being caught in the discourse of metaphysics, and thus had no choice but to reduce ontology to *adequatio*. This explains why he seems to privilege metaphor, insofar as it indicates Being over metonymy, which in his system refers to a constitutive lack, or desire. Lacan preserves an intersubjective adequation made firmer by a pact passed with the big Other of the Unconscious. Truth as *aletheia* offers itself in the self-presence of the pure adequation of a speech that functions as enunciation (*TL*, 143). Lacan imitates Heidegger in his endeavor to remain faithful to *aletheia* by translating what must remain untranslatable. But translation as *homoíōsis* (the likeness of signifieds) misses the essential dimension of *aletheia*, even though it is the destined groundwork for the unfolding of philosophy.

Heidegger's goal was to read the unthought thought of Greek philosophy by reading *logos* against itself. His "destruction" of metaphysics would lay bare the philosophical field and enable a fresh beginning; one would then question any positive or scientific system of signs. Lacan's logic duplicates that of Heidegger for whom un-concealment cannot avoid getting caught up in the coordinates of *adequatio* or *homoíōsis*. Even when Lacan insists on the difference between the small other and the big Other, this

Other is then invoked to reinstate a higher *homoíōsis*. Lacan trusts the power of the Other to usher in an enunciation beyond language, a pure speech, whereas what he has been doing is to create a text.

Nancy and Lacoue-Labarthe locate the question of Lacan's relation to the unthought as a beyond-the-text, a beyond that would always be forgotten or repressed. How could one have an experience that withdraws from re-presentation, or that presents itself only by withdrawing? Psychoanalysis always provides an answer by way of desire. Hence the forceful conclusion reached by Lacoue-Labarthe and Nancy: "(Freudian) desire occupies the same *position* as (Heideggerian) truth" (*TL*, 138). The beyond of discourse that defines the experience of impossibility in Heidegger would for Lacan be an "experience" of presence, which recurs symptomatically in Lacan's often repeated phrase, "in our experience." By means of this idiom, the psychoanalyst parades a knowledge of the ineffable, a knowledge in which all subjects meet their constitutive limit.

What is the truth of Lacan's text, if it refuses to be determined by the economy of truth? On this point, Nancy and Lacoue-Labarthe hesitate at times, recognizing that there is a poetic textuality at work in Lacan's writings that prevents them from closing it upon a doctrine defined by its alleged "scientificity." At times, they see the appeal to Truth as a way to assert the psychoanalyst's mastery:

> We shall speak therefore, in the end, of *text*—if the text (is what) does not allow itself to be comprehended in the economy of truth. This has nothing to do with that "text" that Lacan led us to qualify as a discourse. Rather it is a text which Lacan's discourse, despite the disruptions of its enunciation, the gaps in its language, the detours of its process fails to rejoin—or rather in which his discourse never loses itself. Certainly, all discourse is always, also, a text. But *as discourse*, it can only "be" this text insofar as it constantly says, with respect to the text it implies: *I do not want to know,* if we may here single out Freud's text in the discourse we are (inevitably) holding, or by which we are (inevitably) held. And isn't this "denial" precisely what brings Lacan's text (discourse) to a close with the very formula of ontology, that is, with the definition of metaphor?
>
> (*TL*, 144–45)

These questions, left open, will sketch a theoretical program to which Nancy will return with greater frequency after 2001 (with "The 'There Is' of Sexual Rapport") but also in a number of assessments of Freud himself. This entailed reconsidering Freud when read within a larger tradition, the tradition of German Romanticism.

Romanticism and Psychoanalysis: Freud, from *Witz* to *Trieb*

Witz is the concept chosen by Nancy to open a recent collection of essays, *Expectation: Philosophy, Literature,* which spans thirty-five years. In this early essay, Nancy discusses the term in the context of an exploration of German Romanticism.

"*Menstruum universale*: Literary Dissolution," from 1977, provides the blueprint for a section of the 1978 book that Nancy jointly wrote with Philippe Lacoue-Labarthe. Indeed, *The Literary Absolute: The Theory of Literature in German Romanticism*[7] has a section entitled "The Fragmentary Exigency" in which the *Witz* is placed at the core of German Romanticism. Friedrich Schlegel had developed in the *Athenaeum* a theory of the reduction of the philosophical system à la Kant or Hegel to a series of dense and independent fragments. Such fragments could be even more condensed as *Witze*:

> *Witz* is concerned with the fragment, first of all, in that both of these "genres" (insofar as they can be given such a name) imply the "sudden idea" (*Einfall*, the idea that suddenly "falls" upon you, so that the find is less found than received). The "motley heap of sudden ideas" implies something of *Witz*, just as, because "many witty sudden ideas … [*witzige Einfälle*] are like the sudden meeting of two friendly thoughts after a long separation," *Witz* seems to imply within itself the entire fragmentary, dialogical, and dialectical structure that we have outlined.
>
> (*LA*, 52)

Thus, the main feature of the *Witz* is its brevity. As Nancy sums up in *Expectation*, there is a long tradition of similar analyses from Shakespeare to Freud: "Ever since Shakespeare's famous 'maxim' in *Hamlet* (repeated endlessly until Freud)—'brevity is the soul of wit'—the sole 'genre' or the sole 'form' that is always recognized as typical of *Witz* is concision, the rapidity of the statement that carries the *point*."[8]

We are reminded here that *Witz* stems from *Wissen*, meaning knowledge; it is related to the French *esprit* and to the English *wit*, terms that all refer to knowledge, but here is a different knowledge, a knowledge that is in some way always "other." It is a witty knowledge that eschews the stale and systematic discursivity of Reason, an unconscious knowledge, as it were. Romantic *Witz* thus brings to a climax the metaphysics of the *Idea*, the Idea's self-knowledge emerging poetically in its auto-manifestation. Therefore, the most bizarre or baroque manifestations become compatible with the highest knowledge, which is capable of reaching the infinite. "'*Witz* is creative, it produces resemblances,' Novalis writes in *Grains of Pollen*. *Witz* is an immediate, absolute knowing-seeing [*savoir-voir*]; it is sight [*vue*] regained at the blindspot of schematism and, consequently, sight gaining direct access to the productive capacity of works" (*LA*, 53). Thus, *Witz* gives birth to a poetry capable of "losing itself in what it presents," and in which irony is a key component. Romantic irony supposes the identity of the creative self and of the nothingness of works in what they saw as a "transcendental buffoonery" (*LA*, 56), a phrase that captures Nancy's efforts in the poems collected in *Expectation*.

---

[7] Lacoue-Labarthe and Nancy, *The Literary Absolute: The Theory of Literature in German Romanticism*, trans. Philip Barnard and Cheryl Lester (Albany: State University of New York Press, 1988), originally published in 1978. Hereafter *LA*.

[8] Nancy, "A Kind of Prologue. *Menstruum universale*: Literary Dissolution," in *Expectation: Philosophy, Literature*, trans. Robert Bononno (New York: Fordham University Press, 2018), 19.

At the same time, *Witz* appears caught up in a dilemma, for it entails a sacrifice, as dire as that outlined by the references to Bataille facing Lacan in *The Title of the Letter*:

> On the path toward the absolute, toward absolute fragmentary absolution, romanticism will now follow two distinct and continually crossing paths. The first, that of Novalis, redefines *Witz* as simultaneous combination and dissolution: "*Witz*, as a principle of affinity, is at the same time *menstruum universale*" (*Grains of Pollen*) [*Blüthenstaub* fragment 57]. The universal dissolvent undoes the systematic, undoes the identity of the poet and sweeps it toward the "dissolution in song" … a dissolution that includes the sacrifice, in all its ambiguity, of the poet ("he will be sacrificed by savage peoples"). The ambiguity of sacrifice (sanctification), however, corresponds to the ambiguity of the motif of dissolution, which leads the chemistry of the *Witz* back to the alchemy of the *menstruum*, and therefore to the Great Work, while at the same time leading back to *Auflösung* (dissolution) in the sense, found notably in Kant, of organic assimilation, of "intussusception."
>
> The second, Schlegelian path might be indicated by *Athenaeum* fragment 375 as the path leading toward "energy" or toward "the energetic man," defined by the "infinitely flexible … universal power through which the whole man shapes himself," well beyond the "genius" who "shapes a work." Energy extends to the limit of the work and of the system; its "infinite flexibility," linked to "an incalculable number of projects," effects an infinite fragmentation of work and system. But what is this flexibility, if not an infinite capacity for form, for the absolute of form; and what is energy, *en-ergeia*, if not the putting-into-work itself, the completed *organon*, whose works (of genius) are mere potentialities?
>
> (*LA*, 56–57)

This double postulation, dissolution or energy, is not an alternative, for both can be combined: dissolution *and* energy. Such a combination brings *Witz* closer to Maurice Blanchot's concept of "unworking" or *désœuvrement*, a manifestation of latent irony and parody. If *Witz* creates resemblances, it endlessly splits itself in half, thereby generating a process of dissolution that can never avoid chaos. It was such a chaos that Lacan's system was dangerously flirting with when attempting to read Freud philosophically, that is, in a Hegelian manner.

Given his solid grounding in a longer German tradition, Freud would appear to be a belated Romantic. We can see this feature in his younger years, when he was not only reading Feuerbach and Hoffmann, but also quoting Jean Paul and Goethe. In Freud's correspondence with his childhood friend Eduard Silberstein, when Freud was between fifteen and twenty-five years old, a specific Romanticism marked by the *Witz* creeps in. Freud wanted that he and his friend should enter into an epistolary pact that would lead to weekly confessions.[9] Such a regular exchange was to remain in the "spirit

---

[9] Sigmund Freud, *The Letters of Sigmund Freud to Eduard Silberstein, 1871–1881*, ed. Walter Boehlich, trans. Arnold J. Pomerans (Cambridge: Harvard University Press, 1990), 57–58.

of romanticism."[10] Freud was following a Romantic tradition marked by a mixture of humor, fantasy, and poetry. One of his predecessors was E. T. A. Hoffmann, whose tale of "The Sandman" became the main literary evidence for a definition of the Uncanny. Hoffmann had published "News from the Most Recent Fate of the Dog Berganza"[11] in 1814 in his groundbreaking *Fantasy Pieces in the Manner of Callot*. The stories were introduced by Jean Paul, another Romantic writer who would provide a stylistic model. Freud's juvenile letters are in the spirit of Jean Paul and Hoffmann; they are self-consciously humorous and critical at the same time. This would require a whole chapter by itself, but I would simply like to suggest at this point that Nancy did not go on with a project that might be called a deconstruction of Freud. On the contrary, he reads Freud in a positive manner, looking for stable and strong foundations.

What is striking is that when Nancy had to present Freud to a Japanese audience, he insisted on two new elements: Freud's doctrine is seen as predicated upon one main factor, the theory of the drives; Freud's thought is characterized as being the most non-religious thinking of the twentieth century. And so Nancy, working at the cusp between poetics and deconstruction, has cleared a new path for French phenomenology in that he has sharpened its edges without falling prey to the "religious turn" that lay in wait for most French phenomenologists, from Emmanuel Levinas to Jean-Luc Marion.[12] Nancy's readings of Freud and Lacan owe to Freud their distancing with the religious itself. Nancy states: "the Freudian invention is the most clearly and resolutely unreligious of modern inventions. It is also for this reason that it cannot even believe in itself."[13] Conversely, we can say that it is precisely when psychoanalysis started to believe in itself that it became imperative to make it see its delusion, whether religious or not.

So when Nancy points out the need for a Freudian mythology, it has to be a mythology of the drives. Indeed, Freud famously announced in his *New Introductory Lectures on Psycho-analysis* that his way of referring to the drives was reminiscent of myth: "The theory of the drives is so to speak our mythology. The drives are mythical entities, magnificent in their indefiniteness."[14] Freud is of course referring to *Triebe*, a term still translated as "instincts" in the earlier version of the Standard Edition, soon to be updated. He explains in the same lecture, XXXII, that *Trieb* is a good word because it evokes a strong pressure: "We picture it as a certain quota of energy which presses in a particular direction. It is from this pressing that it derives the name of '*Trieb*.'"[15]

---

[10] Ibid., 58.
[11] E. T. A. Hoffmann, *Fantasiestücke* (Frankfurt: Deutscher Klassiker Verlag, 2006), 101–77.
[12] See Dominique Janicaud's accurate assessment, "The Theological Turn of French Phenomenology," trans. Bernard G. Prusak, in *Phenomenology and the "Theological Turn": The French Debate* (New York: Fordham University Press, 2000), 16–103.
[13] Nancy, "Freud—so to speak. Introduction to the Japanese edition of S. Freud's 'Complete Works'" (2010), trans. Gianmaria Senia, *European Journal of Psychoanalysis*; online, accessed December 2, 2021: https://www.journal-psychoanalysis.eu/freud-so-to-speak/.
[14] Freud, *New Introductory Lectures on Psycho-Analysis and Other Works* (Standard Edition, Volume XXII), ed. and trans. James Strachey (London: The Hogarth Press and the Institute of Psycho-Analysis, 1964), 95; translation modified.
[15] Ibid., 96.

Nancy dismisses the Lacanian notion according to which everything hinges on the concept of the *Unbewußt*, the Unconscious seen as the source of Truth, beyond rationalization and philosophy—a thesis that led Alain Badiou to call Lacan's theory an "anti-philosophy." Rejecting this elegant but drastic solution, Nancy wants to keep philosophizing with Freud, even as he is aware of the slipperiness of the terms used. For him, Freud did not "discover" a dark continent that would be either sexuality or the Unconscious, but he provided a new narrative:

> there is no Freudian discovery and ... the unconscious is not an organ. But Freud did make an invention: he invented man's narrative. Before, it was a Creator or Nature that had created Man, before, man was promised a celestial afterlife or the survival of his species, but instead, Freud gives man another origin and another destination. Man comes from a momentum [*élan*] or a surge [*poussée*] which surpasses him, which surpasses in any case much of what Freud designates as the "self" [*moi*].
> He calls this momentum or surge the *Trieb*.[16]

Nancy inherited from Lacan the strict rejection of any ego-psychology. The foundation he is looking for exceeds the human self, even any kind of subjectivity. It seems in fact closer to a Bergsonian (hence Romantic) *élan vital*:

> The notion of *Trieb*—or of the *Triebe* complexes—signifies a movement that has come from elsewhere, from the non-individuated, from what is the hidden archaic state of our origins, proliferating and confused—and that is: nature; the world; the whole of humanity behind us, and behind it what makes it possible; the emergence of the sign and the gesture; the call of all of us to the elements, to forces, to the possible and the impossible; the sense of infinity lying ahead of us, lying behind and amongst us; the desire to answer to this call, and to expose oneself to it. We originate from this movement, from this momentum, from this surge. In the final analysis, it is within this movement and as such a movement that we can *grow*—as we say in French when talking about plants: it is thanks to this movement that we rise, and become what we are capable of being.
> This surge comes from elsewhere than us. It makes of us a grown individual, a being which has not been "produced" by a set of causes, but led, launched, projected, or even "thrown" (to reuse a word of Heidegger's). This "elsewhere" is not a "beyond," it is neither a theological transcendence, nor a simple immanence as some atheistic negative theologies have understood it to be. This "elsewhere" is inside us: it forms within us the most creative and the most powerful engine driving this momentum, which is what we are.[17]

---

[16] Nancy, "Freud—so to speak."
[17] Ibid.

Freud provides a new conceptual lever for Nancy—he allows him to rethink Heidegger's ontology:

> This is because it [this elsewhere] is nothing less than our being, or it is being in itself once it has detached itself from its ontological moorings. It is "being" considered in the meaning of the verb "to be": it is a motion, a movement, an emotion, the shock and rise of desire and fear, waiting and attempting, trying, accessing, even crisis and exaltation, exasperation or exhaustion, the forming of forms, the invention of signs, the incoercible tension moving to an unbearable point where it fragments or lays itself down.[18]

Hence the main point for Nancy will not be to launch a new ontology but to rethink the nexus between being and sexuality—one of the key points of the Freudian intervention in culture. It will entail a certain "return to Lacan."

Returning to Lacan via Sexuality

This occurs when Nancy reads Lacan once more, this time not as a "text" but as a thinker working with cryptic one-liners, as when he insisted that "there was no sexual relation." In "The 'There Is' of Sexual Relation,"[19] Nancy tackled Lacan's paradoxical statement squarely. Again, a disciple of Lacan might be tempted to see in Nancy's title nothing more than a negation. While Lacan repeatedly stated since the end of sixties that "there was no sexual relation," Nancy affirms the exact opposite: "there is a sexual relation." As the translator observes, the key here is the term *rapport*, as Lacan keeps referring to "*rapport sexuel*," which means both "relation," "relationship," and "having sex" (*C II*, 109). Nancy begins his examination with a battery of observations that sound critical. He notes that Lacan's expression, "There is no sexual relation," has the air of a provocation or of paradox, flying in the face of common sense (*C II*, 2). After all, what we call "sexual relations" happens every day. The expression is intended to shock by stating that "What there is, is not," a gesture that can be inscribed in a long philosophical genealogy. It is typical of claims we find in Hegel and Heidegger to the effect that Being, in some ways, is not. A well-known Heideggerian logic suggests that we should consider the "sexual relationship" as a "being" whose "Being" is not. The real Being coupled to the human subjects engaged in an active sexual life does not allow itself to be seen, counted, or even defined.

Being as such can be approached via a word that can be read either as a verb or as a noun: *baiser* or "(to) fuck" (*C II*, 2). From its classical sense, *baiser*, to give someone a kiss, has taken a current slang meaning to fuck, in all its senses. This noun-verb

---

[18] Ibid.
[19] This was published as a book in 2001 and translated into English by Anne O'Byrne in *Corpus II – Writings on Sexuality* (New York: Fordham University Press, 2013), 1–22. Hereafter *C II*.

condenses the Lacanian paradox provided we conjugate it in the active and the passive voice. Nancy nimbly concludes his semantic overview as follows: "the foundational expression of psychoanalysis is that I am kissed every time I kiss, fucked every time I fuck" (C II, 3). What does Nancy mean here? Deploying a logic that is more Freudian than Lacanian (one might think here of the letters Freud sent to Fliess while they were exploring the inversion and demultiplication due to bisexuality), this utterance means that, according to psychoanalysis, I am severely mistaken if I believe in any sexual relation. For to believe in that, romantically as it were, one would have to believe that there is such a thing as One—i.e., union—when in fact there is only two—i.e., separation. And there is a second critical intervention: at the end of his reflections on passivity and activity, Nancy adds that the provocative force of the Lacanian utterance does more than shock: it also prohibits and interrupts: the pragmatic effect of this prohibition is tantamount to a *coitus interruptus* (C II, 3–4) in light of incest taboos, castration threats, and all the Freudian panoply of concepts. A certain castration in sexuality corresponds to a renunciation of the straightforward empirical evidence.

Having reached this point, Nancy knows that the Lacanian analyst will cry foul at this hermeneutic scandal and denounce the errors of such a partisan reading. Has Nancy deliberately misunderstood Lacan's lesson? After long detours through Aristotle and Kant on the concept of "relation," which never refers to a thing but to a rapport between two subjects or entities, it seems possible to reconcile Nancy's analyses with the passages in which Lacan makes love the ideal means men and women have found to overcome this fateful "There is no." As if noticing that he had strayed too far from the dynamics of the Lacanian text, Nancy then backtracks and tackles the idea of "relation" in sexuality. "Relation" might appear as Nancy's key concept since the *Literary Absolute*. "Relation," whether sexual or not, is not reducible to an "act," even if common French usage treats them as synonyms. Finally, Nancy comes much closer to Lacan's original meaning. If common usage assumes that the "relation" is something, it is in fact an action, and not a product. Nancy thus proceeds to unpack the intertwined meanings that Lacanians recognize in "There is no sexual relation." As Nancy explains at some length, the claim that there is no sexual relationship means that there is no return, no report, no conformity, or pre-established proportion for what is involved when a couple mates. If the claim is about the relation of two subjects in the sexual act, this act asserts, as Lacan stated, that *rapport* as a measured homology between two beings is impossible. Jumping from Hegel to Heidegger, Nancy reiterates the critique of *homoiōsis*, but this time applied directly to sexuality:

> The sexual is not a variety of the genre known as relation, but in the sexual we see the extent of relation and see it fully exposed. I could say that the sexual relates [*rapporte*] what there is of relation [*rapport*], but its report—its account and its narrative—is not totalizing and does not close the circle.
>
> …
>
> The sexual is not a predicate, for it itself is no more a substance or a thing than relation is a substance or thing. The sexual is its own difference, or its own distinction. Being distinguished as sex or sexed is what makes sex or sexed-ness.
>
> (C II, 9)

Any critical attitude toward Lacan disappears at this point. Nancy offers a profound and subtle philosophical commentary of Lacan's sentence, one that remains entirely in accord with its logic. For Lacan's sentence, whether we stress the beginning ("*There is no sexual relationship*") or the end ("There is no sexual *relationship*")—in other words, whether we stress the ontology (the being of the relationship) or the epistemology (the nature of this relationship, or the possibility of calculating the relationship by framing it as a fraction or as complementarity, as the homology between the two sides of a straightforward and clear-cut opposition, that is, masculine-feminine, active-passive, lover-beloved, etc., namely pairs of opposites that must, of course, be applied to subjects of the same biological sex)—always presupposes a dialectical relationship between two terms: "no" and "sexual." In short, it is a matter of fully rethinking the negativity and restlessness stated by the original maxim. If "relation" leads us to sexual difference, it shatters any belief in a pre-existing "One." But whereas Lacan reserved some room for this One and gave it the name of "Love," for Nancy there is a shattering brought about by the sensual experience of sex itself. There is no need to elevate it, be it in the name of Love.

Nancy thus prefers to talk about "fucking" and "jouissance," finding in the phenomenology of sexual enjoyment as "coming" a more secure (and materialist) foundation. He nevertheless acknowledges that Lacan does not exclude this idea: "The finitude of relation or jouissance (which is, after all, what Lacan wants to make us understand) must be understood as what punctuates (finishes, terminates, *and fines*, that is, refines) sexual infinity" (*C II*, 15). Such a jouissance is not infinite, it is not reserved for women and mystics, as Lacan seems to say at times; it is divided and predicated upon its impossibility. Concluding with a rephrasing of the initial statement ("*the sexual is the 'there is' of relation*" (*C II*, 21), we could add that there is no "there" there: no subject, no *Dasein* will be present to recuperate it. Another concluding statement confirms this: "Jouissance is not something we can achieve. It is what achieves itself and consumes itself in that self-achieving, burning its own sense, that is, illuminating it even as it burns it up." (*C II*, 21).

Nancy makes this more explicit in his dialogue with Adèle van Reeth about "coming":

> I don't think that what Lacan says about feminine *jouissance* means it's only the woman who *jouit*. If I were to rephrase it in my own words, I would say of feminine *jouissance* that it is neither the possession nor appropriation of something, but rather openness to an alterity, since the woman is in the position of what Lacan calls "the Other," the big Other. *Jouissance*, then, would make woman into that big Other, that is, that which remains outside of language and meaning, and which for that reason escapes any capture by a subject.[20]

The meaning of *jouissance* would thus lie beyond satisfaction, bringing us closer to an ecstasy that would differ from itself, thus remaining ungraspable. Nancy reiterates this

---

[20] Jean-Luc Nancy and Adèle van Reeth, *Coming*, trans. Charlotte Mandell (New York: Fordham University Press, 2017), 21.

analysis in *Sexistence,* ironically pointing out that Lacan had anticipated this move in a February 1973 seminar where he said to his audience: "There is a jouissance, since I am confining myself here to jouissance, a jouissance of the body that is, if I may express myself thus—why not make a book title out of it? it'll be the next book in the Galilée collection—'beyond the phallus.' That would be cute, huh?" (*S 20*, 74). Quoting this allusion to the *Title of the Letter,* Nancy quips that his present book should be "cute" enough to please Lacan's spirit.[21] Finally, as we have already seen, it is the very notion of jouissance that becomes an equivalent of Derrida's *différance,* a point underlined in a note of "The 'There Is' of Sexual Relation" in which Nancy alludes to Derrida's unfinished treatment of *Geschlecht* (sexuality in German, and many other meanings) in Heidegger: "Derrida's différance must therefore be sexual … Therefore being is sexed and/or sexing" (*C II*, 109n6). Sexual difference becomes ontological difference: Freud and Hegel merge with Heidegger.

To conclude, we see Nancy distinguishing himself not only as a brilliant commentator and sharp critical reader but also as an original thinker who understands why psychoanalysis is relevant today. He implicitly rejects the vulgar philosophy of jouissance as simple enjoyment deployed by a bad but successful philosopher like Michel Onfray.[22] Onfray has attempted to debunk Freud, to expose him as a fraud, while praising a *jouissance* obtainable without any repression. Nancy, of course, remains closer to Derrida, whose recent publication of *Geschlecht III*[23] shows that Nancy has understood him. At the same, he has managed to combine the two main references of Lacanian discourse, Freud and Heidegger. What emerges from the confrontation between a Romantic Freud and a Heideggerian Lacan bridges the gap between a science of the Unconscious and a new mythology. If the Unconscious is the modern equivalent of the ancient "soul," what does this insight yield? Nancy forces us to return to that obscure hinge, the locus where we try to make sense of the links between language and body, drives and pleasure, life and death, culture and individuals, in an unfinished narrative aiming at questioning the roots of all religions.

In *Sexistence,* Nancy quotes countless passages from literature, religion, and philosophy, as he did in "The Birth of Breasts" (*C II*, 23–69), in order not only to mobilize his immense culture but also to point to numerous attempts by writers who wish to go beyond language when evoking sexual desire, passion, and "coming." Language and the drive thus remain the two fundamental incompatibilities, even when one attempts to return to a before-language, or an archaically undifferentiated sexuality. Nancy finds this wish and its undoing both formulated ironically in a first draft of Joyce's *Finnegans Wake,* where Shaun, the blustering Irish tenor, plays the role of Tristan in love with Isolde, both ready to melt in Wagnerian *Liebestod.* Shaun says this:

—Isolde, O Isolde, when ~~theeupon~~ **theeuponthus** I ~~do~~ oculise my most inmost Ego most vaguely senses the profundity **deprofundity** of multimathematical

---

[21] Nancy, *Sexistence,* trans. Steven Miller (New York: Fordham University Press, 2021), 136.
[22] See Michel Onfray, *L'Art de jouir* (Paris: Grasset, 1991).
[23] Jacques Derrida, *Geschlecht III: Sex, Race, Nation, Humanity,* trans. Katie Chenoweth and Rodrigo Therezo (Chicago: University of Chicago Press, 2020).

immaterialities whereby in the pancosmic urge the Allimmanence of That Which Is Itself exteriorates on this here our plane of disunited solid liquid and gaseous bodies in pearlwhite passionpanting intuitions of reunited ‡ Selfhood in the higherdimensional Selflessness.[24]

If the first kiss of doomed Romantic lovers always rests on an illusion of oneness, Joyce's parodic language reminds us that the "ego" is always shattered by "multimathematical immaterialities." This is what Nancy is talking about, mostly, when he is talking about love.

---

[24] From David Hayman's *A First-Draft Version of* Finnegans Wake (Austin: University of Texas Press, 1963), 209; final version of the passage in James Joyce, *Finnegans Wake* (London: Faber, 1939), 394; quoted by Nancy in *Sexistence*, 134.

10a

Streams of Consciousness: River Poetry from Heidegger to Nancy and Lacoue-Labarthe

John McKeane

> *If I think of Germany in the night,*
> *I am jolted from my sleep,*
> *I can no longer close my eyes,*
> *and my hot tears flow.*[1]
>
> —Heinrich Heine

Surprising as it may seem, rivers are a consistent presence in the work of thinkers from Friedrich Hölderlin and Martin Heidegger to Jean-Luc Nancy and Philippe Lacoue-Labarthe. Other natural features (mountains, hills, plains, sea) feature in the Romantic poetry of Hölderlin or others but are not taken up with anything like the same persistence. And indeed, for Heidegger, Nancy, and Lacoue-Labarthe, rivers take us beyond questions of nature, allowing for the interrogation of notions such as landscape, technology, the specificity of humanity, and the presence (or absence) of divinity. If "these sinuous lines ... penetrate territory like nothing else does," they also penetrate and carry us far into key twentieth-century thinkers' approach to such topics.[2]

The poetry of Hölderlin is—as it were—the source of this mini-tradition of thinking rivers. He writes hymns dedicated to major European waterways the Rhine and the Danube (under its alternative name the Ister), to the source of the Danube, and to Bordeaux's Garonne ("Remembrance"), as well as poems of different genres

---

[1] The first strophe of the poem "Nachtgedanken." The quotation is given anachronistically but appositely at the opening of the film by Hans-Jürgen Syberberg, *Hitler: A Film from Germany* (Berlin: TMS film/Bernd Eichinger, 1977).

[2] The quotation is from a writer associated with Lacoue-Labarthe and Nancy, Jean-Christophe Bailly; J.-C. Bailly, *Le Dépaysement. Voyages en France* (Paris: Seuil, 2011), 343. The work discusses, among others, the Loire, the Loir, the Seille, the Rhône, the Loue, the Vézère, and the Oise. All translations from French are mine unless indicated otherwise.

on the German rivers Main and Neckar, and on "The Fettered River."³ Now, if one of the more common ways in which rivers become metaphorical is via the trope of *water under the bridge*, speaking to the loss and irrecuperability of what went before, Hölderlin pursues an alternative approach. Instead of loss and dissolution, the flowing of the river represents an increase of breadth and depth, the river rushing onwards to become ever more itself, affirming worldhood over any essence. These opposite poles are conceptualized in various terms—as homely and foreign, modern and ancient, natural and technological, German and Greek, human and divine. With the Danube or Ister in particular, linking as it does the Black Forest and a province of ancient Greece, there is scope for a fruitful encounter between these various declinations of same and other.

The rivers discussed have a raw power that is conducive to both industry and sublimity (as for Scotland's Clyde: see Coleridge, Wordsworth, and Robert Owen). They provide opportunities for the advancement of geographical knowledge, as European explorers saw the great African rivers Nile, Niger, and Congo as doing.⁴ And they allow or provoke some consideration of the divine (as with India's Ganges and its sacred status in Hinduism).⁵ But the rivers discussed by Hölderlin and Heidegger, Nancy and Lacoue-Labarthe are never only powerful, epistemic, or divine. The poet and his later philosophical interpreters use rivers to think through the existential or phenomenological topics of humankind's relation to the world in which we dwell and the mode of questioning that sets humankind apart.

In addition to the Hölderlin poems mentioned above, rivers see extensive treatment in three of Heidegger's lecture courses on the Romantic poet: on "The Rhine" (1934–5), "The Ister" (1942), and "Remembrance" (the Garonne poem; 1943). Lacoue-Labarthe and Nancy, for their part, feature heavily in the filmed travelogue *The Ister* (2004).⁶ We shall look at the latter's contribution to this film alongside his work *The Creation of the World or Globalization*, before moving to the question of landscapes and homeliness or unhomeliness in Lacoue-Labarthe's writing (specifically the essay "Le Dépaysagement"). Addressing first Heidegger, then Nancy, then Lacoue-Labarthe, we shall see the multiple and sometimes unexpected ways in which they travel along these philosophical rivers, these streams of consciousness.

---

³ See Friedrich Hölderlin, *Selected Poems and Fragments*, trans. Michael Hamburger (London: Penguin, 1998).
⁴ There is a more skeptical reading, which is that they were used to enable colonialism. On the topic, see Joseph Conrad's *Heart of Darkness*, which is discussed by Lacoue-Labarthe, a discussion itself extensively explored in Nidesh Lawtoo, *Conrad's Heart of Darkness and Contemporary Thought: Revisiting the Horror with Lacoue-Labarthe* (London: Bloomsbury, 2012).
⁵ An interlocutor of Jean-Luc Nancy, Divya Dwivedi, has rightly signaled to me the dangers of the sacralization of rivers in the context of contemporary *Hindutva*.
⁶ I will try to distinguish typographically between the Ister (the river itself—the Danube), "The Ister" (Hölderlin's poem), Heidegger's lecture course on "The Ister" (Hölderlin's poem), and *The Ister* (the film featuring Nancy and Lacoue-Labarthe which addresses at once river, poem, and lectures). For full references, see below.

Martin Heidegger: The Same Through the Other

It is impossible to learn the dates of Heidegger's lectures on Hölderlin's river poetry without questioning their relationship to nationalism and National Socialism: 1934–5 on "Remembrance," 1942 on "The Ister," 1943 on "Germania" and "The Rhine."[7] Does the first lecture course show any signs of reconsideration, following his resignation from the rectorship of Freiburg University earlier in 1934? How did the lectures given at the height of the Second World War relate to the Nazi project (he remained a member of the party until 1945)?[8] Quite apart from their author's abhorrent politics, the lectures show a strange blindness: even as he discusses Greek thinkers and analyzes phenomena applicable across the (Western) world, there is barely any attempt to make the conclusions relevant for readers located in different traditions. The radical thinking of indeterminate being-in-the-world was in fact already determined by its author as German thought, for the Germans.

We shall look at the 1942 lecture course on "The Ister," partly due to its alignment with the film featuring Nancy and Lacoue-Labarthe, but also due to the complex interactions with otherness it proposes. In the eponymous poem, Hölderlin compares the Ister (or Danube) and the Rhine: both rise in the mountains, close to one another. The Rhine for its part "has gone away / sideways," plunging down into the plain, irrigating and making fertile (of which more later). As for the Ister, it "cling[s] to the mountains, straight," and rather than rushing downstream, it moves so slowly, dwelling and whiling, that it "seems / to travel backwards." This causes the poet to speculate that "I think it must come from / the East" (this is what led the 2004 film to start at the Black Sea and travel upriver). These opposing characteristics, as well as the epic scale of the two rivers, cause Heidegger to refer to them as *the* rivers: standing for and containing within themselves all the possibilities of riverdom.[9]

The ultimately German horizon or destination of Heidegger's thinking does not mean that there is any simple refusal to consider or encounter otherness (that refusal, when it comes, is invested with all Heidegger's philosophical weight, making it all the more repellent). The encounter with otherness is precisely what Heidegger sees taking place in Hölderlin's poem. The thought that the Ister might flow backwards, importing foreignness from faraway lands, chimes with the multiple mentions of exotic lands in

---

[7] Martin Heidegger, "Remembrance," *Elucidations of Hölderlin's Poetry*, trans. Keith Hoeller (Amherst: Humanity, 2000); Heidegger, *Hölderlin's Hymns "Germania" and "The Rhine,"* trans. William McNeill and Julia Ireland (Bloomington and Indianapolis: Indiana University Press, 2014); Heidegger, *Hölderlin's Hymn "The Ister,"* trans. William McNeill and Julia Davis (Bloomington and Indianapolis: Indiana University Press, 1996). References to the latter are henceforth abbreviated *HHI*.

[8] Such questions have had even greater urgency since the publication of *The Black Notebooks* in 2014; see Donatella Di Cesare, *Heidegger and the Jews: The Black Notebooks*, trans. Murtha Baca (Cambridge: Polity, 2018). Di Cesare notes the disturbing values given to landscapes by Heidegger: the German forest, weald or *Wald* as the secluded home of thought, and the desert, a space of the vacuity and rootlessness he associates with Judaism. See Di Cesare's work, *passim*, but in particular the passage on the notion of "without world," 161ff.

[9] The Danube and the Rhine are in fact only the second and eleventh longest in Europe, but the rest of the ten longest are in Eastern Europe and likely were not considered by Heidegger.

his river poetry.[10] In turn, this can be understood as part of a wider Romantic thinking of *Bildung*, with an encounter with foreignness representing a formative experience.[11] This is the context in which Heidegger writes that "The Ister *is* that river in which the foreign is already present as a guest at its source, that river in whose flowing there constantly speaks the dialogue between one's own and the foreign" (*HHI*, 146[12]). It is important for this dialogue to exist in order for what is one's own not to be a simply closed, unknowing identity or sameness (an idiocy, according to the etymology).[13] In Heidegger's formulation, "the Ister satisfies the law of becoming homely as the law of becoming unhomely" (*HHI*, 164). This is to say that the greater one's experience of or connection to the foreign, the more fully one is able to become oneself. The Ister, flowing backwards from the Black Sea—a province of ancient Greece—shows this process in action, irrigating Germany with its own dialogical becoming.

While we might expect a lecture-course on rivers by a nationalist or Nazi philosopher to underline the importance of the landscapes of the homeland, this is not the case. The rivers do not act as straightforward symbols of anything (e.g., national character or German exceptionality). He writes that "these river poems are not simply depictions of landscapes, which evidently they are not intended to be … the river poems cannot be poems 'about' rivers, in which the rivers are already familiar in their essence and are taken as images or emblems signifying something else" (*HHI*, 26). The rivers discussed therefore have a strange status in Heidegger's thought: he makes it quite clear that they are not to be read symbolically, loaded with metaphysical freight in the classic tradition of Western philosophy, made to stand in for something they are not, or to represent abstract concepts. In this sense, he tells us that Hölderlin's poems *really are about rivers*, rather than rivers as a way toward something else. However, inasmuch as the rivers lead their own existence, pursuing their own specificity heedless of the rest, they provide a pointer as to how humans might exist. To see how this works, first of all it is necessary to say what rivers are not. Heidegger does this as follows: "[rivers] are not gods. They are not humans. They are not occurrences of nature, nor are they parts of the landscape. Nor, indeed, are they 'symbolic images' of the 'earthly journey' of human beings. To say what the rivers in each instance are *not* … is of some help" (*HHI*, 33). It is indeed helpful to recap what rivers are not, in Heidegger's reading of Hölderlin: they are not a straightforward expression of the German homeland, they are not part of a landscape, they are not symbolic, they are not metaphorical or

---

[10] Both the Neckar and the Main are said to long for Greece; the Garonne in "Remembrance" is associated with India; "At the Source of the Danube" mentions Ionia, Arabia, Asia, and the Caucasus; and the poem "The Ister" itself refers to two non-German rivers, the Alpheus (Greece) and the Indus (of the Indian subcontinent). See Hölderlin, *Selected Poems and Fragments*.

[11] See Antoine Berman, *The Experience of the Foreign: Culture and Translation in Romantic Germany*, trans. Stefan Heyvaert (Albany: SUNY Press, 1992).

[12] Italics original throughout.

[13] Heidegger quotes another Hölderlin poem to make this point:
> at home is spirit
> Not at the commencement, not at the source. The home consumes it.
> Colony, and bold forgetting spirit loves (*HHI*, 126).

In other words, staying at home, remaining fixed in sameness and not encountering the other, "consumes" spirit, exhausts its resources. The quotation is from a draft of "Bread and Wine".

metaphysical. While such an interruption of or resistance to such modes of reading is frustrating, and might tip over into obstructiveness if pursued indefinitely, Heidegger continues the passage as follows: "Initially, what emerges is that any determination of the essence of the rivers must appear alienating. Our claim is this: the river is the locality of the dwelling of human beings as historical upon this earth" (*HHI*, 33). This seems to be suggesting that, rather than participating in the lofty but ultimately fragile constructions of metaphysics, so many views from nowhere, a thinking of rivers allows human beings to fully inhabit or dwell in our specificity.

What then, in Heidegger's eyes, is this specificity of human existence? Here we are confronted with the classic Heideggerian theme, familiar to readers of *Being and Time*: human beings are the beings for whom their existence is a question. We have no determined or fixed nature but must locate it in and through a *being-in-the-world*, with the truth of that situation not being a formal *adequatio* (a correspondence to some pre-existing reality), but a living *aletheia* (a revelation or remembering), an attunement to what really is, to what is really the case.

Nature is often taken to represent this real state of things. But for Heidegger this is a false construction, one that fails to take account of the world which we humans have built for ourselves. This is what places the topic of technology at the center of his lectures on Hölderlin's "Ister" poem. This is literally the case, with two sections on the poem itself bookending a middle section looking not at the German poet, but at Sophocles's *Antigone*. At one point Heidegger explains this in terms of the foreign (the Greek) being needed at the heart of the homely (the German) in order for the latter to be fully itself. But the most important characteristic of the notions discussed is surely not their Greekness—at least if understood as one national identity among others. Instead, it is the fact that the section of the *Antigone* discussed is that sometimes known as the "Ode to Mankind," praising the latter's various technological achievements (ploughing, ensnaring birds, hunting, farming, navigation, governance). While these activities can of course be seen as a form of metaphysical domination or rationalization of nature—and sometimes are by Heidegger, in the right conditions a thinking of them allows what is proper to mankind, what he calls our destination, to emerge.[14] If such a thinking is to emerge, it must pass through what the chorus in the *Antigone* mentions at its outset:

Manifold is the uncanny, yet nothing
More uncanny looms or stirs beyond the human being.[15]

The uncanny, *to deinón* or *das Unheimliche*, is what defines mankind, and finds expression in the technology that we alone create. The Greek term translated here is

---

[14] A criticism of modern technology specific to rivers can be found here: "The hydroelectric plant is not built into the Rhine River as was the old wooden bridge that joined bank with bank for hundreds of years. Rather the river is dammed up into the power plant. What the river is now, namely, a water power supplier, derives from out of the essence of the power station" (Heidegger, *The Question Concerning Technology and Other Essays*, trans. William Lovitt [London: Garland, 1977], 16).

[15] English translation of Heidegger's translation; *HHI*, 58.

sometimes rendered as "the monstrous," and the German *Unheimliche* is cognate with the English "unhomely" (although "uncanny" is often used as the translation because it better recreates the German expression's double sense of something being strange, but also strangely familiar).

In addition to framing this discussion of technology, Hölderlin's poem explicitly discusses technology (and its attendant questions: humankind's construction of a world, and the uncanniness of that world). Rivers in general provoke the statement that

> … here we wish to build
> For rivers make arable
> The land.

As previously seen, the Rhine is shown going away from the mountains—the line "not for nothing rivers flow / through dry land" suggests that the river is somehow destined to bring fulfillment to the land by making it fertile. The final strophe of the poem then contains the lines

> But the rock needs incisions
> And the earth needs furrows,
> Would be desolate else, unabiding.

These Hölderlinian lines are clearly attractive to Heidegger, as they depict the river as a site of nature, but also as allowing humans to undertake technological activity (and we think of everything from breweries to mills to hydroelectric dams to nuclear power stations). Rather than seeing agriculture (and behind it technology in general) as the imposition of a rational plan, the lines suggest that it is a response to what is already there, arising from it, in a strangely familiar way. The river is both of the land and always flowing to (or from) an elsewhere. It is a supplement, without becoming transcendent.

For Heidegger, then, "the river '*is*' the locality that pervades the abode of human beings upon the earth, determines them to where they belong and where they are homely [*heimisch*]. The river thus brings human beings into their own and maintains them in what is their own" (*HHI*, 21). Humans are uncanny, unhomely, *unheimlich*, or monstrous because we are unsettled, living in a world of betweenness: between nature and technology, between animals and gods, having characteristics of all and yet belonging entirely to none.[16] Similarly, communing with otherness, but linking that other to the same, rivers can be understood not as fully divine, but as demigods. With dazzling bravura, Heidegger abandons the slow pace adopted in much of this lecture course to collapse the categories at this point. If humans occupy this middling world, then poets (and Hölderlin's river poems) are particularly important in understanding

---

[16] Major thinkers nonetheless go against this reading: Emmanuel Levinas arguing that Heidegger's opposition to metaphysics leads him to a version of paganism, and similarly Jean-François Lyotard, who states: "Heidegger-Hölderlin's god is merely pagan-Christian, the god of bread, wine, earth, and blood." See Di Cesare, *Heidegger and the Jews*, 176, 240.

this human being, because humans and poets and rivers each represent, to different degrees, this middleness. In Heidegger's words, "the demigod, the river, the poet: all these name poetically the one and singular ground of the becoming homely of human beings as historical and the founding of this ground by the poet" (*HHI*, 154). He puts these phenomena all on the same level, in a way that is challenging for many readers, but nonetheless reveals what was motivating the previous lengthy discussions. The demigod, the river, and the poet are all figures of betweenness: each one is an other, but in Heidegger's words, "this Other who is needed" (*HHI*, 156). This is to say that they do not remain austere and remote in their otherness, but in the fact of being needed, enter a relation. It is this sense of relationality that is explored by Jean-Luc Nancy with his thinking of world.

Jean-Luc Nancy: Producing the Uncanny

Do Hölderlin's rivers run through Nancy's world? To start exploring this question, we shall look at Nancy's contribution to the film *The Ister*, in which the section featuring him uses as its title Hölderlin's line—quoted above—"here we wish to build." His contribution focuses to a large extent on technology, and in so doing is also a response to Heidegger and his reading of Hölderlin. The thinking of rivers as demigods is also germane to Nancy's interest in the withdrawal or deconstruction of a direct relation to the sacred. Accordingly, we shall see Nancy recounting the shift between two types of politics: that based on a firm mythological foundation, and that based not on *mûthos* but on *logos*, which is without firm foundation, and therefore constitutes what he means by world. In this sense, he picks up on Christianity's disparaging habit of referring to the world or what is worldly: "the Christian sense of *world* as that which precisely lacks all sense or has its sense beyond itself."[17] But rather than demonstrating the limited or unfulfilling nature of the world, this lack of any beyond is precisely what is interesting for Nancy. It is not just a question of setting concreteness in opposition to abstraction, but of seeing how this concreteness can be gathered into a supplementary world or worlding (a supplementarity that is weaker than full-blown transcendence). In order to explore this before discussing the film *The Ister*, let us briefly look at Nancy's work *The Creation of the World or Globalization*.[18]

This work takes as its starting point the observation that, with *mondialisation*, questions of technology and economic rationalization are no longer confined to the West alone. This is to say that by extending its technologico-rational approach to all corners of the world, the West has also ceased to exist as a particular area of that world. Its dominance is so complete that it becomes self-erasing. As we have seen, Heidegger denounced the earlier stages of this process in the name of a thinking intended for

---

[17] Jean-Luc Nancy, *The Sense of the World*, trans. Jeffrey S. Librett (London: University of Minnesota Press, 1997), 54. See also the chapter "Touching," which is particularly important (pp. 59–63).

[18] Nancy, *The Creation of the World or Globalization*, trans. David Pettigrew and François Raffoul (Albany: SUNY Press, 2007). Hereafter *CW*.

the Germans alone (as supposed spiritual leaders of Europe or the West), and on the basis of Hölderlin poems that refuse conceptuality and metaphysics in favor of *really*, that is, non-metaphorically, being about rivers. For his part, Nancy does not have any such solid foundations on which to base a resistance to *mondialisation*—for him, this process has long since eroded any such foundations, and to seek to return to them would be a treatment more harmful than the disease.

Nonetheless, two notable definitions of world that he gives in this work do retain strikingly Heideggerian language. The first ties world to the question of inhabiting:

> a world is a world only for those who inhabit it. To inhabit is necessarily to inhabit a world, that is to say, to have there much more than a place of sojourn: its place, in the strong sense of the term, as that which allows something to properly take place. To take place is to properly arrive and happen [*arriver*]; it is not only to "almost" arrive and happen and it is not only "an ordinary occurrence." It is to arrive and happen as proper and to properly arrive and happen to a subject.
>
> (CW, 42)

This is to say that to inhabit is weightier than simply to sojourn or stay in a given place; it is to arrive properly as a subject, to arrive at that status of subjecthood. In turn, this is said to be necessary for there to be world: "a world is only a world for those who inhabit it." In other words, there is no world if we are just sojourning ephemerally, but only if there is (in)habitation by subjects. Although deprived of its reference to a particular locality such as Germany or the West, the model here is strikingly Heideggerian. Similarly, a little later, Nancy provides a formulation that removes world from the sort of direct representation that the earlier thinker denounces as metaphysical:

> the world is no longer conceived of as a representation. A representation of the world, a worldview, means the assigning of a principle and an end to the world. This amounts to saying that a worldview is indeed the end of the world as viewed, digested, absorbed, and dissolved in this vision.
>
> (CW, 43)

This is to say that to represent world is to posit that it has already come to an end, that one is able to stand outside it and capture a stable image of it. This is impossible, because we are always-already and always-still within the world, not separate from it but at best providing a way for the world to relate to itself (to give itself sense, in Nancy's term). The subjecthood previously mentioned means to be subjects in the world, not subjects standing outside it. This is where the literalness of Hölderlin's river poems can act as a guide: for we are also here, now, not in some abstract evertime from which we could look back on the world and on ourselves.[19]

---

[19] Another way of putting this would be that there is no safe redoubt from which we could watch climate disaster unfold. For a treatment of the ways eco-criticism has drawn on Nancy's work, see Martin Crowley, "The Many Worlds of Jean-Luc Nancy," *Paragraph* 42, no. 1 (March 2019): 22–36.

In his chapter in *The Ister* entitled "Here We Wish to Build," Nancy gives something like a lesson to the camera, interspersed with footage from the travelogue up the Danube (Ister), and with on-screen quotations from Heidegger's lecture course on the Hölderlin poem.[20] He is careful to distinguish the importance placed on the river from a straightforward Romantic mythologization of nature: the river is not directly sacred, nor is it part of any nationalistic landscape. Instead, Hölderlin and Heidegger's thinking is tied in with a narrative of the West (presumably in its extended form) as lacking any direct mythological foundation: "The beginning of the West is also the beginning of a question of the institution, or of foundation ... The question of foundation appears as a question at the moment when foundations have disappeared." This situation is contrasted to that of the empires of early recorded history (Egypt, Assyria, Babylon, the Hittites). Of these, Nancy states that "Empires in this sense are precisely the orders of a clearly given foundation. The empire always has its foundation behind it, it is founded by the gods, it has always been there, and its order is installed once and for all." He takes the advent of technology to be responsible for this shift away from *mûthos* or mythology: technologies such as writing, navigation, numeracy and accountancy, up to and including sophistry and philosophy, mean that the world of *mûthos* becomes a world of *logos*.[21] This is to say that rather than relying on what was given by nature, up to and including the presence of the gods, mankind stepped into a new dispensation: the discourse or logic of *logos*, meaning that the surrounding world would no longer just be that given by nature, but that shaped and created by technology. Instead of everything conforming to its own nature, pursuing its own destination or destiny, this notion of things being destined to certain ends would be questioned and overturned. In Nancy's words:

> *tékhnē*, to say it in one word, is what has no end, it is *savoir-faire* towards some given thing, but precisely this thing is not given, it must be produced. And perhaps the entire history of the West as a history of technology, is the history of an endless end, of the endless production of new ends, which means also the absence of ends.

Thought is presented as being generally applicable—indeed, as that within which generalization or universalization is always at work. These are categories that are (or at least should be) open by definition, as for them to refuse to integrate an emergent or newly discovered phenomenon would undermine the claim of being universal.

This has consequences for the way in which Hölderlin and Heidegger, to whom Nancy is responding here, are interpreted within the history of ideas. For it would

---

[20] The quotations that follow are my transcriptions from David Barison and Daniel Ross, *The Ister* (Fotzroy: Black Box, 2004). The film features Nancy, Lacoue-Labarthe, Bernard Stiegler, and Hans-Jürgen Syberberg.

[21] This term is famously untranslatable—Barbara Cassin glosses it as follows: "If we look up *logos* in a Greek-French dictionary, we find a mass of equivalents: 'discourse, language, tongue, speech, rationality, reason, intelligence, foundation, motivation, proportion, calculation, account, value, report, recounting, narrative, thesis, reasoning, argument, explanation, statement, proposition, definition, term,' etc." (*Éloge de la traduction – compliquer l'universel* [Paris: Fayard, 2016], 39).

be difficult for these figures, with their thinking of the Ister (Danube) river as the site of humankind's move from *mûthos* to *logos* by way of technology—a thinking of "an endless end ... [an] absence of ends"—to be interpreted as allowing only Romantic or nationalistic readings.

This can be seen most of all in the conclusion at which Nancy arrives in this mini filmed lecture, having insisted on the distinction between the known and accepted foundations and goals of a mythologically based society or politics, and the unknown, shifting, or absent foundations and goals of a technological, discursive society: one in which nothing is a given. Speaking of this second dispensation, here is Nancy:

> [in the logical world] the production of the proper doubtless has an aporia behind it, an aporia of violence, and before it, a confrontation with the foreign [*l'étranger*] and with total or absolute foreignness—*das Unheimliche* or *das Unheimische*. This means that, with the West, with what we can call philosophical—or politico-philosophical—technology, there appears an institution which is the endless demand or search for a proper that can only ever be presented via a foreignness to itself.

In other words, in a mythological world (or rather place, for it is not fully a world in Nancy's sense) the "proper" or one's own is given, available, recognized as such. In the world of *logos*, on the other hand, because this properness has none of these characteristics, it must be produced artificially, and there is an unavoidable element of violence in doing so. This has direct political consequences: any attempt to draw on a foundation myth, in the modern world, is also a writing or creation of that myth (or to use Lacoue-Labarthe's term, a fiction of the political). In short, if it is to explore and question its true status, this modern world must instead prepare for a "confrontation" with "*das Unheimliche* or *das Unheimische*": the uncanny or the unhomely. This is why in Nancy, rivers—and particularly the Ister—are the occasion less for a mythologizing, Romantic, nationalistic approach to landscape, than for what has been called *le dépaysement* or *le dépaysagement*. But to understand the term fully, we must turn to Lacoue-Labarthe.

Philippe Lacoue-Labarthe: Rivers Draining Landscape

This is a thinker who engages extensively with Hölderlin's river poetry, both through and against the influence of Heidegger's readings. Indeed, across his work multiple documents in multiple genres address the interaction of place and thought: for instance, his contribution to the film *The Ister*, looking at Mauthausen concentration camp, which is located next to the Danube. But there is also his translation of "Andenken," Hölderlin's poem on the Garonne at Bordeaux and the subject of a Heidegger lecture course, a translation which eschews the title's normal sense of remembrance and instead emphasizes the literal *an-denken*: "Je pense à vous" (I am thinking of you). A reading of this translation with footage of the Garonne constitutes the short film

Andenken/Je pense à vous. Beyond this, no fewer than three further films feature Lacoue-Labarthe engaging with the notion of place: *Voyage à Tübingen*, concentrating on Hölderlin's secluded existence in a tower above the river Neckar for nearly forty years; the *Entretiens de l'Île Saint-Pierre* see Lacoue-Labarthe in dialogue with Jean-Christophe Bailly by Lake Geneva (and elsewhere); and *Altus* is a travelogue about the *hauts lieux* of (Western) European spirit, featuring the Vosges, Sils-Maria in the Alps, Jena, and Tübingen again.[22]

Although many of the locations featured might seem apt for a post-Romantic thinking of landscape and inspiration, and although Lacoue-Labarthe does write extensively on Romanticism, his approach is a different one. He does not wish to marvel at the grandeur of epic landscapes, but instead to consider the horrific deeds committed by those claiming to be inspired by this European spirit. This is how the section on the concentration camp at Mauthausen by the Danube takes its place, Lacoue-Labarthe speaking of a Europe that is no longer inspired, but short of breath, emphysemic (not a little dramatically, he drags on a cigarette as he does so). Indeed, given all his work on Hölderlin, rivers, landscapes, and so on, we might have expected these questions to feature more heavily in his section of the film. Instead, the fact that he concentrates on technology and on Heidegger's failure to recognize the gravity of the Holocaust speaks to a growing distancing from Heidegger in Lacoue-Labarthe's mind. Although he had dedicated many publications to the philosopher, the concepts of being-in-the-world, existence as a question, "whiling" (*HHI*, 162, 163, 164), and so on, were increasingly contaminated by a conception of dwelling that was not only exclusive to the Germans, but murderously, genocidally so. In thus rejecting Heidegger, Lacoue-Labarthe also rejects all notions of a landscape in which one might dwell.

We can follow Lacoue-Labarthe's thinking by looking at a short text named "Le Dépaysagement," which has two immediate interlocutors: the first is photographer Thibaut Cuisset, whose publication featuring interspersed photos of barren scenes in Namibia and Iceland is prefaced by Lacoue-Labarthe's text.[23] In this light, *dépaysagement* would be an "un-landscaping," an emptying-out of the activities that traditionally define a landscape—ones that are apparently bucolic but in fact already technological and rationalizing. The second interlocutor is Jean-Christophe Bailly, a regular collaborator of both Lacoue-Labarthe and Nancy, and author of *Le*

---

[22] Barison and Ross, *The Ister*; Christine Baudillon and François Lagarde, "Entretiens de l'Île Saint-Pierre," featuring Lacoue-Labarthe and Jean-Christophe Bailly, and Baudillon and Lacoue-Labarthe, "Andenken/Je pense à vous," both in Baudillon and Lagarde, *Proëme de Philippe Lacoue-Labarthe* (Montpellier: Hors œil, 2011); Baudillon, *Philippe Lacoue-Labarthe: Altus* (Montpellier: Hors œil, 2013)—Lacoue-Labarthe's spoken prologue is printed and translated for the first time in this volume; Michel Deutsch, *Voyage à Tübingen, un portrait de Philippe Lacoue-Labarthe* (2009), online, accessed November 2, 2010: http://www.filmsdocumentaires.com/films/434-philippe-lacoue-labarthe. It must be said that *Voyage à Tübingen* is in many respects mawkish, showing a Lacoue-Labarthe suffering from illness, and revolving around Hölderlin's madness in the German city in a teleological and mythologizing way.

[23] Philippe Lacoue-Labarthe, "Le Dépaysagement" in Thibaud Cuisset, *Le Dehors absolu* (Trézélan: Filigraines, 2005), reprinted in *Écrits sur l'art* (Geneva: Les Presses du Réel, 2009), 249–55.

Dépaysement. Voyages en France.[24] The title of this travelogue evokes being *dépaysé*, lost, disorientated, not at home, literally "un-countried." It also responds to the German terms *das Unheimliche* and *das Unheimische*; Bailly speaks of the difficulty of national identity for a member of the '68 generation, who only much later in his career came to write this book of passages through France (rather than a book about France). In other words, the classic symbols of Frenchness for him provoke not homeliness but a sense of unhomeliness or unease.

What does Lacoue-Labarthe say about *paysage* and *dépaysagement*? He starts by making a clear distinction between a landscape as a human creation, and unadulterated nature (that which from Romanticism on has been seen as an indicator of real or authentic existence). In his words,

> [a landscape] is always homogeneous, it has its own identity: its vegetation and fauna, its contours and the shape of its land, the nature of its ground and the way it is divided up, the architecture of its habitat, the way people speak there and their customs. This is obviously without forgetting its climate and its light, the air one breathes there; even, just as much, the type of activity that predominates there. It is a land that is essentially inhabitable, and inhabited: habitual too, familiar.[25]

This suits perfectly the discussion of rivers as what—in Hölderlin's words—"make[s] arable / the land," allowing for a large number of agricultural and industrial techniques, and responding the quasi-mystical, Hölderlinian sense in which, as we have seen, "the rock needs incisions." As he continues, Lacoue-Labarthe softens or even erases the distinction between this sort of mainstream human activity, and the Romantic defenses of nature that are often attempted in opposition to this activity. Yes, nature is pushed to the margins of exploitable land, but this is only a temporary stage: "until such time as ... a late Romanticism invents an exoticism of elsewhere and a sense of the picturesque, both based on this brute nature."[26] In other words, a Romantic love for nature is not an act of insubordination against technological exploitation, but instead a more refined version of it, a way of extracting cultural value where no other form of material value is available. In short, a Romantic affection for nature—and the tourism associated with it—does not allow for a sufficiently robust critique of technology's destructive planetary dominance.[27]

---

[24] The river theme is continued by a collaboration this time between Cuisset and Bailly, based around the former's photographs of the banks of the Loire; see Jean-Christophe Bailly, "La Loire de Thibaut Cuisset," (2001), online, accessed July 13, 2020: http://andrea.nfrance.com/~eq26451/texts/Cuisset_49-1.pdf.

[25] Lacoue-Labarthe, "Le Dépaysagement," 250.

[26] Ibid., 250–51.

[27] In 2019, Nancy remarked to me that neither he nor Lacoue-Labarthe had written on the Rhine—which after all flows past their adopted home city of Strasbourg and is heavily laden with cultural associations—because they saw it as a commodified tourist attraction, suitable only for narrated river cruises.

In view of such an apparently promising external position becoming unavailable, the only possible alternative is to push onwards, searching for what Cuisset used as the title of the photographic album that Lacoue-Labarthe is prefacing: *Le Dehors absolu*.[28] And beyond daffodils and waterfalls, the heritage-industry version of Romanticism, it is the work of Schelling that allows Lacoue-Labarthe to do this. It seems highly significant that he draws on a term that we have already seen passing between the oeuvres of Sophocles and Hölderlin, Heidegger and Nancy (not to mention Freud, who made it most famous): *das Unheimliche*. Lacoue-Labarthe writes:

> In the canonical definition that Schelling gives once and for all of *Unheimlichkeit*: it is the revelation of what must not revealed, and what might secretly lie in this vision of the outside—or of this "search for the absolute" ... Before the measureless distance of the desert and beneath its unlimiting limitlessness, before the sky's incommensurable insubstantiality, in which the ab-solute is sketched out, no subject is operative any more.[29]

In other words, it is not sufficient to simply posit an alternative type of subjectivity, for example Romantic rather than technological: this is still all-too rationalizing, it still brings everything back home beside the hearth of human activity. Despite the dangers present in a search for the absolute, one must understand this not as a total systematization but instead as a fragmentation or suspension, an "ab-solute." And accompanying Schelling in the article here is perhaps the central figure in Lacoue-Labarthe's thinking, Hölderlin. We are reminded that it is necessary to recuperate him from "Heideggerian overinterpretation," for instance of his poems on the Rhine or the Ister, and instead consider him overlooking the banks of the river Neckar, during his long exile from sanity in Tübingen.[30] Here, we read that "Hölderlin constantly came back to the intuition about what he once called 'the open': *das Offene*. He did so with a disarming simplicity, which is the most just response to the call of the outside."[31] In other words, the river should not be seen as a pretext for human technology, nor as some mystical divine otherness. But above all, it should not be limited to given landscapes, even as it continues to run through and shape them. Instead, it undoes the landscape as much as it contributes to it; it leads away from any given locality, breaking down the unity of place, draining it figuratively as well as literally.

It is in this sense that we must always remember to speak of *dépaysement* and *dépaysagement*, with Nancy and Lacoue-Labarthe, and against Heidegger. We might take this, with Nancy, as an invitation to think the groundless subject of *logos*, in and through an open-ended process of worlding where nothing is given, but which nonetheless sees the humming of constant activity and production. Or we might take it

---

[28] Thibaut Cuisset, *Le Dehors absolu* (Trézélan: Filigranes, 2005).
[29] Lacoue-Labarthe, "Le Dépaysagement," 254–55.
[30] Ibid., 255.
[31] Ibid.

more in Lacoue-Labarthe's sense, according to which there are not only no givens but no giving, no originary donation of being, via an *es gibt* or an *il y a*. For Lacoue-Labarthe, it is a matter of unworking the subject's operativity ever more thoroughly, rather than—as he would see Nancy as doing—merely recasting that subject as groundless rather than grounded. Such were the dialogues that animated this remarkable pair of thinkers, and which through their works, now equally posthumous, continue to flow.

Altus*

Philippe Lacoue-Labarthe

Altus, en latin, dit à la fois le haut et le bas; *altitudo*, c'est l'élévation et la profondeur. On parle ainsi, en français, de « la haute mer ». Et il est arrivé à Hölderlin d'écrire: « on peut aussi bien tomber dans la hauteur que dans la profondeur ».

Qu'est-ce que regarder d'en haut ? Qu'est-ce que chercher à voir au plus profond ? Dans l'un et l'autre cas, n'est-ce pas sombrer ? Atteindre la clarté même ? Évoquant la marche de Lenz à travers les Vosges, Büchner indique, dès les premières lignes de sa nouvelle: « seulement il lui était désagréable parfois de ne pas pouvoir marcher sur la tête ». Et Celan commente, dans *Le Méridien*: « celui qui marche sur la tête, Mesdames et Messieurs, celui qui marche sur la tête, il a le ciel comme un abîme sous lui ».

Vers où, sur quoi, l'écriture et la langue orientent ou dirigent notre regard, et selon quels modes de pensée ?

Que voudrait embrasser Rousseau du regard depuis le sommet des Alpes ? La vue que prend Hölderlin sur Bordeaux et la Garonne, est-ce dans l'attente du retour vers la terre natale, ou dans l'impossible espoir de la découverte d'un autre monde ? À Sils-Maria, « six mille pieds au-dessus de la bêtise humaine », quelle révélation Nietzsche veut-il provoquer ? Et la hauteur de vue de Hegel, déjà, quelle histoire permettait-elle d'accomplir ? Celle qu'avait ouverte Homère, l'*aède* aveugle ? Car, à l'inverse, qu'est-ce que s'engouffrer (Baudelaire), se terrer (Kafka), se dissimuler au regard (Blanchot) ? Qu'est-ce que s'acharner à s'enfuir dans sa propre chair (Artaud) ? Et qu'allait donc chercher Bataille dans la crypte inviolée depuis des millénaires de Lascaux ?

C'est un voyage (visionnaire). Il passe par Bordeaux, Genève et Sils-Maria, Iéna et Tübingen. Il pourrait tout autant rester immobile. La vulgate de ces trente dernières années nous a soumis à la question: « d'où tu parles ? » On tente de lui substituer cette autre: « d'où tu vois ? » C'est-à-dire, peut-être: « quel espace entends-tu ? »

---

* This text by Lacoue-Labarthe is read out by the author at the beginning of the film *Altus*. The camera pans slowly away from a lake in Switzerland's Engadine valley, while Lacoue-Labarthe dictates the text by phone with great emphasis on the punctuation. Full details of the film are: Christine Baudillon and François Lagarde (Hors oeil éditions), *Philippe Lacoue-Labarthe: Altus*, produced 2001, released in France 2013, sixty-seven minutes. I am grateful to Christine and to Claire Nancy for permission to include the text here. [Translator's note.]

Altus, in Latin, means both high and low; *altitudo* is both height and depth. Thus we speak, in French, of the "high seas." And Hölderlin came to write: "one can fall into height as well as into depth."

What is it, to look from on high? What is the attempt to see in great depth? In both cases, does this not mean to go under? To reach clarity itself? Evoking Lenz's walk across the Vosges, Büchner remarks in the first lines of the novella: "only it was unpleasant for him not to be able to walk on his head." And Celan commentates, in *The Meridian*: "he who walks on his head, Ladies and Gentlemen, he who walks on his head, has the sky for an abyss below him."

Where, toward what, do writing and language orientate or direct our gaze, and according to what modalities of thought?

What did Rousseau try to encompass in his gaze from the summit of the Alps? Was Hölderlin's view over Bordeaux and the Garonne one awaiting to return to his native land, or did it hope, impossibly, to discover a new world? At Sils-Maria, "six thousand feet above human stupidity," what revelation was Nietzsche trying to provoke? And what narrative did Hegel's lofty gaze allow to be completed? That begun by Homer, the blind *aóidos*? Conversely, what is it to be engulfed (Baudelaire), to go to ground (Kafka), to hide from view (Blanchot)? What is it to persist in fleeing one's own flesh (Artaud)? And what was Bataille looking for in the crypt of Lascaux, untouched for millennia?

This is a (visionary) voyage. It passes through Bordeaux, Geneva and Sils-Maria, Jena and Tübingen. It could just as easily have remained immobile. The vulgate of these last thirty years has subjugated us to the question: "where are you speaking from?" We try to replace it with this other one: "where are you looking from?" Which is to say, perhaps: "what space do you hear?"

(Translated by John McKeane)

11

The Regime of Technique: Nancy, Science, and Modernism

Ian James

Writing in *The Cambridge Companion to Modernism*, Michael Bell makes a striking claim about the relation of modernism to its supposed successor: "the change from Modernism to postmodernism is not a difference in metaphysic so much as a different stage in the digestion of the same metaphysic."[1] Published in 1999, at the turning point of the new millennium, the *Companion* itself offers a wide-reaching critical and scholarly evaluation of modernism in the twentieth century and does so across different genres and art forms (e.g., the novel, poetry, plastic art, and film) but also different and overlapping cultural spheres (e.g., politics and economy, gender). From the point of view of intellectual history, therefore, it gives an interesting snapshot of how leading Anglophone scholars across the globe gave a reckoning with modernism and its aftermath at the very end of the century of modernism itself and did so in a moment of inevitable looking forward to the century and millennium to come.

Bell's contribution, "The Metaphysics of Modernism," offers a rich and supremely informative account of the various philosophical figures that shaped modernism (most obviously Freud, Marx, Nietzsche, Bergson, and Heidegger) and examines how these influences informed key pre-occupations in the period: human worldhood, language, history, myth, tradition, innovation, and so on. He also gives an account of the influences of early twentieth-century science and scientific thought on modernism and in so doing he identifies an intellectual-historical trajectory in which fundamental philosophical understanding, scientific knowledge, and the creation of aesthetic forms are closely interwoven. What follows will trace the line of this trajectory in order to give a more precise sense to Bell's claim that modernism and postmodernism in the twentieth century may be different stages in the digestion of the same metaphysic. In this way it will shed light on Nancy's relation to the modernist legacy. It will also argue that this legacy may be a resource for thinking with and after Nancy in response to the challenges of the twenty-first century.

---

[1] Michael Bell, "The Metaphysics of Modernism," in *The Cambridge Companion to Modernism*, ed. Michael Levenson (Cambridge: Cambridge University Press, 1999), 9.

Nancy and Science

Nancy's philosophy, opening up as it does in the wake of Derrida, might most obviously be thought of as post-deconstructive and therefore even as post-postmodernist. Yet the decisive engagements with both Nietzsche and Heidegger that mark Nancean thought from its earliest moments shape some of its most fundamental concerns. These are concerns which are also those of modernism and, indeed, of what one might call "modernist" science. These include a preoccupation with a fragmentation of unity and, along with this, an emphasis on multiplicity and plural being. Fragmentation and plurality are articulated in an understanding of being which is relational and in which relation and relationality are themselves originary. In this context, notions of ontological substance and ground give way to an affirmation of ontological void and groundlessness.

Nancy's relational account of being, of course, unfolds in different ways across his career, most notably in the context of his re-working of Heideggerian *Mitsein* and Kantian freedom in the 1980s and of his thinking of finite being, the sense of the world, and of being-singular-plural in the 1990s.[2] His Derridean readings of the 1970s and the engagements with Kant and Heidegger in both the 1970s and 1980s do not immediately suggest an alignment of Nancean thought with science or with scientific knowledge. It is in *The Sense of the World* that he begins explicitly to invoke the question of whether something like a philosophy of nature can be renewed within contemporary thought and in which he introduces cosmological references and calls for a renewed cosmology that would be consistent with the ontological fragmentation and loss of ground or foundation that his thinking has always articulated and affirmed.[3] It is only in his 2011 collaboration with the theoretical physicist and cosmologist Aurélien Barrau that the possible alignment of Nancean thinking with contemporary scientific theory becomes explicit and is explicitly developed as such.[4]

Yet, despite the fact that these explicit references to science may appear to emerge more marginally in Nancy's discourse, it should be noted that, from the beginning of the twentieth century at the very least, the relational understanding of being is by no

---

[2] See in particular, Jean-Luc Nancy, *La Communauté désœuvrée* (Paris: Christian Bourgois, 1986), trans. Peter Connor et al., *The Inoperative Community* (Minneapolis and Oxford: University of Minnesota Press, 1991); *L'Expérience de la liberté* (Paris: Galilée, 1988), trans. Bridget McDonald, *The Experience of Freedom* (Stanford: Stanford University Press, 1993); *Une pensée finie* (Paris: Galilée, 1990), trans. Simon Sparks, *A Finite Thinking* (Stanford: Stanford University Press, 2003); *Le Sens du monde* (Paris: Galilée, 1993), trans. Jeffrey S. Librett, *The Sense of the World* (Minneapolis: University of Minnesota Press, 1997); *Être singulier pluriel* (Paris: Galilée, 1997), trans. Anne O'Byrne and Robert Richardson, *Being Singular Plural* (Stanford: Stanford University Press, 2000).

[3] Nancy, *The Sense of the World*, 37–38, 40.

[4] Jean-Luc Nancy and Aurélien Barrau, *Dans quels mondes vivons-nous ?* (Paris: Galilée, 2011), trans. Travis Holloway and Flor Méchain, *What's These Worlds Coming To?* (New York: Fordham, 2015). For a more extended discussion of the interplay between Nancy's account of relational being, sense, and things and of scientific accounts of these within both biology and fundamental physics or cosmology, see Ian James, *The Technique of Thought: Nancy, Laruelle, Malabou, and Stiegler After Naturalism* (Minneapolis: University of Minnesota Press, 2019), 55–119.

means alien to science and to scientific thinking.[5] The notion that being is relational and with this also liable to a plurality of constructions and approaches on different levels of thought and perception emerges in a distinctive and decisive manner during the modernist period that spanned the first four decades of the twentieth century.

"Construction in a Void": On Modernist Technique

Michael Bell's chapter in *The Cambridge Companion to Modernism* gives an excellent account of the influence of early twentieth-century scientific discovery and theories on the emergence of modernist thought and aesthetics. The most obvious points of reference here are, of course, Einsteinian relativity and quantum mechanics. It is not simply that these rapidly became famous and influential within the scientific outlook or worldview but rather that they precipitated a wider shift in worldview, as Bell notes: "Einstein's relativity theory was to catch the headlines and, like Heisenberg's 'indeterminacy', it seemed to have an analogical application to other, nonscientific spheres."[6] In relation to both Einsteinian relativity and quantum mechanics, it can be said that they may have precipitated a thoroughgoing decomposition relative to what might be called "perceptual faith," the notion that what is real is what is given to us pre-reflectively in the senses. These sciences reveal different levels of reality that are not accessible to the world of ordinary perception or to the received Euclidean geometry and the notions of perspective used to represent that world. Non-Euclidean geometries (Riemannian, Lobachevskian), Minkowski spacetime, multidimensional Hilbert space, all challenge the pre-reflective perceptual faith of our everyday and immediate sensorium. As Bell puts it: "It became evident that the universe at these levels behaved in a different way from the common-sense world of everyday experience while the necessary questioning could only be asked through highly speculative theory."[7]

This decomposition of common-sense and everyday experience and perception had, according to Bell's account, a number of consequences. First, the multiplication of geometries beyond the Euclidean geometry used by Newtonian physics reinforced the "recognition that science is a construction of the human mind before it is a reflection of the world."[8] There is an apparent reinforcement of the Kantian perspective here that would insist that the world we can know is a product of our categories and of a priori logical structures of the human mind. This is consistent with a wider

---

[5] In the light of this and the analysis of modernist science and its legacy that follows, Quentin Meillassoux's claim that modern science has, thanks to its grounding in mathematics, taken over from (pre-Kantian) philosophy as a means of accessing the absolute appears rather partial and reductive, ignoring the historical and contemporary development of debates within both the philosophy of science and mathematics.
[6] Bell, "The Metaphysics of Modernism," 11.
[7] Ibid.
[8] Ibid.

neo-Kantianism of the period and opens the way for those strands of twentieth-century philosophy of science that might go under the name of constructivism or conventionalism.

Second, the multiplicity of possible perspectives implied by scientific constructivism also inaugurated a more wide-reaching fragmentation of metaphysical unity and ground or foundation, and with this a fragmentary multiplication of the notion of world: "Different world conceptions are held together in a mutually defining, mutually testing, relation ... it becomes necessary to speak not of *the* world so much as of the human 'world.'"[9] *The* world breaks apart, the center cannot hold, and we are confronted with the idea of different historical worlds, diverse possibilities of *Weltanschauung* or worldview, and even with the notion that there are human worlds and non-human worlds. Heidegger, of course, famously claimed that humans were world-building (*weltbildend*) and that animals were world-poor (*weltarm*). Heidegger was not at all sympathetic to science in general and, as such, rejecting biologistic accounts of human being and aligning quantum theory with the metaphysics of presence and with the techno-scientific and nihilistic mastery of being that he held to be the essence of metaphysics and its instrumental rationality. Yet it should be recalled that his notion of world as a surrounding environment experienced as such has some considerable indebtedness to von Uexküll's biological understanding of *Umwelt* (developed from his famous account of the tick). In any case, Bell directly relates the Heideggerian concept of world and Dasein's being-in-the-world (later so important to Nancy) to the more generalized fragmentation and pluralization that modernist science helped to inaugurate.[10]

Third, the recognition of the constructedness of human scientific views of the world, and the multiplicity and relativity of worldhood as such, necessarily also calls into question the place of the human in the cosmos. On this point, Bell's account is clear: "the relative status of the human was a central recognition of Modernism."[11] One could argue that there are both a centering and de-centering of the human at play here. On the one hand, it is recognized that our worlds, worldviews, and scientific constructions of reality are inevitably human-centered. On the other hand, the human itself does not enjoy any privileged perspective over the totality of being; it is cut loose, unmoored, and cast directionless into the abyss of the universe in a manner evoked by Nietzsche's madman in the parable of that name in *The Gay Science*.[12] So while there may remain a humanism within modernism, it is no longer one in which the human is the measure of all being and not one which affirms the cosmos as an anthropic home: "humanism ... is acknowledged in its ultimate groundlessness" and any human home is "a construction within a void."[13]

---

[9] Ibid., 12; italics original throughout.
[10] Ibid.
[11] Ibid., 13.
[12] Friedrich Nietzsche, *The Gay Science*, trans. Josephine Nauckhoff (Cambridge: Cambridge University Press, 2001), 119–20.
[13] Bell, "The Metaphysics of Modernism," 14.

Bell's account is not only useful for its analysis of the way scientific developments heavily influenced the metaphysics of modernism. It also gives brief but illuminating indicators of the many ways in which these influences were played out within the realm of art and aesthetics—e.g., the use of mathematical terms in the "Ithaca" episode of Joyce's *Ulysses*, the impact of psychoanalysis on D. H. Lawrence, Mann's literal and metaphorical references to X-ray technology in *The Magic Mountain*, or Proust's scientific analyses.[14]

Yet, the scientific revolutions of the modernist period are perhaps most clearly marked in the reconfiguration of space and time and its representation within literary and pictorial aesthetics. Non-Euclidean geometries and Einsteinian relativity not only fragmented our sense of a unified world and our apprehension of reality, they also opened up new possibilities of representing the perception of world and reality. So when Marinetti proclaims in his *Futurist Manifesto* of 1912 that "Time and Space died yesterday" and ushers in the Futurist aesthetics of speed, he may certainly be evoking the advent of Einstein-Minkowski space-time and its transformation of absolute Newton space into the space of relativity theory.[15] Looking beyond Bell's account and the more obvious references to Einstein and Heisenberg, it is in fact the thought of the mathematician, theoretical physicist, and philosopher of science Henri Poincaré that can be seen to exert the most decisive influence throughout the modernist period.

Described by Gary Gutting as "a founder of the philosophy of science that became so central in twentieth-century analytic philosophy," Poincaré's longer-term influence is in fact so great as to be hard to gauge in its entirety.[16] As a practicing mathematician and scientist, Poincaré was not trained in philosophy, had little interest in the French spiritualist and idealist philosophies of his preceding and contemporary milieu, but he was very well informed in relation to current philosophical issues, in particular those which concerned science and scientific epistemology.[17] In their essay on Poincaré for the *Stanford Encyclopedia of Philosophy*, Gerhard Heinzman and David Stump explicitly highlight his "modernist-sounding views" and "[t]he modernist character of Poincaré's approach."[18] These are most explicitly present in his geometrical conventionalism and his relationalism, that is to say, the insistence that "we have no pre-axiomatic understanding of geometric primitives" and that "[w]hen we speak of space, all we can talk about is the relations of physical bodies."[19]

Heinzmann and Stump also point out that Poincaré's conventionalism and relationalism are two different aspects of his structural approach leading to the influence attributed to him in the emergence of structural realism later in the century.[20] The

---

[14] Ibid., 12.
[15] *Futurist Manifestos*, ed. Umbro Apollonio (Boston: MFA, 2001), 22.
[16] Gary Gutting, *French Philosophy in the Twentieth Century* (Cambridge: Cambridge University Press, 2001), 27.
[17] Ibid.
[18] Gerhard Heinzmann and David Stump, "Henri Poincaré," in *The Stanford Encyclopedia of Philosophy*, ed. Edward N. Zalta, online, accessed December 6, 2021: https://plato.stanford.edu/entries/poincare/.
[19] Ibid.
[20] Ibid.

"modernist character" of Poincaré's scientific thinking is already a distinctive feature of his 1902 work *Science and Hypothesis*, a work whose influence on modernist pictorial art makes it exemplary in relation to the interplay between fundamental philosophy, science, and aesthetics being highlighted here.[21]

On the face of it, Poincaré's position appears to be Kantian and his relational ontology clearly points to a separation between what is knowable and what will always be unknowable: "the things themselves are not what [science] can reach ... but only the relations between things. Outside of these relations there is no knowable reality."[22] This would be consistent also with his conventionalism and his self-avowed constructivism as when he insists that "the first principles of geometry are conventions" or that "[m]athematicians proceed ... 'by construction.'"[23] This neo-Kantian character of Poincaré's thinking needs to be qualified, however. As Gutting points out, he was without doubt influenced to a large degree by the Kantianism of his milieu but, while his conventionalism clearly gives the activity of the human mind a central role in the constitution of empirical objects and truth, his work derives from reflections on scientific experimental practice rather than on purely abstract philosophical reflection and his "a priori categories ... are more a function of pragmatic utility than of transcendental conditions of experience."[24] This is very significant since it indicates that there is a distinct absence of idealism and philosophical foundationalism in Poincaré's conventionalism. The axioms of geometry, Poincaré notes, "are *conventions*; our choice among all possible conventions is *guided* by experimental facts; but it remains *free* and is limited only by the necessity of avoiding all contradiction."[25] In fact, rather than an idealism or a priori philosophical foundationalism, there appears to be a realist pragmatism at play here in which the choice of convention, the empirical real, and an applied rationality that abhors contradiction combine to co-constitute the object of scientific knowledge. Importantly, Poincaré does not appear to be interested in the laying of metaphysical or universal a priori foundations.

Indeed, he is clear that when it comes to space and the location of points or objects in space there is no primitive orientation or absolute positioning of said points or objects. All that can be said of these arises from the axioms we ourselves have chosen. Poincaré says of the positioning of bodies in space:

> among the data which enable us to define this position we shall, moreover, distinguish the mutual distance of these bodies, which define their relative positions, from the conditions which define the absolute position of the system and its absolute orientation in space.

---

[21] Henri Poincaré, *Science et hypothèse* (Paris: Flammarion, 1902), trans. George Bruce Halsted, *Science and Hypothesis*, in *The Foundations of Science* (Cambridge: Cambridge University Press, 2015 [1913]).
[22] Poincaré, *Science and Hypothesis*, 28.
[23] Ibid., 29, 41.
[24] Gutting, *French Philosophy*, 27.
[25] Poincaré, *Science and Hypothesis*, 65.

> The laws of the phenomenon which will happen in this system will depend on the state of these bodies and their mutual distances; but, because of the relativity and passivity of space, they will not depend on the absolute position and orientation of the system.
>
> In other words, the state of the bodies and their mutual distances at any instant will depend solely on the state of these same bodies and on their mutual distances at the initial instant, but will not at all depend on the absolute initial position of the system or on its absolute initial orientation. This is what for brevity I call *the law of relativity*.[26]

This absence of an originary, absolute, or primitive orientation within space implies an ontological equivalence between the multiplicity of new geometries and with this an irreducible absence of overarching or unitary metaphysical foundation. Geometry does not give us a truth about an already known object positioned in absolute space. Rather, as Heinzmann and Stump put it, Poincaré formulates a new view that "geometry does not express true or false propositions and that there are no special objects which geometry studies. Rather, geometry is just a system of relations that can be applied to many kinds of objects."[27] Here, in the context of scientific and pragmatic or experimentally oriented scientific theory, the key ingredients that have here been associated with the metaphysics of modernism are implicitly but unambiguously present: the fragmentation of unity, multiplicity, thoroughgoing relationalism, and along with all of these the absence of any primitive foundation or ground within being.

Poincaré's immediate reception within the sphere of philosophy of science and physics was variable and equivocal, as exemplified in Einstein's 1921 article "Geometry and Experience," in which Einstein endorses the ideal in-principle truth of his conventionalism but argues that not all contemporary physics is in accord with it.[28] His influence within the realm of wider modernist thought and aesthetics was far-reaching, however.

Perhaps the most important figure for the transmission of Poincaré's thought into modernist, avant-garde cultural circles was Maurice Princet, an insurance actuary born in 1875 who, according to the editors of *A Cubism Reader*, "was probably the source of the cubists' interests in the fourth dimension and non-Euclidean geometries, based on his reading of Poincaré's *Science and Hypothesis* (1902) and other mathematicians' works."[29] Specifically: "Before 1909 he conveyed his enthusiasm for the new mathematics to André Salmon, Guillaume Apollinaire, and Pablo Picasso."[30] Princet also influenced Albert Gleizes and Jean Metzinger, whose 1912 essay *Du "Cubisme"* was the first

---

[26] Ibid., 83.
[27] Heinzmann and Stump, "Henri Poincaré."
[28] Albert Einstein, "Geometry and Experience," in *Sidelights on Relativity*, trans. George Barker Jeffery and Wilfrid Perrett (New York: Dover, 1983), 27–56. On this, see also Heinzmann and Stump, "Henri Poincaré."
[29] Mark Antliff and Patricia Leighten, *A Cubism Reader* (Chicago: Chicago University Press, 2008), 234.
[30] Ibid.

theoretical work on the movement and drew heavily on Poincaré's thinking and on the terminology of *Science and Hypothesis*. Gleizes and Metzinger note that, when it comes to pictorial form and pictorial space, "People have carelessly gotten into the habit of confusing that space with either pure visual space or with Euclidean space."[31] Indeed, they very explicitly align the techniques of cubism to non-Euclidean geometries: "If we wished to tie the painter's space to a particular geometry, we should have to refer it to the non-Euclidean scientists; should have to study at some length certain of Riemann's theorems."[32]

In assimilating Poincaré alongside other well-known influences on modernism such as Nietzsche and Bergson, Gleizes and Metzinger are representative of a broader theoretical consensus that was shared amongst critics as well as practicing artists of the time.[33] To this extent, they are indicative of the way in which, throughout the period of the early twentieth-century modernist avant-gardes, renewed philosophical and scientific understandings of space and time informed innovations in aesthetic form. Nietzschean becoming and Bergsonian *durée*, combined with Poincaré's conventionalist defense of non-Euclidean geometries and Einstein-Minkowski spacetime, contributed to the emergence of not just cubist pictorial technique but also variably to Delaunay's simultanism or the stream of consciousness techniques within novels that align narration with the duration of first-person internal time consciousness.

This combination or coming together of elements drawn from philosophy, science, and art is not a unifying synthesis of these distinct domains but rather a confluence which gives rise to an open-ended and experimental proliferation of new forms and ways of grasping, conceptualizing, and representing reality on multiple, at times incommensurate levels, based on a profound recognition that reality itself is irreducibly incommensurable. Nor is it just, as Bell indicates, "an analogical application" of new scientific theory "to other, nonscientific spheres."[34] What is perhaps at stake here, decisively, is the way in which philosophical discourse, scientific theory and experiment, and aesthetic production can all be understood as different techniques. Insofar as they apprehend different aspects of a fragmented, multiple, and non-unified reality, they are themselves irreducibly plural. In turn, with each technique being able to influence the other in an open-ended way, they are able to invent further experimental techniques and further images or representations of what one might ultimately call a "plural real." In his introduction to *The Cambridge Companion to Modernism*, Michael Levenson attributes "the recurrent act of fragmenting unities" to the common devices of modernism but also to a general preoccupation with "technique." By "technique" here is to be understood the material technicity of any given form, that is, not just its formal aspects in relation to "content," but rather the fact that "every element of the work is an instrument of its effect and therefore open to technical revision."[35] This

---

[31] Ibid., 423.
[32] Ibid., 424; translation modified.
[33] Ibid., 438.
[34] Bell, "The Metaphysics of Modernism," 11.
[35] Levenson, "Introduction," in *The Cambridge Companion to Modernism*, 3.

recognition of the material technicity of aesthetic forms leads Levenson to ascribe to modernist culture a "regime of technique" and a "passion for technique."[36] Arguably then, the notion of technique understood as material technicity of aesthetic form which is declined always in the plural (paint, canvas, framing, brushwork or typographic print forms, celluloid, and so on) offers the key to understanding the way in which, within modernism, the fragmentation, plurality, relationality, and groundlessness of being were both experienced and represented.

"Phenomenotechnique": Realism at the Limit

That a concern with technique and technical production is not limited to the aesthetic sphere alone but also emerges clearly within philosophy and the philosophy of science becomes evident in the thought of the most prominent French philosopher of science of the interwar years, Gaston Bachelard.[37] Already at this point in the discussion it might be possible to retroactively assimilate the notion of technique to the pluralization of geometry beyond its Euclidean form, to apply it to Poincaré, and thereby to speak of "techniques of space" in relation to the new geometries. Bachelard's work itself is firmly rooted back within the tradition associated with Poincaré (as well as Émile Meyerson and Émile Boutroux) and his concept of "phénoménotechnique" can also be understood as a critical response to the conventionalism of Pierre Duhem and Édouard Le Roy.[38] Bachelard influenced diverse later French thinkers such as Michel Foucault, Louis Althusser, Jacques Derrida, and Pierre Bourdieu. His immediate philosophical inheritor and successor Georges Canguilhem likewise exerted a decisive influence on all these, more broadly being a key figure in the rise of French structuralism, and specifically being an important, albeit somewhat hidden, influence on Nancy himself.[39] In this way, Bachelard can be taken as a key staging post, within the interwar years, in a trajectory that leads from Poincaré's modernism, through to the structuralist, poststructuralist, and postmodernist thinkers of the postwar decades, and then on to Nancy in the last decades of the twentieth century and first decades of the twenty-first.

Bachelard's 1934 work *Le Nouvel Esprit scientifique* (*The New Scientific Spirit*) contains many of the key elements that have been encountered in the context of

---

[36] Ibid., 3, 5.
[37] This concern with technicity and technique is representative of a wider philosophical critique of instrumental rationality within modernity. For a synoptic account of this, see James, "Tekhnē," *The Oxford Research Encyclopaedia of Literature*, February 2019, online, accessed December 6, 2021: https://oxfordre.com/literature/ view/10.1093/acrefore/9780190201098.001.0001/acrefore-9780190201098-e-121.
[38] See Gutting, *French Philosophy*, 85. See also, Lucie Fabry, "Phenomenotechnique: Bachelard's Critical Inheritance of Conventionalism," *Studies in the History of Philosophy of Science Part A* 75 (June 2019): 34–42.
[39] For an extended discussion and analysis of Nancy's thinking in his confluence with that of Canguilhem, see James, *The Technique of Thought*, 75–90. Nancy has acknowledged his debt to Canguilhem in a recent special issue of the review *Angelaki* that has been dedicated to his thought; see James, "Affectivity, Sense, and Affects," *Angelaki* 26, nos. 3–4 (2021): 155–61, 161.

Poincaré and pre-First World War modernist, avant-garde activity. So, for instance, he affirms that scientific "experimentation is always dependent on some prior intellectual construct" in a manner that clearly echoes Poincaré and the conventionalist position.[40] He also affirms that the plural relationality of given phenomena requires a plurality of method or technique: "When the object under study takes the form of a complex system of relations, then it can only be apprehended by adopting an appropriate variety of methods."[41] Similarly, Bachelard, like Poincaré, sees in mathematics and geometry a purely relational way of knowing space: "Put simply, algebra contains all relations and nothing but relations. The equivalence of different geometries is defined in terms of relations, and it is as relations that geometries have reality, not by reference to any object, experience, or intuition."[42] This in turn leads him to affirm that fundamental (i.e., quantum) reality is itself purely relational and not composed of objects or things, as when he argues that "objects only have reality in their relations"[43] or that it is "necessary to renounce the notion of object or thing, at least in the study of the atomic world."[44] In Bachelard's universe, then, there are no primitive substances or substantive entities that would ground our understanding of the being of being, only relational forms.[45] Finally, and as a result of this, Bachelard also affirms the necessity of technique as a means of approaching reality: "In this way the qualities of the scientific real are, in the first instance, functions of our rational methods. In order to constitute a definite scientific fact, a coherent technique needs to be implemented."[46]

The emphasis on "some prior intellectual construct" in relation to scientific experimentation and the implementation of "coherent technique" in the production and constitution of scientific facts might make one think, as was initially the case with Poincaré, that Bachelard's position is unambiguously Kantian. However, as Dominique Lecourt has pointed out, Bachelard's position is in fact radically anti-Kantian and, in a perhaps unusual manner, realist and objectivist.[47] What is at stake here is, to use Bachelard own denomination, an "applied rationalism" according to which objective scientific knowledge is constituted in a dialectic between a non-human, independent real that imposes itself on our experience and upon the rational constructions or conventions that are embodied in material, experimental technologies and techniques.

---

[40] Gaston Bachelard, *Le Nouvel Esprit scientifique* (Paris: Presses Universitaires de France, 1934), trans. Arthur Goldhammer, *The New Scientific Spirit* (Boston: Beacon Press, 1984), 41.
[41] Ibid., 12.
[42] Ibid., 29.
[43] Ibid., 132.
[44] Marcel Boll, *L'Idée générale de la mécanique ondulatoire et de ses premières explications* (Paris: Hermann, 1932), 32; quoted in Bachelard, *The New Scientific Spirit*, 128; translation modified.
[45] Bachelard emphatically repeats his rejection of the notion of objective individuality and of the categories of substance and unity in a later work, *La Philosophie du non. Essai d'une philosophie du nouvel esprit scientifique* (Paris: Presses Universitaires de France, 1940), 64, 90, 93; trans. G. C. Waterston, *The Philosophy of No: A Philosophy of the New Scientific Mind* (New York: The Orion Press, 1968), 54–55, 76, 78–79.
[46] Bachelard, *The New Scientific Spirit*, 171; translation modified.
[47] Dominique Lecourt, *Bachelard ou le jour et la nuit. Un essai du matérialisme dialectique* (Paris: Grasset, 1974), 62, 88.

In his 1949 work, *Le Rationalisme appliqué* (*Applied Rationalism*), Bachelard redefines the Kantian noumenal and suggests that the real, far from being unknowable, is always imposing itself as a corrective to our existing constructs and is known in and through the production of phenomena that result from those corrections. As he himself puts it: "The real is a mass of objections to already constituted reason."[48] This, then, is not an idealism, and it is here that the notion of "phenomenotechnique" takes on a decisive importance. For Bachelard, scientific knowledge and its objects are experimentally produced in a combination of abstract and rational (that is: theoretical or mathematical) form and experimental-technical activity: "All primary experimentation must first be *transposed* into a domain of rationality in order to then be *re-posed* as an element of a realist technique."[49]

In this context, the noumenal is not understood as an unknowable Kantian thing-in-itself but rather as a rationally (theoretically, mathematically) knowable objective reality that is given phenomenal and material form in an experimental situation. So when we observe a quantum event, or subatomic wave or particle, such phenomena are, insofar as they are not in any way available to ordinary perception, both objective and real *and* the production of the mathematical theory that has conceived them along with the technical apparatus used to perceive them as such. They are at once objectively real and rationally technically produced in such a way that Bachelard would understand the mathematics of quantum theory and mechanics as "the noumenal preparation of technically constituted phenomena" and would insist that quantum phenomena must therefore be "technically produced" and that they are in this way "reified theorems."[50] This, clearly, is not at all Kantian insofar as Bachelard's understanding of "phenomenotechnique" combines prior rational constructions that are contingent and conventional (and not transcendental conditions) with the technical production of empirically observable phenomena. In the domain of phenomenotechnique "one thinks before realizing, in order to realize. The noumenon is an *object* of thought just as the phenomenon is an *object* of perception" and in this way: "With phenomenotechnique … everything is developed according to an applied rationalism."[51]

Although *Le Rationalisme appliqué* is published in 1949, the concept of phenomenotechnique dates back to the early 1930s and is elaborated in response to the new quantum physics in a manner similar to Poincaré's elaboration of conventionalism in response to the new non-Euclidean geometries. So in the short essay "Noumenon and Microphysics," published in the 1931-2 edition of *Recherches philosophiques*, Bachelard explicitly notes that the mathematical formalism of quantum mechanics is a "noumenology" and one which "clarifies a phenomenotechnique by means of which new phenomena are not simply found, but invented and completely constructed."[52]

---

[48] Gaston Bachelard, *Le Rationalisme appliqué* (Paris: Presses Universitaires de France, 1949), 65. My translation.
[49] Ibid., 125.
[50] Ibid., 103.
[51] Ibid., 168, 169.
[52] Gaston Bachelard, "Noumène et microphysique," *Recherches philosophiques* 1 (1931–1932): 55–65. Reprinted in Bachelard, *Études* (Paris: Vrin, 2002), 11–22, 18. My translation.

Again, this might point to a thoroughgoing constructivism rather than a realism, but one might also say that, being completely constructed, new phenomena may *not simply* be found but that they *do uncover* an independent reality that in this construction *is* nevertheless objectively found. Dominique Lecourt puts this in the following terms: "Bachelard proposes without equivocation the thesis that the truth of scientific truth 'imposes itself' by itself; this means that it does not need to wait for a philosophical 'foundation' or 'guarantee'. Scientific knowledge as such is scientific, it is objective."[53] What this means is that Bachelard does not impose an idea of the limits of knowledge or a separation between the phenomenal and the noumenal that would be discerned and legislated upon by philosophy as it is in Kant. Insofar as science reflects upon itself and becomes philosophy of science, then, it "must in a certain way systematically destroy the limits that traditional philosophy has imposed upon science."[54] In this way, Bachelard develops an understanding of scientific activity which proceeds without metaphysical or philosophical foundations to produce objective and realist knowledge of the real through the multiple contingent constructions of its rational forms and experimental techniques. It also does this without regard to any philosophical demarcation of epistemological frontiers or limits. As such, science and scientific experimentation in a certain manner always work at a limit or frontier, that between the known and unknown. They are a kind of un-grounded but realist limit practice in which both sides of the limit of knowledge are always at play: "Only science is used to tracing its own frontiers. For the scientific spirit, to trace a distinctive frontier is already to exceed it."[55]

Despite their differences, Bachelard's thinking resonates with key elements of Poincaré's position: relationalism, metaphysical non-foundationalism, a non-idealist thought that responds to a plural real in a plurality of technique. When taken together with Bachelard's characterization of science as a practice at the limit of thought, these elements may all sound quite familiar to readers of Nancy. In this way they give a clear sense of a modulated line of scientific thought and cultural practice that runs from Poincaré and the modernist avant-gardes through to Bachelard (and his successor Canguilhem) and then through to core Nancean concerns: the preoccupation with ontological ungroundedness, the relationality and singular plurality of being, the practice of philosophy at the limit.

What is perhaps most important in the context of this modulated line of thought and culture is the way in which the understanding of the real as plural and the multiplicity of technique that this necessitates implies not only a realism of thought and knowledge but also an absence of hierarchy between scientific technique, on the one hand, and artistic technique, on the other. It could be argued here that this trajectory of scientific and artistic modernism that runs from Poincaré to Bachelard is antithetical to

---

[53] Lecourt, *Bachelard*, 66. My translation.
[54] Gaston Bachelard, "Critique préliminaire du concept de frontière épistémologique," in *Études* (Paris: Vrin, 2002), 76. This is also where Bachelard sharply differs from some of the conventionalist thinkers who precede him such as Duhem and Leroy; on this see Fabry, "Phenomenotechnique."
[55] Bachelard, "Critique préliminaire du concept de frontière épistémologique," 71.

scient*ism*, that is to say, the notion that scientific knowledge can exhaustively describe reality and human being in its entirety, without remainder, and in a coherent unity that would leave no ontological authority for other ways of knowing or presenting the real.

Bachelard's later work on aesthetics bears this out. In *Poetics of Space*, for instance, he draws on Eugène Minkowski's notion of *reverberation*, a concept that articulates a profoundly relational understanding of the physical universe and the manner in which different elements of reality resonate with each other. Bachelard does so in order to describe the status of the poetic image.[56] Invoking Minkowski's phenomenology, Bachelard finds in reverberation a means of understanding "the real measure of the being of the poetic image," namely that the poet "speaks on the threshold of being" and that "[t]he poetic image places us at the origin of the speaking being."[57] Where scientific phenomenotechnique involves the production of real objective knowledge and truth in relation to the being of the physical universe through a constant tracing and exceeding of the limit between the known and the unknown, so the poetic image occupies a limit-point between the logic of the speaking (human-)being and being. Both poetic images and scientific experimentation here could be called "techniques of the real," each taking a measure of the real in a different manner within a plural non-hierarchical regime of technique.

The Modernist Legacy

This discussion began with Bell's observation that the change from modernism to postmodernism is not a radical break but a difference of stages "in the digestion of the same metaphysic." Leaving aside the fact that the modernism highlighted here is characterized by an abandonment of metaphysical foundationalism as such, one might also wish to highlight the differences of "digestion" that are at stake in these two stages.

So, somewhat schematically, it might be noted that modernist artworks and aesthetic theory often appealed, albeit equivocally or in a mode of self-conscious failure, to myth, to syncretism, and to a horizon of synthesis as a means of overcoming the experience of fragmentation, disunity, and abyssal disorientation. In this context one might cite, amongst others, Guillaume Apollinaire's synthesis of Christian and pagan motifs in the early section of *Zone*, T. S. Eliot's appeal to Hindu myth at the end of *The Waste Land*, André Breton's Hegelian evocation of the "surreal" as a synthesis of opposites in *The Second Manifesto of Surrealism*, or Thomas Mann's extensive exploration of myth in the *Joseph and His Brothers* quartet. In postwar aesthetic contexts one might discern,

---

[56] Eugène Minkowski, "Retentir (L'auditif)," *Vers une cosmologie. Fragments philosophiques* (Paris: Éditions Payot et Rivages, 1999 [1st edition, Aubier-Montaigne, 1936]), trans. Deborah Bouchette, "To Reverberate," 2018, online, accessed December 6, 2021: https://www.researchgate.net/publication/323675730_Minkowski_Eugene-To_Reverberate_Retentir_translated_by_Deborah_Bouchette_copyright_2018. Although Bachelard speaks of the poetic image, the concept of *reverberation* would allow his arguments to be extended to all kinds of aesthetic images and forms.

[57] Gaston Bachelard, *Poétique de l'espace* (Paris: Presses universitaires de France, 1957), trans. Maria Jolas, *Poetics of Space* (New York: Penguin, 2014), 2, 8.

on the contrary, a radicalization of fragmentary form that is shorn of any attempt at the restoration of unity (in the French Nouveau Roman, for instance, in exemplary or iconic authors such as Thomas Pynchon, or in the painting of American abstract impressionism).

In philosophy, a similar shift can be discerned. In this context, it might be noted that the pre-Second World War emphasis on the "vital" of Bergson's "élan vital," or the voluntarism of Nietzsche's "will to power" both came to be associated with the possibility of creating or returning to more unified organic forms, with notions of life-force and the collective will of national identity, politicized notions that would be discredited in the cultural-political aftermath of the 1930s and 1940s. In the postwar period, the legacy of Bergson and Nietzsche was taken up by thinkers such as Gilles Deleuze in an affirmation of pluralized and impersonal becoming rather than life-force, and through his engagement with eternal recurrence rather than with will to power. Configurations of organic identity and the regressive affects of national community are, for evident historical reasons, absent from postwar, postmodernist thought and Deleuze's thinking is exemplary in this regard insofar as it privileges "active" over "reactive" forces and affirms a decomposition of subjectivity and identity.[58]

In a similar vein, the emphasis we find in Heidegger's thinking of the 1930s on figures of sheltering, oneness, originary gathering, and "enowning" (*Ereignis*) gives way in Derrida's thinking to motifs of *différance*, dissemination, and originary dispersal.[59] It is as if the response to the abyssal ungroundedness of being (the Heideggerian *abgründlich*) shifts from its attempted overcoming in a centripetal drawing together of thought in the poetic saying of being (Beyng/*Seyn*) in Heidegger to the affirmation of a radically centrifugal scattering of being in Derrida according to which the very use of the term and any possibility of ontology are suspended or placed under erasure.

This "digestive" shift from equivocal or failed attempts at synthesis in art and, in philosophy, from organic life-force to impersonal becoming or from centripetal gathering to centrifugal scattering is, however, not reflected in the postwar legacy of Poincaré or that of the modernist posture of science that has been evoked here. Poincaré, it was noted earlier, was hugely influential on the later analytic philosophy of science tradition. From the perspective of contemporary debate, he is perhaps most clearly noted as the founder of structural realism and its legacy in ontic structural realism.

---

[58] See for instance Gilles Deleuze, *Nietzsche et la philosophie* (Paris: Presses Universitaires de France, 1965), trans. Hugh Tomlinson, *Nietzsche and Philosophy* (New York: Columbia University Press, 1983); *Différence et répétition* (Paris: Presses Universitaires de France, 1968), trans. Paul Patton, *Difference and Repetition* (New York: Columbia University Press, 1994). For an account of the shift in interest from the doctrine of will to power to that of eternal recurrence, see Douglas Smith, *Transvaluations: Nietzsche in France 1872–1972* (Oxford: Clarendon, 1996).

[59] See Martin Heidegger, *Contributions to Philosophy (of Enowning)*, trans. Parvis Emad and Kenneth Maly (Cambridge: Cambridge University Press, 1998), 138. See also Jacques Derrida, *De la grammatologie* (Paris: Minuit, 1968), trans. Gayatri Spivak, *Of Grammatology* (Baltimore: Johns Hopkins University Press, 1998) and *La Dissémination* (Paris: Seuil, 1972), trans. Barbara Johnson, *Dissemination* (London: Athlone, 1981).

In his highly influential 1989 article, "Structural Realism: The Best of Both Worlds," John Worral argues that Poincaré's mathematical relationalism offers a realism which runs counter to the anti-realist instrumentalism that, he claims, has often been attributed to him.[60] This is because, Worral argues, Poincaré's approach, insofar as it insists that relations are all we can know of the physical universe, is successful in accounting for both the predictive successes of theories and the survival of mathematical equations across the changes from one scientific theory to another. Worral points to Poincaré's discussion of theory change in *Science and Hypothesis* and in particular to his discussion of Fresnal and Maxwell. While the theoretical assumptions underpinning their different perspectives may have radically altered, Poincaré notes: "The differential equations are always true; they can always be integrated by the same procedures and the results of this integration always retain their value."[61]

So structural realism, as defended by Worral and attributed by him to Poincaré, argues that the relational knowledge of mathematics gives us knowledge of the real structure of the universe. Mathematical structure and real physical structure are therefore assumed to be non-contingently isomorphic and this is why science can predict from theoretical-mathematical hypotheses how the universe will behave and also why equations survive theory change.

It was argued earlier that Poincaré conventionalism was not really Kantian but rather a pragmatic realism that combined convention, empirical content, and rationality but which avoided metaphysical foundationalism or idealism. While Worral's defense of structural realism is not devoid of empirical reference insofar as it insists that "ultimately evidence leads the way," the isomorphism he poses between mathematical relations and the physical real does allow him to posit the existence of theoretical "primitives" and to attribute this also to Poincaré in a manner which runs against the geometrical conventionalism that was described above as a key characteristic of his thinking.[62] Thus, where earlier it was argued that Poincaré's conventionalism was plural and not subject to any overarching unity or metaphysical ground, Worral's argument relating to the survival of equations across theory change arguably represents a marginalizing of Poincaré's conventionalism, which holds that there is no pre-axiomatic understanding of *geometric* primitives. It moves structural realism toward something that might begin to resemble a mathematical idealism and opens the possibility of posing a philosophically and scientifically grounded and unified account of the physical universe. This, of course, runs directly counter to the emphasis on ungroundedness, fragmentation, and multiplicity that has been shown to characterize Poincaré's modernism and its legacy.

---

[60] John Worral, "Structural Realism: The Best of Both Worlds?," *Dialectica* 43, nos. 1–2 (1989): 99–124, 117.
[61] Poincaré, *Science and Hypothesis*, 140.
[62] Worral, "Structural Realism," 123, 122.

"Struction in a Void": Nancy, Barrau, and the "More Than One"

If Worral's structural realism represents a turning away from the modernist legacy of Poincaré's thought, its development into the "ontic structural realism" championed by James Ladyman and Don Ross in *Every Thing Must Go* represents its complete abandonment.[63] In direct contrast, Nancy and Barrau's *What's These Worlds Coming To?* can be seen to carry forward and further develop all the key aspects of the trajectory of modernist science that has been sketched out here in relation to both Poincaré and Bachelard.[64]

The two key concepts that structure the dialogue between Nancy and Barrau in *What's These Worlds*, "more than one" [plus d'un] and "struction," also resonate strongly with Nancy's philosophy as a whole. So the "more than one" for Nancy is thought in terms of a questioning of the figure of the "One" such as it has been deployed within European philosophy from its pre-Socratic origin in Heraclitus onwards. The "One" at stake here is the unity and totality that philosophy and cosmology have, across the European tradition, ascribed in different ways to the concepts of world, cosmos, and being. Nancy glosses the (now decapitalized) "more than one" in terms that recall his thinking of the singular plural. So, a given singular is one but only insofar as it is in relation to another singular, and that to another in such a way that any possibility of posing the one is always also implying a more than one. A singular is an inherently relational entity simply because it can only exist as such by way of its differential relation to another singular. The singular one, therefore, "is the transporting of itself and out of itself ... Each singular is itself 'one' in this sense: in that it repeats the initial transporting ... as it is itself a prelude to other profusions."[65] The constitution of a singular can only take place in an unlimited profusion and proliferation of relation.

In this way Nancy suggests that any unity we give to the world must always be of the order of this unlimited profusion. Being and beings are, once more, always, and necessarily, declined in the singular plural. Barrau ripostes by transposing the "more than one" into the domain of science and by suggesting that if the one is always *more* than one, then it is always also *less* than one insofar as it can never be posed as a closed, unified, and unique totality. This is true, he argues, in the current state of contemporary theoretical physics and particularly in relation to the notion of a "law" of physics. The existence and diversity of symmetry breaks, for Barrau, radically undermine the notion of universal law: "symmetries are indeed shattered. That they can be shattered in several ways and that this diversity is not at all insignificant. That

---

[63] James Ladyman and Don Ross, *Every Thing Must Go* (Oxford: Oxford University Press, 2007). Interestingly, Ladyman and Ross also dispute Worral's characterization of Poincaré as a structural realist, 123.

[64] For a more extended comparative discussion of Nancy and Ladyman and Ross, see James, *The Technique of Thought*, 61–71.

[65] Nancy and Barrau, *What's These Worlds Coming To?*, 19.

laws, therefore, reemerge as simple, environmental parameters: a contingency lying at the heart of formal necessity."[66]

Such a loss of unitary and universal laws within physics is accompanied by a profusion of theories in a manner which exemplifies the "more than one" in relation to the physical universe: "The profusion of complementary theories," Barrau writes, "contributes to the plural, numeric, and numeral dynamic of the 'more than one.'"[67] This suggests an irreducible disunity that is characteristic of science as a whole and is borne out in "the co-existence of models that pertain to the *same* phenomena."[68] In this regard, Barrau cites a number of theories relating to quantum gravity, all of which offer variable and differing explanations of the same observational results. This leads him to conclude, with regard to the multiplicity of theories within fundamental physics, that "no model can be absolutely and eternally correct."[69] This emphasis on the plurality and contingency of scientific theories and models is entirely consistent with Nancy's thinking of the singular plural, with the plural character of Poincaré's conventionalism, and with Bachelard's emphasis on a necessary multiplicity of method or technique.

It is entirely incompatible, however, with Worral's account of mathematical continuity across theory change and with his (mis)appropriation of Poincaré as a founder of structural realism. As an inheritance from Worral, the ontic structural realism of Ladyman and Ross appears in stark and distinctly un-modernist contrast to Nancy and Barrau. In *Every Thing Must Go*, ontic structural realism emerges on one level as quite similar to the relationalism of Poincaré and Bachelard. Like Bachelard, they draw on quantum theory, to argue that "relational structure is ontologically fundamental," and that "individuals are nothing over and above the nexus of relations in which they stand."[70]

Here, however, the similarity between Ladyman and Ross and the modernist science of Poincaré and Bachelard ends rather sharply. Like Worral, they posit an isomorphism between mathematical relational structure and real physical structure in order to affirm a metaphysical, scientific realism. This comes with an ambition for a total scientific knowledge of the universe and its contents alongside an insistence that whatever cannot be known scientifically is, from the perspective of ultimate metaphysical reality at least, nonexistent. As they themselves put it: "Science respects no domain restrictions and will admit no epistemological rivals ... scientific institutional processes are absolutely and exclusively authoritative."[71]

On this basis, Ladyman and Ross defend a scientistic metaphysics that affirms the unity of both science and cosmos. Ontic structural realism, they argue, "is the

---

[66] Ibid., 35. Symmetry breaking refers to fluctuations acting on a physical system that determine the fate of the system. As fluctuations that are unpredictable and apparently arbitrary, symmetry breaking, Barrau is arguing, runs counter to the idea of a deterministically unfolding universal law.
[67] Ibid., 36.
[68] Ibid.
[69] Ibid., 37.
[70] Ladyman and Ross, *Every Thing Must Go*, 130, 138.
[71] Ibid., 28.

hypothesis that science provides a unified account of the world by modelling structures" and their underlying argument is that it should aim to provide the "metaphysical glue" that will undergird the greater unity of science as a whole.[72]

If it is true that the shift from modernism to postmodernism involved a radicalization of fragmentation and multiplicity into a more pronounced scattering and dispersal of being that was shorn of residual attempts to restore unity and synthesis, then the pluralism of Nancy and Barrau in *What's These Worlds* can be seen as a culmination of the line of modernist science that runs through Poincaré and Bachelard into contemporary thought. By contrast, Ladyman and Ross's ontic structural realism, despite its relationalism, offers an un-modernist image of physical and metaphysical unity which is given a full philosophical foundation in mathematical realism and what comes very close to Platonism.[73]

These contrasting positions, it could be argued, represent a fault-line within recent and contemporary philosophy of science which opposes ontological disunity and plurality to metaphysical unity and totality. Opposed here, then, are an open, pragmatic, and experimental realism that carries forward the legacy of modernist science and at times Platonistic or quasi-theological scientism that seeks the closure of total unified knowledge.[74]

The anti-metaphysical, anti-foundationalist posture of Nancy and Barrau is summed up in the concept of "struction," which once again, and for one final time, returns this discussion to the modernist preoccupation with technique, technicity, and technology. Technicity or technique (*la technique*), Nancy argues, is not an artificial supplement to physical nature but rather "has a place within nature," it is "one of nature's ends because it is from nature that the animal capable of ... technology is born."[75] Human technical capacity, its invention of art, technology, science and the diverse techniques proper to each, is understood here as an extension of nature. As Nancy puts it: "We have been inserting ourselves into a technosphere"[76] and on this basis all human activity or production, artistic, scientific, but also social, cultural, political and economic, should be understood in the mode of technical "struction" which prolongs the profusion of physical nature into our own distinct sphere. This is no longer the perspective of constructivism where forms are made according to all too human-centered artifice because the human is no longer centered on itself but is rather dispersed back into the natural world that precedes it. Nor is it the perspective of deconstruction where forms are disarticulated, exposed in their groundlessness and rethought outside of the

---

[72] Ibid., 251, 275.
[73] Ibid., 236–37.
[74] For discussions of recent and contemporary thinkers who might be placed on either side of this fault-line (Lee Smolin, Bernard d'Espagnat, Nancy Cartwright, John Dupré on the one side and David Wallace, or Paul and Patricia Churchland on the other) see James, *The Technique of Thought*, 95–113, 140–56, 159, 72, 181–84.
[75] Nancy and Barrau, *What's These Worlds Coming To?*, 43. This insight can be seen as a further development of Georges Canguilhem's concept of "technical life" and as an extension of Nancy's thinking of "ecotechnics."
[76] Ibid., 57.

hierarchy of their constitutive oppositions. Rather, "struction" is an ungrounded and fragmentary production that arises from a plural technicity or technique: "Struction offers a dis-order that is neither the contrary nor the destruction or ruin of order: It is situated somewhere else in what we call contingency, fortuity, dispersion, or errancy."[77]

***

This discussion of modernism and science began with the decomposition of world into worlds, and the experience of fragmentation, multiplicity, and ungroundedness in both science, philosophy, and art. It ends with the singular plurality of the "more-than-one," and the dis-order of "struction" as articulations of contingency, fortuity, dispersion, and errancy. If "struction" and the "more than one" can be viewed as intensifications or a radicalization of modernist fragmentation, what is also carried over from one to the other is "the regime of technique." The "regime of technique" can be traced along the modulated line that passes from "techniques of space" in Poincaré and modernist aesthetics, through to Bachelard's "phenomenotechnique," and then to Nancean ecotechnics and his affirmation of technical life as an unlimited profusion. This line has not been traced in order to express a nostalgia for the experimental openness and ontological pluralism of modernist technique, nor simply to glorify its vestiges or remains. Rather, it has been traced in order to pose the question of whether the legacy of modernism within contemporary scientific thought and Nancean philosophy is in fact best placed to help us in the twenty-first century to confront what one might call the infinitude of our finitude: the limitations and limits, but also the unbounded multiplicity, of shared biological life. Will a metaphysical, idealist, and totalizing desire for unity and (re)foundation within scientific knowledge, but also within philosophical, aesthetic, and cultural or political forms, best help us to respond to the challenges of the present and of the coming decades? Or will a pragmatic and plural realism that takes up the modernist legacy be better placed to do so according to a posture that views science as one technique amongst others with which we can know and understand the multiple dimensions of the world and our place within it? This modernist legacy such as it has been identified here tells us that only a plurality of technique across philosophy, science, art, and indeed any other realm can allow us to account for and respond to an irreducibly plural real. What Nancy and his modernist inheritance may show us is that we need to abandon our illusions of human finality and total mastery once and for all, embrace our groundlessness, and proceed according to the "struction in a void" that is the regime of technique.

---

[77] Ibid., 54.

12

Le fond du film: Worlds, Images, and the Machining of Grounds (or: Blanchot Not/Beyond Nancy)

Jeff Fort

Ultimately, all that we have called "matter" and "life" as well as "nature," "god," "history," and "humankind" has fallen into the same grave.
— Jean-Luc Nancy, "Of Struction"

... "artificial intelligence" (a tautology perhaps?) ...
— Jean-Luc Nancy, "Of Struction"[1]

One of the most important senses in which Jean-Luc Nancy's work and thought can be linked with modernism may be indicated as follows: this work sets out to think transcendence in entirely worldly terms. This is of course also an essential aspect of its Heideggerian inspiration, an aspect which in Heidegger's early work can be situated squarely within the heart of modernism, indeed of "high modernism," considered as an epochal frame, a period, and a mode of experience or reflection. *Being and Time*, published in the late 1920s as an open confrontation with mass society (urbanized, industrialized, technified, mechanized, and above all standardized society), and thus as an attempt to articulate within that context the possibility of authentic experience and unleveled singularity, is for these and other reasons something of a modernist classic. Nancy, of course, did not take up this "jargon of authenticity" from Heidegger, recognizing as any critical reader must (and as Adorno certainly did) that such talk is itself the height of inauthenticity, or rather that by now the very category has been more or less liquidated, for reasons that we will touch on later.[2] Nancy did, however, take

---

[1] These quotations are found in Jean-Luc Nancy and Aurélien Barrau, *What's These Worlds Coming To?*, trans. Travis Holloway and Flor Méchain (New York: Fordham University Press, 2015), 55 and 98n9, respectively. Nancy's texts (with a couple of exceptions) will be cited here with references to both French and English. Translations have occasionally been silently modified in order to provide more literal readings when needed.

[2] I am referring of course to Theodor Adorno's *The Jargon of Authenticity*, trans. Knut Tarnowski and Frederic Will (Evanston: Northwestern University Press, 1973), first published in German in 1964.

very seriously the imperative to think the question of "world," and he brought to this task certain of the remnants, one might say, of the para-phenomenological structures that Heidegger had laid out, including "finite transcendence" above all. That is (to put it somewhat obliquely): the sense that the world has nothing beyond it, but that world itself as such must comport a moment or dimension of originary opening, such that it does not simply coincide fully with itself as mere positive presence. Heidegger's name for this opening was of course *Dasein* or, as he preferred to write it later, *Da-sein*, thus setting off the "there" which opens the "in" (a relation not to be understood as mere spatial containment) of our being in the world. Transcendence, for both Heidegger and Nancy (and despite the differences which the latter has long worked to elaborate), is simply this opening of the world which does not go beyond the world, but which makes the world as something constituted by a beyond that is "internal" to it, in the sense of an immanence that is also a limit. And in that sense, the world is necessarily and immanently structured by something that, to speak with Blanchot, takes a step/ not beyond: a step (*pas*) that somehow does and yet does *not* (*pas*) go beyond the world thus opened, a step "into"—or rather always being taken within—an opening which, it should be added immediately, Nancy prefers to speak of in the more localizing and less totalizing terms of spacing and exposure, just as he came to speak of transcendence more transversally, one might say, as *transimmanence*.

Now if I begin with this broad reminder, in order to situate Nancy's work in relation to modernism and to what in that work might still be considered residually modernist, it is to point to a particular dimension of this worldly transcendence—this difference of the world from itself that is entirely *of* the world, or this folding of what-is back onto or into its very own being-what-it-is—a dimension that has preoccupied Nancy for some twenty years or more, namely, that of images. For what are images if not the world's own internally resemblent alterity to itself? One might even say that images "open" or constitute a world of their own, and thus a fold or pocket of world that, while certainly not anything other than or outside the world, also do not quite entirely coincide with this world of which and in which they show themselves—and this by way of a constitutive disjunction which they *also* show. In this regard we can indeed see them as a distinctly visible mode of transcendence, and thus a preeminent way in which that transcendence shows itself as such. This is essentially the role, function, or presentative force that Nancy assigns to art in many of his texts.[3] To stress further a word I just used and which Nancy foregrounds in his writing on images, we can say that they make up something of a *distinct* spacing of the world, one that has a peculiar and deeply ambiguous relationship to the world it is (they are) *of*.[4] Nancy characterizes

---

[4] See "L'image—le distinct" in *Au fond des images*, 11–32; "The Image—the Distinct," in *The Ground of the Image*, 1–14.
[3] Beginning with *Les Muses* (Paris: Galilée, 2001 [1994]; hereafter *LM*), trans. Peggy Kamuf, *The Muses* (Stanford: University of Stanford Press, 1996; hereafter *M*) on art more generally, and passing through works on portraiture (*Le Regard du portrait* [Paris: Galilée, 2000], *L'Autre Portrait* [Paris: Galilée, 2014]), film (*L'Évidence du film / The Evidence of Film: Abbas Kiarostami*, multilingual edition, trans. Christine Irizarry and Verena Andermatt Conley [Brussels: Yves Gevaert, 2001]; hereafter *EF*), drawing (*Le Plaisir au dessin* [Paris: Galilée, 2009], trans. Philip Armstrong [New

this *distinction* as separation and framing, as a drawing up, detachment or "extraction" from a ground and a cutting out within a frame (see *FI*, 22; *GI*, 7). The ambiguity in question is condensed into this small word: what is the *of* here (or likewise, the *from*, which is the same in French: *de*…), in this image-space that is *of* the world? On the one hand, it marks provenance, location, continuity, appurtenance, and participation (a kind of constitutive *methexis*), as well as, on the other hand, something like resemblance, reflection, or reproduction, a relation that we can in turn condense into the term *mimesis*, as long as this term is properly complicated and qualified—precisely through a certain effective merging with *methexis*, and a consequent "grounding" of their difference in self-relation (and vice versa).[5] One purpose of the present analysis will be to indicate the convergence of these two modes, and to do so especially in terms of a *mimesis* that "covers" them both, that seeps from one to the other, and that undermines the ground of images as such (through immanent or "underground" forms of space that will have to be explored, such as a cave or a grave…), and especially our *sense* that this ground itself is in the end and entirely *of the world*. The possibly unworldly and even dangerous force and draw of the ground that images also show, and which may be *at bottom different* from the world that images are of (a difference that can in turn be called *mimesis*), may require a rethinking of the internal limits in question.

Image/ground, Nancy/Blanchot

Nancy's notion of a "ground" (*fond*) of images functions in multiple ways, in order to indicate a "background" in the sense of spatial depth or a ground-against-which specific forms or figures appear, as well as that of a broader world-space within or from which images as such are separated and framed, in such a way, Nancy says, as to bring the distancing of space at large into the intimacy of a single cut-out segment (*FI*, 27; *GI*, 10). The term also evokes the philosophical concept of a ground, a grounding *reason* in the sense of *ratio* or *Grund*, as when Heidegger interrogates *Der Satz vom Grund*, the

---

York: Fordham University Press, 2013]) and various other essays on painting and photography, including *Noli me tangere* (Paris: Galilée, 2003), which revolves around paintings that depict the biblical episode of the resurrection of Christ and the command with which he greets Mary Magdalene: "do not touch me." The figure of resurrection, or reanimation, will reappear at the end of the present essay through resonances with film that I will not be able to develop at any length, though *L'Évidence du film* may allow us to touch on a certain limit in Nancy's thinking on images. But as my title indicates, the commentary here is inspired especially by *Au fond des images* (Paris: Galilée, 2003; hereafter *FI*), a text I translated some years ago as *The Ground of the Image* (New York: Fordham University Press, 2005; hereafter *GI*), using a title that Nancy favored, though he regretted, as I did, both the loss of a certain localization (*au fond*…, *in* the ground, *at* [the] bottom…), and the reduction of the plural to the singular. This plurality of images in relation to (a) ground with its own peculiar spacing should be kept in mind.

[5] See Nancy, "L'image : mimesis & methexis," in *Penser l'image*, ed. Emmanuel Alloa (Dijon: Les presses du réel, 2010), 69–94; "The Image: Mimesis and Methexis," trans. Adrienne Janus, in *Nancy and Visual Culture* (Edinburgh: Edinburgh University Press, 2016), 73–92.

principle of (sufficient) reason—a meaning which remains rather in the background (so to speak) of Nancy's analyses of images, but which at the same time retains its interrogative force in relation to the grounding conditions of the elements in question (whether of the world itself or of the "subject" who vehiculates, forms, and/or is figured in images). The present discussion aims as well to indicate a point of convergence between these senses of ground—let's refer to them in shorthand as aesthetic and metaphysical—a necessarily unstable point where both categories are undermined by the bottomless pluralities that images in their originary dimensions set in motion. Now, in order to locate this convergent point, it will be necessary to radicalize Nancy's discourse around the first, the "aesthetic" sense of ground, whereby Nancy sees images as "distinct" and "separated" from their world by being "withdrawn from this world," as a world of things "considered as a world of availability," that is, a world "available to use" (*FI*, 27; *GI*, 10). While this sense does apply, the distinction and otherness of images to world as such that I mean to evoke goes further, not only neutralizing the use and availability of things (image-things, images as things turned into images), and exiting images from settled significations, but rendering them incommensurate, in a radical otherness that threatens worldliness and scrambles the very possibility of sense, even as it "grounds" this possibility within the limits of its operability. Put succinctly, and as a question: do images ruin the world or do they make it be the world that it is? The answer is that they do both, because images are not only separated off from a world out of which they are cut or formed into commensurate and continuous image fragments, but also because they are already lodged, as foreign bodies and as hollowed abysses, into the space of transcendence that no world can do (can be) without. This ambiguous paradox of images is far from new, having been inaugurally inscribed into Plato's terminological fluctuation between two vision-oriented terms, *idea* and *eidos*; but its problematic "ontological" dimension reaches a new level of explicitness in the age of philosophy's dissolution. It is not by chance that the figure in whose writing this happens most intensively (I would argue) is not a philosopher but a writer who very deeply and directly influenced Nancy: in Blanchot's version of image and ground, one finds a thinking, or perhaps rather an articulated experience, of images that not only invests the latter with an "ontological" or "grounding" structure—or at least with the inescapable semblance of one, and this changes everything—but also severs them from the world by rendering them more radically originary than the "Ideas" they supplant and whose autonomy they cannibalize. While similar to what Nancy calls the "distinction" and "withdrawal" of images, this is different from the latter in that its disruption of the world that images are *of* leaves nothing worldly, nothing *of the world*, intact, not even its uselessness and unavailability, nor its intimacy in distance, terms which in Blanchot are so *hyperbolized* that they both cancel and maintain one another indistinguishably. For Blanchot, the alterity of images opens a space, which he calls both imaginary and literary, that has (literally) no place in the world, that even opens onto something he calls "the other of every world," a radically impersonal space mediated by fascination and collapsed into the images that all things there become.

This is certainly not to say that for Nancy the ground of images is stably set in a world that would assign them a fixed place or a readily displayed sense. Nancy's image ground does have its own forms of bottomlessness, infinite mobility and displacement (see for example *FI*, 31; *GI*, 13), even violence (see "Image and Violence" in the same volume), and one can argue that his writing on images gives them a specific positioning force in a philosophically derived thinking of metaphysical groundlessness (or of the epoch of the "death of God"), especially insofar as images are a *technique*—technics being for Nancy the operator and manifestation of this groundlessness (and of the death just mentioned…). At the same time, one wonders whether Nancy's continual foregrounding of *world* and *sense*, even in the form of their threatened dispersion into globalized catastrophe,[6] might not foreclose the articulation of an otherwise profoundly troubling dimension of the experience of images, and of *mimesis* in general—that is, in an originary generality that we find more directly dramatized in Blanchot, which Nancy would nonetheless have absorbed from this important predecessor.

The most succinct way to indicate the difference I am pointing to is to say that while for both Blanchot and Nancy images have an ontological dimension in that they show the ground of the world's originary opening (although Blanchot does not use exactly this philosophical language), and whereas for Nancy images remain within the domain of *sense* even as they exceed that of signification (and even when they breach into senselessness), and thereby press through the worldly margin between signification and nothingness, for Blanchot images ultimately *lose sense* by entering into a radically depersonalized totality, a totality that Blanchot projects as an interminably roiling element drawing one into an unworldly space of endless repetition. Put even more succinctly, and to use a single phrase as a provisional shorthand: whereas Blanchot thinks images in relation to what he and Levinas call the "*il y a*" (the "*there is*"), the obsessive and entrapping ground of experience that takes the place of "being" in their more poetic or literary "ontologies," Nancy de-dramatizes this conception,[7] displacing the terrorizing "*il y a*" into the more *mundane* register of *sense* (in every sense of both of these words). Such a de-dramatization and displacement are surely desirable insofar as Nancy legitimately sets out to articulate forms of transcendence that eschew any risk of reifying a beyond or an outside of the world, as the "*il y a*" may well appear to do. And yet again one may wonder whether Blanchot's more fanciful and *hyperbolic* formulations ("the opaque and empty opening onto what there is when there is no more world, when there is not yet world" [*EL*, 31; *SL*, 33], or again: "the other of every world" ["l'autre de tout monde"] [*EL*, 89–90, 303; *SL*, 75, 228])—whether such formulations remain true in the end to an extremity that images also reveal by opening in the world an outside-(of)-world, a space in which there is nothing but an incessant and senseless stream of only apparently sense-making appearances. Blanchot spoke of this stream as an anonymous and multiplicitous *murmur*, and there is little reason why this figure,

---

[6] See for example *La Création du monde, ou la mondialisation* (Paris: Galilée, 2002), trans. François Raffoul and David Pettigrew, *The Creation of the World, or Globalization* (Albany: State University of New York Press, 2007) and *L'Équivalence des catastrophes (Après Fukushima)* (Paris: Galilée, 2012), trans. Charlotte Mandell, *After Fukushima: The Equivalence of Catastrophes* (New York: Fordham University Press, 2014).

[7] A conception that is in fact clearly derived to a considerable degree from French Romanticism, a fact somewhat disguised by the Anglophone references (Poe and Shakespeare, *Hamlet* and *Macbeth*) used by both Blanchot and Levinas in texts where they evoke this experience (*L'Espace littéraire* and *De l'existence à l'existant*, respectively).

itself something of a projective and totalizing image, should not be transposed into the register of a *murmur of images*, a roiling river of shadows continually traversing and vacating (effacing through erosion) every modality of sense. This phrase-figure thus indicates as well the *methexic* force of the originarily *mimetic* realm that Blanchot locates in the abyssal ground of literary experience, cast as the eccentric extreme from which any experience in its possibility is precariously derived.[8]

Images, Underground

Nancy comes very close to evoking such a totalizing image world, or image as condition of world in general, when he writes, in reference to the earliest cave paintings:

> Image, here, is not the convenient or inconvenient double of a thing in the world: it is the glory of that thing, its epiphany, its distinction from its own mass and its own appearance. The image praises the thing as detached from the universe of things and shown to be detached *as is the whole of the world* [ainsi que l'est le tout du monde]. (The whole of the world is detached from itself: it is detachment.)
>
> (*LM*, 125; *M*, 73)

The image in its singular detachment thus imitates the detachment of the entirety of the world from itself, its originarily mimetic self-separation in self-coincidence.[9] Does this imply that the world, in its entirety, necessarily presents itself as an image (of)

---

[8] This may be the place to refer to a work that presents a much more strident critique of Nancy in relation to Blanchot, who is passionately defended by its author: Leslie Hill's *Nancy, Blanchot: A Serious Controversy* (London: Rowman and Littlefield, 2018). That book's terrain is rather different from that of the present essay (it deals especially with the question of community and the exchange between the two authors around this question), but the hesitations regarding Nancy's work expressed here also derive in part from concerns that are ultimately political. This will have to be addressed elsewhere, except to note the following: Nancy appears to believe that art, along with the thinking that seeks to locate its philosophical specificity (i.e., his own work), can inhabit some discursive or aesthetic zone outside of ideology; this tendency in Nancy is explicitly summed up in an article by one of his most astute readers: Ian James, "The Evidence of the Image," *L'Esprit créateur* 47, no. 3 (2007): 79. Nancy's own setting-aside of the crucial question of social, economic, and institutional conditions is something of an inaugural gesture in his discourse on art, in *Les Muses* (136–37) / *The Muses* (82), and one finds a similar sidelining of the entirely central role of capitalism in modern techno-disasters in his book on Fukushima (*L'Équivalence des catastrophes*, 17), despite the equivalence in question in the title being at bottom that of money. In terms of Nancy's philosophical positions, two of the more severe critical responses to Nancy that I have seen, separated by their approaches but linked in many of their concerns, are Simon Critchley, "With Being-With? Notes on Jean-Luc Nancy's Rewriting of 'Being and Time,'" *Phänomenologische Forschungen* 3, no. 2 (1998): 198–210, and Peter Hallward, "Jean-Luc Nancy and the Implosion of Thought," *Oxford Literary Review* 27 (2005): 159–80. For a recent critique of Nancy's writing on sexuality, one that intersects with the aforementioned insofar as it seeks to bring out a number of political limitations, see the remarkable essay by Peter Banki, "Pornosophy: Jean-Luc Nancy and the Pornographic Image," in *Nancy and Visual Culture*, 109–28.

[9] Elsewhere I have attempted to articulate this generalized mimetic logic in relation to a well-known "ontology" of photography and film in "André Bazin's Eternal Returns: An Ontological Revision," *Film-Philosophy* 25, no. 1 (February 2021): 42–61.

itself, singularly and as a whole? This whole, constituted as detachment from itself and in its entirety, is also the ground—or something like the generalized aspecting—from which any specific image comes to appear. This *mimesis of self-detachment* that is carried out in any specific image is figured by Nancy in the same essay:

> From the painter to the wall, the hand opens a distance that suspends the continuity and the cohesion of the universe, in order to open up a world. The surface of stone becomes this suspension itself, its relief, its nuance and its grain. *The world is as if cut, cut off from itself, and it assumes a figure on its cutaway section* [le monde est comme tranché, retranché de soi, et prend figure sur sa tranche], flattened, freed from its inert thickness, form without ground [*forme sans fond*], abyss and shore of apparition [*plage d'apparition*].
>
> (LM, 128–29; M, 75–76; my emphasis)

This cutting off of the world from itself forms a space of forms "without ground," forms that hover suspended over the whole from which they are cut out, separated, distinguished, both covering it over and raising it into visibility (Nancy will say something very similar in "The Image—the Distinct"). And while this groundless form is figured as an "abyss," it is also a delineated zone or *plage* that contains, as much as it borders, a still dense and turbulent space of separation and dispersion.

Nancy locates this space in a cave,[10] that is (as he writes in a suspended sentence/paragraph): "Beneath the earth, as if touching on the rupture of any support and on the foundation of any distance [*au fondement de tout écart*], the whole world surfaced [*le monde entier faisait surface*] …" (LM, 127; M, 74). The cave is something like an internal fold of the world whose very depths are turned to surface, depths thus made continuous, albeit across a "rupture," with a universal "surfacing" of the earth, the becoming-surface of every worldly aspect, even of buried and enclosed spaces, of every interior, which is conversely the making-world (or making-image) of every exterior, however "interior" (or underground) it may be. And since this space of underground images cannot be far from another more allegorical but no less cavernous one, we can say that the internal image space surfaces as well into the exteriority that has been called the Idea. Nancy does not fail to make the comparison with Plato,[11] drawing these different image caves into each other, by cross-contaminating their central graphic trajectories: on the one hand, painting as the thing glorified through the *éclat* of distinct visibility and, on the other, Idea as the hidden movement and formation, the formal order and force, of painting. Nancy concludes the section thus: "the first Idea was a painting and the first painting was an Idea. Painting is not a copy of the Idea: the Idea is the gesture of painting" (M, 78). To reconfigure and expand a famous poetic formula, we could transpose thus: no ideas but in things, but likewise no things

---

[10] This is in accordance with the context of an invited talk, on Bataille and aesthetics, and in particular with his chosen topic, which works off from Bataille's writing on the Lascaux cave paintings.

[11] Especially in a section of the book that was for some reason excluded from the second French edition of *Les Muses* (2001), but that is included in the English translation.

without the Idea that makes them visible as what they are, that makes them images (of) themselves.[12] In this sense, Ideas too are "of the world," insofar as they space out the forms of things, not by crossing a chasm of supersensible intelligibility, but by giving shape to the gesture that cuts the world into each and all of them.[13] In this sense too, each thing, as indiscernibly itself and image of itself, is the visibility of its own *mimesis*. At the same time, to pose somewhat precipitously a question that begins to emerge here, between similar but distinct images: could the gap ("tout écart") of this indiscernible difference also be the strange "underground" into which the world, having surfaced from it, could collapse, as though into a grave?

The Wall of Images: Image Ideas and Cinematic Distinction

The deathly implication of this question, whereby the image cave echoes the grave through a ground of images that continually *surfaces*, is a bit premature here; I signal it in anticipation, as it will guide us if not out of the cave then toward an internal difference that may cut through the ground-image distinction to reveal a more radical experience of image alterity. This cut passes through an art form that Nancy has discussed extensively, namely, cinema, in which the cutting out of images puts their relation to the world they are *of* directly in view. In the one book that Nancy has published on film, he calls this relation *évidence*, which he defines in terms similar to those that will appear in the essays of *Au fond des images* (none of which, curiously, is devoted to cinema). Evoking the Latin origin of the word, Nancy explains (in language that clearly echoes *Les Muses*):

> *Evidentia*: the character of what is seen from afar (giving a passive turn to the active meaning of *video*, "I see"). The distance implied by evidence gives both the measure of its spatial removal and the measure of its power. Something *distinguishes* itself from far away because it detaches itself, is separated … Something strikes [one] because of its distinction: an image is also, always, that which is cut away from a context and cut out against a ground [*ce qui se retranche d'un contexte et qui tranche sur un fond*]. It is always a cut-out, a framing [*une découpe, un cadrage*].[14]

In *Au fond des images* this distinction of the image, its *découpe* and *cadrage*, will be taken up in terms that emphasize the image's imbricated heterogeneity (*FI*, 15; *GI*, 3),

---

[12] "Say it, no ideas but in things." This is the well-known adage from the first pages of William Carlos Williams's *Paterson*—or rather it is an adage preceded by an imperative that already renders the message much more complex than it may seem.

[13] In *Le Plaisir au dessin / The Pleasure in Drawing*, Nancy elaborates on this intimate interaction of form and idea through the process and movement of drawing/design.

[14] Nancy, *L'Évidence du film / Evidence of Film*, 43 / 42; emphasis Nancy's. This book features the French and English texts on facing pages, as well as a translation into Persian in a separate section; it will be cited henceforth as *EF* followed by the respective page numbers, with the odd-numbered French pages given first.

or one might say its heteromorphism with respect to the ground (in that the image first opens the spacing of form). What distinguishes this discourse of evidence in cinema is that it must also reckon, simultaneously and inversely, with a certain intensified *homomorphism* in the cinematic image with respect to the ground of the world from which it was cut out.[15] The camera's cut is distinguished from the painter's first by its instantaneousness and then by the sequential distension of the instantaneous in time (*EF*, 43 / 42), all of which amounts to an intensified resemblance to the world from which it is distinguished and cut away. In the cinema, the ground is (in) the image[16] in a way that can be seen as somehow *less* distinguished, however "evident" the image may be. This intensified diminishment of distinction (if I can put it thus) is the source both of cinema's evidence and of its sharpened ambiguities, its sameness-in-otherness to the world it appears to show, or as what Nancy later describes more generally as "la dissemblance qui habite la ressemblance" / "the dissimilarity that inhabits resemblance" (*FI*, 24; *GI*, 9). And this is why, having highlighted the underground images on the wall of the cave, we are all the more proximate to Plato's allegorical staging, although now we can see that there is no allegory, only (image) worlds within (image) worlds whose transcendences with respect to each other are all the more equivocal, and equivocally immanent, in their involuted separations. What is the status of this cavernous wall of images in the age of its techno-mimetic reflexivity?

> Until our time the wall of images was solid and it bore witness to an outside or a deepmost depth of the world [*un tréfonds du monde*] ... With the cinema, the wall becomes an opening cut out in the world and opening onto this world itself. That is why the comparison often made between the cinema and Plato's cave is not pertinent: the depths, the ground [*le fond*] of the cave attest precisely to an outside of the world, but as a negative, and precisely thereby sets up Plato's well known discrediting of images, or the demand for a consideration of higher and purer images called "ideas." The cinema operates in the opposite sense: it does not reflect

---

[15] Quickly stated, and without putting too fine a point on the matter for the moment, one can say that Nancy's characterizations of cinema are rigorously if somewhat diffusely Bazinian, though Bazin is not cited in *L'Évidence du film* (nor anywhere else in Nancy's work, as far as I am aware). This influence may have been transmitted partly through Deleuze, whose imprint is more directly apparent. One also sees very Bazinian language in a brief and curious text devoted to photography in *Le poids d'une pensée* (1991): "Georges" features what appear to be Nancy's own photographs of an older man sitting at a table drinking and smoking. See "Georges," trans. Simon Sparks, in *Multiple Arts: The Muses II*, ed. S. Sparks (Stanford: Stanford University Press, 2006), 131–42. The relation between Bazin's "realism" and Nancy's thinking on photographic and cinematic images calls for further elaboration. Rosalind Galt makes some helpful remarks in this direction in "The Obviousness of Cinema," *World Picture* 2 (Autumn 2008): online, accessed December 14, 2021: http://www.worldpicturejournal.com/WP_2/Galt.html. Ian Balfour also refers to Bazin in "Nancy on Film: Regarding Kiarostami, Re-Thinking Representation (with a Coda on Claire Denis)," *Journal of Visual Culture* 9, no. 1 (2010): 29–43, where he also points to images of an entrance to a cave, in Denis and Courbet, that would be worth exploring.

[16] Later in this essay on Kiarostami Nancy refers to "[les] paysages qui ne sont 'au fond' de l'image que pour être mis en vue ... en de larges plans" / "[the] landscapes are 'in the ground' of the image only so as to be placed in view ... in very wide shots" (*EF*, 55 / 54).

an outside, it opens the inside onto itself. *The image on the screen is itself the idea* [L'image sur l'écran est elle-même l'idée].

(*EF*, 45, 47 / 44, 46; my emphasis)

This last statement runs parallel with those quoted above from "Painting in the Grotto" ("The first Idea was a painting and the first painting was an Idea. Painting is not a copy of the Idea: the Idea is the gesture of painting" [*M*, 78]),[17] but it brings into greater focus the collapse of allegorical difference that it operates, and the paradoxical involution thus indicated. This involution is one in which a radically heterogeneous outside (Ideas as purely intelligible) is recast as immanent to an "inside" that opens not to a higher reality but "onto itself." The internal fold of a cave is thus reconfigured as an opening onto a space that is simultaneously homogeneous and distinct, continuous and separated, internal and external. This is very close to an image of the worldly transcendence we began with, and it is equally problematic, or enigmatic, in terms of the precise sort of opening in question, and the persistent strangeness and "outsideness" of ideas as these are "internalized" in images, and into the "inside" in general. If the opening here is first marked by a frame, and specifically a screen, it is also marked within the screen by the "ideas" that distinguish its forms as abstractions, that is, as the internal spacing of their forms. Ideas are thus the very force of their formation as such, what Nancy calls in *Le plaisir au dessin*, "La force formatrice" or "Formative Force." But from where do they receive this "force"? Insofar as it is transmitted in and through ideas, it maintains a dimension external to the plane of images that it also internally constitutes (opens). But Nancy's gesture here does not point in the direction of a *mise en abyme*, a structure of frames within frames, but rather to the selfsameness (the *à-mêmeté*, one could say) of ideas and images, a sameness to self of every imaged thing, and a sameness across the border of the screen. In this sense, this "internal" distinction is precisely coextensive with that of the frame by which an "inside" opens "onto itself," for this formative "ideational" distinction is what conditions the possibility of an "itself" in the first place. The allegorical chasm is thus reduced to the thin margin of difference by which a frame opens any "inside" and any "itself"—and this opening, *as idea*, therefore continues to press as something of an outside, one that both inhabits specific images and traverses the entire difference between inside and outside. In this respect, one thing that Nancy is indicating here is that all images—and cinematic images in a particular and perhaps preeminent way—give to be seen the ideas that make them be (that form them as) what they are. At the same time, it is clear that the giving-to-be-seen of the idea-structure (or one could say, more dynamically, of the formative spacing) that are formative of images is not exclusive to cinema, as the example referring to cave painting indicates. And yet we note right away a difference in the parallel examples mentioned above, between the "gesture" of the idea in painting (visible in the painting and yet indicating a prior external mediation) and the direct

---

[17] See also *Le Plaisir au dessin*, in the section titled "La force formatrice," which begins: "Le dessin est donc l'Idée : il est la forme vraie de la chose" (19); "Formative Force": "Drawing is therefore the Idea: it is the true form of the thing" (10). Nancy specifies that this form comes through the gesture of a search, which is that of drawing itself.

equivalence of idea and image attributed here to cinema, a difference that hinges around the simultaneity of idea-image and its visible formation in time, and thus a difference that intensifies the visibility of images' resemblance to themselves, as one traced along the dimension of time.[18] This is a self-resemblance thus determined above all by a temporal self-formation, by which *at bottom* film images are most forcefully distinguished. In addition to being homomorphic with respect to the ground of world from which they are cut out and onto which they open, film images are also *automorphic*: they appear to *form themselves* in time, and this is their distinguishing "gesture," their manner of immanently marking themselves as the conjunction of an "auto" and a "form"—a selfsameness determined in part by the abstraction of an idea in the process of forming whatever the idea itself already is (of).[19]

What I have called a "collapse" is thus an infinite internal expansion, one that is not circumscribed only by the framing/framed space of the wall but that intimately traverses the entire world in question. Now, in that sense, "the image on the screen" emphatically *does* show something of an outside, the internal outside of the idea-image and of the world "onto" which it opens as an endlessly expanding space of images in formation. While Plato's "outside" is a supersensible order that lends its greater reality to the shadowy inside that can only allegorize it, Nancy's cinema-cave, devoid of that allegorical projection, becomes an image of image-ideas, in other words, an image of how the world is made *in its own image*; or further: an image that strangely shows (shows through estrangement, separation, abstraction) the image-constitution of the world at large. The chasm of allegory is reduced to the faultline of abstraction, which is thus also the minute linkage binding all images to whatever world they could be *of*, and this means that every *thing* is "grounded" in its own possibility as an image (image-idea). It is in this sense as well that the world as a whole is made in its own image, and the wall that shows this is one that bears forth images both as themselves and as self-forming abstractions that reveal, across a faultline of self-sameness, their distinction into images.

Cinema, then, is a gesture of abstraction in time. But we also know that this "gesture" is operated, in part but necessarily, by a machine—and it is here that another kind of heterogeneity enters the picture, as it were. For if what is peculiar in film images is that they are mediatized in time, this is true not only in that they are by nature mechanically repeatable (recurrent), time being *what is cut out* along (with) these images, but also because time, in its originary dimension, is *what cuts*, thus bringing the cinematic machinery, in a broadened sense, into the very ground of film images. The "gesture" of their idea is time itself, and this gesture of distinction (which has only relatively rarely been effected by marking or drawing directly on a surface or image support) is necessarily both "transcendental" and mechanical.

---

[18] In a word, and to anticipate the following sections, the kind of self-resemblance that Blanchot attributed preeminently to the corpse, and in rare moments to someone in life, is the general condition of cinema.

[19] On automorphosis as a distinguishing characteristic of cinema, see Christophe Wall-Romana, *Cinepoetry: Imaginary Cinemas in French Poetry* (New York: Fordham University Press, 2013), 16.

Time and Image

The element of time is thus fundamental, because time, as both the operator and the operated of distinction, is the milieu in which a thing is constituted as the intersection (the disjointed identity, the abstracted embodiment) of image and idea. Nancy first takes up this question (though not in relation to cinema) in the essay "Image and Violence," beginning with this quotation from the section of Kant's first *Critique* on the schematism: "the pure image ... of all objects of the senses in general is time." This is because, Nancy explains, "time is the very movement of synthesis, of the production of unity." In this regard, it is time that cuts first and deepest into the ground of images, forming them from out of the "dispersed multiplicity" (*FI*, 50; *GI*, 23) that precedes them, in a strange violence—the violence of originary estrangement itself—which in Nancy's text is rendered in the images of an earthquake, and of a cut sliced through a densely gathered involution. I give this passage at some length (with one interruption for comment):

> This pure image is the image of images, the opening of unity as such. It violently folds together the dismembered exterior, but its tightened folds [*son pli, sa fronce serrée*] are also the slit that unity cuts in the continuity of extension. The pure image is the earthquake in being that opens the chasm or the fault of presence [*la faille de la présence*] ... Time is in many respects, violence itself.
>
> (*FI*, 51; *GI*, 23–24)

These images are striking. They correspond to nothing less than the "detachment" or tearing away that is a condition for any images as unified objects, or (one might say) as ideas. Unity and self-resemblance thus converge, across a separation that marks out objects as they turn toward the violent "*arrachement*" or "tearing away" that has made them be what they are:

> Unity forms (*bildet*) the image or the picture [*tableau*] (*Bild*) of that which in itself is not only without image, but without unity or identity [and therefore without world—JF]. Consequently, the phrase "the image of" signifies not that the image comes after that of which it is the image, but that "the image of" is, first of all, that in which, and as which, what is presents itself [*cela en quoi ... ce qui est se présente*]—and nothing presents itself otherwise. In presenting itself, the thing comes to *resemble itself* [*se ressembler*], and therefore to be itself. In order to resemble itself, it *gathers itself* [*se rassemble*], it gathers and brings itself together. But to gather itself it must withdraw from its outside.
>
> Therefore being is torn away from being [*arrachement de l'être à l'être*]; and it is the image that tears itself away. It bears within itself the mark of this tearing away: its ground monstrously opened to its very bottom, that is, to the depthless underside [*au revers sans fond*] of its presentation (the picture's back or "blind side" [*le dos aveugle du tableau*]).
>
> (*FI*, 51; *GI*, 23–24; Nancy's emphasis)

From here, from the blindness of this depthless ground, Nancy goes on to evoke the death mask that makes an appearance in Heidegger's analysis of the Kantian schematism (to which Nancy will give more attention in "Masked Imagination" and to which we will return in a moment). The violence that Nancy points to brings us as close as we will get to the terror evoked earlier in reference to Blanchot's thinking of images, and Blanchot's name will not fail to appear in these analyses, albeit only in passing (as is so often the case when Nancy touches on Blanchot's texts). But here this violence is one that remains largely concealed in the gap between a thing and itself, insofar as its "coming to resemble itself" tends toward an indiscernibility that covers over the disjointed equivalence posited here between resembling itself and being itself.

Most things, then—or I should say most experiences of things on most days—do not make evident this gap of self-co-incidence, or this *dis-con-juncture*, as we might call it. Art is the general name given to objects that do this in a preeminent way, and it is indeed possible that cinema has a heightened capacity to show precisely this *evidence*, if only because, as mentioned above, it shows things as images (in the relative unity and intelligibility of their formative ideas) and it does so in time, that is, in the medium of their fundamental self-estrangement—a term that in this context is essentially synonymous with self-resemblent. It is possible that cinema shows things in such a way as to make evident that any "self" presents itself as self-resemblent—that is, as "self-evident" in this slightly modified sense—or does not present itself at all. This amounts to saying that cinema shows the "ground" of images in the formative emergence of the latter, and in the "violence" of the "pure image," the "image of images," that opens the interval of their self-relation, that is, of their immanent possibility. If cinema shows this image, then we could say that such a violence, as a kind of primordial ontological violence, is in some sense inherent or endemic to the experience of cinema. It is surely to this that the legends of public panic before the first film images attest (regardless of whether these legends refer to any empirical events).[20] For the train hurtling toward you in a movie theater has indeed and in all evidence already flown off its rails.

Blanchot with (and without) Nancy

Before addressing cinema more directly in this regard, it will be illuminating to lay out in more detail how Nancy's thinking of ground and image in terms of self-resemblance both derives and differs from Blanchot, whose reflections in *L'Espace littéraire* on the self-resemblance of the *corpse* had already introduced a particularly uncanny deathly dimension into these questions. Blanchot evokes cadaverous self-resemblance as a forceful manifestation of the relation of image to ground, which appears more generally, he says, in *fascination*, that is, when "la chose que nous fixons s'est effondrée dans son

---

[20] For a detailed and persuasively skeptical discussion of this legend, see Tom Gunning, "An Aesthetics of Astonishment: Early Film and the (In)Credulous Spectator" in *Viewing Positions: Ways of Seeing Film*, ed. Linda Williams (New Brunswick: Rutgers University Press, 1995 [1989]), 114–33.

image [... et ...] l'image a rejoint ce fond d'impuissance où tout retombe" / "the thing that we stare at has collapsed into its image [... and ...] the image rejoins that ground of powerlessness into which everything falls back" (*EL*, 343; *SL*, 255). What the corpse introduces into this experience is a peculiar projection or animation of this ground, which begins to move and take up its own space, insinuating itself "between" what we call the "departed" and the image-body that precisely thereby *remains*. Blanchot writes:

> The departed [*le défunt*], they say, is no longer of this world. He has left it behind [*derrière lui*], but left behind is precisely this corpse which is itself not any more of this world [*pas davantage de ce monde*]—even though it is here—which is rather behind this world, what the living (and not the departed) has left behind himself and which now affirms, from here [*à partir d'ici*], the possibility of a back-world [*un arrière-monde*], a world in back of the world, a turning back, an indefinite, indeterminate, indifferent substance ...[21]

Moving quickly we can say that on the basis of the corpse that is here, that instantiates "à partir d'ici" a here that is also always elsewhere, that both is and is not of this world—Blanchot opens a kind of eerie transcendence, a world within or "behind" the world that is "no longer of this world." We can already discern an important resonance with what Nancy says not only about the blind backside of the image, but also about the cave-space of cinema, a space in the world that opens onto its own inside but never quite corresponds with it, since it exists only across the gap between thing-world and image-world while also "collapsing" one into the other. The difference is that Blanchot emphatically stresses the irreducible otherness of this world-onto-which *that we see here*, precisely by placing it in intimate proximity with what he calls a "ground of powerlessness," one that turns every image into a kind of "turning back," a compulsive turning and returning, a kind of perpetual *revenance*. Later in the same essay, Blanchot refers to this intimate proximity as being "close to a dangerous neutral region" (*EL*, 347; *SL*, 258) (he says this, by the way, in reference to anyone who, in a rare moment, comes to resemble oneself *in life*, like their own revenant). The image compulsively returns to the ground of its own powerlessness, a ground itself structured by repetition and endlessness, a kind of after-world on a loop (Blanchot's repeated evocation of a *ressassement éternel*, which could be translated as an *eternal rehashing*, is highly relevant here). In this sense we could sum up by saying that in Blanchot the frame of fascination, which opens the image onto its own specific dimension of worldly otherworldliness, is itself subject to (in a relation of passivity with) a danger and a violence that make it possible but only by becoming *inescapable*, indeed in a way perhaps a kind of prison, utterly unbounded though it may be. This may well be the most salient version of the in-finity of "transimmanence" that Blanchot has to offer.

---

[21] Blanchot, *L'Espace littéraire* (Paris: Gallimard, 1988 [1955]), 345; *The Space of Literature*, trans. Ann Smock (Lincoln and London: University of Nebraska Press, 1982), 257. Hereafter *EL* and *SL*, respectively.

Nancy's reflections intersect with this aspect of a deathly image of images in Blanchot's texts through the very specific figure of the death mask. In "Masked Imagination," Nancy notes the strange appearance of a death mask in Heidegger's analysis of the Kantian schematism, while also bringing this image, that of a dead face with its blind and empty look (in both senses of this word), down into the ground of all image-making, in the "transcendental imagination"—the ultimate fold or turn, perhaps, in the involuted cave of images we have been exploring. Nancy thus places the death mask in much the same position that Blanchot gives to the corpse (and, indeed, elsewhere to the death mask), an immanent image that marks a limit of all images and shows something of the structure and conditions of their originary formation, while also suggesting that the ground from which they are imagined, in the sense of being made as images (*eingebildet*), is inhabited at bottom by a nonlooking blindness uncannily looking out (*aussehen*) of all images and all vision.[22] An essay with a broader scope than the present one would follow the details of Nancy's analysis (and of Heidegger's discourse on Kant) in order to situate it in close relation to the Blanchot of *L'Espace littéraire*, which Nancy mentions only briefly in a note (*FI*, 168n1; *GI*, 152n18). What I would like to do here, having noted the proximity of Nancy and Blanchot on this point, is to specify a divergence as well, one that emerges when the ground turns into a grave that remains open, where no resurrection is possible, and yet where there is nothing but return. I will do this by referring to film examples that show how this return takes the form of a strange technical cinematic reanimation.

First, then, in order to point us back toward cinema, let us look at one further movement of convergence and divergence, as evidenced particularly in a passage from the Blanchot text I have been referring to. What is fascination for Blanchot? His description immediately brings to mind Nancy's discourse on touch—and even more directly the scholarly attempts to link Nancy to film by way of touch and contact[23]—but it leaves us in what we cannot help seeing as a rather different topography. In the following paragraph, the first under the section titled "The Image" in the chapter "Essential Solitude," the convergence resonates clearly, as does, already, the experience of cinema:

> Why fascination? Seeing presupposes distance, decisiveness which separates, the power to stay out of contact and in contact avoid confusion. Seeing means that this separation has nevertheless become an encounter. But what happens when what you see, although at a distance, seems to touch you with a gripping contact, when

---

[22] In this regard, Nancy's analyses resonate with those proposed by Jacques Derrida in *Memoirs of the Blind*, trans. Pascale-Anne Brault and Michael Naas (Chicago: University of Chicago Press, 1993).

[23] See especially Laura McMahon, *Cinema and Contact: The Withdrawal of Touch in Nancy, Bresson, Duras and Denis* (London: Legenda, 2012). For an insightful and circumspect discussion of Blanchot in relation to cinema, see Calum Watt, *Blanchot and the Moving Image: Fascination and Spectaroship* (London: Legenda, 2017), which relevantly brings out the question of self-resemblance in Blanchot as "originary doubling" (27). It is worth recalling too that the striking resonances between Blanchot's description of fascination and the image in *L'Espace littéraire* and the experience of the cinematic spectator were indicated by Raymond Bellour, particularly in an essay from 2003 titled "L'image," in *Maurice Blanchot : récits critiques*, ed. Christophe Bident and Pierre Vilar (Tours and Paris: Éditions Farrago and Éditions Leo Scheer, 2003), 133–41.

the manner of seeing is a kind of touch, when seeing is contact at a distance? What happens when what is seen imposes itself upon the gaze, as if the gaze were seized, put in contact with the appearance? What happens is not an active contact, not what still remains of initiative and action in real touching, but rather the gaze gets pulled along, absorbed into an immobile movement and a depthless ground [*un fond sans profondeur*]. What is given to us by this contact at a distance is the image, and fascination is the passion of the image.

(*EL*, 28–29; *SL*, 32)

What Blanchot says here has the most curious, oblique, and (I would suggest) disruptive relation to Nancy's notion of touch. The capaciousness of the latter, its sense of opening on all sides, and of all "sides," edges or limits being the form and spacing of an exposure that both brings into contact and withdraws, in a reserve that likewise prevents fusion—all of this is here strangely magnetized, so to speak, by another kind of relation, one that may well contaminate the difference Blanchot himself evokes here between the contact of fascination and "real touching," presumed to be active but only insofar as it "remains" so in relation to this more fundamental relation, upon which wilfull action and initiative appear to be thinly grafted as a kind of alibi. It is not enough, then, to say that Blanchot is projecting a virtual or imaginary touching, nor even to specify that this imaginary touch is, as such, a direct and forceful pull of "real" things as the images they also always are. For we have entered into an encounter where this forceful contact at a distance also radically abolishes distance, and with it the openness and spacing of contingent borders—or rather, it turns spacing inside-out, renders a world that is nothing but spacing, a pure "outside" that nonetheless envelops *absolutely*. Hence Blanchot's frequent talk of the "absolute" nature of such an experience, which is not of course meant in the sense of a self-sustained plenitude or Hegelian fulfillment, but rather merely as pure *separation*—but a separation so strange and extreme that it also *suffocates*. Blanchot takes exposure so far in the experience he calls "literary" that it loses all reciprocity, all symmetry, and every grounding in sense, leaving one (or "someone" as he puts it) abandoned in something other than a world, though nowhere beyond it either. It is in terms of such abandonment of sense that he expresses this in the paragraph following the one just quoted, where he continues:

What fascinates us robs us of our power to give a sense. It abandons its "sensory" [or sensible, *sensible*] nature, abandons the world, draws back from the world [withdraws to the hither side of world, *retire en deça du monde*], and draws us along [*nous y attire*, attracts us into it, this hither side]. It no longer reveals itself to us, and yet it affirms itself in a presence foreign to the present of time and to presence in space.

(*EL*, 29; *SL*, 32)

Withdrawal, which is often evoked by Nancy in a Heideggerian mode, is presented here not only as something that *being* does (to put the point crudely), but as something that *happens* to "one" (to someone...), and as such it opens onto a "space" that is without sense and without possibility, a space in which one is *lost to sense*, where nothing is revealed but the affirmation of a presence foreign to appearance but in no way ideal, in-itself, or transcendent. This is the sort of ground that opens "immanently" or "internally" for Blanchot, a sub-phenomenal obtrusion (or perhaps the ultimate *intruder*) that radically undermines any such philosophical categories, leaving only what he elsewhere calls "le harcèlement de l'indéfini" / "the harrassment of the indefinite" (*EL*, 26; *SL*, 30).[24] It is a ground to which one is nonetheless drawn and *attracted*, as though to an irreducibly forceful remainder of being's stripping away (its leftover *dépouille* and image-ground)—or as though to a death that cannot ever quite happen. That is, to a death that goes on, just as life always does—or so we like to say.

Grounds, Graves, Effacements

Let us turn from here back toward the cavernous image-world with which we began, and back toward cinema as the opening of the inside onto itself, while keeping in view the strange harassing draw of this ground. Is it after all a draw into the grave? What if the ground of the image were best framed as just that, the opening of a ground dug up as a grave, but one in, around, or after which "life goes on…," perhaps terrifyingly so? This language is meant to evoke two of the films by Abbas Kiarostami that Nancy comments on in *L'Evidence du film*: *And Life Goes On*, whose original title translates more literally (and perhaps with a subtle note of Blanchotian inescapability) to "Life and Nothing But," and *Taste of Cherry*. More than the other films discussed there by Nancy, these two allow us to broach the question of *the ground* in a very direct, literal, possibly naive, but revealing way, in that both films are constructed around its violent opening: *And Life Goes On* was shot in the aftermath of a catastrophic earthquake, a real and quite devastating one that occurred in northern Iran in 1990. The notion of the ground opening, fissuring, yawning, and engulfing life, along with the dusty piles of rubble and ruin, literal graves for thousands, take on very concrete forms in this film, as does the sense that life does go on—although, I would add, with a hint that this message may not be the unequivocal affirmation it appears to be, particularly when linked with the strange endless mechanical movement embodied in the automobile's continuous tracking down long indefinite and repetitious dirt roads, and by extension with the cinematic machinery tightly implicated in this movement.[25] But it is especially *Taste of Cherry* that I would like to comment on, for it not only tracks even more relentlessly such a mechanical movement, it revolves around a death to come and an

---

[24] Ann Smock translates this nicely as "the exhausting insistence of the indefinite." This insistent demand, and the continual exhaustion in the face of it, is itself a fundamental condition of the experience in question.

[25] The use of the phrase "life goes on" for the title is not arbitrary in that it is spoken by one of the characters in the film. On the ambivalence implied in this phrase in relation to cinema, see Laura Mulvey, *Death 24x a Second: Stillness and the Moving Image* (London: Reaktion Books, 2006), where she directly juxtaposes the end of *A Taste of Cherry* with that of Rossellini's *Journey to Italy* (in which the camera abandons the main characters and fixes on a dense and endless stream of passersby). *Journey to Italy*, with its skulls, excavations, and corpse images, is also very much a film about grounds as graves and the images extracted from them.

open grave, and it features images of "the ground" in the most concrete sense possible, along with those of a man's form merging into and emerging out of this ground as though to live on despite all. This cinematic afterlife brings the question of ground and image, and that of their transimmanent in-folded worlds, not so much into focus as into a potentially troubling indistinction.

Taste of Cherry is from the beginning a story about ground as dirt and dust, about a grave and a burial: Mr. Badii, a middle-aged man about whom we know virtually nothing, has decided to kill himself. This central fact itself we do not learn until well into the film, throughout which we accompany him in his car as he searches for someone to help him carry out his plan. That is to say: not to help him with the killing—he'll take care of that with pills—but rather to bury his body in a grave he has already dug next to a dirt road on an isolated hillside, where he will lie down that night, when the time comes. He is willing to pay this helper, if only he will show up at the grave in the early morning, shout his name (three times) and then, if he does not respond, cover his body by filling the grave with dirt. This image of himself, of the shell of a man he has become, and also essentially as a character (as mentioned we know nothing at all about him, and he remains very impassive and affectless throughout most of the film), wants thus to rejoin the ground that he himself has opened. His concern is to do precisely that—not so much to have what one would call a "proper burial," and certainly not a proper Muslim burial (suicide being forbidden in Islam), but rather most basically a burial that covers over his corpse. It is unclear why he wants even this much, he never explains this, but he most emphatically does want it, along with the possibility of being found and lifted out if he does not die. Aside from considerations one could guess at, such as the scandal or indecency of leaving a corpse for others to deal with, or for animals to find, and so on, I would propose that it is essentially in order to *disappear*, to cover over the image that he is, to remove it from the visible circulation that the film so continuously engages as he drives around, and so to exit the circuit of the gaze which he himself so intensely embodies (a large portion of this film simply shows him *looking*, out the car window, across the scrubby landscape, at the people he sees and encounters and the like). The fact that this burial never happens in the film, and could never happen (it is very difficult to imagine such an ending, with Badii's grave filled in, his up-to-now continuous visibility definitively effaced), only reaffirms this endless circulation of images and of Badii as an image, the impossibility, henceforth, of his disappearance within the unspooling logic of this film as a visual artifact, a logic it seems intent on making explicitly manifest. A certain survival is inscribed into this logic, which is not only that of the physical existence of the film—sole index of its otherwise eternal unfolding—but also of its internal construction, whereby Badii as image confronts the conditions of his own ongoing visibility. Even death could not eliminate this condition, and perhaps he knows this, and no doubt so do we.[26]

---

[26] It is something along these lines that Mulvey indicates when, in an undated interview following the publication of *Death 24x a Second*, she describes cinema in its cumulative history as "a vast receptacle of the living dead." See "Death 24x a Second: In conversation with Laura Mulvey," in *Four by Three Magazine*, accessed December 17, 2021: http://christine-jakobson.squarespace.com/issue/death/laura-mulvey-interview.

There is however one moment when such an invisibility through burial comes over him, but it occurs not when he places himself in the open grave at the end, but earlier, during the remarkable sequence at the cement factory.[27] This sequence is often said to take place at a quarry, but what we see in the images is not so much a quarry, in which digging and excavation would be taking place, as a factory site with large dump trucks, loaders, and conveyor belts (the last two being prominent in the first images of the sequence), where dirt and stones are hauled, dumped, and *poured into* a pit and then through a machine designed to prepare this material for industrial cement production (to confirm all this, the worker who eventually shoos Badii away from the site says that if he wants cement, he'll have to go to the office). I stress these points not only because of the frame in which we've approached them here—wherein we could say that the *ground*, as stone, dirt, and dust, has been cut out of itself and here becomes ground-*as*-image, a highly fascinating sight for the captivated Badii—but also because this ground is not immanent, self-enclosed earth, not even in the freshly extracted form of quarried stone, but rather mechanically labored construction material that is being industrially "spaced" (one could say) by these machines into ever finer gradations (we see everything from large stones to the fine dust that begins to surround Badii). The thoroughly mechanical nature (so to speak) of this operation shows that (the) ground is being rendered *entirely* over to image—and "earth" over to "world," to use Heidegger's lexicon—while also paralleling, at least (if not in fact interpenetrating more deeply), the image-making machinery of the cinema. Ground, made image, now *openly flows*, as the constant pouring and tumbling of dirt and stones make manifest, just as the passing clouds of dust do, as they by turns invade the image and dissipate. Indeed, Badii's intense fascination with these sights is first triggered when he sees himself in the form of an image, a shadow projected onto the wall of the pit, cast as an upright figure standing right next to the pouring dirt and *its* shadow, in a play of desubstantialization and intimate contact which appears to jolt into focus his at first wandering attention.

No better clue is needed to indicate that we are in the strange "ground" of an image world in which things and images coexist on the same plane of visibility: Plato's cave both opened and flattened onto "itself." The element of projection is significant as well, not only in that it evokes cinema—the cinematic image showing something of its own work in rendering ground as images—but also because in showing Badii his shadow it casts his image directly "into the ground," anticipating a kind of merging

---

[27] I am indebted to Hamish Ford's detailed discussion of this film in his article "Driving into the Void: Kiarostami's *Taste of Cherry*," *Journal of Humanistics and Social Sciences* 1, no. 1 (2012): 1–27. Another useful resource is Mathew Abbott, *Abbas Kiarostami and Film-Philosophy* (Edinburgh: Edinburgh University Press, 2017). I would like to note as well that the initial inspiration for linking the concrete factory images with the motif of the ground in Nancy, and laterally with the topos of resurrection, was sparked in part by the image chosen for the cover of the recently released Criterion DVD of the film (figure below), which shows not an image from the film but a production still re-dramatizing Badii's emergence/withdrawal from the dust, as though stepping forth from it (or, in a remarkably ambiguous gesture, reaching out, or simply displaying the gesture of an upheld hand), whereas in the film, as we will see, this dust fully enshrouds and then quickly releases his hunched immobile form. This is a dramatization meant to sell DVDs, to be sure, but it also points toward a central dynamic, and a certain cinematic truth, engaged by the film.

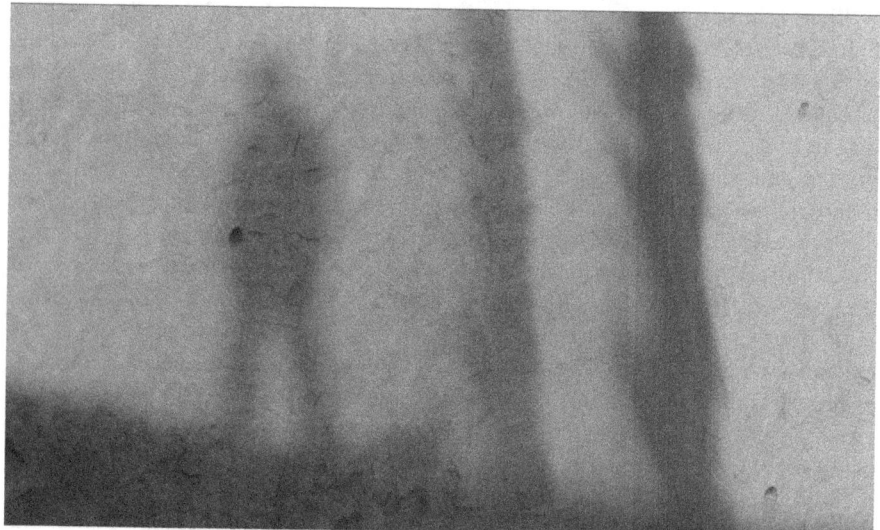

Figure 12.1 *Taste of Cherry*: shadow image and earth, 1.

with the element of his burial (surely one source of his initial fascination), while also distinguishing this image, inscribing it as such, indeed making it into a kind of mechanical effect he can no longer escape. In that vein we see him move back and forth as though to manipulate this image he is now locked into, to set it in motion and make it operate as such, in a movement that inextricably attaches him to it even as it appears to give him some mastery over it—just as the machine does to the stones it works (and just as the camera does as it cuts out and records all this). In that sense, he is like a man in the Platonic cave who has discovered a reality and a freedom that confirm all the more implacably his inability to exit its machinations. The grinding and repetitive machinery used in the operation becomes more evident in the next image of his shadow, this time cast just below him toward a metal grate through which stones and dirt pour onto a flat bin beneath it that rhythmically oscillates back and forth, disappearing when the flow overwhelms it.

As all this happens, the imposing but somehow muffled sound of flowing dirt and the loud clanking of stones on the grate are, I want to say, *excruciatingly tactile*, and the sense of submersion—the relentless burial of dirt with dirt—becomes intensely palpable. Badii turns away. He goes to sit on a large stone and watches as a dump truck perched high on a huge mound of loose rocks unloads its cargo, which flows like a river down the side of the hill, raising thick dust that we then see (in a cut to a close-up) accumulating around him. Enormous truck wheels roll by in the foreground, the dust thickens, Badii bows his head. A second load is dumped on the hill which pushes the dust to a kind of saturation point, its thickness becomes more palpably unbreathable than ever—and it is here that the first and only "burial" of this film occurs, as Badii disappears completely, enshrouded, one might well say, in the impenetrable ground of

Figure 12.2 *Taste of Cherry*: shadow image and earth, 2.

Figure 12.3 *Taste of Cherry*: buried by dust.

its dirt-borne images. Three consecutive screen shots (occurring within three seconds or so) give a sense of this quickly passing moment.

In my view, this sequence is far more terrifying than the penultimate one of the film, when Badii lies in the open grave at night—a disconcerting moment, to be sure, but one whose melancholy pathos is somehow comfortably Romantic, with its ordinary clouds overhead (more skydrift than earthbound matter), lit by an exaggeratedly enlarged full moon, and with its final black screen softened by the sound of rain, all rendered familiarly dramatic with thunder and lightning. The earlier moment is more terrifying not only because it evokes the topos of being buried alive (admittedly no less Romantic in some respects), but because it does so in a way that also shows, in the midst of this strangely industrial burial, a superimposition (perhaps a coincidence) of indefinite dying over the banal and implacable continuation of living in time. And it does this as well through the submersion and reemergence of an image, something of a living corpse (a film image), from or against a ground that is itself shown in the sequence at large to be thoroughly mechanized, a domain of repetitious and automated movement that renders the world over to the order of its equally mechanically produced image.[28] My point here, I should say to be clear, is not so much that we have entered the regime of the Debordian spectacle; while certainly not untrue (we entered it the moment we started watching the film, or picked up the DVD, or even the moment when film was invented and commodified, etc.), such an observation occupies a different register from the one I am trying to indicate, which in any case surely overlaps in the end with the former, and no doubt conditions it. My point is rather that this sequence shows a kind

Figure 12.4 *Taste of Cherry*: production still/DVD cover: commodified reanimation.

[28] There is a distinct lack of human presence throughout the scene until the worker appears to "harass," however politely, the deeply distracted Badii. In terms of the scene's mechanistic elements, it's worth noting as well that it is initially introduced through the sudden intrusion of a loud and repetitive machine-like pumping/clanking noise first heard over a tracking shot of the dirt road on which Badii approaches in his car.

of death and return to life, a sinking into the ground, or a raising of ground into what is meant to be *distinct* from it, a ground, then, that never stops being world and image, and that in the process is thoroughly determined as a form of industrial operation. Life returns not as redeemed or resurrected, but as mechanically reanimated, as something merely persisting, but implacably so, through its own fascinated effacement. Life does go on, and it does so in an intersection of living death, radical estrangement in images, industrial production, and the machinery of cinema in its accumulating eternities—that "vast receptacle of the living dead," to cite Mulvey again.

Compared to this scene, the infamous coda of the film—in which the dark screen closing over Badii's face in the grave unexpectedly fades back into colorful springtime video footage of the shooting of the film, featuring the actor who plays Badii along with crew members, extras, and Kiarostami himself—is neither more disturbing nor more uplifting as an image of endless continuation (one might well recall Beckett here), but it does underscore the dimension of cinematic production in this troubling impression of eternal reanimation: neither heaven nor hell, only an infinitely repeatable moment cut away from the flow of life "going on." In this regard we might think again of Blanchot, when he evokes the reanimation of Lazarus in a metaphor for the action of a reader who, simply by reading, attempts to call the living-dead *oeuvre* out of the tomb of a book (an action with which one can readily analogize that of the film viewer[29]), but who says that what emerges is neither a living body nor even a stone door falling away from an opening, but rather "[un] déluge démesuré de pierre" / "an overwhelming deluge of stone" (*EL*, 258; *SL*, 195)—this impossible image that sweeps away all but a futile semblance of sense and, on its way to an inaccessible silence, leaves a pure luminous opacity in its wake. Absorbed into it, we are as much opened to light as buried in earth.

---

[29] Indeed Kiarostami himself, quoting Godard, says precisely this to Nancy: "Godard dit que ce qui est sur l'écran est déjà mort, c'est le regard du spectateur qui lui insuffle la vie" / "And Godard says that what's on the screen is already dead—the spectator's gaze breathes life into it" (*EF*, 85 / 84). Nancy comments on this section of *L'Espace littéraire* and the "Lazare, veni foras" that draws the work from the stone that entombs it, reflecting on Blanchot's reference not to a miracle but to "thaumaturgy"—a move that likewise could well be translated into the idiom of cinema and its "magic," thus also into its radically technical and repetitive forms of reanimation. See "Blanchot's Resurrection" in *Dis-Enclosure (The Deconstruction of Christianity)*, trans. Bettina Bergo, Gabriel Malenfant, and Michael B. Smith (New York: Fordham University Press, 2008), 94–95.

13

Nancy('s) Surfaces

James Martell

Thin as a Dissolving Host

Let us be humble. See, feel the paper or screen on which what is printed or projected here appears to you. This chapter aspires to be as humble as possible. In keeping with Jean-Luc Nancy's recurrent use of etymology, it wishes to remain as close as possible to the Latin *humus*, the earth, but also to the ground, the background, and the surface. To be as close as possible to the ground means, as Freud "posthumously" said of Psyche, to be "laid out," "extended," *ausgedehnt*.[1] But how close can this closeness be, especially to a ground-as-surface on which we lie extended, supine or prostrate, perhaps moving or crawling slowly or merely immobile on our backs, listening to a voice in the dark—like Samuel Beckett's character in *Company*? The etymology of *ausgedehnt* ties it to *dünn* (thin, like a film), the ancient Greek τείνω (to stretch, to extend), and the Latin *tenuis* (fine, thin, clear—hence "tenuous" in English). With these semantic hues in mind, when we are stretched out on a surface—in an attempt to be as close as possible to it, thinning ourselves out as far as possible, becoming surfaces ourselves—how close can we get before thinning out completely and disappearing like a transparent film or skin? In other words, how do we measure our closeness to the surface or surfaces on which we stand, lay, sleep, love, or die?

These questions are already betraying our initial intentions. Indeed, let us be humble and remain close to the surface instead of attempting to find a profound answer or a yardstick with which to measure all surfaces. Thus, my thesis in this chapter will not be a regular hypothesis (*hupóthesis*), whereby a general claim is posited, like a foundation on which to build something new or something old anew. Because what I wish to do is to remain as close as possible to some of Nancy's surfaces, my thesis will not be a "putting down" (*hupotíthēmi*), but rather a kind of extending, a spreading, as thinly as possible, on the surfaces we want to examine, becoming as thin as a film or glass that we might see them, and perhaps even touch them—without ever touching them, of course.

---

[1] Sigmund Freud, *Schriften aus dem Nachlass* (*Gesammelte Werke*, Band 17) (London: Imago, 1946), 152.

How many surfaces does Nancy have? It is hard, perhaps even impossible to count them, which is why I do not intend to examine them all here, nor do I believe this possible. Let us split or layer some of them so we can see them better.

There is the page.
There is the fabric.
There is the canvas.
There is the body.
There is the skin.
There is the ocean and Aphrodite.
There is the sky or air.
There is the scene.
There is the cogito and the Chaos: the *chaogito* or the dark side of the canvas.

There is also, to the extent that Nancy's corpus is in dialogue with Heidegger, the indecision between the opening or revelation (*Offenbarung*) and its place or possibility of opening (*Offenbarkeit*).

Figure 13.1 *Nancy Surfaces I*. James Martell, 2021.

Surface ~~is~~ ground ~~is limit~~

In Nancy's body of work, at some point or another, all these surfaces rise, sometimes appearing (as a visible phenomenon), sometimes merely touching, touched or felt. Sometimes they present themselves alone, and sometimes they mirror another surface, as when, through the parallel movement of a pen's opposite ends, the air is inscribed, or written on, at the same time as the paper itself: "*the characters traced in ink become at once, at the other extremity of my pen, pure aerial graphisms.*"[2]

In Nancy's work, this performance or thinking of the surface is linked to a philosophical and writerly preoccupation with *sub*stances and *sup*ports that extends across ethics, aesthetics, politics, and ontology. As early as 1979, in *Ego Sum*, when Nancy began distinguishing his project from those of his contemporaries and co-thinkers of modernity and modernism (a thought of the body à la Merleau-Ponty, of the death of man à la Foucault, or a thinking of the subject as constituted by the structures of psychoanalysis, both Freudian and Lacanian), he conceived their differences in terms of substances as surfaces (a topology) that must, before everything else, support (*soutenir*): "all these instances impose a topology of the *substance*: somewhere, in some place, *that* [*ça*] is supported by something. *Unum quid* supports itself with nothing, and yet 'it takes' place every day."[3] Thus, when he redubs the Cartesian *cogito* as *chaogito*, it is not only because it stands apart from an already ordered world (one *substantivized* into subjects and objects) but also because chaos (χάος) betokens an undecidable, etymological, and ontological confusion of its own between (1) a sufficiently solid surface upon which God created the world, and (2) the abyss, chasm, or ultimate opening into which everything ineluctably gets swallowed. The dual and contradictory value of chaos allows Nancy to deftly follow Descartes's own optic-narratological strategy of the dis/appearance of ego in his own oeuvre. As Nancy shows, in the Cartesian corpus, the author's ego only appears through a mask (*larvatus prodeo*) that conceals chaos as the everyday "support" *through* and *on* which the subject takes place ("a lieu"), or, in other words, as the chaotic grain on whose surface (veil or canvas) the light of illumination is painted.

> [L]ight painted in *trompe-l'œil* can only let its relief be seen by dissimulating this obscure reverse side, the unnamable support (this *substance*) upon the chaotic grain of which it paints itself. It will therefore never be possible to remove or to lift the veil or the picture, without running the risk of not seeing anything anymore, of seeing only darkness—a darkness that no light has yet separated from itself, and which does not even take the *figure* of a shadow. And yet it is also by means

---

[2] Jean-Luc Nancy, *Ego Sum*, trans. Marie-Ève Morin (New York: Fordham University Press, 2016), 34, translation modified; *Ego sum* (Paris: Flammarion, 1979), 55; italics in the original French version. Italics original throughout unless otherwise noted. From this point on, I will provide the translation's pagination and then, when possible, the page of the original French. Translations have occasionally been silently modified.

[3] Ibid., 110; 160–61.

of the "vision," of this invisible support—*formless substance of the eye itself*—that illumination begins. Behind the picture, what does Descartes's face actually *resemble*? Behind the dead eye that deceives the eye, what does the eye (of the) subject resemble? Which *chaogito*?[4]

As we can see, this aesthetic/ontological oscillation between the surface-*behind*-which-something-appears and the surface-*on*-which-something-appears merges the mask, the support, the substance, the ego, and the eye, truly exposing them as supported by no preceding substance or support but themselves. As implied by the confusion between the values of chaos (solid surface or gaping abyss), and the two prepositions linked to the surface (*behind* and *on*), this does not mean that there is no depth or (back)ground here, but rather that one does not exist without the other, and that neither of them can exist without being observed by the others: "For it is 'true' that the surface is that which forms the ground, and that in order for the ground to see itself, it must see its surface, and that in order to see the surface, it has nothing but

Figure 13.2 *Larvatus prodeo*. James Martell, 2021.

4   Ibid., 54–55; 83.

the gaze of others."⁵ As we know, this interdependence—bordering on confusion—between (back)ground and surface will become a central theme or motif in Nancy's reflections and writings on art, while also affecting his writing on other topics, such as politics and technology. My focus in this chapter on Nancy's surfaces is a way of exposing that interdependence—and confusion.

Looking closely, this early superficial (in terms of surface, not of lightness or carelessness) example of the *chaogito* already contains at least five of the surfaces listed above: the fabric of the veil, the canvas of the portrait, the body and skin of Descartes, and the scene where he presents himself (*ego sum, ego ipse*). However, in its presentation or exhibition of the blurred threshold between ground and background, or between the *on* and the *behind* or *within*,⁶ the *chaogito* also already includes Nancy's later version of Aphrodite in "Péan pour Aphrodite" and, with her, the surface of the ocean: "The goddess inverts the sense of depth. In her, depth (*l'enfoncement*) becomes surface; *makes itself* surface [it surfaces, one could say], it rises and is carried off by the foam at the foot of the rock of Paphos in Cyprus. It is not Aphrodite who rises from the abyss, it is the abyss that rises in her."⁷ She thus behaves or exists as the *chaogito*. *In* her, the reversion through which the ground rises and becomes surface takes place. Moreover, this inclusion of Aphrodite and the ocean with and within the other Nancean surfaces is necessary because, in accordance with what Nancy calls "the law of touch" (which I am tempted to call "the law of surfaces"), every being touches every other. This law of touch ties into the previous question: how close we can get to the surfaces upon which we extend ourselves? In the end, it does not matter how close we get (or it matters only in terms of how many surfaces we can touch through that contact), since the law of touch—or law of surfaces—will always dictate separation. Even as we become, like Aphrodite, surfaces ourselves, it is not "us" (as identifiable, definite, self-made and self-sustained sovereign subjects/objects) but our superficial heterogeneity that makes contact:

> All of being is in touch with all of being, but the law of touching is separation; moreover, it is the heterogeneity of surfaces that touch each other. *Contact* is beyond fullness and emptiness, beyond connection and disconnection. If "to come into contact" is to begin to make sense of one another [or one for the other], then this "coming" penetrates nothing; there is no intermediate and mediating "milieu." Meaning is not a milieu in which we are immersed. There is no *mi-lieu* [between place]. It is a matter of one or the other, one and the other, one with the other, but by no means something from one to the

---

⁵ Ibid., 59; 88.

⁶ This confusion among prepositions in English becomes clearer when we think of the different meanings of the French preposition *à* and its polyvalent use in Nancy's oeuvre.

⁷ Nancy, "Paean to Aphrodite," in *Corpus II: Writings on Sexuality*, trans. Anne O'Byrne (New York: Fordham University Press, 2013), 71; *La Naissance des seins* suivi de *Péan pour Aphrodite* (Paris: Galilée, 2006), 102.

other, which would be something other than one or the other (another essence, another nature, a diffuse or infuse generality).[8]

Surfaces of the world, we are one *or, and, with, on, behind, within*, etc., another. Contact is what separates us as limits, whose relations are described or drawn with a variety of prepositions. Nothing and nobody can escape this (pre)positionality, from the very beginning, foundation, or grounding[9] of the world:

> The world, moreover, is but surfaces on surfaces: however far one penetrates behind the wall, there are only other walls, other slices, and strata beneath strata or faces on faces, indefinite foliation of layers of evidence. By painting the wall, the *animal monstrans* does not set a figure on a support; rather, he takes away the thickness of this support, he multiplies it indefinitely, and it is itself no longer supported by anything. There is no more ground, or else the ground is but the coming about of forms, the appearance of the world.[10]

This world of absolute prepositionality is the "being-*toward* of being itself" ("être-à[11] de l'être même").[12] It is also what Nancy calls "aréalité,"[13] that which extends or spreads itself on and as surfaces: the world, a painted wall or rock.

Thus, we must add a new surface to the list: the wall or rock where the *animal monstrans* drew or pressed its hand before blowing paint on it—at Chauvet or Lascaux, for example. But in those landscapes (Vallon-Pont-d'Arc, Dordogne), around the

---

[8] Nancy, *Being Singular Plural*, trans. Robert D. Richardson and Anne E. O'Byrne (Stanford: Stanford University Press, 2000), 5–6; *Être singulier pluriel* (Paris: Galilée, 1996), 23–24.
[9] Needless to say, Nancy's thought on surfaces is directly related to the grounds in German Idealism and Heidegger work, such as *Grund, Ungrund, Urgrund*, and *Abgrund*. Unfortunately, I do not have the space here to develop such relations, which would constitute a full study of its own.
[10] Nancy, *The Muses*, trans. Peggy Kamuf (Stanford: Stanford University Press, 1996), 76; *Les Muses* (Paris: Galilée, 2001 [1994]), 130.
[11] "*World* means at least *being-to* or *being-toward* [*être-à*]; it means rapport, relation, address, sending, donation, presentation *to*—if only of entities or existences *to* each other. We have known how to categorize being-*in*, being-*for*, or being-*by*, but it still remains for us to think being-*to*, or the *to* of being, its ontologically worldly or worldwide trait," as Nancy writes in *The Sense of the World*, trans. Jeffrey S. Librett (Minneapolis and London: University of Minnesota Press, 1997), 8; *Le Sens du monde* (Paris: Galilée, 1993), 18. As the translator's occasional inclusion of two options shows (*to, toward*) when the *à* changes language it must embrace different and varied pre-positions to carry similar meanings (as if the pre-positions were inseparable from a locality, a geography, and a topography). I would argue that, in English at least, the French *à* also conveys meanings closer to the surface, and that it could also be translated by way of *on* or *in* in certain cases, when location and transport are involved, that is, "à Paris"/"in Paris," "à cheval"/"on horseback," etc. Nancy's insistence on the *à*, together with the role of surfaces in his thought, would point to this variegated yet "superficial" dimension of the being-*à*. For a development of the relations between being and prepositions in contemporary thought, see Irving Goh, *L'Existence prépositionnelle* (Paris: Galilée, 2019).
[12] Nancy, *The Sense of the World*, 180n35; emphasis mine; *Le Sens du monde*, 73.
[13] "… being takes place [*a lieu*], but its place spaces it out. Being is, each time, an area, and its reality gives itself in areality [*aréalité*]. It is thus that being is body" (ibid., 35; 58).

caves, there is also the presence of vegetation and, with it, flowers—yet another kind of intricate surface-on-surface event (a foliation of layers) we must keep in mind.[14] If we wish to understand the full notion of the surface in Nancy's corpus, we must touch on all these surfaces on (or against, behind, toward, with, etc.) other surfaces very carefully. Without an ultimate foundation or stable sub-stance beneath them, supported by nothing but themselves and their distance and separation, each of them is not an already stable or grounded entity or representation, but a presence in the Nancean sense, that is to say, a coming-into-being, a birth. As we know, for Nancy, birth is not a noun, a finished or circumscribed past event. It is an undecided and undecidable active verb (whereas death is a name): "To be born is not to have been born, and to have been born."[15] This rising as birth is presence, and here, in this being that is a place "('space' is here the name of 'Being'),"[16] there is no ultimate stable (back)ground (*fond*) or substance. Consequently, on these surfaces that are coming-into-presence, on this rising-of-the-ground, there lies an irresolvable or undecidable question. On the one hand, "[t]here is no more ground, or else the ground is but the coming about of forms."[17] On the other hand, "[w]hat is born has *no form*, nor is it the fundament that is born. 'To be born' is rather to transform, transport, and entrance all determinations."[18] What exactly is a form in this corpus? Is it traced, given, cut out? And where, exactly? On which matter? What is matter (*hýlē*) in a world of surfaces-on-surfaces without substance?

Here lies the humblest aspect of surfaces, the one that is closest to the ground. On, through, against, for, in, toward, etc., there is no solid matter, merely its exterior, its outside, an "impenetrable element" as Ian James explains:

> for Nancy, matter or materiality is always an outside or an impenetrable element, since we know that objects are touched, seen, sensed and given sense only from the outside and from this relation of exteriority, of objects touching each other in a mutual distance or separation (if we open them up, dissect, X-ray, scan, or hugely magnify them we are simply creating another exterior surface or relation of contact-separation of sense).[19]

---

[14] The inclusion of surrounding surfaces such as these vegetal ones underscores the impossibility of detaching one textual surface from other surfaces, like the flowers attached to Nancy's corpus across different collaborative works, such as this gentiana included in a letter from Hantaï to Nancy, reproduced in *La connaissance des textes*: "Sitting on the threshold, seeing nothing but the effects of light going through the holes between the leaves, turning the others translucid, with parallel traits as though engraved on wax with a needle, or accentuating the blue of the gentiana's sepal. And thus afterwards and lasting. The ground and the extension lost." Simon Hantaï, Jean-Luc Nancy, and Jacques Derrida, *La Connaissance des textes* (Paris: Galilée, 2013), 75. My translation.
[15] Nancy, "Introduction: The Birth to Presence," trans. Brian Holmes, in *The Birth to Presence* (Stanford: Stanford University Press, 1993), 2.
[16] Nancy, *The Muses*, 19; *Les Muses*, 39.
[17] Ibid., 76; 130.
[18] Nancy, "The Birth to Presence," 2; emphasis mine.
[19] Ian James, *The Fragmentary Demand* (Stanford: Stanford University Press, 2006), 143.

Without solid or substantialized matter, how does a form take place? On this corpus where "'space' is ... the name of 'Being,'"[20] what exactly is the relation between form and place? How are they different or distinct? Why is form affirmed and immediately effaced within Nancy's corpus?[21] What are the conditions of possibility for both, for a form to take place (*avoir lieu*) and for it to disappear?

Let us get close to the traits, marks, lines, and cuts that make up a form (as the photographs of Simon Hantaï's canvas force us to do when we leaf through the pages of *La connaissance des textes* [Knowing Texts]). Notwithstanding the particularities of its surface (its chaotic grain), it seems as though for any form to appear or to "open," a previous opening as possibility had to already be in place. To speak in Heideggerian terms, for any revelation or opening as *Offenbarung* to occur, the possibility of an opening or revelation, *Offenbarkeit*, must precede it. Unless it is in fact the other way around, and the-possibility-of-opening emerges only through a previous event-of-opening.[22] But what exactly is this opening, how is it de-fined? Precisely by a certain de-finition, a limiting, a tracing as contouring, a co-t(o)urn as a bringing-together not dissimilar to the juncture of concepts and intuitions at play in Kant's schematism. In order for the opening to occur, a line has to be drawn or pulled, a line that resembles a round point, an opening—like a mouth. What exactly triggers or begins this opening, or where—on which exact surface, provided there is a surface before the opening in the first place—is not clear. There is a demand, a request for the line or trait to exist or be drawn. The request for the opening is a call for an act of tracing, for a drawing of a closed line into a contour; in other words, a call for (a) form:

> the opening is what calls for its contour in order to open up, just as the mouth opens and gives its contour, for which it itself takes on contours ... what else is the demand, the call, or the injunction for an opening if not the demand or injunction to have to trace contours, and thus forms, for a revelation, if you will, but I would simply say contours for something of the Open in general to present itself? Otherwise, nothing would present itself at all.[23]

Let us draw this line carefully. The opening demands contours and delimitation, and it does this (requests, calls for it) by precisely taking (*prendre*) contours, by drawing a limit as a closed line resembling a mouth. These contours or closed lines are forms, perhaps setting the scene for a revelation, or, as Nancy says, at least for something of an Opening (of the Revelation) to present itself. But then (what temporal

---

[20] Nancy, *The Muses*, 19; *Les Muses*, 39.
[21] For a development of the question of the birth of forms in Nancy's work, see "Le désir des formes. Entretien avec Jean-Luc Nancy," in *Cosa volante. Le désir des arts dans la pensée de Jean-Luc Nancy* ed. Ginette Michaud (Paris: Hermann, 2013), 241–59.
[22] This reversibility is part of Nancy's and Derrida's discussion in "Responsibility—Of the Sense to Come," in Jacques Derrida, *For Strasbourg. Conversations on Friendship and Philosophy*, trans. and ed. Pascale-Anne Brault and Michael Naas (New York: Fordham University Press, 2014).
[23] Nancy and Derrida, "Responsibility," 78–9; *Penser à Strasbourg* (Paris and Strasbourg: Galilée and the City of Strasbourg, 2004), 191.

boundary or moment is marked by this "then"?), following the previous shift we saw in Nancy's thought on forms, these disappear, transform, transport. Looking at it from another angle, we could say: "first" (and it is not clear if this really is an origin) something of the Opening presents itself, surfaces, thanks to its contours. It exists or is born through these contours, as its proper form. Then (when exactly is this "then"? Is it consecutive, simultaneous, repetitive?), the contours blur, the limit is eroded, and the forms that came to presence transform, transport, entrance all its determinations, limits, closed lines and mouths. What surfaced through, and as its surface, ceases to exist. Where does it go?[24] Is this a measurable transport or transformation? But where and how do we measure it? And where exactly, on which surface or plane does this trans-movement occur?[25]

If we look at this Opening as a cosmogonic surface, we cannot help but recall, in our tradition, one of its most significant names. This primary matrix surface whence all surfaces arise is called *khōra*, the (cosmogonic) "place" par excellence. Derrida invokes it twice in *Le toucher, Jean-Luc Nancy*: once, early on, between the day and the first night, calling it "room, place, space, or an interval,"[26] and then again, near the end, referring to it/her as the space of a substitution or replacement without sacrifice, the "neutral spacing"[27] of hospitality. As we know, in Nancy's body of work, *khōra* does not appear as often as in Derrida's. Just like the mother's name,[28] that of *khōra* is rarely mentioned by Nancy. For Derrida, this is strange, seeing as, when conceiving of the opening (or Revelation) of the figure of the mouth, "it is the mother, in every case, who opens the bordering edges as well as the lips of a mouth first described as an opening … this happens before any figure—not before any identification, but before any 'identification with a figure.'"[29] Before any figure (or identification with one), as before any form, the mother(-like) *khōra* opens in every case, each time, a set of limits,

---

[24] This undecidability between the Opening and its condition of appearance, as well as between the nascent forms and their immediate transformation, resonates in contemporary physics, e.g., with Stephen Hawking's information paradox. In a brutally simplistic way, we could say that the problem of this paradox was precisely the apparent nonexistence of a surface of inscription that could register the transformations in the universe that are effected by black holes. Ultimately, if this surface as register or record could not be proven (with information ultimately disappearing), according to Hawking, scientific determinism would break down, and with it, not only our capacity to predict the future, but also our certainty of the past. In Hawking's words: "The history books and our memories could just be illusions. It is the past that tells us who we are. Without it, we lose our identity," as he writes in *Brief Answers to the Big Questions* (London: John Murray, 2018), 119. Hawking's ontology also appears to be a topology: "the universe we experience is just a four-dimensional surface in a ten- or eleven-dimensional space" (ibid., 117).

[25] For a similar examination of the surfaces of transformation but on Catherine Malabou's corpus, see my "Malabouian Plasticity Without Surfaces," *Mosaic: A Journal for the Interdisciplinary Study of Literature* 54, no. 1 (March 2021): 93–112.

[26] Derrida, *On Touching—Jean-Luc Nancy*, trans. Christine Irizarry (Stanford: Stanford University Press, 2005), 3; *Le Toucher—Jean-Luc Nancy* (Paris: Galilée, 2000), 13.

[27] Ibid., 262; 293.

[28] Ibid., 28; 41.

[29] Ibid., 41–42.

borders, contours. Yet *khōra* does occasionally appear in Nancy's corpus, although not in the context of ontology. Instead, it appears in or as art:

> The painter reproduces the discretion of presence because he imitates it, because he repeats it, and because these two gestures are one and the same. Of presence in general ... it imitates the line drawn by withdrawal, the silent coming and going in which presence exchanges itself ceaselessly with its own disappearance, leaving and coming back ceaselessly from farther away, from the space of *chora*, where the pure separation of forms and colors would be rigorously equal to the total indistinction of a single material mass.[30]

And a decade later in an interview with Jérôme Lèbre, it appears yet again:

> Everything jostles instantly into a chaos impossible to untangle, from which innumerable forms emerge, only to dive immediately into the maelstrom of this ever-so-strange (hi)story of art ...
>
> As if there were—there or underneath, or rather: there as the beneath of all possible theres, as the non-place and non-time of an extraordinary, exorbitant reserve, not of the possible but of the unexpected, the unpredictable, remaining ever unforeseeable in every moment, in every burst of a coming and an expansion that pulls itself together so as to replay, reform, transform itself somewhere else in the same place, a Platonic *khōra*, or rather *Khōra* in person, as Derrida wishes to call it/her, calling nobody really, nor any determined thing—not so much an informity [*informité*] as how it offers and lends itself prior to any distinction of forms.[31]

The painter imitates by repeating (it is in fact the same gesture), back and forth. Painters imitate/repeat the movement of presence *in general*, the marking that is an immediate, if not simultaneous, effacing of the line that exchanges, substituting itself over the *khōratic* surface. This coming and going is not just a to-and-fro; it is also a back and forth over and into the surface-maelstrom (like the *chaogito*), from the space where we distinguish colors and forms, to the space of total indistinction, a space of "non-place and non-time" that is not exactly matter but made of a material mass. Yet *khōra* is not exactly the latter space, but rather the equalizer of the two (surface and chaos) and, ultimately, of all spaces. "In this place, which is at once without place and in a hundred places ... *the transcendent and the immanent would imitate each other*, in an impossible and tenacious imitation."[32] This is *khōra* as Nancean transimmanence. It is the canvas (or notebook, paper, wall, rock, subjectile, copying machine, etc.) as surface of painting and inscription, but also the brain, the hand, the palette, the painter's skin, the viewer's

---

[30] Nancy, "On Painting (and) Presence," in *The Birth to Presence*, 348.
[31] Jean-Luc Nancy and Jérôme Lèbre, *Signaux sensibles. Entretien à propos des arts* (Montrouge: Bayard, 2017), 109–10. My translation.
[32] Nancy, "On Painting (and Presence)," 349.

eye, their mouth and every other rim (*bord*) in and around a given opening. It is the "farther away" where presence is equal to its disappearance. However, if *khōra* is the elsewhere of everywhere, why does it appear exactly here in Nancy's corpus, in other words, in and as art, at the hands of painters, sculptors, videographers, etc.?

As we know, art and aesthetics occupy—and embody—a special space in Nancy's oeuvre. As Martta Heikkilä shows us in *At the Limits of Presentation*, Nancy's "philosophical views even come so close to the way he explains an artwork that they finally prove indissociable."[33] Or as Ian James explains: "his thinking on art is inseparable from *the manner* in which he conceives of thinking per se, and thus inseparable from his thinking of sense, body, materiality, world-hood, and so on."[34] Such an intricacy within his corpus and thought begs the question as we endeavor to remain close to some of Nancy's most relevant surfaces: is there any surface (in this corpus) that is not an *a(i)esthetic*[35] surface—or even an art sub-ject or ob-ject? If to paint is to imitate

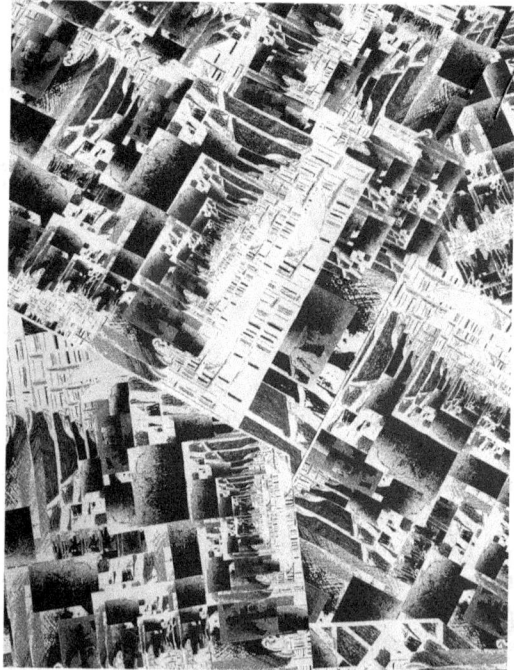

Figure 13.3 *Nancy Surfaces II*. James Martell, 2021.

---

[33] Martta Heikkilä, *At the Limits of Presentation* (Frankfurt am Main: Peter Lang, 2008), 150.
[34] James, *The Fragmentary Demand*, 204; emphasis mine.
[35] By means of "aiesthetic" I want to mark, like Ginette Michaud in "Le désir des formes," a certain preference for a thinking of the aesthetic that is not necessarily coopted into art history. However, I use the parentheses to question if that separation is possible anymore, especially in our hyper-imaged social-media life, where each picture gets "exhibited" to potentially millions of people (alive or to come), mere seconds after it is taken.

and repeat the discretion of presence, can there be a presence (*praesum, praesse*: to be in front, even of oneself)[36] that is not always already the repetition or a rehearsal of a painting? Is the pre-positionality of presence as *prae-sum* an ex-hibit that trans-forms each presence—as aiesthetic/thinking surface—into an artwork or a work of *tékhnē*? In other words, is what distinguishes Nancy's surfaces from those of Derrida, Heidegger, and Kant (among others) precisely the fact that they cannot *not* be artistic, that there is nothing non-artistic, non-technical, "natural" about them—there is something in them, sometimes, not even *written* in a Derridean sense of (arche-)writing, but just surfaced, extended, spread like a canvas or a body? Is the inextricability of philosophical thinking and art in Nancy's work an idiomatic trait constantly remarked by his thinking of and on surfaces (of the body, the world, the ego, the imagination, communities, etc.), that is to say, by his performative affirmation of an inseparability between (the subject of) thought and its surface(s) of inscription/appearance?

The Place: Without Sacrifice

When, at the end of a discussion of flesh in *On Touching*, Derrida reinvokes *khōra* as the place of the gravest Temptation in our tradition, the place of a substitution without sacrifice, he is hinting at a substitution of the classical tradition of ontotheological substitution (exemplified here by Jean-Louis Chrétien) by Nancy's own thinking of substitution. Such a sacrifice of the sacrifice, in Nancy's thought, is essential to art. Or, in other words, it is the closest we get to an essence of art and *tékhnē*, inasmuch as they present us with a resistance against the essential operation of metaphysics that denies sense and the senses. In Nancy's corpus, this resistance is existence itself, "insofar as it *is* the without-essence."[37]

> Art is the presentation of presentation insofar as presentation—the eternally intact touch of being—cannot be sacrificed ... This is indeed why, moreover, the entire tradition has stumbled over the sacrifice *of the senses* that it required in the name of truth and the good, a sacrifice, however, that art has not ceased to refuse to grant the tradition, withdrawing this sacrifice from the tradition in virtue of the breaking [*frayage*] of a completely different path.
>
> This is indeed why "art" is also *ars* or tekhne: that which takes place wherever the essential and sacrificial—essentializing—operation that "meta-physics" projectively supposed to be the operation of a *phusis* does not take place.[38]

"... that which takes place whenever the essential and sacrificial—essentializing—operation ... does not take place." Where is this place? "[W]herever (there) ... does

---

[36] Nancy, *The Sense of the World*, 13; *Le Sens du monde*, 28.
[37] Nancy, *The Gravity of Thought*, trans. François Raffoul and Gregory Recco (New Jersey: Humanities Press, 1997), 76; *Le Poids d'une pensée, l'approche* (Strasbourg: La Phocide, 2008), 11.
[38] Nancy, *The Sense of the World*, 138–39; *Le Sens du monde*, 211.

not take place" [*là où n'a pas lieu*]? If this "place" is no longer determined by the metaphysical operation, that is to say, if it is not a place understood from the perspective of *physis* or nature, is it still a place as space, or is it something else, an "*espacement*" without space? Where does the (Nancean) substitution lie or take place, and what is its relation to painting's and presence's imitation *and* repetition of each other, *as*—quite literally—each other? Is this the place where participation (*methexis*) and imitation (*mimesis*) "meet"? Etymologically, as we know, a substitution, like a hypothesis (*hupóthesis*), is a putting down (*sub-statuo*). But without a sacrifice to sustain or substantivize it, to "harden" the place,[39] where exactly is this sub-stitution happening, upon which surface as limit is it put down?

Here lies, precisely, another surface I have not mentioned explicitly, but that is essential to the body in Nancy: the limit. As can be easily inferred, even if I have not mentioned the limit explicitly in my initial list of surfaces, it has been there the whole time. It was there from the beginning, when we began with a command to be humble and remain close to the earth, the ground, the page, or the screen. Later, the limit also appeared under another of its common guises: the contour, the line that, starting at (or as) a point, ends up reaching itself after going through a certain circuit. As we know, *Margins of Philosophy* begins with an analysis of the limits of philosophy, where Derrida pictures these limits as the "domestic page of its own tympanum."[40] For both Derrida and Nancy, the limits of philosophy are the limits of their own writing, both insofar as they remark them and as they constantly try to pass—or pierce—them. However, when the structure under discussion is that of Psyche outstretched (unbeknownst to her) as it appears in Nancy's philosophy, the limits become nothing but surfaces that create "the *interiority effects* of a structure made up of nothing but surfaces and outsides without insides. The superficies of these surfaces ... are limits—exposed, as such, to a touch that can only ever leave them intact, untouched and untouchable."[41]

But how exactly is the limit constituted for Nancy? Considered as a surface, it has a singularity that distinguishes it from other surfaces (e.g., it is not a bank or a *rivage*).[42] At the same time, the limit is precisely what constitutes or delimits all singularities: "the limit is in sum both inherent to the singular and exterior to it: it ex-poses it."[43] However, the limit is not only what constitutes them, but also their very place, where singularities take (or have) place as limits, becoming bodies in the process: "*Bodies*

---

[39] Yet, on these surfaces, there is a "hardening" or "thickening," which is that of sense through exscription: "It is the point where all writing *ex-scribes* itself or is *ex-scribed*, where it comes to rest outside of the meaning it inscribes, in the things whose inscription this meaning is supposed to form. This *ex-scription* is the ultimate truth of inscription. Made absent as discourse, meaning comes into presence within this absence, like a concretion, a thickening, an ossification, an induration of meaning itself" (Nancy, *The Gravity of Thought*, 79–80; *Le poids d'une pensée, l'approche*, 15).

[40] Derrida, *Margins of Philosophy*, trans. Alan Bass (Chicago and Sussex: The University of Chicago Press and The Harvester Press, 1982), xii; *Marges—de la philosophie* (Paris: Les Éditions de Minuit, 1972), III.

[41] Derrida, *On Touching—Jean-Luc Nancy*, 14; *Le Toucher—Jean-Luc Nancy*, 26.

[42] See Jean-Luc Nancy, "Banks, Edges, Limits," trans. Gil Anidjar, *Angelaki. Journal of the Theoretical Humanities* 9, no. 2 (2004): 41–53.

[43] Ibid., 46; "Rives, bords, limites (de la singularité)," in *Le poids d'une pensée, l'approche*, 130.

don't take place in discourse or in matter. They don't inhabit 'mind' or 'body'. They take place at the limit, *qua limit*: limit—external border, the fracture and intersection of anything foreign in the continuum of sense, the continuum of matter. An opening, *discreteness*."[44] To have or take place (*avoir lieu*): is this then what distinguishes—by embodying it—a limit, what creates both the opening and its possibility? Is Nancy's corpus, against and in front of phenomenology (and post-phenomenology), nothing but a topology?

> The place, the big place, open to their multiplied enclosures [*clôtures*], all tangent among each other. Everywhere the place shifted between them, quickening the touching of their ever-sensitive membranes. Of their films [*pellicules*], minuscule epidermises, surfaces of contact between us, between the world and the world, places stretched into membranes too fine to contain the time of an opening, a single time [*le temps d'une fois*], a single time each time reprised and replayed, of one unique view taken again, reframed, coated with a new gel, a new glassy humor.
> Neither sight nor appearance [*le paraître*] are at play here: phenomenology has no place there where being is topological.[45]

It is certain that, even among the extraordinary catalog of paintings, sculptures, videos, drawings, and films in Nancy's corpus, we are not there, whenever we visit it, merely to *see*. Thinking in Nancy is not a matter of *eidos*, even though Derrida was right not to completely exclude Nancy (and himself and anyone else who writes philosophy) from the desire to retain "the sense of touch within sight so as to ensure for the glancing eye the fullness of immediate presence required by every ontology or metaphysics."[46] Nevertheless, a *topos* and a topology, as a thought, logic, or bundle of surfaces, is a matter never only of seeing and touching, but also—and perhaps more importantly—of walking, crawling, swimming, and, in general, of moving. A topological thought is a moving thought going at a speed that, in Nancy's view, does not belong to time: "To think: a speed for which no time can account. And thus, not a speed. A gap, a dis-location: here is another place, another *topos*."[47] Yet, if this is a topology, it is different from Lacan's.[48] Here, it is not the knots that multiply the surfaces, but rather the surfaces that—in their "original" multiplicity—create and multiply knots (as in a painting by Hantaï). In other words, if—as I said at the beginning—it is impossible

---

[44] Nancy, *Corpus*, trans. Richard A. Rand (New York: Fordham University Press, 2008), 17; *Corpus* (Paris: Éditions Métailié, 2000), 18.
[45] Nancy, "L'approche," in *Le poids d'une pensée*, 122–3. My translation.
[46] Derrida, *On Touching—Jean-Luc Nancy*, 120; *Le Toucher—Jean-Luc Nancy*, 138.
[47] Nancy, "Espace contre temps," in *Le poids d'une pensée, l'approche*, 86. My translation.
[48] Perhaps they are not completely different, however. There is an insight in Lacan's topology of the disappearance of the background or depth as third dimension in our regular human experience, at least: "The sense of depth, of thickness, is something we lack, much more than we believe. This to put forward what I want to tell you at the start: that we are beings, you as well as me, of two dimensions, despite appearances," as transcribed in Jacques Lacan, *Seminar XXI: Les non-dupes errent*, trans. Cormac Gallagher, December 11, 1973, 3; *Le Séminaire. Les non-dupes errent*, séance du 11 décembre 1973, 18).

to count the surfaces of Nancy's corpus, it is because this body of work is not exactly topological but topographic. That is to say, before any *logos* or *ratio* can describe or measure it, it exists as the tracing, scratching, cutting, drawing, inscribing, imprinting of an originary *grapho* (γράφω) that creates (the) surface(s): "There is not 'the' body, there is not 'the' touch, there is not 'the' *res extensa*. There is that there is: creation of the world, *tékhnē* of bodies, weighing without limits of sense, topographical *corpus*, geography of multiplied ectopias—and no u-topia."[49]

The question for us is—not necessarily in front of, but against, on, for, under and above all these surfaces and their marks, stains, wounds, valleys, and so on—how does a topographic thinking like Nancy's take place (*topos*), and how exactly is it written, marked, printed, etc.? How does such a thinking affect our modern and modernist traditions not only of thinking and writing, but also of painting, engraving, printing, filming, touching, tattooing, walking, kissing, etc.—and of everything that happens on, against, etc., a surface? How does this "superficial" thinking affect our own notion

Figure 13.4 *Nancy Surfaces III*. James Martell, 2021.

[49] Nancy, *Corpus*, 119; *Corpus* (original French edition), 104.

of modernism (and modernity), if we consider the latter as a departure, a taking off from a previous foundation, an abandonment of a previous soil and tradition? In other words, what happens when we, in and as the world, no longer distinguish a radical break or clear elevation (above the past, tradition, the dead, what has been overcome, *aufgehoben*, etc.) but become instead surfaces on surfaces against surfaces toward surfaces, and so on? What happens when surfaces rise without any foundation, tradition, or ultimate ground other than their "own" superficiality? Does the new spatiality of this Nancean topology not affect necessarily our own historicity too? Perhaps, from our positions, prostrate or supine on the ground, the page, or the screen, we cannot answer this question. Perhaps it is not the right question anymore. This close to the surface, there is no clear "what," no ontological or historical event that can rise higher for us to distinguish it clearly—there is no separate tradition to distinguish from our modernisms (at least not before we have deconstructed these terms and their complex co-implications). Here, any event that arrives arrives *on us* aesthetically; it gets inscribed or exscribed on us, as us, as a tattoo on our multiple corpora. A tattoo on our backs, on our punctum caecum, can only be seen, read, and/or touched through the sight or touch of the other, the one who, no matter how close, remains infinitely distant in their finitude.

However, is there any clear tattoo-like inscription or mark in or on the whole oeuvre or written (visual or tactile) corpus of Nancy's work, something we could call a Nancean tattoo? If our thesis is correct and the essential structure of Nancy's oeuvre is a topography of infinite surfaces, and, according to it, our own bodies are a primary surface of inscription, is the tattoo (not only as a writing, but also as any kind of tracing—figurative, abstract, or in between) not a fit description of the surfaces' reciprocal effects on each other? In *Corpus*, however, when explaining exscription and the *partes extra partes* of bodies, masses, and senses, Nancy makes an exception for the corpus itself as surface. It is not a complete exception, as if the corpus were not a surface at all in this case. It is merely a restriction.[50] The corpus remains a surface, just not one for the inscription of a signification, namely, for writing. This exception foregrounds the tattoo, at least within the envelope of a parenthesis. Here, Nancy does not deny that tattoos exist or are inscribed on the body. In this exceptional context, he merely separates them from a writing on the body as inscription of signification. As for the tattoo itself, we have not yet started discussing it properly, to do it justice.

> In this anatomy of masses, which is the same thing as saying a space of emotions, the corpus is no longer anything like an inscriptive surface—**as a recording of signification**. No "written body," no writing at the body, and nothing whatsoever

---

[50] Earlier on in the same book, Nancy had made another singular exception to the surface. In this case, it was to subsume it into category of extension. "The body is the being-exposed of the being. / This is why 'exposition' is very far from simply taking place as the extension of a surface. This very extension exposes other kinds—such as, for instance, that mode of the *partes extra partes* that is the singular dis-assembly of the 'five senses'" (Nancy, *Corpus*, 35; *Corpus* [original French edition], 32–3). The question for us, looking at the further development of surfaces in Nancy's later corpus is: can an extension completely avoid being a kind of surface?

of a somatographology into which the mystery of the Incarnation was sometimes converted *à la moderne*, and the body, also, into a pure sign of the self, the pure self of the sign. Just so, therefore: the body's no place for writing (it's certainly clear, for example, that we have to start here, if we hope to do justice to tattooing). *That we write*, no doubt, is the body, but absolutely not *where* we write, nor is a body *what* we write—but a body is always what writing *exscribes*.[51]

If the body is not, thus, *where* we write, but rather that which writing exscribes, what kind of surface does this exscription constitute or create? Is the risk of the tattoo as a *signifying* writing on the body its putative permanence—a harbinger of identity? For Nancy, the body as surface of exscription is rather like a screen (like the one where I, and potentially you, are seeing these words "appear" as I type and you read) instead of a skin pierced with metal and ink.[52] The risk of the surface as skin, parchment, page, as with Freud's writing pad, or the Levinasian (and perhaps Derridean) trace, is its potential ineffaceability, that is to say, the threatening permanence of its traits. Even if, as in Beckett's oeuvre, it seems that a new utterance or trait would efface the mark of the previous one ("all you have to do is say you said nothing and so say nothing again"[53]), on the inscribable, material surface, unlike on an electronic screen, the trace or writing remains, like a mark unto and potentially beyond death.

Thus, if, as we saw, the paradigmatic surface of Nancy's corpus is the place, and his oeuvre a topography, it is because, in the reciprocal coming and going of us and/as places, we become (each other) screens, not pages: "The value of the place is an approximate value. It is a value of proximity. One comes on the places, a view offers and disposes itself, the whole of being comes next to us. The whole of being disposes itself on the screen we have become."[54] Thus, to us, the whole of being comes. *On* us, as its exscription, the whole of being extends (*dehnt aus*, like Psyche) ("from the andesite idols of uncertain sex up to us, who grasp the foam of their names on the shining screen of a computer")[55] without knowing it (*weiss nichts davon*).[56] This is the Nancean approach. Come close. Let us be humble. Nevertheless, perhaps there is still a tattoo somewhere on this corpus. After all: "Existence is its own tattoo."[57]

---

[51] Nancy, *Corpus*, 85, 87, bolds mine; *Corpus* (original French edition), 75–76.
[52] For an analysis of tattooing, Nancean exscription and Derridean grammatology in the context of Jeff VanderMeer's oeuvre, see Cosmin Toma, "Jeff VanderMeer's Southern Reach Trilogy: Writing Out the Body Between Grammatology and Exscription," in *Tattooed Bodies: Theorizing Body Inscription Across Disciplines and Cultures*, ed. Erik Larsen and James Martell (New York: Palgrave Macmillan, 2022), 245–64.
[53] Samuel Beckett, "Texts for Nothing 6," in *The Complete Short Prose*, ed. Stanley E. Gontarski (New York: Grove Press, 1995), 124.
[54] Nancy, "L'approche," in *Le poids d'une pensée, l'approche*, 120.
[55] Nancy, "Paean to Aphrodite," 77; *Péan pour Aphrodite*, 111.
[56] Freud, *Schriften aus dem Nachlass*, 152.
[57] Nancy, *The Sense of the World*, 58; *Le Sens du monde*, 98.

14

The Poetics and Politics of Disenclosure: Nancy, Mbembe

Michael Krimper

If it has become a refrain of the neoliberal age that it is easier to imagine the end of the world than the end of capitalism, then perhaps Jean-Luc Nancy could be said to alert us to the gaps, intervals, and ruptures within these very conditions of enclosure. An excess of sense, he argues, always runs counter to the circulation of money presiding over the ends of the world. This counter-circulation of sense tends to suspend the principle of general equivalence, undermine the transcendental reign of monovalue reducing everyone and everything to measurable units of exchange, and elicits an experience of the common that has otherwise been captured, appropriated, and extracted by the logic of property. It opens onto the incommensurability of the outside that each and every being shares in common, for the outside constitutes what the world is and what all things are, that is, the finitude and materiality of coexistence. In Nancy's view, the affirmation of infinite openness to the outside of the world offers an immanent exit from the nihilism that defines the era of the closure of metaphysics—an era in which the forces of technical-economic and political domination set the world to work according to the rational and indefinitely expanding processes of globalization. It is from this perspective that Nancy broaches the task of the "disenclosure" (*déclosion*) of metaphysics, reason, and the globalized civilization of the West in his two volumes on the *Deconstruction of Christianity* (*Dis-Enclosure*, 2005 and *Adoration*, 2010).[1] Disenclosure concerns the trace of writing that dismantles and reopens the closures blocking off our being-in-common or, as he puts it in a succinct formula, brings about the "[d]econstruction of property—that of man and that of the world" (*DE*, 161) so as to make sense of the world anew.

---

[1] Jean-Luc Nancy, *Dis-Enclosure (The Deconstruction of Christianity)*, trans. Bettina Bergo, Gabriel Malenfant, and Michael B. Smith (New York: Fordham University Press, 2007) and *Adoration (The Deconstruction of Christianity II)*, trans. John McKeane (New York: Fordham University Press, 2013). Hereafter *DE* and *A*, respectively. See also "On Dis-enclosure and Its Gesture, Adoration: A Concluding Dialogue with Jean-Luc Nancy," in *Re-treating Religion: Deconstruction Christianity with Jean-Luc Nancy*, ed. Alena Alexandrova, Ignaas Devisch, Laurens ten Kate, and Aukje van Rooden (New York: Fordham University Press, 2012), 304–44.

The questions of writing and sense-making traverse Nancy's methodology of "disenclosed metaphysics," shaped by his sustained research on the ontological, political, and ethical implications of modern literature and art. Over the course of nearly fifty years, he explored how a certain itinerary of literary and aesthetic experience from Romanticism to modernism and beyond interrupts the totalizing narrative structure of myth and communicates the "inoperativity" of the work, its *désœuvrement*, leaving sense unfinished, interspersed, and open-ended. Rather than producing meaning as fixed signification or representation, the modern literature and art under question for Nancy dis-encloses the metaphysics of meaning as presence, all the while making sense in common. This transmission of sense passes through words, bodies, and things, propelling them outward, where they are put in contact with the infinite from which the motion, emotion, passage, transport, and dynamic impulse at the source of existence are generated. Moreover, in his writing on democracy, Nancy locates a disjunction between the sphere of politics, which is not everything, and the sphere of sense, which enlarges the scope of modern literary and aesthetic experience to embrace a much more capacious field of poetics and praxis including multiple modalities of the arts and expressive cultures in everyday life. Democratic politics, according to Nancy, must then be charged with the task of holding open this space of sense without circumscribing its form, determining its content, or privileging any figure of the people. This is because the space of sense safeguards the demands of justice and equality—the demands to acknowledge the nonequivalence of singularities and to sustain the improper that is the most proper to each and every being. The disenclosure of metaphysics therefore entails (though this remains implicit) a poetics and a politics that warrant further attention.

One of the few contemporary thinkers to pick up on Nancy's study of disenclosure is Achille Mbembe, who likewise holds out on the promise of a "democracy to come"[2] predicated on the ethos of being-in-common. But Mbembe links disenclosure (*déclosion*) to yet another wide-ranging theoretical term marked by the negative prefix *dé*, namely *décolonisation*, as elaborated above all by Frantz Fanon and his successors. Disenclosure, he maintains, introduces strategies for breaking apart the globalized structures, institutions, and forces of enclosure underlying the racializing and (post)colonial configurations of sovereign power and violence in modernity. These regimes of power exclude certain human populations and groups from fully partaking and sharing in the common, rendering them fungible and disposable, consigned to the region of nonbeing. Disenclosure, however, lets what has been foreclosed surge into the open where each one of us can dwell together in the common. Such an emergence or insurgency of sense, the sense of being-in-common, sketches the edges of our co-inhabiting and belonging to the world. To tease out the poetics and politics of disenclosure in this essay, I will examine the

---

[2] Achille Mbembe, *Out of the Dark Night: Essays on Decolonization*, trans. Daniela Ginsburg (New York: Columbia University Press, 2021), 90.

still underappreciated convergence between Nancy and Mbembe,[3] both of whom consider notably inoperative ways of making sense, of doing and being in common, or even of reimagining the human and world divested of property. In my concluding section, I will turn to Mbembe's approach to decolonial and modern literary and aesthetic practices in Africa and particularly his remarks on listening and writing to urban Congolese music as a tangential way of illustrating and deepening Nancy's poetics of disenclosure.

The Writing of Disenclosure

Nancy's treatment of the disenclosure of metaphysics submits to critical reassessment the "disclosure" (*Erschließung*) of the meaning of Being as elucidated by Martin Heidegger.[4] After Heidegger and Friedrich Nietzsche, he interrogates how the metaphysics of presence purports to establish a transcendental foundation on the basis of which the entirety of beings appears in the world. Insofar as metaphysics attempts to bring about its own closure as the accomplishment of a totality, it cannot help but remain susceptible to a field of instability that threatens to undermine the whole system and open it onto something else. If, as Nancy asserts, "metaphysics sets a founding, warranting presence beyond the world" that "stabilizes beings, enclosing [*referme*] them in their own beingness [*étantité*]," then "[d]is-enclosure denotes the opening of an enclosure [*enclos*], the raising of a barrier [*clôture*]" out of which being-in-common can be exposed, felt, and shared (*DE*, 6). This is why, he explains, metaphysics deconstructs itself, or the closure of metaphysics discloses itself, for it is tied to the excess of sense from which it stems and yet which it cannot rationally grasp, appropriate, or master. "In truth, metaphysics deconstructs itself constitutively, and, in deconstructing itself, it dis-encloses [*déclôt*] in itself the presence and certainty of the world founded on reason" (*DE*, 7). It is in this way that disenclosure exhibits the groundlessness of metaphysics, or absence in the place of the supposedly transcendental foundation, surpassing both humanity and the world. However, Nancy goes further in unraveling the ontological difference between Being and beings—the fundamental relation at the heart of Heidegger's existential analytic—without revealing anything at all. In contrast to the disclosure of the meaning of Being, disenclosure lays bare the infinite expanse of nonbeing (i.e., *nothing*) out of which beings are pushed into existence, pass through one another, and become sensible as always already being-with. It does not lay bare the enclosure of everything within the confines of pure immanence either, but rather the mutual entanglement of

---

[3] I am indebted here to Michael Syrotinski who begins to think their convergence around the notion of disenclosure in "Mbembe's (Re-)Writing of Postcolonial Africa," *Paragraph* 35, no. 3 (2012): 407–20; and "Postcolonial Untranslatability: Reading Achille Mbembe with Barbara Cassin," *Journal of Postcolonial Writing* 55, no. 6 (2019): 850–62.

[4] See Michael B. Smith's useful foreword (*DE*, ix–x).

all things exposed to the outside of the world in the midst of the world. Disenclosed metaphysics and reason let us think an immanence with an outside.[5]

Nancy's reiteration of *déclosion* as "disenclosure" thereby displaces the *Destruktion* of ontology initiated by Heidegger within another configuration of sense oriented around the ethos of being-in-common. In this respect he expands on Jacques Derrida's approach to deconstruction through the prism of writing, frequently turning to literature (and art) in his elaboration of the experience of language as trace and, somewhat at odds with Derrida, as the *exscription* of sense. "[O]ur world," Nancy proposes, "is the world of literature" (*A*, 41) because it interrupts the mythological narrative structure in which language is harnessed to assign meaning to the origin and destiny of a communal existence—any particular social, ethnic, religious, national, racial, or linguistic group based on fixed relations of common belonging and ownership. By contrast, the strand of modern literature and art under question for Nancy, extending from Friedrich Hölderlin to Stéphane Mallarmé to James Joyce, among many others, communicates the "opening of the voices of the 'with'" (*A*, 41) deprived of all foundation and identity. On the one hand, it ruins the logic of property according to which the individual and collective subject could be mythologically constructed as a self-unifying and totalizing whole. And, on the other hand, it conveys senses of relation, as shared separation, touching the infinite out of which the rhythm, pulsion, and élan of finite coexistence reverberate without closure.

The way Nancy puts into play the interweaving terms of disenclosure and deconstruction within this context resembles his usage of the untranslatable word *désœuvrement* or "inoperativity." He borrows the doubly active-passive sense of *désœuvrement* as "unworking" and "worklessness" from Maurice Blanchot in his critical readings, first of all, of the Jena Romantics with Philippe Lacoue-Labarthe (*The Literary Absolute*, 1978) and, secondly, of Georges Bataille's failed experiments with community (*The Inoperative Community*, 1986). In the latter book, Nancy links *désœuvrement* more broadly to the concern with writing in Derrida, Blanchot, and Roland Barthes, all the while emptying Bataille's meditations on the sacred of their sacrificial and religious dimensions. Subsequently, *désœuvrement* for Nancy comes to signal the "*in*" of "being-in-common," that is, the spacing of the common that no one owns but is shared and divided between us as *partage*. Writing, then, involves the exscription of the passage between, across, and through a plurality of singular voices whose openness to each other and to the outside defies integration into the work as a whole. This is why Nancy unfolds *désœuvrement* as "the unworking of literature," "the unworking of works," of "all unworked 'communication.'"[6] *Désœuvrement* gives rise to the unworking of the work, not only as the work of literature or art, but also as the overall program of humanity whose enormous effort of self-production and realization

---

[5] On broken immanence in Nancy, see Frédéric Neyrat's important book, *Le Communisme existentiel de Jean-Luc Nancy* (Paris: Éditions Lignes, 2013).

[6] Nancy, *The Inoperative Community*, ed. Peter Connor, trans. P. Connor, Lisa Garbus, Michael Holland, and Simona Sawhney (Minneapolis and Oxford: University of Minnesota Press, 1991), 39. Hereafter *IC*.

derives from the work of the subject or organic substance. At certain junctures, Nancy puts the unworking of literature under the header of "literary communism," that is, "the sharing of community in and by its writing, its literature" (*IC*, 26). However, literary communism does not refer to the literature belonging to any community in particular, nor to "the myth of the literary community" introduced by Jean-Jacques Rousseau and German Romanticism up to "the idea of communism (of a certain kind of Maoism, for example), and revolution inherent, *tels quels*, in writing itself" (*IC*, 64). On the contrary, writing shatters those myths of community, including the enclosures of national literary traditions, republicanisms, the avant-garde groups, and their disparate postwar afterlives, indicating altogether different ways of partaking in the common and commons.[7]

It is worth underscoring that Nancy's usage of *désœuvrement* in his study of Bataille's search for impossible literary, aesthetic, and erotic communities during the 1930s and 1940s proceeds from his earlier application of the term in his study of the search for the literary absolute in the fragments of the Jena Romantics at the dawn of the nineteenth century. Across this long century of the avant-gardes, the affinity between the inaugural moment of Romanticism in Jena and the twilight of modernism signaled by Bataille implies the significance of literary communism for Nancy. At the interstices of these literary-aesthetic movements and periodizations, we can glimpse the ruptures wherein the work (including the work of the avant-garde group) induces its own fragmentary dissolution and breakdown, improvises other ways of making sense in common, and contributes to the disenclosure of metaphysics. Furthermore, in turning to early Christian texts, Nancy registers the proximity between disenclosure and *désœuvrement* in his reading of faith, or *pistis*, according to Saint James. "Faith," rendered "in a Blanchotian idiom," he specifies, is "the inoperativity [*désœuvrement*] that takes place in and as the work [*dans et comme l'œuvre*]." And, returning to Derrida, he restates "that faith, as the praxis of *poiēsis*, opens in *poiēsis* the inadequation to self that alone can constitute 'doing' ['*faire*'] and/or 'acting' [*l'agir*']" (*DE*, 52). What Nancy's elaboration of inoperativity suggests throughout, as distilled most recently in the book *Doing* (2016), is the possibility of "both transitive and intransitive" modes of making, creating, or doing (*faire*) that amount to neither a poetics characterized by the production of a work adequate to its concept, nor a praxis characterized by the effectuation of a goal-oriented project.[8] Rather, the word "inoperativity" approximates the creative production of a work in which what is at stake is the manifestation of its own praxis, that is, a nonproductive mode of doing or being devoid of finality. It transmits the sheer materiality of language, or sensorial experience, whose exposition

---

[7] On the ethical, political, and ontological stakes of Nancy's hitherto abandoned expression of literary communism, see my essay "Senses of Relation: 'Literary Communism,' Democracy, and the Common" in the special issue "Jean-Luc Nancy: Poetics, Politics & Erotics of Exscription," ed. Philippe P. Haensler, Stefanie Heine, and John Paul Ricco, *Parallax* 26, no. 4 (2020): 449–65.

[8] Nancy, *Doing*, trans. Charlotte Mandell (London: Seagull Books, 2020), 56. Nancy's revisiting of Lenin's famous revolutionary question "What is to be done?" around mode, or the *how* of doing, resonates to some extent with Agamben's treatment of modal ontology in *The Use of Bodies* (2014) and Tiqqun's call to mobilization "How is it to be done?," reprinted in *Introduction to Civil War* (2006).

of being-in-common resists the identity and community formation of the subject and affirms the freedom to co-fashion the sense of the world here and now. What it offers to thought, Nancy proposes, is "'causing to exist' [*faire exister*] without principle or goal, without author or project, but where *existing* is asserted as the adventurous and daring 'shoreless doing' (*uferlosem Tun*) of which Celan speaks."[9] He calls this unbounded making of existence, stripped of all teleology, *adoration* or *fervor*.

Sense, Justice, Democracy

Nancy's analysis of the literary aesthetic of sense-making (*faire sens*) thus leads him to lay out an inoperative poetics and praxis that recasts doing (*faire*) at a distance from politics. He detaches inoperative poetics and praxis from re-productive activity or labor, from the social management and organization of the common, as well as from the work of the subject. And, in doing so, Nancy avoids reorienting the retreat of the political and politics around the ethical ontology of being-in-common. Instead, he contends that democratic politics, or "'communism' as the truth of democracy,"[10] must undertake the task of holding open the space of sense without determining its meaning or privileging any figure of the people. "Democracy," he claims, must be reinvented and "assume a dimension that it cannot integrate for all that, a dimension that overflows it, one concerning an ontology or an ethology of 'being-with,' attached to that absolute excedence [*excédence absolue*] of sense and passion for which the word *sacred* was but the designation" (*DE*, 5). The sphere of sense, as I mentioned beforehand, embraces not only modern literary and aesthetic forms, but numerous ways of existing "outside" politics—"almost anything you like,"[11] Nancy suggests, such as love, thought, play, leisure, dreams, sexuality, friendship, and so on. These ways of existing, doing, and making sense run counter to the circuit of general equivalence and exchange, because they furtively elide, curtail, and resist the calculation and regulation of value. They communicate the incommensurable value of any singularity whatsoever, whose irreducible plurality cannot be represented within the political domain where everyone is supposed to be deemed equal and interchangeable as individuals, persons, or citizens under the abstraction of the law.

What can be heard in the sphere of sense is another call for equality and justice than that which can be discerned or achieved by politics. This is the infinite demand to feel and acknowledge the common impropriety at the heart of someone's most proper being. If "politics is far from being everything," Nancy estimates, then democratic politics "becomes precisely a place of detotalization" and the disenclosure of the world responding to the demand of "incommensurable 'justice.'"[12] And he distinguishes the

---

[9] Nancy, *Doing*, 72. Italics original throughout.
[10] Nancy, *The Truth of Democracy*, trans. Pascale-Anne Brault and Michael Naas (New York: Fordham University Press, 2010), 30.
[11] Ibid., 26.
[12] Ibid., 51.

freedom of sense-making, in response to that exigency of justice, from the political administering of systems of domination and unequal power relations:

> Freedom is arriving at a heteronomy of meaning: being free from oneself so as to enter into the intelligence and sensibility of the unknowable, the undeterminable, even the unnamable—but because it is to such an opening that meaning exposes itself. Politics is an administration of possibilities that doesn't impose a higher order on them but opens them to this opening: not what is out of reach, but what reaches us by coming from nowhere and going nowhere. Neither a dream of happiness nor a triumph of mastery, but still and always justice—which is also justice of forms, relationships, emotions, in short, justice of meaning. It is infinitely just that we all can not merely produce a unique meaning but also exist in a circulation of meaning where there is no question of mastering or subjecting.[13]

The circulation of sense that safeguards the "justice of meaning" exposes an elsewhere, coming from and going nowhere, both within and without the structures of confinement and enclosure instituted by neoliberal regimes of governance, both within and without the ceaseless production and consumption driving the technical-economic configuration of the world as an indefinitely expanding totality, both within and without the conditions of globalization in the era of the closure of metaphysics. It attunes us to the opening from which the common that we are is disenclosed and shared—the common to which anyone belongs and in which anyone can partake without mastery, subjection, or possession. "It is existence and the sharing of this existence," Nancy remarks, "that can alone lay claim to the 'proper,' that is, to meaning. A meaning that is not available and not discoverable otherwise than in its passage and its sharing."[14] What is most proper to us is the improper that we cannot help but give away and share together. This is why democratic politics, according to Nancy, stems from an "equality of incommensurables" outlining "a communism of nonequivalence."[15] It does not produce any common identitarian form but sustains a gap out of which uncountable reconfigurations of the people, a sense of being-in-common, can be provisionally engendered. This tension marks how the spheres of politics and sense are at once separated from and conjoined to one another.

It is precisely Nancy's ethical reframing of politics that Mbembe takes up from the standpoint of decolonization, community, and democracy to come. His approach to an "ethics of encounter" characterized by an "aesthetics of singular plurality" and "dispersing multiplicity" similarly emphasizes the sharing of the outside as what is held in-common. This is why Mbembe proposes that "if, as Nancy suggests, justice

---

[13] Nancy, *Doing*, 34.
[14] Ibid., 42.
[15] Nancy, *After Fukushima: The Equivalence of Catastrophes*, trans. Charlotte Mandell (New York: Fordham University Press, 2015), 40–41.

must be done both to the singular absoluteness of the proper and to the common impropriety of all, then democracy must once again find what, at the origin, has always made it an ethical event."[16] Or, in another formulation, a "planetary democracy" has to rediscover the ethos of being-in-common harboring the inescapable "demand for justice and reparation."[17] Ultimately, the common furnishes a compelling alternative to the impasses of the politics of abstract universalism and of difference shaping the terrain of contemporary debates on community. For the "*in-common*," Mbembe claims, implies the "communicability" and "shareability"[18] of relation without assimilating the other into an already constituted community delimited by fixed relations of attachment and belonging. Nor does it reify and essentialize difference under the rubric of communitarianism, multiculturalism, or identity politics in its most restricted sense. Democracy to come for Mbembe is therefore incompatible with either the universalist model of the state or liberal humanism, each of whose calls for inclusion steadily recognize and integrate the other into an established socio-juridical and economic order that always presupposes and conceals a particular ethnonational, cultural, linguistic, or racial identity. Instead, it is predicated on the acknowledgment of the equality of singularities without common measure.

Mbembe would seem to hold, even if he is less explicit on this point than Nancy, that democratic politics must then keep open the space of the common where unheard forms of existence can be made anew. "[T]he *sharing of singularities*," he specifies, "is indeed a precondition to a *politics of relation and of the in-common*."[19] But Mbembe resitutates Nancy's communism of nonequivalence within the theoretical framework of postcolonial thought geared more acutely toward the question of race and the prospect of a "postracial democracy." He unfolds this intervention as a multi-staged effort: "enunciating the plural of singularity becomes one of the most effective ways of negotiating the Babel of races, cultures, and nations"[20] that are increasingly entangled with one another in the age of globalization. Under the material circumstances of widespread global migration and displacement, Mbembe seeks to align the politics of the in-common with the task of abolishing race and more specifically of the sovereign configuration of necropolitics—the subjugation of life to the power of death— approximated by the expression *white supremacy*. One could trace the origins of white supremacy at least as far back as to the advent of Enlightenment reason and technical-scientific mastery in Europe, which sought to elect a specific people, as the white race, to represent all of humanity and fulfill what is proper to Man, thereby justifying the reign of colonial imperialism and the transatlantic slave trade. In Mbembe's view, this metaphysical paradigm of sovereignty at the source of the modern era constructed race as a hierarchal ordering and dividing of human populations "according to *a logic*

---

[16] Mbembe, *Out of the Dark Night*, 111.
[17] Mbembe, *Necropolitics*, trans. Steven Corcoran (Durham: Duke University Press, 2019), 40.
[18] Mbembe, *Out of the Dark Night*, 110.
[19] Ibid., 109.
[20] Ibid., 106–7.

of enclosure"²¹ governed by the principles of capture, predation, and commodification. And it continues to produce forces of extraction and containment, relations of enmity and hatred, and the violent material destruction of the work of death systematically exercised over groups deemed to be surplus (e.g., Black, native, immigrant, etc.). For these reasons, Mbembe holds that the "myth" of "the absolute superiority of so-called Western culture,"²² understood as the culture and technological power of "the white race," lies at the basis of not only fascism and Nazism, as Nancy would emphasize, but also the colonialism to which democracies are inextricably bound. To abolish white supremacy, Mbembe seems to suggest, the politics of the in-common would require ethical interventions of the social, aesthetic, and literary praxis of decolonization, that is, the disenclosure of the world.

Mbembe's theory of decolonization draws in part from Nancy's essay on "Disenclosure," which briefly treats the ecotechnical and colonial dimensions of "the 'conquest of space'" (*DE*, 159). There, Nancy links the installation and proliferation of global satellite communication networks back to Europe's imperial expansion into the Americas and, in turn, settler colonialism. He puts forward that with the so-called discovery of the new world, its eclosure (*éclosion*) in the sense of the hatching or blossoming of the new becomes a function of the technical-economic instrument, namely Christopher Columbus's boat *The Santa Maria*, which serves to divide, possess, and transform space. The figure of the boat indexes the ways in which the larger technological spatialization of nature and the given (including human and nonhuman species) makes everything and everyone available as standing reserve for the extractive forces of capital. But, against this ecotechnical determination of space, Nancy considers another sense of eclosure, as self-eclosure, which exhibits the mutual entanglement of all things in the ordinary everyday. "The separation and distinction of all things is not a banal, de facto given," Nancy observes. "It forms, on the contrary, the gift, the giving of things itself. It is the permanent eclosure of the world" (*DE*, 159). Such an eclosure of the world traces "the spacing of space," the shared edges at the limits of the outside, opening onto the impropriety of the common over which no one has power. This is why "dis-enclosure," Nancy sums up, is the "dismantling and disassembling of closed bowers, enclosures, fences [*des clos, des enclos, des clôtures*]. Deconstruction of property—that of man and that of the world" (*DE*, 160–61). But what would it mean to dismantle the apparatuses of enclosure and reopen them to the outside of being-in-common that they incessantly try to exclude, appropriate, and dominate? What would it take to think and enact the deconstruction of property from the perspective of decolonization as the disenclosure of both humanity and the world?

---

[21] Mbembe, *Critique of Black Reason*, trans. Laurent Dubois (Durham: Duke University Press, 2017), 35. For a critical take on Mbembe's humanist argument from the lens of Blackness in this book, see David Marriott "The becoming-black of the world? On Achille Mbembe's Critique of Black Reason," *Radical Philosophy* 2, no. 2, online, accessed June 2018: https://www.radicalphilosophy.com/article/the-becoming-black-of-the-world.

[22] Mbembe, *Necropolitics*, 120.

In addressing these questions, Mbembe aims to retrieve and renew the theoretical stakes of decolonization in terms of disenclosure. His concern lies with the event of decolonization not so much as the historical transfer of power from empire to formerly colonized states as the ongoing "struggle for freedom" and "revolution"[23] that withholds the creative insurgent potential to transfigure the globalization of Western Christian civilization. This is what leads Mbembe to connect the "disenclosure of the world" and of humanity to the chance of their "rebirth" along the lines of a postracial humanism, as arguably upheld by Frantz Fanon. After citing Nancy's formulation of disenclosure as the dismantling and disassembling of all sorts of closures, Mbembe teases out its relationship to decolonization in the following way:

> The term *disenclosure* is synonymous with opening [*éclosion*], a surging up [*surgissement*], the advent of something new, a blossoming. To disenclose is thus to lift closures in such a way that what had been closed in can emerge and blossom. The question of the disenclosure of the world—of belonging to the world, inhabitance of the world, creation of the world, or the conditions in which we make a world [*faisons monde*] and constitute ourselves as inheritors of the world— is at the heart of anticolonial thought and the notion of decolonization. One could even say this question is decolonization's fundamental object.[24]

Mbembe's theory of decolonization as disenclosure corresponds to the eclosure of the world, that is, the emergence of a shared common world in the making of which anybody can freely partake. By way of Fanon, he develops this point in drawing our attention to the movement of uprising or surging forth [*surgissement*] whereby the colonized subject awakens to consciousness and asserts self-ownership. Yet the struggle for self-determination and autonomy on the part of the dispossessed, Mbembe specifies, involves an *"ascent into humanity"* given over to the impropriety of "the *Open*."[25] The "return to oneself," he points out, is above all to "leave oneself,"[26] to relinquish identity, to inhabit the space between self and other, at the cusp of the outside. The task of decolonization, then, is to exit the *"enclosure of race"* in which the colonized had been closed off, captured, exploited, oppressed, and commodified. If racialized signs like "Black" indicate that which exceeds all signs—an "operation of injustice,"[27] according to Nancy, which fixes and names the unpresentable, foreclosing any share in the common—then the disenclosure of race would have to signal the unpresentable escaping all figuration. "The universalism of the name 'Black,'" Mbembe explains, "depends not on repetition but on the *radical difference without which the dis-enclosure of the world is impossible*." In the name of "this *radical difference*," he continues, we must reimagine Blackness as always being "on the road,"[28] stolen away, in

---

[23] Mbembe, *Out of the Dark Night*, 43.
[24] Ibid., 61–62.
[25] Ibid., 62, 63.
[26] Ibid., 75.
[27] Nancy, "The Compearance," trans. Tracey B. Strong, *Political Theory* 20, no. 3 (1992): 392, translation modified.
[28] Mbembe, *Critique of Black Reason*, 160.

passing. Subsequently, Mbembe registers a new beginning for the creation or invention of existence, no longer rooted in the land, blood lines, language, heritage, nor ethnic or racial belonging, but uprooted, dispersed, and migratory, much like Celan's shoreless doing. And though this "dream" of a planetary and postracial humanism prefaced on the affirmation of being-in-common, insurgency, and "sharing"[29] (*partage*) borrows and departs from Nancy (who adamantly steers clear of any humanism), Mbembe reminds us that human being is imbricated with other living species, incessantly surpasses itself, and stays suspended as an open question.[30]

Mbembe elucidates the disenclosure of the world within a wide field of inquiry comprising not only the French deconstructionist thinkers of the democracy to come, but also multiple trajectories of Black study. He finds affinities between Nancy's ethos of being-in-common and Léopold Sédar Senghor on the cultivation of the care of belonging; Édouard Glissant's poetics of relation; and Paul Gilroy on convivial life.[31] From the other side of the Atlantic, we could also bring into the fold Fred Moten on insurgent social life and Saidiya Hartman on the wayward and unmanaged life of Black feminist anarchy. These writers, despite their many divergences, all contest the logic of property from the lens of the common. Mbembe, for his part, distills these intersecting revitalizations of the common in "an ethics of the passerby [*passant*]" according to which passage, crossing, and translation assert the solidarity of "passing life,"[32] which traverses a shared humanity and world to come. He thereby brings Nancy's inoperative poetics and praxis of "making common" to bear on the chance of a disenclosed and "*decolonized community*"[33] that would confirm our co-inhabiting and belonging to a world whose sense is always still in the process of being made. Disenclosure, then, would involve a nonsovereign way of making common—of making sense, community, people, humanity, and world—detached from all property. But what remains to be thought is how the poetics of disenclosure can be affirmed in specific modern literary or aesthetic practices.

Infinite Rhythm

Mbembe alludes to the political stakes of the poetics of disenclosure in a semi-autobiographical essay where he incisively displaces and rethinks Heidegger's commentary on Hölderlin concerning the role of the poet "in times of distress."[34] Following Nancy, he cautions against the mythologizing power of poetry elucidated

---

[29] Mbembe, *Out of the Dark Night*, 75.
[30] We can hear echoes of Nancy's insistence on the excess of *humanitas* in Heidegger's letter on humanism, as well as his frequent references to Pascal's formulation that "man infinitely surpasses man."
[31] Mbembe, *Out of the Dark Night*, 63–64.
[32] Mbembe, *Necropolitics*, 188.
[33] Mbembe, *Out of the Dark Night*, 224.
[34] This insightful essay, "À partir du crâne d'un mort. Trajectoires d'une vie," introduces the French version of *Out of the Dark Night* but is not included in the English translation. See Mbembe, *Sortir de la grande nuit. Essai sur l'Afrique décolonisée* (Paris: La Découverte, 2010), 31–53. My translation.

by Heidegger, for whom the language of the poem as song is meant to disclose the destiny of a people rooted in its proper and authentic being, a view which entails the "enchantment" that arguably underpinned his commitment to Nazism. By contrast, Mbembe gestures toward a literary or aesthetic practice of errancy that would acknowledge and share the impropriety at the heart of being singular plural. His own writing proceeds from this rupture of identity, from the noncoincidence of the self, whose fundamental pre-originarity has become all the more exposed due to the migratory flows of global capital. In refusing the aestheticization of politics based on myth, Mbembe considers and performs an African decolonial writing that discloses the world from the guise of "Afropolitanism," understood as a transnational, diasporic, and antiracist stance of solidarity.[35] To illustrate and deepen the poetics of disenclosure, I would like to conclude by turning to Mbembe's statements that listening to the modern sounds of urban and popular African music animated his writing of the book *On the Postcolony* (2000).[36] The experience of listening to this music guided him to think with the bodily senses and, returning us to Nancy's own reflections on music, to channel the infinite rhythm of the outside in and through the resistance of writing.[37]

With the decline of Afro-Marxism in the early 1990s, Mbembe would register the political implications of altogether different transmissions of senses of being-in-common in literature, the arts, and many other ordinary forms of expressive culture and experience. He points out that his critique of the sensorial life of power in *On the Postcolony* draws on innovations in the Francophone novel and writing in Africa from the 1980s onward, alongside the loose filiation of French theory from Bataille to Nancy with which he had become familiar as a student in Paris. Moreover, Mbembe claims that his book would not have been possible without the experience of listening to pathbreaking African musicians like Fela Kuti, Pierre Akendengué, and Ray Lema, but especially the vibrant postwar mutations of Congolese music, whose dual expression of joy and pain invents a tragic variation on beauty. Congolese music would let him hear the "social memory of the present" in which the drama of African self-making and unmaking was being played out across national, linguistic, aesthetic, cultural, and geopolitical borders.[38] After all, each of these emergent musical forms, be it Fela Kuti's revolutionary protest songs dubbed "Afrobeat" or Franco Luambo's polyrhythmic deviations on rumba, taps into heterogeneous genres and traditions spanning the modernist innovations of Black American jazz to Latin and Caribbean dance styles to

---

[35] Mbembe, *Out of the Dark Night*, 209.
[36] See the interview "Achille Mbembe in Conversation with Isabel Hofmeyr," *South African Historical Journal* 56, no. 1 (2006): 177–87; and Mbembe, *On the Postcolony*, trans. A. M. Berrett, Janet Roitman, Murray Last, and Steven Rendall (Berkeley: University of California Press), 2.
[37] Nancy, according to Ginette Michaud, touched on his own habit of listening to music—"bathed, surrounded, and carried away by music, that of opera in particular"—while writing together with Lacoue-Labarthe. See her essay "Ek-phraseis de Nancy," in *Cosa volante. Le désir des arts dans la pensée de Jean-Luc Nancy* (Paris: Hermann, 2013), 218. My translation. Many thanks to Mahité Breton for this reference.
[38] "Achille Mbembe in conversation with Isabel Hofmeyr," 178.

European classical composition and Christian hymnology to indigenous folklore. These juxtapositions would make sensible the rapid material transformations and historical fluctuations of everyday urban life in Africa, whether in Kinshasa, Brazzaville, or elsewhere. "A good reader," Mbembe notes, "can hear the sounds of Congolese music late in the night behind many a chapter of *On the Postcolony*. Some days, while writing this book and listening to this music, I could literally feel the transitory rhythms of earthly life in Africa."[39] He goes on to stress that Congolese musical performance does not have recourse to the myth of Black nationalist politics, economic-technical developmentalism, or the postcolonial dream of Pan-African racial redemption. Rather than rooting the destiny of a people in the language, land, and nation to which they would authentically belong, the song archives the syncopated rhythms and breaks of passing daily life, the ethics of the passerby, in the postcolony.

In an essay dealing at length with Congolese music, Mbembe examines how its mixture of sounds, noises, and screams occasions certain effects on the listener up to the point of eliciting an "experience of *listening*" with the whole body.[40] The music performed by Papa Wemba, Koffi Olomidé, or Zaïko Langa Langa, just to name a few, put the senses in motion; they generate overwhelming waves of energy that affect, assail, and pass through the listening and, most often, dancing body. Calling attention to the sensual dance steps of women in particular to the rhythms known as soukous, Mbembe proposes that the experience of listening renders tactile the ways in which the history of power and violence is inextricably entangled with the senses in the everyday struggle for life in the postcolony. With a nod to Nietzsche (if not Bataille) on the Dionysiac frequencies of music, he maintains that the dancing body expresses the desire for fugitive release, escape, and joy in the throes of abjection; "dancing becomes a way of journeying outside the self."[41] The dancing body's unproductive expenditure of energy destroys the relations of servitude and mastery underlying the subject as work. "For, to dance in a regime of the ugly and the abject, is to rid oneself, in an instant, of the labour of the slave," Mbembe contends. "Shaped and sculpted by sound, the subject relinquishes himself, erases from his face the expression of destitution."[42] Congolese music, then, evokes a "celebration of the flesh" in search, he specifies, of "perpetual genesis" and the "serenity"[43] of beauty or happiness within the prevailing sociopolitical and economic conditions of enclosure.

Yet wouldn't such a celebration of the flesh run the risk of producing the ecstatic communion or enchantment against which Mbembe had warned us from the outset? Nancy, for his part, cautions against the interiorizing dangers of music, which is liable to be subsumed by the immanentism of myth making. This is because music's expression of sentiment can be "understood as collective and unique to a defined

---

[39] Ibid.
[40] Mbembe, "Variations on the Beautiful in the Congolese World of Sounds," *Politique africaine* 100 (2005): 73.
[41] Ibid., 86.
[42] Ibid., 91.
[43] Ibid., 85.

community, or rather, defined by being experienced in its own song."[44] In spite of these risks, inherent to the participatory absorption of *methexis*, we could emphasize the radically exteriorizing effects of music in Mbembe's reading of Congolese musical performance. To celebrate the life of the flesh in undergoing an ecstatic physical experience of listening, feeling, and dancing with others is to be carried outside and abandoned to the space of the common. The festival opens up and affirms the sphere of existence where senses of being-in-common can be heard and affirmed underneath the violent structures of domination in the postcolony, without congealing into the sentiment defining any newly forged community. One could argue that the poetics of disenclosure hereby implies the underside of necropolitics, not the subjection of bodies to regimes of terror, but the insurgency of forms of life mobilizing other ways of coming together, making sense in common, and beginning the world anew.

Mbembe thus evokes the dynamic interplay between multiple registers of the senses traversing the experiences of writing, reading, listening, dancing, and sensorial life in general. His point of departure of writing from "a rift" (*faille*) of identity cannot help but "explode received language"[45] and lead him to experiment with thinking in the form of a song that provokes the senses. "Congolese musical imagination taught me how indispensable it was to *think with* the bodily senses, to write the musicality of one's own flesh if we are to say anything meaningful about life in contemporary Africa" and to "write a book in which the song carries with it the flesh that gives it life."[46] To think musically is to communicate the finitude and materiality of life propelled by the force of transport between porous bodies, words, sounds, ideas, and things. The cadence of rhythm, its intermittent withholding of tension and bursting in the break of the present, its discontinuity and irregularity, consigns the senses to constant remaking according to a futural temporality at the interstices of living and dying that remains unknown, inappropriable, and open-ended. It would seem, then, that the poetics of disenclosure courses through Mbembe's writing and thought, lending to it a certain sonority and pacing of resistance, just as much as the music to which he had been listening.

Mbembe's reading of Congolese musical performance shows how the poetics of disenclosure implicates another way of embracing, sharing, and celebrating different senses of existing at a remove from politics. He touches on the poetical manifestation of "a veritable politics of freedom" that could exceed and suspend the necropolitical killing machine of human sacrifice or extermination. And it refuses the generalized circulation of death in decolonial or emancipatory struggles on which the sovereign self-actualization of the human is usually based. This politics of freedom and the in-common would have to keep open the space of sense in which the work of death can be rendered inoperative and the unsacrificeable fact of existence felt, written, and affirmed. This is because, Mbembe explains, the call for "*disposing-of-death itself*

---

[44] Nancy, *Listening*, trans. Charlotte Mandell (New York: Fordham University Press, 2007), 55. Hereafter *L*.
[45] "Achille Mbembe in conversation with Isabel Hofmeyr," 187.
[46] Ibid., 178.

[donner la mort à la mort]" can only be read "figuratively" or "poetically,"[47] such as in the decolonial African novel or Congolese music and dance, exhibiting the precariousness and confusion of life in the postcolony. And yet they improvise at the same time the freedom and resistance of disenclosure, a common spirit of uprising, whose opening onto the outside sustains the infinitely demanding exigencies of justice, reparation, and equality.

I would venture that this is the outside to which Nancy speaks and listens in his own ontological meditations on music. "Music is the art of making the outside of time return to every time, making return to every moment the beginning that listens to itself beginning and beginning again. In resonance the inexhaustible return of eternity is played—and listened to" (*L*, 67). Even though his analysis relies for the most part on examples of European classical music and opera, Nancy embraces a range of high and low art forms, mentioning at various points contemporary genres of Black music, including rock, techno, and rap. Furthermore, his elucidation of rhythm in terms of the temporality of the outside, punctuating an interval that is out of time, corresponds to Mbembe's remarks on the antisystematic beat of urban African music.

Nancy, too, is well aware of the contact zones where music and writing, sound and thought, communicate with one another across the senses. All of the senses can animate and shape certain discourses as philosophical, literary, or aesthetic practices attuned to the ethos of being-in-common. Thus, it is in writing and thinking with the bodily senses that Nancy contributes to the deconstruction of property or the disenclosure of both the human and world. Writing becomes an experience of listening to the pulse, thrust, and drive of sense-making in the unmediated temporality of the here and now. This is why writing, as Nancy reiterates once more, "is nothing other than making sense resound beyond signification, or beyond itself" (*L*, 34–35). For writing vocalizes a sense, or insists on a way of existing, whose resisting and shattering of meaning continues to resound and sound out with others. "Here, no doubt," he specifies, "literary writing and musical writing touch each other in some way" (*L*, 36). At this confluence, Nancy's musical and literary writing, accompanied by Mbembe's, touches and channels the infinite rhythm of the outside from which the sense of existence, always still in the making, surges into the open.

---

[47] Mbembe, "*On the Postcolony*: A Brief Response to the Critics," trans. Nima Bassiri and Peter Skafish, *Qui Parle* 15, no. 2 (2005): 19.

15

Between Modernism and *Modernité*: An Interrupted Dialogue with Jean-Luc Nancy

Jean-Luc Nancy and Cosmin Toma

What follows is an unfinished conversation. A mere few months before the Covid-19 pandemic broke out, I sent Jean-Luc Nancy a set of pointed questions on the topic of modernism and/or modernity, with the understanding that he would revise his answers shortly prior to the manuscript's submission, and that I would append a handful of additional, last-minute questions in response to his initial replies, to which he would then respond in turn. The aim was thus to provide an up-to-date reflection of his thoughts on the matter, in keeping with modernity's transience and velocity.

This was sadly not to be. What remains, presented here in translation, is a semi-fragmentary snapshot of a strand cut short.

Cosmin Toma: When I first got in touch with you about this edited volume, you replied that your work is "entirely immersed" in modernity—so much so that it is impossible to tackle it head-on. Is this immersion something of an unthought for us "moderns"? And what does this "us" mean here in light of statements you've made in the past, which paint modernity as something that is "ours"? Allow me to cite a few examples: "No culture has lived as our modern culture has in the endless accumulation of archives and expectations"[1]; "Deconstructing belongs to a tradition, to our modern tradition"[2]; "our community, if it is one, our modern and postmodern humanity"[3]; "A veritable romantic *unconscious* is discernable today, in most of the central motifs of our 'modernity.'"[4]

Jean-Luc Nancy: This "us" or "we" [*nous*] is equivalent to the "modern" ever since it—culture, discourse—started calling itself "modern." This word means that we cannot

---

[1] Jean-Luc Nancy, *After Fukushima: The Equivalence of Catastrophes*, trans. Charlotte Mandell (New York: Fordham University Press, 2014), 40.
[2] Nancy, *Dis-Enclosure: The Deconstruction of Christianity*, trans. Bettina Bergo, Gabriel Malenfant, and Michael B. Smith (New York: Fordham University Press, 2008), 148.
[3] Nancy, *The Inoperative Community*, ed. Peter Connor, trans. P. Connor, Lisa Garbus, Michael Holland, and Simona Sawhney (Minneapolis and Oxford: University of Minnesota Press, 1991), 52.
[4] Philippe Lacoue-Labarthe and Jean-Luc Nancy, *The Literary Absolute: The Theory of Literature in German Romanticism*, trans. Philip Barnard and Cheryl Lester (Albany: State University of New York Press, 1988), 15.

detach ourselves from this sign of demarcation because we are too conscious of coming after… in a certain sense: after all. We know all too well that an entire history is behind us. Your quotes clearly show that I am distancing myself from "modernity": I speak of "tradition," I add quotation marks. We could almost even get rid of the word *modern* altogether: it no longer constitutes a subject of interrogation or discussion; it is only the index of a situation. At bottom, this situation is somewhat analogous to old age: when we grow old, we know ourselves to be at the end of a past and with but a short future ahead. And so we say "at my age," etc. I would say that "modern" means "at our age…"

CT: Perhaps the problem of immersion in modernity and/or the unconscious harks back to what Georges Bataille says of sovereignty:

> in general modern man has given first importance to a domain that the advancement of learning extended, organized and made ever more coherent, this being the domain of consciousness—clear and distinct, of course. Archaic man was mainly taken up with what is sovereign, supernatural, with what goes beyond the useful, but that is precisely what a consciousness enlightened by the advancement of learning relegated to a dubious and condemnable semidarkness, which psychoanalysis named the *unconscious*.[5]

Do you share this effectively psychoanalytic articulation of the archaic and the modern, perhaps even of history in general?

JLN: No, because I don't think we may speak in such a way of "archaic man," who certainly had many "useful" preoccupations and for whom even what Bataille calls the "supernatural" [*merveilleux*] hinged on the "useful." Everything had to be useful for the sake of a pressing concern with survival. Since we have more or less devised a system where survival appears relegated to the background—for all those who do not suffer from hunger or thirst or other extreme conditions—we have dissociated the "useful" from the "supernatural." We look after life, health, work, leisure… Everything is in this upkeep. And it is a source of disquiet for us in the end…

CT: If we give in to the temptation of etymology, modernity stems from the postclassical Latin *modernus*, which points back to *modus*—measure and manner—as well as to the instantaneity of *modo*. On the one hand, every measurement is retrospective; it distinguishes, mathematically and rhythmically as it were, between the manner "before" and the manner "after." And yet, modernity nonetheless construes itself as a kind of "absolute present,"[6] to quote Mallarmé's *Igitur*, and hence as a perpetual present, ceaselessly leaping beyond itself in order to respond to the call of that which is to come [*l'appel de l'à-venir*]. Does this tangled and paradoxical temporality fundamentally differ

---

[5] Georges Bataille, *Sovereignty*, in *The Accursed Share: An Essay on General Economy*, vols. II (*The History of Eroticism*) and III (*Sovereignty*), trans. Robert Hurley (New York: Zone Books, 1991), 226. Translation slightly modified.

[6] Stéphane Mallarmé, *Igitur*, trans. Mary Ann Caws; online, accessed February 15, 2022: http://www.studiocleo.com/librarie/mallarme/prose.html.

from that of a hypothetical "pre-modernity"? From an anthropological standpoint, for instance, Bruno Latour has argued that "we have never been modern," rejecting one of the most traditional criteria we use to distinguish the modern era from what preceded it, namely the "nature/culture" coupling.

JLN: When did the "call of that which is to come" begin? It seems possible to think that the Roman Empire began with a vision of expansion at once political and technical, which previous expansions (the Persian one, for example) had ignored. Christianity grafted a "future to come" [*un "à venir"*] onto it, one that was non-earthly at first but already imbued with the expectation of a "coming." Later it becomes historical—while, by way of an interesting contrast, Islam, on the one hand, and Byzantium, on the other, represent dispositions less turned towards "progress" and more towards conservation. There is something like a split [*un partage*] between East and West here that is also a split relative to the motif of God's "incarnation."

CT: There are, as we know, countless *manners* of defining modernity. Its taxonomy varies from one country, from one field of study to the next. Thus, this term does not convey quite the same meaning depending on whether we happen to be in France, in the United Kingdom, in Egypt or in Japan, whether we study history, literature, politics, philosophy, anthropology, the visual arts, theology, music, the so-called "hard" sciences, etc. Is this plurality, which may well point towards a disagreement that is impossible to overcome, constitutive of modernity *as such* (assuming it is possible to speak of it in the singular)?

JLN: I don't know whether this plurality is truly plural. It seems to me that everywhere and in all registers this word conveys a value of difference of nature between a given past and a currency that is innovating in a decisive manner—a difference that is like a leap or a mutation more so than an evolution. It is parsed by some as a promise, by others as a deterioration. I don't think we can find a comparable concept/affect in the histories of other long civilizations, in which it's true that there were evolutions, transformations, but never (and I may well be wrong here) the awareness of a mutation of nature rather than of degree.

CT: More so than the French tradition, its Anglophone counterpart uses the term *modernism* to name twentieth-century art's most demanding forms, as if this becoming "-ism" formed the ground of aesthetics in the modern era. Under this umbrella are gathered writers such as Ezra Pound (whose programmatic motto, "make it new," inspired many poets), James Joyce, Virginia Woolf, T. S. Eliot, Gertrude Stein, and Samuel Beckett (to name but a few), visual artists like Pablo Picasso, Georges Braque, and Marcel Duchamp, or composers: Arnold Schoenberg, Alban Berg, Anton Webern, Igor Stravinsky, Béla Bartók, etc. It goes without saying that this brief enumeration is anything but exhaustive, if only because of the Muses it glosses over, but I would like to at least dwell on Beckett's case, because it opens onto two questions that strike me as unavoidable here: 1) how does the word *modernisme* resonate in French?; and 2) what are we to make of the self-described internationalism of this movement, which Beckett so exemplarily embodied?

JLN: It seems to me—and this remains to be verified, once again—that early on the "modern" was an English value—whether it be in matters of language or, independently of language, in political, social, or cultural matters. Francis Bacon (and even, before him, Roger Bacon!), Hobbes, Locke, and Shakespeare bear witness to an incontestable English anteriority in the awareness of what I would call a "change of nature," even if the Italian Renaissance holds other titles through which it may lay claim to "modernity." The *New Atlantis* is an invention of Bacon's.

How does *modernisme* resonate in French? It strikes me as a worn term, which is all I can say. It was overtaken by the "avant-garde," until the latter disappeared along with the idea of revolution in general. As for internationalism, it is ultimately inherent to modernity.

CT: In Beckett's wake, once again, we may revisit the (increasingly less ubiquitous) notion of "postmodernism." Indeed, Beckett has often been singled out as the twentieth-century author who best subverted the modern/postmodern distinction, ushered in by Jean-François Lyotard (among others) then taken up by the English-speaking world, where it made an even bigger splash. In *After Fukushima*, you write that "[t]o speak of 'postmodern' is correct if we mean by that giving up any aim for a future conceived of as the unity of a meaning to come. But it is not enough, since that remains trapped in a scheme of succession, of before and after."[7] More than a decade later, what remains of this demarcation line [*ligne de partage*] today?

JLN: "Postmodernism" was invented by architects who wished to get out of a "modernism" they deemed rigid, authoritarian, or even totalitarian. It sought to loosen the self-assured principles of a modernity already certain of being its own coming [*avenir*]. I would say that the modern was the future [*futur*] close at hand (as was indicated by the word *futurible*, now largely forgotten) and that the postmodern replaced the future with games played with the present. But all *post* are mere acknowledgments of the powerlessness to find other categories. Today the future becomes present to the point where it obliterates that which is to come. We feel that nothing more can come if already our future lays waste to us—to the planet, to the cosmos and history along with them…

CT: What sense are we to ascribe to the "today," or to the "contemporary," or even to the "extreme contemporary," expressions that appear in many ways to have supplanted the "modern," which we tend to ascribe to the past century. And if we hazard that a certain modernity has withdrawn—entirely or in part—and is so ungraspable that it might as well be absolute self-evidence, what are the "ends" of this interrogation? What enclosure does it trace or sketch out or write—and why?

JLN: Either there is no more history or there is another history. In either instance it's unforeseeable. There was a time when the forecast limited itself to the return of the same, then came the time of the forecast of something calculable or at the very least estimatable (this is modernity), and now a time of un-foreseeability is opening…

---

[7] Nancy, *After Fukushima*, 37.

CT: In a recent *Le Monde* article, Nicolas Truong writes about the "new conservatives" who "seek to ward off the 'perverse effects' of modernity," to such an extent that "some of them have become genuine 'neoreactionaries.'"[8] In other words, it is no longer merely a matter of preserving the old ways in the face of the metamorphoses that the modern world continually brings about but also, and especially, of "restoring," argues Truong, who stresses the symbolic force of Notre-Dame-de-Paris in this scheme. On the other side of the political aisle, where the struggle against climate change is at its height, restoration means something else entirely. There is talk of an "ecology of restoration," which also targets techno-industrial modernity: the decade that has just begun has incidentally been dubbed the "Decade on Ecosystem Restoration" by the United Nations. In every instance the aim is to turn back the clock and to erase the harmful effects of an era that is also that of the two World Wars, and of the Holocaust, in particular. How are we to understand this nostalgic "temptation," which is at once so modern and so anti-modern?

JLN: It is a manner of hiding the unforeseeable from oneself… For even the effects of a supposed "restoration" are unforeseeable.

CT: In *Banality of Heidegger*, you analyze the German philosopher's resistance to modern technics, a resistance that is to be thought via his connection to Nazi ideology. What do you make of the concept of *das Riesenhafte* (the gigantic) in his thought, which he deploys in his *Beiträge zur Philosophie (Vom Ereignis)* and, less forcefully, in *Holzwege*? More specifically, to what extent is this measureless, gigantic, or colossal measure (which goes so far as to exceed the very *modus* of modernity) characteristic of the modern world? Moreover, is there a difference—dare I say of degree—between this excessive, even over-the-top modernity and the exacerbated amplification that characterizes the "present moment" (put simply: the first two decades of the twenty-first century)?

JLN: Perhaps there is no difference except, as you say, one of degree: violence and dislocation become ever more manifest. "The desert grows," Nietzsche said: yes, it is a growth—one that will impel "degrowth," or ever greater violence. The two are *somewhat* foreseeable but we cannot foresee their respective proportions…

What is surprising is the extent to which the forebodings not only of Heidegger, but of Freud, Orwell, Henry Miller, Günther Anders, Jacques Ellul, Rachel Carson, Marshall McLuhan, Ivan Illich, etc., have been underacknowledged. Notwithstanding the outrageousness of some and the vaticinating stances or the approximations of others, there has been an impressive deafness, despite a few specific moments of trendiness, simply because modernity was profoundly imprinted upon the state of things and upon mindsets for several centuries already. And there were very strong reasons for that!

CT: This excess—this "TROP" or "TOO MUCH," to evoke the title of an exhibition devoted to your work, alongside those of François Martin and Rodolphe Burger—yields

---

[8] Nicolas Truong, "Restaurer plutôt que conserver, la nouvelle arme idéologique d'Eric Zemmour," *Le Monde*, October 3, 2019; online, accessed February 15, 2022: https://www.lemonde.fr/idees/article/2019/10/03/restaurer-plutot-que-conserver-la-nouvelle-arme-ideologique-d-eric-zemmour_6014038_3232.html. [Translator's note: my translation.]

"horizontality" more so than "horizons,"⁹ per *Dis-Enclosure*. Yet this spatial extension, which exceeds (itself) in every sense and direction, is inseparable from the *body* for you, which in *Corpus* inspires this Rimbaldian *élan*:

> From now on, it is no longer a question of anything but being *resolutely modern*, and there's no program, just necessity, urgency. Why? Just turn on the television, and you'll get the answer every day: in a quarter or a third of the world very few bodies circulate (only flesh, skin, faces, muscles—bodies there are more or less hidden: in hospitals, cemeteries, factories, beds from time to time), while everywhere else in the world bodies multiply more and more, the body endlessly multiplied (frequently starved, beaten, murdered, restless, sometimes even laughing or dancing).¹⁰

Could you specify what you meant by this "being *resolutely modern*," which seemingly articulates an ethical imperative, no less?

JLN: You are quoting a book from twenty years ago, and even though this isn't much compared to others that are fifty years old, this nonetheless represents a serious gap since these first twenty years of the twenty-first century have precipitated the course of things. What had been advancing slowly but surely over the previous twenty years has taken on an accelerated rhythm. So much so that the "resolutely modern" has become increasingly more pressing, so to speak, in the process of its deconstruction. Indeed, modernity has definitively disappeared as the time of the advance, of the "step (not) won" [*pas gagné*], as Rimbaud puts it, as a time that projects itself ahead of itself and opens a new path in every moment.

One must always be resolutely modern in the sense that the modern of the modern is another time entirely—by no means a "postmodern" one, as some thought we could call it (this concerned but a small intellectual trend, not an epoch as such). We have entered a process of mutation, hence an end and a beginning. We must be in it. We must end and begin.

CT: In "The Poet's Calculus," you return to Hölderlin's poetry by dwelling on what is incalculable within calculation. Inasmuch as all poetry hinges on numbers¹¹—more so than narrative, even though it cannot escape it altogether—"the measurement standard that is the work can be used to calculate the relationship of the incalculable (of sense) to a short word gap."¹² Has the sense of this "incalculable" radically changed since Hölderlin, be it in poetry or elsewhere?

JLN: No, certainly not. This sense never changes, it is given with the poem, with man, perhaps even with life or with the cosmos: a star gives the measure of the flare out of

---

⁹ Nancy, *Dis-Enclosure*, 145.
¹⁰ Nancy, *Corpus*, trans. Richard A. Rand (New York: Fordham University Press, 2008), 9.
¹¹ In French, *le nombre* (the number) is a rare synonym for poetry.
¹² Nancy, "The Poet's Calculus," in *Expectation: Philosophy, Literature*, ed. with the assistance of Ginette Michaud, trans. Robert Bononno (New York: Fordham University Press, 2018), 87.

which it was born and of the flare where it becomes extinguished, as well as of the millions of light-years that separate it [*l'écartent*] from other stars.

The gap [*écart*] between the incalculable and calculation—this gap and the necessity of its two poles—is more ontological than any ontology, more creative than any creationism, and it is against this gap that poetry measures itself, so to speak.

CT: You provide no fixed, axiomatic, or dogmatic definition of modernity. However, you occasionally adopt a most affirmative tone when talking about it, as if it were necessary for you to take a firm stance, be it only in passing, so as not to betray its ephemeral and fragmentary facets. Thus, in *Dis-Enclosure*, you write that "'modern' signifies a world always awaiting its truth of, and as, world [*sa verité de monde*], a world whose proper sense is not given, is not available, is, rather, in project or in promise."[13] Yet such a "definition" (provided this is the *mot juste*) seeks in fact to backtrack to "a resource that could for at once the buried origin and the imperceptible future of the world that calls itself 'modern.'"[14] It is thus the world that calls *itself* modern, between quotation marks. Would it be correct to state that modernity is a "so-called" [*un "soi-disant"*]? And since you give us this "definition" in a context pertaining to Christianity, can we think the latter outside of modernity, all the more when one remembers that the Roman senator, monk, and writer Cassiodorus is one of the first to have used the term "modern," thus articulating the undoable politico-theologico-literary nexus that is still ours?

JLN: Indeed! Modernity is a "so-called" [*"soi-disant"*], but it is a so-called that pre-dicts [*pré-dit*] itself, in a sense. For instance, "Antiquity" referred to itself neither as "antique" nor as "modern" (even though there doubtless was, from the perspective of a certain Greek self-comprehension, a kind of modernity…). Or perhaps more clearly still: a people that refers to itself as "mankind" does not pre-dict itself, nor an empire that calls itself the "Middle Empire": these so-calleds situate themselves; they do not announce themselves as being yet "to come" to themselves.

Christianity, by contrast, lies entirely in the advent: the Redeemer came, and he ceaselessly comes and comes back, supervening [*sur-venir*], one might say, in all the senses of its "over" or "on" [*sur*]. The modern supervenes [*survient*]: comes as an addition, comes by surprise, does more than come since it is also already there…

But today we supervene ourselves [*nous nous sur-venons*] via a modality of deception, of disquiet. Our modernity no longer expects much from itself… In this sense, it is no longer modern.

CT: In "Noli me frangere," a dialogue-pastiche from 1982, the two neo- or post-Romantic figures you stage converse around the topic of the Blanchotian fragment. Whereas Ludovico states that he "can't, finally, dissociate the fragment from the closure of the modern world,"[15] Lothario argues that "the fragment, even in Blanchot, is too much the

---

[13] Nancy, *Dis-Enclosure*, 34–35.
[14] Ibid., 34.
[15] Nancy, "Noli me frangere," in *Expectation*, 140.

mark of the modern. It's impossible to tear it free from modernity."[16] Do you feel closer to one or the other of these voices or should we instead think them as voices of the neuter (*neutre*), understood here as *ne uter*? Is the neuter—in Blanchot's sense—"absolutely modern"?

JLN: In fact, these two voices concur: they both state that the fragment belongs to the modern—and this clearly means in this context that Modernity is already past, that it represents a belated belief… It is thus difficult to say *ne uter* here.

I would say that since 1982 this question has disappeared from my horizon. First, Philippe Lacoue-Labarthe himself has disappeared (he was more of a Lothario). But even if he were here, I think he would no longer see the right question in the "neuter." As far as I'm concerned, I would point to an article where I wrote that "the Neuter … neutralizes (itself)"[17] to suggest that we cannot settle for it. No more than for the Modern or for anything else of the kind. We are on the cusp of a wholly other time.

CT: As you know, the notion of "modernity" durably held Philippe Lacoue-Labarthe's attention. How do you situate your thought relative to his approach in *The Imitation of the Moderns*, in particular? In other words, does *mimesis* also occupy a privileged position in your way of addressing the modern?

JLN: *Mimesis* has always been Philippe's question and I was happy to receive his lessons on the matter. I wholeheartedly agree with what—today, at least, without rereading his writings—strikes me as having characterized Modernity as an interminable race towards models to be imitated and/or towards the absence of any and all models as the ultimate truth of *mimesis*. I remain true to this thought. I could even push it further still, towards the "self" as a *mimesis* of what may be said through the Freudian term *id*. This is a whole other chapter that would need to be opened…

CT: I am writing these lines the day after the massive strike that marks the beginning of the pushback against pension reform in France. Much is made, as ever, of the counting of crowds, since there is strength in numbers, as La Boétie intimated. Yet in *The Possibility of a World*, your book of conversations with Pierre-Philippe Jandin, you argue that it is the "mode of gathering," even the "the true witness from the point of view of being-together [*l'être-ensemble*] in our modern and contemporary era," before adding: "We're still in the era of crowds, even if these crowds have taken on certain aspects that have transformed them into something else perhaps."[18] What is this hypothetical "something else"? Should we ascribe it to the digital (*le numérique*: the number, yet again) and to the internet in particular, which has made possible a whole new conception of the crowd and of community?

---

[16] Ibid.
[17] Nancy, "The Neutral, Neutralization of the Neutral," in *Expectation*, 189. More specifically, this quote is taken from Blanchot's *The Step Not Beyond*, trans. Lycette Nelson (Albany: State University of New York Press, 1992), 75.
[18] Nancy, *The Possibility of a World: Conversations with Pierre-Philippe Jandin*, trans. Travis Holloway and Flor Méchain (New York: Fordham University Press, 2017), 40.

JLN: First, I am replying to you much later, since after two months of lockdown, in France as well as in other countries, and in the midst of a viral pandemic, the phenomenon of crowds has taken on a few additional traits. We live amid numbers of sick people, of deaths, of caregivers, of those forced into unemployment, of face mask supplies, etc. And we live amid a deafening hubbub of speeches, complaints, solutions, recriminations, incriminations, calls, addresses, invectives, forecasts... The circulation of discourses is frightening...

At the same time, this wandering and this scattering are gripping, all the more so because they are simultaneously social, psychological, political, technical, and even scientific (at least in the sense we ascribe to this word when we speak of medicine...).

CT: Does the debate surrounding "post-truth," which has been raging for a few years now and is in many ways unthinkable without the extreme acceleration of "news" made possible by the generalization of the Internet, mark another "time" in the history of modernity (and if there is any, as Jacques Derrida would say)? I am thinking here of a passage from *Ego Sum* where you cite Spinoza—"truth reveals its own self"—before going on to argue that "[p]erhaps no expression has remained more foreign to the modern world as this one."[19] What does this "strangeness" mean for us today?

JLN: It seems to me that "post-truth" is but a twist of language to say something that everyone knows or senses, namely that THE Truth, unique, absolute, first or last, is merely the illusion of finding an object that our understanding [*entendement*] would match perfectly. It is a poor, sub-scientific model that has imposed this belief. It will not last! Everyone knows or senses that truth isn't the adequacy of an object to our measure but rather that which stands within an encounter and within a dazzlement [*éblouissement*].

At the same time, we have "discovered" that those in power lie and that the knowledgeable are sometimes wrong or do not know everything. In fact, we have always known this. But for a long time, we put up with what we deemed a regrettable yet ineluctable necessity. We were able to put up with it as long as we thought that elsewhere, be it in the infinite, there lay THE truth, which would one day do justice to everything.

But the lies of the powers-that-be and the scholars' shortcomings became unbearable precisely because there is no longer any faith in "the" truth. So we believe in a factual, debatable, or provable truth. We forget that "facts" [*les "faits"*] are always factitious [*faits*], constructed, thought, perceived, even according to implicit judgments.

All this will pass, you can be sure of it! Or we will lose our minds in the process...

CT: Lastly, to return one more time to the question of "modernism," because it raises modernity to the level of an absolute program, so to speak, but also because of its essential complicity with aesthetics, do you think we ought to view it, to paraphrase Hegel, as a thing of the past? In any event, which future should art—and literature in particular—keep in store for itself?

---

[19] Nancy, *Ego Sum, Ego Sum: Corpus, Anima, Fabula*, trans. Marie-Ève Morin (New York: Fordham University Press, 2016), 14.

JLN: Yes, modernism is certainly a thing of the past. It is the past of a self-overcoming of humanity towards an accomplishment. Yet art and literature have never been beholden to the logic of accomplishment. On the contrary, they always bespeak an acute sense of essential unaccomplishment. Modernity called this the "open work," "work in progress," "worklessness" (terms that are not equivalent, but I won't dwell on this point). They hinge, to segue from what came before, on an overcoming through the outside or through the other.

A philosophical system may tend—and always tends—to overcome itself, even if it critiques Hegelian, Marxian or Heideggerian overcoming. But a real philosopher also knows quite well that there is no such thing as metaphilosophy… A novelist, on the other hand, doesn't even think about that—even when they appear to be most drawn to the prospect of an integral accomplishment.

Whereas the quest for a "total work of art" is fated to fail because it closes on itself and it chokes… Wagner is exemplary in this regard, or (albeit in a different manner) Zola, even if neither of the two amounts to that. Roberto Bolaño said of his books: "stories like this don't have an ending."[20] Indeed, those that end are fairy tales—which is something else.

(Translated by Cosmin Toma)

---

[20] Roberto Bolaño, "The Secret of Evil," in *The Secret of Evil*, trans. Chris Andrews and Natasha Wimmer (New York: New Directions, 2012), 11.

Part Three

Glossary

16

Art (and Its Deliverance)

John McKeane

Nancy's approach to art insists less on its qualities, characteristics, or subject matters, than on its status—the way it comes to be. His question is not *what is art?*, but instead: *how is art possible?* Art therefore provides an invitation to develop his phenomenological reflections, his thinking of world and sense. How is it that art comes to be in the first place? Where, and from where, does it appear or present itself? In attempting to answer such questions, Nancy discusses the presence of art, the process of becoming-present that is operative whenever there is art. But for him, art is not simply presentation—instead, his interest lies in art as "the presentation of presentation."[1] This is to say that art is capable of reflecting on its own presentation, without needing philosophy to intervene on its behalf. The value and ambition of this approach are that seeing art as "the presentation of presentation" means that it is able to enlighten us with regard to presentation in general (i.e., any and all instances of coming-to-presence or being-in-the-world).

Nancy reflects on such topics in the critical anthology of early German Romanticism *The Literary Absolute*, co-edited with Lacoue-Labarthe, and in several key texts which pursue this line of thinking further.[2] One of these is the chapter "Art, a Fragment" in *The Sense of the World*, a text that pulls together much of Nancy's thinking on art, and on which we can focus here.[3] The chapter's title is playful, first referring to the fragmentary Romantic writing discussed by Nancy and Lacoue-Labarthe, second suggesting that the chapter itself is a fragment on the topic of art, and third proposing that art itself be seen as a fragment. This third sense is the most important currently. If art is a fragment, what precisely might it be a fragment of? Nancy thus opens the question of art's relation to a broader totality, the notion that it fits comfortably into some broader political, theological, or philosophical system. In short, this is Hegel's thesis on the aesthetic religion of ancient Athens: the notion that particular art forms

---

[1] Jean-Luc Nancy, *The Muses*, trans. Peggy Kamuf (Stanford: Stanford University Press, 1996).

[2] Where Nancy speaks of the presentation of presentation, Lacoue-Labarthe takes up the Romantic term "presentification"; see among others Philippe Lacoue-Labarthe, "Sublime Truth (Part 2)," trans. David Kuchta, *Cultural Critique*, no. 20 (Winter 1991–2): 218.

[3] Nancy, "Art, a Fragment," in *The Sense of the World*, trans. Jeffrey S. Librett (Minneapolis: University of Minnesota Press, 1997), 123–39.

(notably tragedy and statuary) must be understood in the context of their roles in establishing and maintaining a civic religion.

In one sense this vision of aesthetic religion is familiar, thanks to the classical tradition; in another, it is utterly foreign to us in the modern world. Nancy responds to this situation by arguing that modern art arises out of the breakdown of any metaphysical system: any system based on Sense. In Nancy's words, "aesthetics and art appear in our history … when the intelligibility of sense, in its cosmocosmetology, vanishes. This is what happens between the eighteenth century and Hegel."[4] This is to say that not only does modern art happen to take on fragmentary form, but that the categories of art and fragmentation begin to strongly resemble one another. Whenever there is fragmentation, there is art (this explains the Romantic valorization of ruins as having aesthetic value). Indeed, there must be fragmentation for there to be art—for when it is lacking, we are too likely to be distracted by the religious or metaphysical freight that the proposed artwork is carrying.

Nancy discusses this situation as follows: "Hegel *delivers* art for itself: he delivers it from service to transcendence in immanence, and he delivers it to detached, fragmentary truth. Hegel, *volens nolens*, registers and salutes in fact *the birth of art*."[5] This is provocative insofar as Hegel is better known as the philosopher who declared the death of art (or more precisely: that art was no longer invested with a privileged role in the realization of spirit).[6] But in freeing, liberating, or delivering art from this role, Hegel is thought by Nancy to be enacting the *deliverance* of art. We can understand this term as a liberation, but also as a delivery lacking any given end or destination, a destiny that is also an errancy: a *destinerrance*. Its connection to a broader totality of aesthetic religion having been severed, and it therefore having become a fragment, art is not stripped of its role, but instead set free, or indeed—like a baby—delivered.

The attention given by Nancy and Lacoue-Labarthe to Jena Romanticism responds precisely to this situation. They often speak of these figures in terms of birth: the Romantic project is for a new movement, a new art, a new politics to be born. In this way, it establishes the paradigm for all later avant-gardes. But "Art, a Fragment," although clearly informed by the *agôn* between Hegel and the Romantics, develops its thinking of birth in terms of a different figure. In Nancy's words,

> It was not really so naïve of Marx, after all, to be astonished at the effect and affect produced by the works of the Ancients, now that the myths that supported them have fallen into disuse; he understood this effect as the effect of a perpetual childhood freshness. Perhaps art is the *infans* par excellence, the one who, instead of discoursing, fragments instead.[7]

---

[4] Ibid., 130.
[5] Ibid.; emphases original.
[6] See my "Art's Passing for Hegel, Lacoue-Labarthe, Nancy," *Angelaki: Journal of Theoretical Humanities* 26, nos. 1–2 (2021): 101–12.
[7] "Art, a Fragment," 132.

Nancy depicts Marx as marveling at the continued life of art, even though it has been severed from the ancient myths to which it was once connected. But here the emphasis is less on the birth of art than on its infancy. The term is significant as, in addition to referring to a newborn or small child, it insists on the *in-fans*, the inability to speak which is therefore said to lead art not to "discourse," but to "fragment."[8] This fits well with the conception of art with which we began: not as something that exists in this or that particular way, or makes this or that particular statement, but instead that simply *is*. The infant says nothing, makes no sense, but insists through its sheer presence, through a fragmentary burbling that demands our attention, not at a time that is convenient to us, or in any rationally sanctioned way, but now, right now.

---

[8] See the work by Nancy and Lacoue-Labarthe's colleague: Sarah Kofman, *L'Enfance de l'art. Une interprétation de l'esthétique freudienne* (Paris: Payot, 1970).

17

Body

Juan Manuel Garrido

Jean-Luc Nancy's conception of the body can be traced back to a single fundamental postulate: bodies are separate entities. We isolate and identify a body whenever we distinguish it from other bodies, thereby inscribing its separation, for example, from those bodies that obstruct its passage or from those more subtle bodies that open the way for it. A body is not an abstract concept or the concept of an object. A body is a singular thing that moves or rests, flows or evaporates, and separates itself from other bodies that move or rest, flow or evaporate. Bodies exist insofar as they are positioned or located through their singular, concrete ways of being separated from each other. Bodies result from the set of operations that define their separation.

A body's properties (e.g., luminosity, roughness, shape, size, weight, sound, acceleration, etc.) stem from the circumstances that define its relationship to other bodies. A body is always a term of the interaction between bodies, and is added or juxtaposed to other bodies; it is near or far, inside or outside, above or below, in front of or behind, to their right or to their left. It lies among other bodies, and co-appears with them. This holds true even for the invisible interior of a body, since it establishes a kind of interaction with its visible exterior. And the visible exterior is such only to the extent that it is separated from an invisible interior. Exterior and interior are relational concepts—if I divide a body, if I open it up, I will not find something that would in itself be interior; rather, I will redefine the circumstances that define the body's interior in relation to its exterior.

The language we use to refer to bodies and their properties (i.e., the language through which we describe interactions among bodies) is also a body. Language is made of the visible marks that a surface registers, sounds that propagate through the air, mental or intentional contents displayed according to a process ordered in time. Correlatively, the exercise of decoding a message follows the rules that determine the spatial and temporal sequencing of perceptual or mental marks. The phenomenon of meaning is inseparable from the matter that inscribes, transmits, or emits it, which is to say: there is no meaning apart from the signifying body that conveys it. There is no disembodied meaning, no spiritual or mental substance embedded in a signifying material substance. This aspect is crucial: the "meaning" of a body in general, particularly the meaning of a signifying body, consists of its exposure. We can never treat a body as the mere vicar of some disembodied, non-extended ideal meaning.

But the ideality of meaning does not consist in a sort of immaterial abstraction that the concrete and localized reality of bodies belies (if we consider the ideality of meaning to be illusory) or betrays (if, on the contrary, we consider that we must account for the ideality of meaning). Supposedly, the ideality of meaning concerns an objective, universal, intentional content independent of its signifying exteriorization. As such, it must be a structure that differentiates between particular instances that bring about its materialization. Ideality is meant to be something identical to itself and not something always other in each of its different instances. But if the ideality of meaning differs from its particular instances, is it not then something "separate," which would mean that it is a body rather than an ideality? The answer to this question is not simple. Ideality must certainly be something that exists separately from its instances, but it is not something separate from the singularity of these instances. Ideality refers to the concrete plurality of the singular instances that embodies it. It is not a disembodied entity but the *corpus* of its own realizations. No ideality subsists apart from the plurality of singular instances that materializes it. It does not matter whether this plurality is real or fictitious, perceived or imagined, physical or simulated, discrete or continuous, finite or infinite, statistical or apodictic. For a singular instance to refer to an ideal content, for "this to be that," "this" must be different from its properties, and the properties must be different from the objects that instantiate them. Properties need to be thought of as different from the objects on which they are predicated. Moreover, and principally, properties, precisely in order to be properties and not terms, in order to be idealities and not particular materializations, need to be non-exhausted by any of their particular instances. Ideality supposes that every instance of it must always and a priori be one-among-other instances (possible or real), one-among-many instances (possible or real) of itself. And what does this mean, if not that ideality consists in the separation of bodies, the singularity that materializes and executes the indefinite plurality of instances that defines it as ideality? Similarly, truth—the truth of a thing, of a proposition, of a body of propositions—does not exist apart from the singular instances that verify it. But a singular instance is, by necessity, plural, for an unrepeatable verifying instance would not be verifying, and a repetition that did not imply singularity in each occurrence would generate instances unable to differentiate each other as multiple instances of the same, that is, would not be a repetition. A truth is verified—it becomes true or is produced as truth—only by means of its singular plural instances.

In the sphere of political life, the singular plural embodiment of meaning in no case leads to the negation of collective projects. No incompatibility exists between the political idea of the common good and the separate existence of this idea in its multiple instances (state apparatuses, institutions, social movements, local communities, minorities, etc.). On the contrary, without embodiment, the idea of a common good would lose all political opportunity. A political project presupposes the participation of many, many different "ones" who are not reducible to one (however powerful this "one" might be), and the existence of many presupposes separation. The common good does not exist apart from the plurality of bodies that move for it, fight for it or ally around it, recognize themselves in it, deliberate about it, institute it, transform it, vindicate it. The common good is never simply a slogan, or an empty signifier; it diffracts in the multiplicity that makes it exist. Political action is the free creation of instances for the common good. That is why the common good does not exist outside the history of its own transformations. It lives on in the living and the dead bodies it animates.

Exscription[1]

John Paul Ricco

The genealogy of the concept of exscription in Nancy's work dates as far back as 1988, and his essay "L'excrit" ("Exscription," or, more literally, "The Exscribed"), in which he presented a philosophical meditation on the oeuvre of Georges Bataille that, Nancy says, serves as a reminder of the impossibility of communication as the condition for any sense of community. Coming just two years after the seminar on Bataille, which would result in perhaps Nancy's most well-known essay, "The Inoperative Community," along with the accompanying "Literary Communism," the essay on *exscription* brings together two texts written eleven years apart: "Reasons to Write" (April 1977) and "Reasons to Read" (August 1988).

While in "Reasons to Read," the term *exscription* is introduced, by pairing it with the earlier text, Nancy makes clear that we are to understand *exscription* as the reason why there are reasons to write and to read. At the same time, with his neologism and its marking of the opening and exposure of *inscription* to the Outside, Nancy argues that the spacing of community is in-appropriable and therefore impossible to inscribe (or circumscribe, prescribe, and perhaps even impossible to describe). In other words, of community there remains something incommunicable, unemployable, and indeed unintelligible. This limit, suspension, and impossibility at the heart of community are written and read as *exscription*.

In his 1990 essay "Corpus," and again in 2006 in the eponymous book-length elaboration of that text, Nancy re-conceptualizes the tracing/erasing of the force of the Outside in terms of the bodily and the corporeal. Picking up and extending the terminological threads of "L'excrit," Nancy asks: "How are we to touch upon the body? ... Maybe it doesn't happen exactly *in* writing ... We have to begin by getting through, and by means of, the *exscription* of our body: its being inscribed-outside, its being placed *outside the text*."[2] As Nancy leads us to understand: the body *exscribes* itself and is *exscribed* in its expropriated relation to itself and in its resonant rapport and naked exposure to other bodies, places, and things. The articulation of body, existence, and

---

[1] This glossary entry is an alternative and revised version of my introduction to "Jean-Luc Nancy: Poetics, Politics & Erotics of Exscription," ed. John Paul Ricco, Stefanie Heine, and Philippe P. Haensler, *Parallax* 24, no. 4 (2020).

[2] Jean-Luc Nancy, *Corpus*, trans. Richard A. Rand (New York: Fordham University Press, 2008), 11; emphasis original.

exscription could not be more clearly formulated and diagrammed, as when Nancy writes: "'Ontology of the body' = exscription of being."[3] In which it is to be understood that exscription-as-body makes ontology be nothing other than the very opening of ex-istence: "[e]xistence addressed to an out-side (*there*, where there's no address, no destination ... bodies are existence, the very act of ex-istence, *being*."[4]

Erotic pleasure, sexual desire, and carnal sex are just a few of the more familiar ways in which corporeal existence is *exscribed*—an irreducible and essentially illegible ontological condition of ecstatic exposure that Nancy has named "sexistence." This task of writing by un-writing the body is closely interwoven with the challenge to conceive of a new "body of language" or literary corpus, one that is poetically created in and as the unsignifying spacing of *exscription*. Poetic language—not just "addressed to the body-outside," but, itself, thoroughly corporeal—works towards and reflects upon the *poiesis* and *praxis* of all forms of aesthetic creation: drawing, painting, choreography, photography, music.

Partly in response to the current degradation of political discourse and the diminishment of a democratic plurality of voices in the world today, there has been a turn to poetics and its rhetorical, creative, and inventive capacity to combat the impoverishment of language, and to articulate the social in ways that retain a sense of freedom, justice, and truth. From at least as early as 1982 and the publication of his first book, *Le partage des voix* (*The Sharing of Voices*), Nancy remained committed to thinking the relation between poetics and politics. A commitment that is predicated on the supposition that all forms of language and modes of enunciation, speech, writing, and reading are, themselves, the expression and affirmation of existence as always-already shared. For Nancy, voices—like bodies—are exteriorities. They are the sonic, signifying, and a-signifying means of making, creating, and producing sense. It is in the sharing or partaking (*partage*) of this vocative sense that poetics is political, that the ethical is erotic, and that the political is its own poetics of *exscribed* community.

Over thirty years ago, in "L'excrit," Nancy asked, "can there be a call to be heard, how can there be any question of vocation, invocation, or advocation?" That is: can an ethical or political demand—including the exigency of the voice—be heard, when the in-appropriate spacing of the Outside seems to have become so thoroughly colonized and inscribed, thereby revoking its positive expropriating force? This in turn raises the question of Nancy's call and demand—including in light of *Demande* (*Expectation*), his collection of essays on poetry, literature, and philosophy—and what his exscription calls upon us to think, to read, and to write in its wake. Something surely beyond *commentary* (univocal or plurivocal) on a thinker's work, given that this was precisely one of the things that Nancy was critical of in his 1988 essay on Georges Bataille.

Such work entails not writing "on" or "about" exscription in terms of its "meaning" or as a means of exegetical interpretation, but rather by attending to what in writing

---

[3] Ibid., 19.
[4] Ibid.; emphasis original.

and reading—Nancy's, ours, and those others with whom we read and write—persists in and as the slipping of and exemption from meaning, from signification, and from communication's closure or its idiotic virality. In other words, the naked exposure to the Outside that we have been invoking is, as Nancy states, "wholly exscribed in the text"—more precisely in the infinite withdrawal and denuding of meaning. According to Nancy, in this withdrawal anything comes to exist, and any sense of the common is experienced: "Writing is naked because it 'exscribes;' existence is naked because it is 'exscribed.'"[5]

---

[5] Nancy, "Exscription," in *The Birth to Presence,* trans. Katherine Lydon (Stanford: Stanford University Press, 1993), 339.

19

Globalization/*Mondialisation*

Barnaby Norman

... how the end of the world of sense opens the praxis of the sense of the world.
— Jean-Luc Nancy, *The Sense of the World*[1]

The English translation of Nancy's use of the French term *mondialisation* presents both a problem and an opportunity. It is a problem because its usual rendering as "globalization" obscures a process—of world-forming—that is lost with the reference to the "globe" in English. Nevertheless, it emerges as an opportunity in Nancy's prefatory note to the English-language edition of *The Creation of the World* or *Globalization* (*La création du monde ou la mondialisation*) where it provides an occasion to distinguish between the reduction to a sphere of "unitotality" implied by the *globe* and the *world* as a "space of possible meaning for the whole of human relations."[2] For Nancy, the tension between these two possibilities highlights the stakes of an interpretative "wager" on the process of globalization itself, on what is happening to the world, and therefore on the future of its development, and of the *world* itself.

These dual possibilities issue from a common source and respond to the world as we know it, which has become what it is through value displacement, a process Nancy calls *mondanisation* (translated as "world-becoming" in *The Creation of the World*). *World-becoming* describes the internalization of value within the world itself—the process by which it becomes its own subject. This is the story of modernity, so long as it is understood that the roots of this transformation go very deep indeed. In fact, for Nancy, it is the story of the West becoming coextensive with the globe, and its origins are therefore to be sought in the West.

"The West," says Nancy, "has come to encompass the world" (*CW*, 34). For better or worse, this is our reality, and, in a double reference to Heidegger and Marx, Nancy invents the term *ecotechnics* to designate a world or a "global (dis)order" in which "planetary technology" and "world economy"[3] conspire to reduce everything to a

---

[1] Jean-Luc Nancy, *The Sense of the World*, trans. Jeffrey S. Librett (Minneapolis and London: University of Minnesota Press, 1997), 9.
[2] Nancy, *The Creation of the World* or *Globalization*, trans. François Raffoul and David Pettigrew (Albany: State University of New York Press, 2007), 28. Hereafter *CW*.
[3] Nancy, *Being Singular Plural*, trans. Robert Richardson and Anne O'Byrne (Stanford: Stanford University Press, 2000), 133.

state of general equivalence and exchangeability. This is the sphere of *unitotality* we encountered above. In "Urbi et Orbi," Nancy conceives this as the sprawling *agglomeration* of the city that "spreads and extends all the way to the point where ... it tends to cover the entire orb of the planet" (*CW*, 33). Here global humanity encounters the "end" of sovereignty as "ecotechnics washes out or dissolves sovereignty (or rather, the latter implodes in the former)."[4] Drawing on Heidegger (in turn reading Nietzsche), this situation corresponds to a generalized nihilism, or quite simply, for Nancy, "misery" (*CW*, 33), in which the world has lost its sense (simultaneously its direction and meaning). A first question arises here: how did this come to pass?

For most of its history, the West was able to posit a world beyond the world. Transcendent to the sensible world was the suprasensible realm. For Nancy, "Christianity is inseparable from the West"[5] and within this paradigm it found its orientation—indeed, the West derived its sense from this other of the world. While, for Nancy, all monotheisms are ultimately atheisms, Christianity is unique in that it provides a mechanism for the evacuation of the divine. God becomes man and Nancy finds himself in total agreement with Marcel Gauchet (in *The Disenchantment of the World*) that Christianity is the religion of the departure from religion.[6] In *The Creation of the World*, Nancy writes: "the 'God' of onto-theology was progressively stripped of the divine attributes of an independent existence and only retained those of the existence of the world considered in its immanence" (*CW*, 44).

Hegel is the philosopher who, more than any other, articulates an interpretation of Christianity as the axis of history. In his work, the Christian event makes the realization of the Absolute in and as history thinkable as it initiates a process through which the transcendent realm of the Father enters the world through the Son to become Spirit actualized in the world—the concrete absolute. Hegel's philosophy of history, as well as his broader system of thought, is inconceivable outside this context, and, like his French forerunners, Blanchot and Derrida, Nancy takes Hegel's apotheosis very seriously. In *world-becoming*, value is displaced from its position outside the world to become immanent, and in this absorption the world loses its orientation. After the West has come to encompass the world, "in this movement it disappears as what was supposed to orient the course of this world" (*CW*, 34).

Like Blanchot's *disaster*, Nancy's *disorientation* marks the end of everything that sustained the conceptual paradigm of a culture. What is new or at least more explicit in Nancy is that this exhaustion coincides with the global extension of that culture, so that the Hegelian completion that has been so crucial to deconstruction in its French incarnation becomes bound to that process of world-becoming, and, consequently, as we will see below, the Marxian transcription of Hegel comes to the fore in Nancy's thinking of the world (a reference that is also more prominent in Blanchot than in Derrida).

---

[4] Ibid., 137.
[5] Nancy, *Dis-Enclosure (The Deconstruction of Christianity)*, trans. Bettina Bergo, Gabriel Malenfant, and Michael B. Smith (New York: Fordham University Press, 2008), 142.
[6] Ibid.

It is perfectly possible—and in fact this is overwhelmingly the situation of the world of ecotechnics, the world we inhabit—for this displacement of value to issue into nihilism. But crucially, at this very point, something other and totally novel comes to thought: the world itself. From out of the nihilism of ecotechnics, from the "without reason" of the world, comes a radical responsibility to create the world anew, to create the world *ex nihilo*.

For Nancy, Marx represents a crucial step in this thinking of the world, but also a limitation (at least in the way he has tended to be read) which it is necessary to exceed. In "Urbi et Orbi," Nancy articulates a reading of Marx in three steps: 1) Marx identifies the emergence of the global market as an unprecedented integration and interdependence of humanity, creating itself as its own value; 2) it is necessary for this process to come to consciousness and for humanity to become aware of itself as its own end in this creation of value, hence the Communist revolution ("For Marx, the human being, as source and accomplishment of value in itself, comes at the end of history when it produces itself" [*CW*, 38]), and 3) a further displacement, which Nancy finds in Marx's text, but which counters the traditional interpretation: "Our difference with him ... reappears on this very point" says Nancy, since "with him, 'human' implicitly remains a teleological or eschatological term, if we understand by that a logic where *telos* and/or *eschaton* take the position and the role of an accomplishment without remainder" (*CW*, 37–38). As such, and in structural complicity with Hegel's Absolute, the global achievement of the communist community would represent the accomplishment of a final value, and it is precisely this accomplishment that Nancy seeks to displace.

It would not be controversial to say that the major theme of Nancy's work has been the deconstruction of the ideal of community as the accomplishment of a final value. This should not be taken to imply the affirmation of the individual as a discrete entity preceding society, but rather the radical interrogation of the being-with (*Mit-sein*) that is foundational for any community as such, and which undoes the presumed unity of the individual. Like *différance* in Derrida's text, the *with* (the *co-* of community) is an originary spacing which is radically contemporary with what it articulates, and like *différance* it cannot be resumed or subsumed in any final teleology. It opens another thinking of community beyond the teleological closure of an accomplished value, another thinking of justice, and another thinking of what it means to be together in the world. Even more fundamentally, *being-with* implies a re-articulation of ontology, opening the space of the world as such. "The *co-* is implicated in the *ex-*: nothing exists unless *with*, since nothing exists unless *ex nihilo*. The first feature of the creation of the world is that it creates the *with* of all things: that is to say, *the world*, namely the nihil as that which opens [*ouvre*] and forms [*œuvre*] the world" (*CW*, 73; emphasis Nancy's).

***

This entry has been structured as a commentary on a short passage from *The Creation of the World*, which I am now in a position to cite in full:

if the world-becoming (detheologisation) displaces value—making it immanent—before world-forming displaces the production of value—making it universal—the two together displace "creation" into the "without-reason" of the world. And this displacement is not a transposition, a "secularization" of the onto-theological or metaphysical-Christian scheme: it is, rather, its deconstruction and emptying out, and it opens onto another space—of place and of risk—which we have just begun to enter.

(*CW*, 51)

We saw above how the process of the world coming into its own is the process by which the value that had oriented the world becomes immanent, and how, with Marx, the world emerged as the space in which humanity produces itself as its own value. Despite all its theological baggage, Nancy retains the word "creation" to name the absolute novelty of the world producing its own value (and sense) beyond the teleological closure. This movement is the *praxis* of deconstruction as it is reinscribed in Nancy's text. As with his retention of the word "creation" beyond its monotheistic/Christian heritage, Nancy's *praxis* both affirms and exceeds its Marxian reference. Keeping the implications of a transformative process through which humanity changes itself and the world ("the point is to change it [the world]"), Nancy seeks to open a thinking of *praxis* beyond the eschaton of a final value, responding the emergence of a structure of community, of *being-with*, that cannot be resumed in the fulfilment of achieved value. From the end of the world of sense opens the *praxis* of the sense of the world, a "space of possible meaning for the whole of human relations": the *praxis* of a world without end.

20

Sense

Isabelle Perreault

A veritable Gordian knot of modern Western philosophy, the problem of sense occupies a central position in Jean-Luc Nancy's body of thought, inseparable as it is from his open-ended conception of being and the world. Instead of outlining the framework of signification that emerges in the wake of the crisis of sense, impelled by the ruins of transcendence and of the great ontotheological systems of yore, Nancy aims to halt the subsumption of particular states of the world to a system of values or to an outside signification that organizes their course and breathes sense into them. Sense, which is irreducible to signification for Nancy, has withdrawn from dialectics and from the referential articulation that moored it to a determined signification, which now consists in a mere opening, a potential to signify, upheld in inexhaustible abeyance. Over and above what may be appropriated, it does not break with the order of the sensible; it remains beyond sense, yet without issuing forth from a "beyond" of any kind. For Nancy, sense is an existential category, not because being *has* a sense or meaning that philosophers are tasked with determining but rather because it is being as such that demands to be thought *as* sense.

In *The Sense of the World* (*Le Sens du monde*, 1993), where Nancy unpacks the conception of sense that his previous work had already made manifest to some degree, he posits the contiguity of sense and world, maintained at the very limit they share, *touching* and structuring each other. The volume's title is thus a tautology: the world no longer has a claim on sense but *is* sense. The world no longer consists in the work of sense, in a *poïesis*. Rather, it stems from an active sense, whose appearance and existence coincide with its very being and action in the manner of a single event—indeed, it is a *praxis* of sense. Thus, writes Nancy, for as long as the world was envisioned as a *cosmos*, a "here below" relative to a "beyond," or simply a "here" defined in opposition to an "elsewhere," it could derive meaning from its difference or reference—a postulate of the semiotic relation, according to which sense is only relative to some outside given:

> for as long as the world was essentially in relation to some other (that is, another world or an author of the world), it could *have* a sense. But the end of the world is that there is no longer this essential relation, and that there is no longer

essentially (that is, existentially) anything but the world "itself." Thus, the world *no longer has* a sense, but it *is* sense.[1]

If we posit that there is a *sense of the world* no longer, then it follows that there is no *world of sense* ever since the end of history and the advent of globalization (*mondialisation*), and hence since Western civilization began facing its own end. Sense, much like the world itself, cannot be called upon to conceive of experiences exterior, anterior or posterior to the West, insofar as the categories around which it once clustered—God, man, history, progress, myth—have given way, through a long and continuous process of exhaustion. And so sense *is* the world, outside of any dialectical relation or assertion of transcendence or truth—which, according to Nancy, must be understood as an occasional presentation imbued with a given essence or signification, one that sense reopens, divides, and defers (in the Derridean sense of a constant postponement toward the *à-venir*, which preserves its absence of origin and exacerbates dearth within the element to come).

What, then, remains of sense as a "reference to," as a "movement towards," when no extra-sensible authority, *telos*, alterity, or transcendence makes up the world's horizon of apperception and apprehension? How are we to think the *to* (*à*) of sense and meaning without reference to some kind of *beyond*—an enigma, which incidentally compels us to reconsider being outside of any and all ontological or metaphysical signification, and which destabilizes the very definition of being-in-the-world (*l'être-au-monde*)? After all, there is the world (*du monde*) and there is being, which is why it makes sense to cast off the "why?" of this condition, and hence to rethink it through the fact that "there is something, and that alone makes sense" (*SW*, 7). Nevertheless, we must be careful not to conclude that Nancy indulges in pure immanentism or materialism, as being has no existence if not as "being-among, being-between, and being-against" (*SW*, 59). There is thus a sense in which singular being, which is coextensive with the space it occupies and adjoined to the area the other inhabits—its *areality*[2]—is always being-in-common, sharing, contact (co-tact). Sense is the very pathway (*frayage*)— passage and sharing (*partage*), gap and address—that makes for a liaison between self and other, between inside and outside, between here and there. Hence the preposition *à* is itself sense—even as they remain distinct, it binds beings between them (and along with phenomena). It opens them up to resonance, to propagation outside oneself, and makes community possible, for "[s]ense is *common*, or it is not" (*SW*, 30). The being of sense thus resides in the *à* of *être*-au-*monde*, an *à* that is its postponement and its

---

[1] Jean-Luc Nancy, *The Sense of the World*, trans. Jeffrey S. Librett (Minneapolis and London: University of Minnesota Press, 1997), 8. Hereafter *SW*. Italics original throughout unless otherwise noted.

[2] Nancy develops the notion of *areality* in *Corpus* by playing on the double meaning of "the nature or specificity of an *aire* ('area')," on the one hand, and absence of reality (*a*-reality), on the other, thus subverting the duality between outer reality and inner psyche, between body and mind, since being is defined through the occupation of a space, which is itself an opening extended toward its confines. On this, see Nancy, *Corpus*, trans. Richard A. Rand (New York: Fordham University Press, 2008), 43.

opening, the movement through which it simultaneously ties and separates being and the world, as well as beings between them.

Hence the transitivity and transversality that make up the different senses of the word *sense*, especially as *sens* in French: meaning, signification, sensibility, direction, moral or practical sense. Indeed, the experience of sense *qua* sensible sense entails no production of signification that would need to be parsed through hermeneutic activity; rather, it invites us "to suffer a touch of sense that is at once its most proper concern (it is itself the sense, the sensible organ of such a touch) and the very place of its expropriation (it does not exhibit the signification of this touch)" (SW, 11). In other words, to comprehend a given sense is to be affected by it, to be literally *seized with* it (*cum-prehendere*)—it cannot but be sensible insofar as it scans the space where the subject opens up, thus connecting it to the world. Sense names the passage between different modalities of *sensing* and *seizing*, the *différance* of the being that senses itself sensing in a state of perpetual excess relative to one's self, which also implies a callback to the self.[3] By resorting to the Derridean notion of *différance* in his attempt to provide a definition, no matter how provisional and indeterminate, of what we are to understand by "sense," Nancy stresses the etymological irreducibility of the word's various senses and therefore the primordial dearth of its originary oneness:

> The word *sense* has no unity of sense, no original matrix of sense, not even a univocal etymological derivation: the Germanic root *sinno* ("direction"), is attached only conjecturally, if at all, to the Latin *sensus* ("sensation"). As for the sense of "signification," it appears to have been formed, in Old French and then in Middle French, on the basis of several connotations of two different origins (*sensus* in the sense of "thought" as in "the author's thought," *sen* and then *sinn* in the sense of "right direction, clear-sighted understanding, reason.
>
> (SW, 76)

As a pathing force, sense is that which links, which orients, and which touches present beings, without reference to what might exceed the world; and if we presume sense to be itself excessive in its excess, it is like an opening onto that which appears and which always remains to come, with no directionality. Similarly, although sense remains suspended in the withdrawal it opposes to the fixation and appropriation that are proper to truth, this is not tantamount to saying that sense may be outright suspended—an operation whereby we would have access to its origin as though it were an end, in the dual sense of *telos* and *clausula*, configured in such a way as to reveal its orientation. Indeed, to think the sense or meaning of history no longer makes sense for Nancy, who instead favors a "history of sense" that must in turn be apprehended independently of historicity: "there is no 'moral of the story' [*sens de l'histoire*] of the (hi)story of sense" (SW, 26).

---

[3] See Nancy, *Listening*, trans. Charlotte Mandell (New York: Fordham University Press, 2007).

Be that as it may, sense still comes *after* myth and science—to the extent that both acted as truth discourses or, at the very least, as possibilities of signifying (as well as of making sense of) the truth. Nancy argues that ever since the (Nietzschean) end of philosophy, *style* has taken charge of sense: not as an ornamental activity of discourse, nor as a cosmetic gloss applied to language, but rather as a thinking that commits itself to forms, "a matter of the *praxis* of thought, its *writing* in the sense of the assumption of a responsibility for and to this excess" (*SW*, 19). Insofar as they presented themselves as the immediate adequation between truth and sense, as a deposit of sense upon the truth, neither myth nor science made room for the advent of style, which is the spacing, the tension, the difference/*différance* that the presence-absence of a sensing and desiring subject—one caught within the world's reticular structure—opens up within the *said*. This is why writing now occupies the locus of sense "in which and through which sense can reply to itself: desire itself, send itself, and refer to itself indefinitely from singular point to singular point—which also means from singular sense to singular sense."[4] At once a matter of thinking in style and a style of thought, sense—or writing—is the subject's presence-absence in language, through which one responds to the shared desire of sense and rekindles the process and bears witness to an inscription—one that is *ex-scribed*—in the world. Indeed, sense is that which opens, unceasingly opens the "possibility of a resonance,"[5] a resonance that is always already a kind of listening and a response, a listening that doubles as reply and reference, a vibration that *makes* the world as sense.

---

[4] Nancy, "Responding for Sense," in *Expectation: Philosophy, Literature*, ed. with the assistance of Ginette Michaud, trans. Robert Bononno (New York: Fordham University Press, 2018), 147–48.
[5] Ibid., 146.

21

With

Jérôme Lèbre

One is not alone in being born and one cannot be born alone. Each and every time, a being comes into the world, one whose singularity ceaselessly shows that it is preceded by nothing, that it stems from nothing; yet this singularity is also related to the two beings from which it stems; and its very birth repeats, in its own way, that of others and therefore of those who will later tell its tale, giving weight to this original event whose memory each and every one of us has lost. One is not alone in dying and one cannot die alone: each time, a being whose singularity asserted itself takes its leave from the world, returning to the nothing whence it came; yet the experience of this moment also escapes it, and this is an escape only for those—the still living—who know that being to be dead, just as they know themselves to be mortal. In other words, existing or being there means being with others; there are no existences or even any singular experiences, from the cradle to the grave, that are not shared with others; or, to put it differently, appearing and disappearing are the borders of an existence that is always coexistence, which only takes place as com-pearance.

The *with* is therefore a given, the *datum* whence Jean-Luc Nancy's thought unceasingly sets forth and to which it unceasingly returns. One could say: the only given. First, because the sole yet inexhaustible gift of existence is indeed that others are given to us, that we may meet with them in every moment, and this holds true even though that gift is also unceasingly taken away from us by their own momentary or definitive disappearances, until all is taken away from us by our own final disappearance. Further, because *with* is appearance or phenomenon *par excellence*: nothing appears on its own, everything unconceals itself in the plural, starting with ourselves, for without us there would indeed be a number of beings, and even a universe, or several, but no beings for which everything appears in all of its inexhaustible plurality. Lastly, because *with* alone gives meaning [*sens*]: an absolutely isolated thing would be alone in the world and devoid of meaning; every signification requires that various things or different words relate to each other; interrelations and, indeed, significations would simply not be possible at all if beings did not present themselves each *with* the other, if their manifestation was not already plural prior to any determined relationship. In other words, the non-manifestation of relation between all beings that manifest themselves—that is what makes sense prior to all signification. A given passerby arrives "with" another; are they together or is their proximity merely that of two passersby? I do not discern it but it already makes sense to me or else I would not try to figure out their connection based on their way of approaching or withdrawing from each other. Sense is thus born out of the sensible, in the perceptible yet neither visible nor audible nor tangible gap [*écart*] between the beings I am able to see, hear, etc. It hinges on the "areality" of the space that separates them; it is to be found only in the relation without relation of the simple gap between them. We may summarize all this by stating that *with* is self-evident for Nancy: it gives itself without a remainder and thus also for no reason, or for nothing, and this nothing is the void that parts [*écarte*] self-evidence from itself through the parting of beings, therefore giving meaning [*sens*] to their manifestation, ahead of any signification in particular.

As such, there is nothing between us; nothing that unites us, yet nothing that separates us; nothing if not this nothing in common that constitutes being in common, so that we are always two or many, two *and* many: always the ones *with* the others. If there is a reason to return to it again and again, it is because reason itself does not readily accept the obviousness [*ne se rend pas facilement à l'évidence*] of this "nothing": all of History is indeed that of irrational reason discovering that self-evidence and covering it up, or rather, per Nancy, filling it up. The first (and worst) of foregone conclusions is the myth of community, imagined as a work that would fill the void that separates us, but also from which we come and toward which we go: thus, the existence of each one of us is ordered according to the survival of a quasi-eternal (political) or eternal (religious) "we"; community thus asserts itself by ordering death directly, demanding the sacrifice of its members for the sake of its survival. Nationalism and war both rest on this myth, and Nazism, which Nancy analyzed *with* Lacoue-Labarthe, marks the systematic eradication of the *with*, drawing upon the myth of Aryanism in order to set, as a condition for survival (that of "true" Germans), the death of others (Jews, and others still). In contrast to myth, modern reason denies the self-evidence of the *with* for the sake of the Cartesian "I am." The subject deludes itself into the possibility of sating its solitude even as it immediately conjures up an Other along the way (relationship between the finite subject and an infinite God) and thinks itself as another in relation to itself (a thinking soul, granted, but one *with* an extended body). Self-evidence, as Nancy parses it in Descartes, would then mean that the body is but the extension of the soul, to such an extent that each subject ex-poses itself as a corporeal being alongside other thinking bodies; that *we are* is indeed self-evident. As for the quasi-contemporary obstacle to the manifestation of the *with*, it is instead to be found in the thought of existence itself, in Heidegger, who clearly states that "being-with" (*Mitsein*) is an essential dimension of "being there" (*Dasein*); but one where *being-with* loses itself in some anonymous "they" (*das Man*), a collective day-to-day manner of being that allows us to shrink from death by turning existence into something banal, from beginning to end; or it becomes secondary when facing the heroic solitude of the encounter with the horizon of one's own death by way of dread [*l'angoisse*]; or it definitively loses itself in the existence of a people, which determines each destiny and ensures a heroic sacrifice, harking back, in short, to the myth of Community and its Nazi version. Lastly, a false self-evidence must be highlighted here, one that is simultaneously modern and thoroughly contemporary: that of "society." This concept dissolves being-in-common into isolated individuals so as to subsequently rebuild more substantial ties between them (which is what positivistic sociology tries to do) or to confront them with the imperative of "making connections" [*faire du lien*]. What is self-evident is that our coexistence is lawless, so that it gestures toward the expectation that we give it meaning [*sens*] by ourselves; it is that of our freedom as mortal beings and not of our submission to necessity.

Freed from any and all false self-evidence, *with* is merely a gap, yet this gap freely varies; being-with thus turns into various modalities of being-in-common, allowing us to outline—without circumscribing them, however—a number of interlocking spheres to match them. The most intense and most extreme sphere is that of love; lovers do indeed run the risk of forming a small community that stands apart from the world, of possessing each other, of hurting each other; yet they sustain their love by exposing themselves to each other, including through their nakedness; through touching they rediscover that the other cannot be wholly touched; through sexuality, that the other, even when penetrated, remains impenetrable; in *jouissance*, that each one is borne by the other beyond oneself, toward the other, yet without ever reaching them. Throughout all this, love is the farthest—albeit non external—end of being-in-common. At the other end lies the deprivation [*dénuement*] due to commerce, which makes all beings equivalent, stripping them of their qualities and submitting them to the necessity of possessing goods that are themselves equivalent; and this impoverishment of existence does nothing to diminish their desire to live a meaningful life (a desire shared by crowds of migrants, the inhabitants of favelas, etc.). Between love and commerce, one finds an indefinite number of other spheres, other manners of being-with, which do not carry themselves out as defined works, instead opening themselves up to the infinity of sense: that of friendship, or intense communication without *jouissance*; that of literature, which is a "community without community" inasmuch as each writer communicates with other writers through reading or through writing with another, as Nancy also liked to do, thus opening, through the very word, the possibility of a contact without contact with his readers; that of the portrait and the spectator, more generally of the sharing [*partage*] of art; that of the urban crowd, at once indifferent and attentive to its own singularities. The demand of letting these modes of *with* be, but also of fighting against economic deprivation, is how Nancy defines democracy, which is not a regime but the fact of the inseparable coexistence of the desire to coexist; the political powers-that-be must acknowledge this fact and support this desire without submitting them to the identity of a nation and of a destiny.

One should not infer that the *with* only concerns humans: for much as a stone is with its ground, a lake with the trees that hem it, and as we are with all other beings, being-in-common in its very manifestation greatly exceeds humanity. Letting the world be, limiting the destructive sway that technics and business hold over it thus also turns out to be one of the demands of the *with*, which can only be formulated in a democratic manner. The Covid-19 pandemic, which has cornered us among ourselves and without others while in lockdown, has also provided Jean-Luc Nancy with the opportunity to underscore the extent to which we were exposing ourselves to others and with others as sensible and vulnerable bodies, the extent to which the battles that rage between national communities were aggravating matters, the extent to which we were human in this life, which is inscribed amidst so many other lives and so many beings that cannot be mastered—all, living, would-be living as viruses are, or non-living, making up the texture of the "fragile skin of the world."

(Translated by Cosmin Toma)

Index

abandonment 2–3, 56, 68, 111, 119, 212, 235
absolute 3, 8, 10, 13, 18, 19, 20, 21–23, 26, 28, 29, 39–45, 47–53, 56, 58, 60, 63, 66, 68, 69, 72, 96, 127, 129, 131, 153–54, 158, 174, 180n5, 182, 183–84, 194, 212, 225, 240, 241, 242, 244, 252, 260, 265, 275, 276, 282
adoration 11, 29, 36, 110, 122–23, 242
Adorno, Theodor 197
Althusser, Louis 186
Anders, Günther 256
Angelus Silesius 128
Apollinaire, Guillaume 184, 190
Aquinas (Saint Thomas) 70, 116
areality 104, 106, 225n13, 279, 283
Aristotle 114–16, 149–50, 158
Artaud, Antonin 176, 177
Augustine (Saint) 116

Bachelard, Gaston 12, 186–90, 193, 194–96
Bacon, Francis 255
Bacon, Roger 255
Badiou, Alain 77n14, 78n17, 106, 111n6, 156
Bailly, Jean-Christophe 4, 34–35, 36n80, 37, 131, 162, 172–73
Barrau, Aurélien 4, 8, 64, 179, 193–96, 197
Barthes, Roland 29, 240
Bartók, Béla 254
Bataille, Georges 2, 19, 22, 102n48, 107, 132–34, 137, 138, 144, 149, 154, 176, 177, 203n10, 240, 241, 248, 249, 253, 271–72
Baudelaire, Charles 5, 176, 177
Beckett, Samuel 9, 21, 22n20, 41n11, 219, 220, 236, 254, 255
Beethoven, Ludwig van 51
Bell, Clive 52
Benjamin, Walter 22, 62
Benveniste, Émile 96, 103, 149
Berg, Alban 4, 254
Bergson, Henri 156, 178, 185, 191

Blanchot, Maurice 2–3, 10, 11, 12, 13, 19, 21, 22, 23, 26, 29, 30, 31, 41, 50, 110, 118–22, 131–46, 154, 176, 177, 198, 199–202, 207n18, 209–13, 219, 240–41, 258–59, 275
Blumenberg, Hans 112–13
body 1–4, 6, 9, 10, 11, 13, 26–27, 29–32, 61, 65, 73, 76, 77, 85–86, 92–93, 100, 102n49, 104–5, 106, 121, 145, 160, 161, 182, 183–84, 200, 210, 214, 219, 221, 222, 224, 230–31, 232–33, 234, 235–36, 238, 249–50, 257, 268–70, 271–72, 279n2, 283, 285
Bolaño, Roberto 261
Bourdieu, Pierre 186
Braque, Georges 254
Breton, André 190

Cage, John 86
Canguilhem, Georges 186, 189, 195
Caravaggio 62–66
Carson, Rachel 256
Cassiodorus 258
Celan, Paul 10, 24, 36, 130, 176, 177, 242, 247
Chrétien, Jean-Louis 111, 231
Coleridge, Samuel Taylor 163
community 1, 2–3, 6, 11, 13, 19, 21, 23, 27, 30n46, 39–40, 58, 60, 79, 105–7, 117, 118, 131–46, 179n2, 191, 202n8, 240–44, 247, 250, 252, 259, 271–72, 276–77, 279, 283–84
Cuisset, Thibaut 172, 173n24, 174

Deleuze, Gilles 101, 191, 205n15
Derrida, Jacques 8, 13, 18, 21n19, 22, 29, 30, 31, 48, 49, 53, 61, 64, 65, 82, 84, 89, 92, 93, 101, 103n51, 110, 113–15, 138n25, 144n50, 147, 148–49, 160, 179, 186, 191, 211n22, 226n14, 227n22&23, 228–33, 236, 240–41, 260, 275, 276, 279, 280

Descartes, René 11, 87–89, 91, 92, 93–96, 98, 100–1, 104–7, 116, 121, 128, 151, 222–24, 283
désœuvrement (worklessness, inoperancy, idleness, etc.) 2–3, 11, 26, 40–41, 44, 50, 57, 120, 131–34, 137–38, 142–46, 154, 179n2, 238, 240–41, 261
dis-enclosure (*déclosion*) 3, 11, 13, 19, 26, 63n16, 109–15, 118–23, 136n18, 219n29, 237–51, 252n2, 257, 258, 275n5
Duchamp, Marcel 254
Duns Scotus 116

Einstein, Albert 180, 182, 184, 185
Eliot, T. S. 4, 190, 254
Ellul, Jacques 256
exscription 2–3, 9, 13, 24, 27, 32, 33, 37, 232n39, 235–36, 240, 271–73, 281

Fanon, Frantz 238, 246
Faulkner, William 4, 19
Feuerbach, Ludwig 154
Foucault, Michel 89n2, 186, 222
Freud, Sigmund 2, 12, 24, 31, 103–4, 128, 147, 148, 149, 150, 151, 152, 153, 154–57, 158, 160, 174, 178, 220, 222, 236, 256, 259, 267n8
Fry, Roger 52–54

Gauchet, Marcel 112–13, 275
Gide, André 148
Glissant, Édouard 247
globalization (*mondialisation*) 6, 11, 13, 109–10, 168–69, 201, 237–38, 243–44, 246, 274–77, 279
God, god(dess), gods 6, 11, 19, 26, 28, 44, 51, 59, 69, 70, 87, 95, 96, 106, 109n3, 110n5, 111, 112, 113, 114, 115–23, 127, 128, 129, 130, 165, 167–68, 170, 197, 201, 222, 224, 254, 275, 279, 283
Guattari, Félix 101

Habermas, Jürgen 111
Hantaï, Simon 4, 226n14, 227, 233
Hegel, Georg Wilhelm Friedrich 8, 21n19, 61, 62, 69–70, 71, 138n25, 144n50, 147, 149, 153, 154, 157, 158, 160, 176, 177, 190, 212, 260, 261, 265–66, 275–76

Heidegger, Martin 4, 6, 7, 12, 13, 19, 91, 95n25, 104, 106, 113, 114–15, 117, 147, 148, 149, 150–52, 156–57, 158, 160, 162, 163, 164–74, 178, 179, 181, 191, 197–98, 199, 209, 211, 212, 215, 221, 225n9, 227, 231, 239–40, 247–48, 256, 261, 274–75, 283
Heisenberg, Werner 180, 182
Henry, Michel 111
Heraclitus 148, 193
Hobbes, Thomas 255
Hoffmann, E. T. A. 154–55
Hölderlin, Friedrich 10, 12, 18, 28–29, 36n80, 162–74, 176, 177, 240, 247, 257

Illich, Ivan 256

James (Saint) 241
Jean Paul 154–55
Joyce, James 4, 10, 24, 160–61, 182, 240, 254

Kafka, Franz 176, 177
Kant, Immanuel 21, 30n45, 52, 61, 87, 116, 117, 128, 153, 154, 158, 179, 180–81, 183, 187–89, 192, 208, 209, 211, 231
Kiarostami, Abbas 12–13, 198n3, 205–6, 213–19
Kuti, Fela 248

Lacan, Jacques 12, 147–52, 154–60, 222, 233
Lacoue-Labarthe, Philippe 3, 4, 10, 12, 18, 22–23, 29, 39–46, 48–53, 56, 69, 77n14, 79n18, 109n2, 117n28, 147–53, 162–64, 170–75, 176–77, 240, 248n37, 252n4, 259, 265–66, 283
Latour, Bruno 1, 254
Lawrence, D. H. 182
Leibniz, Gottfried Wilhelm 116, 127
Levinas, Emmanuel 101, 111, 155, 167n16, 201, 236
Locke, John 255
Löwith, Karl 112–13
Luther, Martin 113–14
Lyotard, Jean-François 167n16, 255

Malebranche, Nicolas 116
Mallarmé, Stéphane 3, 5, 23, 24, 29, 24, 240, 253

Mann, Thomas 182, 190
Marinetti, Filippo Tommaso 182
Marion, Jean-Luc 111, 155
Marx, Karl 128, 178, 248, 261, 266–67, 274–76
Mbembe, Achille 13, 238–39, 243–51
McLuhan, Marshall 256
Merleau-Ponty, Maurice 222
methexis 2, 66, 67, 199, 232, 250
Miller, Henry 256
mimesis 18–19, 31, 66, 67, 199, 201, 203, 204, 232, 259
Minkowski, Eugène 190
Minkowski, Hermann 180, 182, 185
Moore, G. E. 52

Nietzsche, Friedrich 3, 78, 91, 95, 176, 177, 178, 179, 181, 185, 191, 239, 249, 256, 275, 281
Novalis 22, 26, 48–50, 56, 153–54

Orwell, George 256
Owen, Robert 163

Parmiggiani, Claudio 31, 70–71
Paul (Saint) 1
Picasso, Pablo 184, 254
Plato 13, 51, 79, 87, 101n42, 195, 200, 203, 205, 207, 215–16, 229
Poincaré, Henri 12, 182–89, 191–96
Pound, Ezra 4, 254
Protagoras 6–7
Pynchon, Thomas 191

Rancière, Jacques 90, 107
Ricœur, Paul 111
Rimbaud, Arthur 5, 9, 19, 257
Romanticism 3, 4, 10, 12, 18, 20–22, 26, 29, 39–56, 58, 66, 69, 80, 152–56, 160–61, 162, 163, 165, 170, 171–74, 201, 217, 238, 240–41, 252, 258, 265–66

Salmon, André 185
Saussure, Ferdinand de 147–50
Schelling, Friedrich Wilhelm Joseph 43, 45, 51–52, 53, 61, 174
Schlegel, Friedrich 18, 24, 27, 40, 42–49, 51–52, 59, 153, 154

Schoenberg, Arnold 4, 86, 254
Senghor, Léopold Sédar 247
sense (*sens*) 1, 9, 10, 11, 13, 20–21, 22, 23, 24, 25–26, 29–30, 32–34, 36, 37, 48–49, 58, 62, 63, 64, 65, 66, 69, 71, 74, 75, 76–84, 87, 88, 111, 115, 116–22, 127–28, 168, 179, 198, 199, 201–2, 212, 225n11, 226, 230, 231, 233–35, 237–51, 257–58, 265–66, 272–73, 274–77, 278–81, 282–84
Shakespeare, William 51, 153, 201n7, 255
sharing (*partage*) 18, 20, 25, 31, 33, 77, 122, 133, 137, 139–40, 141, 142, 145, 146, 238, 241, 243, 244, 247, 250, 274, 279, 284
singular plural 4, 6, 9, 10, 12, 57–62, 66–67, 70–72, 76, 107, 133, 139, 145, 179, 189, 193, 194, 196, 199n4, 232, 235n50, 240, 243–44, 248, 268, 269, 279, 282
Sloterdijk, Peter 94
Sophocles 166, 174
Spinoza, Baruch 116, 128, 260
Stein, Gertrude 4, 254
Sterne, Laurence 24
Stravinsky, Igor 4, 254
subject 11, 12, 32, 34, 35, 37, 43, 52, 60, 65, 74–77, 79, 85–87, 88–107, 114–15, 117, 121, 123, 132, 134, 141, 151–52, 156, 157, 158, 159, 169, 174–75, 191, 200, 222–23, 224, 231, 240, 241, 242, 246, 249, 274, 280–81, 283

Taylor, Charles 112
technics/technique 10, 12, 18, 28, 57, 58–59, 60, 67–70, 74, 76, 78, 81–83, 84–86, 173, 185–90, 194, 195–96, 197, 201, 211, 219n29, 231, 237, 244, 245, 249, 254, 256, 260, 274–76, 284
touch 2, 9, 13, 22, 27, 33, 34, 61–66, 68, 69, 83, 84, 89, 93, 145, 168n17, 199n4, 211–12, 220, 222, 224, 226, 228, 231, 232, 233–35, 251, 271, 278, 280, 284

Uexküll, Jakob Johann von 181

Valéry, Paul 5, 10, 11, 17, 24, 31, 59, 104–5, 107

Wagner, Richard 76, 78–79, 80, 160, 261
Webern, Anton 4, 254
Williams, William Carlos 204n12
with (being-with), 4, 9, 13, 19, 20–21, 32, 58, 71, 86, 117, 122, 142, 145–46, 202n8, 225, 226, 239–40, 242, 276–77, 280, 282–85

Wittgenstein, Ludwig 63
Woolf, Virginia 4, 10, 41, 50–56, 254
Wordsworth, William 163

Žižek, Slavoj 107
Zola, Émile 261

www.ingramcontent.com/pod-product-compliance
Lightning Source LLC
Chambersburg PA
CBHW052152300426
44115CB00011B/1637